Marketing Hospitality

WILEY SERVICE MANAGEMENT SERIES

TOM POWERS, *Series Editor*

Introduction to the Hospitality Industry
Tom Powers

Introduction to Management in the Hospitality Industry
Tom Powers

Purchasing: Selection and Procurement for the Hospitality Industry
John M. Stefanelli

Marketing Hospitality
Tom Powers

Supervision in the Hospitality Industry
Jack E. Miller
Mary Porter
Karen Eich Drummond

The Management of Maintenance and Engineering Systems in the Hospitality Industry
Frank D. Borsenik
Alan R. Stutts

The Bar and Beverage Book: Basics of Profitable Management
Costas Katsigris
Mary Porter

Marketing Hospitality

SECOND EDITION

Tom Powers
PROFESSOR EMERITUS
SCHOOL OF HOTEL AND FOOD ADMINISTRATION
UNIVERSITY OF GUELPH
ONTARIO, CANADA

JOHN WILEY & SONS, INC.
New York | Chichester | Weinheim | Brisbane | Singapore | Toronto

This text is printed on acid-free paper.

Library of Congress Cataloging in Publication Data:

Powers, Thomas F.
Marketing hospitality / Tom Powers. — 2nd ed.
p. cm.
Includes bibliographical references.
ISBN 0-471-12703-5 (cloth : alk. paper)
1. Hospitality industry—Marketing. I. Title.
TX911.3.M3P68 1997
647.94'068'8—dc20 96-36091

Printed in the United States of America

10 9 8 7 6 5 4 3 2 1

This book is dedicated to my wife
Jo Marie
whose support makes life worthwhile
and this book possible.

Preface

This book was written, first of all, for students in hospitality programs. Most of these students expect to work in the industry; many of them already do. The way hospitality businesses are structured, the overwhelming majority of graduates will make their career on the operations side of the business. The point of this text, though, is that marketing, properly understood, is not *really* an activity separate from operations but, rather, an *integral part* of it, especially at the unit level. For this reason, we will combine attention to the body of theory and knowledge that is marketing with a strong emphasis on applications of marketing in hospitality operations.

To students I would say that the body of theory and knowledge *is* important. When you graduate, you will need to be able to deal with the context of your career, which, for most, at one time or another, involves a multiunit company—either a chain or a franchise organization. This larger context requires an understanding of the strategy and the grand design of the business so that, as a manager, you can knowledgeably and purposefully commit yourself to implementing that strategy. This experience, in turn, is the best preparation for the opportunity that comes along, for many after a few years, to develop strategy at a unit or a chain-wide level. Being able to put practical experience together with a sound grasp of theory is eminently practical.

There is, however, another and more immediate element of a graduate's (and working student's) long-term work environment—that is the challenge of day-to-day unit operations, where most people spend several years before moving on to higher corporate responsibility. Because of the importance of achieving success at the unit level, you will find significant emphasis in this text on trade sources, such as industry conferences and the collective wisdom of practitioners garnered from their years of practical experience. Naturally, however, the framework for this material is provided by the body of academic knowledge that makes up marketing.

There is a second very important public for whom this book must serve as a tool, and that is the professorate who teach hospitality marketing. A first concern of theirs is which of their courses a book is designed to serve. This text is intended for the first course in *hospitality* marketing and has been designed for a one-quarter or one-semester course.

Most hospitality programs offer at least two courses in marketing. The first is a principles of marketing course. *Marketing Hospitality* provides the basic foundations of marketing theory necessary for the principles course when it is taught by *hospitality* faculty.

In many programs, however, the principles course is taught by business administration faculty and then hospitality faculty teach a second course, often called Hospitality Marketing Management or Advanced Hospitality Marketing. This text is suitable for this course in those programs that wish to emphasize the *applications of marketing.*

A second problem for the instructor is how useful this text will be: Will students learn from it? In today's educational environment, knowledge must be packaged in a way that serves the students' *interests,* as well as their career needs, if we want them to expend the energy needed to understand a subject, in effect, to "buy" marketing. I have used the first edition of this text in the classroom for several years and have been very pleased with students' reactions to it. They say (even anonymously!) that they like it and find it easy to read; others who have used it report similar results. I have worked hard to achieve the same outcome in this second edition. Because our students are interested in the industry, I have placed significant emphasis on examples from the field in the main body of the text. In addition, in Case Histories and Field Practice Notes, I have tried to bring into the classroom contemporary issues and practices that are related to the subject matter of the particular chapter in which they appear. Examples are drawn from both food service and lodging, and, where practice is different between the two sectors, topics are analyzed separately.

Hospitality students seem to learn best by doing, and this text, particularly in the chapters on marketing planning, location analysis, and unit level marketing, provides ample resources for field-based term projects. (See the *Instructor's Manual.*)

The field of service marketing has evolved since the first edition, and practice in hospitality has changed even more. Virtually all of the text has been rewritten to reflect contemporary hospitality industry practice. New chapters have been added on distribution in the hospitality industry and on unit level marketing. A major section has been added to the chapters on product to reflect the growing importance of brands in hospitality. Database marketing is discussed in both the chapter on marketing information and research and the one on unit level marketing. The topic of marketing communication has been split into two chapters to accommodate the importance of that topic. The emphasis in the first edition on location and site analysis is retained in this edition.

THE PLAN OF THE BOOK

Chapter 1 introduces the field of marketing and some of its basic concepts by way of orienting the student to the text and field. The next five chapters present the foundations on which marketing is based. Chapters 2 and 3 are concerned with analyzing marketing opportunities, covering such topics as consumer behavior, market segmentation, and target marketing. Chapter 4 extends this analysis with an introduction to marketing information and marketing research, including data-based marketing. In Chapter 5, marketing strategy is shown to be based on customer, competition, and the company's offerings, goals, and abilities. Other topics covered in that chapter include competitive structure, resource allocation, strategic foresight versus strategic opportunism, growth strategies, and positioning. Chapter 6 discusses the process of marketing planning and its importance. It also considers the problems of organizing marketing effectively in the hospitality service company, as well as the important topic of internal marketing.

To provide a context for understanding marketing activities in hospitality companies, Chapter 7 addresses the question of the *service product* and service systems, more generally, showing how important the differences between services and manufactured products are to marketing management. The next six chapters discuss the basic elements of the marketing mix. Chapter 8 continues the discussion of the hospitality *product.* Chapters 9 and 10 address issues of *place,* covering channels of distribution as well as location and site analysis. Since the frame of analysis and methods related to place decisions are somewhat different in food service and in lodging, each area is addressed separately. Chapter 11 focuses on price, including the topics of price objectives, the determinants of price, and pricing procedure in both food service and lodging. The chapter also includes an Appendix on break-even analysis. Chapters 12 and 13 discuss marketing communication, with Chapter 12 focusing on advertising and Chapter 13 focusing on sales promotion, public relations, and personal selling.

Chapter 14 discusses an area of long-established importance in lodging and of rapidly growing importance in food service: unit level marketing. Local marketing should be of special interest to students, because it relates to tasks that may be important early in their career and because it relates to experiences and observations readily available among students in most classes. The problems and approaches to unit level marketing have some factors in common, but they are different in many ways for food service and lodging and so separate treatment of some aspects of the topic are necessary for the two sectors.

Tom Powers
Moon River
October 1996

Acknowledgements

Ronald N. Paul, President of Technomic Consultants, has been kind enough to make available to me his company's research. Both in that material and in personal communications, Ron has been a great support to this work.

I would like to thank the Institutional Foodservice Manufacturers' Association for permission to use a considerable amount of the research and insight provided in the *Proceedings* of their annual conference, COEX (Chain Operator's Exchange). George Rice, founder of GDR CREST, was for many years the guiding force in COEX, and I have quoted extensively from his work.

Michael Beckley, President of Commonwealth Hospitality, and Simon Cooper, President of Delta Hotels, have given generously of their own time and have also helped me to gain access to key people in their organizations. Ian Bell of Cara Foodservices and Susan Barclay of Versa Services have helped me to gain insight into the nature of marketing and merchandising problems in institutional food service. I would like to acknowledge the help of the University of Guelph and its Hospitality Industry Founder's Fund, which supported much of the research on which this book has been based. I would also like to thank John Patterson, Director of Management Development Programs (MDP) at the School of Hotel and Food Administration, not only for his support and that of the MDP during the time he served as its Director, but also for his encouragement and advice. Thanks are due to Michael Nightengale in his capacity as Director of the School of Hotel and Food Administration and as Dean of the College of Family and Consumer Studies for accommodating the demands that research for this book made on my schedule. Michael Haywood, who succeeded Michael Nightengale as Director of the School, was also most accommodating.

A number of colleagues have given generously of their time to review portions of this book. Leo Renaghan's advice and assistance throughout the process of the development and redevelopment of this text have been of critical importance, and I am in his debt. Carl Riegel of Washington State University, Ken Hardy of the University of Western Ontario, and Jim Pickworth of the University of Guelph reviewed portions of this text and gave me invaluable assistance.

Claire Thompson, Senior Editor at Wiley, encouraged me to undertake this revision and has provided valuable advice. Donna Conte, who has been responsible for the production process, is the soul of patience, putting up with my periodic panics over matters that invariably turn out to be minor. Maria Colletti helped everyone with everything and I am particularly grateful for her help with the reviews.

Kay Fairfull put up with numerous changes and often tight deadlines as she typed the manuscript, maintaining a cheerful and friendly outlook, despite numerous excuses for becoming impatient. I acknowledge her once again as a wonderful collaborator.

Throughout the process of preparing this revision, I have had the assistance of a number of colleagues as reviewers. Their advice has been invaluable, and their assistance is deeply appreciated.

Contents

Marketing Hospitality

Chapter 1

When you have finished reading this chapter, you should be able to

1. Discuss three basic approaches to the market
2. Describe marketing as a way of thought
3. Explain the differences between service and manufactured products
4. List and discuss the characteristics of service
5. Identify the macroenvironments of the hospitality industry

(Photo courtesy Peter Mendel, Stock Boston)

Marketing—Everybody's Job

If one of the employees in the plant that manufactures your toothpaste is unhappy on the day your tube was made, it is unlikely that you will know about it. It would not affect your toothpaste. However, you have probably had the experience of eating in a restaurant where your server was unhappy—and what a difference *that* can make.

The product in hospitality is the experience of the guest. That experience has both a **goods** component (food, for instance) and the interactive experience we call **service.** In practice, the employee becomes part of the product (experience). In one way or another, *every* employee is a part of the guest's experience because the typical hospitality organization is highly interactive. One sour apple can upset a lot of the other people and, in the end, an unhappy server can upset the guest.

For the moment, we can divide customers into two types, first-time guests and repeat guests. New guests often decide to try an operation as a result of advertising and promotion, but they can also decide because of word of mouth—that is, other people's experience. **Repeat patronage** comes almost entirely as a result of successful experiences. To create those successful experiences and *to secure repeat customers* takes the effort of every person in the hospitality organization. In hospitality operations, everyone is a **part-time marketer.**[1] Because everybody in hospitality is essential to successful marketing in some way, it is important for anyone planning a hospitality career to understand the important subject of marketing.

In the remainder of this chapter, we will look at what the **marketing concept** is and how it can be distinguished from other points of view; what activities are special to marketing and how being a service business affects our approach to marketing. Finally, we will consider how marketing is affected by the environment in which it is carried out.

THREE APPROACHES TO THE MARKET

Some people argue that the key to attracting and keeping customers is the product: "Build a better mousetrap," as the old saying goes, "and the world will beat a pathway to your door." Another common view is that selling is the way to gain customers. These people say, "Nothing happens until somebody sells something." In fact, there is considerable merit to both these views, but they see only a part of the picture. We will consider each briefly and then turn to a third way of approaching the market, the marketing concept.

A Product Orientation

In the years just after World War II, hotel occupancy was at an all-time high. Flushed with success, hotel owners spoke with scorn of the new roadside motels as a passing fad. They *knew* what a good hotel was—and that's what they intended to offer. However, 10 years later, many of these same hotels were on the ropes because the roadside convenience and lower rates of the motels were stealing customers right and left from the "established" hotels. The hotel operators thought that their *product* was the central consideration in planning their business.

Some restaurateurs have suffered from a similar difficulty. They defined what a good restaurant was in terms of their own tastes and preferences—what *they knew* a good restaurant was. For them, the product defined by tradition was sacred. In today's marketplace, these kinds of operations are disappearing and being replaced by those that are successful and in step with changing consumer demand. The fact is that consumer needs, tastes, and preferences are rapidly changing, and it is the consumer who defines what will and will not succeed. Product-oriented people do, however, have a point in that a good product—that is, effective operations—is an essential part of an effective marketing program. For that reason, we will devote considerable attention to the service product in later chapters. Remember, however, the right product alone is not enough for success.

A Sales Orientation

It is quite common in hospitality organizations to find people who think of selling as the whole of marketing. This point of view is typified by the idea that the key to business success is to "get out there and sell." This assumes that, if one just sells hard enough, the guest or customer will buy. Thus, what *we have for sale* is the focus of the sales orientation. Companies that think marketing is just advertising and selling fall into this category, as do operators who look only at the promotional side of their business.

In fact, selling is a tremendously important activity in business, and the really dangerous aspect of this approach is that, *as long as what the operation has to offer fits the guests' tastes*, it can succeed quite well, thus creating an illusion that "sell,

Marketing begins with the customer's needs and wants. (Photo courtesy Pizza Hut)

sell, sell" is the way to prosper. When guests' tastes change, however, or if the operation fails to satisfy the guests for any reason, this approach is doomed to failure. Remember, satisfying the guest is the key to repeat sales and a vital part of marketing.

A MARKETING ORIENTATION

A marketing orientation is one in which the reasoning process about a company's offering begins with consumer needs and wants, that is, discovering their needs and wants and providing products that satisfy them. This is another way of saying that consumer needs, not management's know-how or the salesperson's art, should define a business. One leading hospitality marketing researcher put it this way:

> The sole difference between competitive restaurant volumes is simply the better definition of guests' needs. There may be many today who are foolish enough to believe that consumers continue to come to your restaurants just because of your offering . . . but they don't! Rather, they come to satisfy their own needs, which happen, at the moment, to be satisfied by your products and services.[2]

The three approaches to the market are summarized in Table 1.1.

Table 1.1 Three Approaches to the Market

Approach	Stresses Importance of	Advantages	Weaknesses or Problems
Product	Our product Our know-how	We know how to do this	Doing the best job of offering something customer may not want
Sales	What we have to sell Our commitment	We can decide to make this effort	The best sales pitch in the world will not result in sales if the customer is not satisfied
Marketing	What customer needs and wants Customer's point of view Customer's values	Stimulates demand by recognizing new needs Stresses both product and selling efforts Changes with the consumer	More difficult Requires careful analysis of problems and studied plans Requires more than operating know-how

MARKETING

As we noted earlier, a marketing orientation is really a way of thinking, some would say, a philosophy. That philosophy is translated into action by the field of marketing. The American Marketing Association defines marketing in this way:

> Marketing is the process of planning and executing the conception, pricing, promotion and distribution of ideas, goods, and services to create exchanges that satisfy individual and organizational objectives.[3]

From what we have already said, the process begins with a set of customers—often called a target market. It is the needs of this market that define what product can be successfully developed and brought to market. In manufacturing, marketing is generally carried out by a separate unit of the company. While there are marketing departments in hospitality firms, everyone in the organization is involved in marketing because, as we have said, their actions are needed to secure repeat sales. The activities that comprise marketing are often referred to as the marketing mix, a term that underlines the fact that marketing involves a *number* of related activities.

The Marketing Mix

The problem with the product and sales definitions of marketing we looked at earlier is not that they are wrong, but that they are only partly right. In practice, *marketing* involves mixing a number of key activities. These are commonly summarized as the *4 Ps: product, price, place, and promotion*. The marketer mixes these elements into a solution that will satisfy the consumer in the face of the competition. Early definitions of the marketing mix in the 1960s included as many as 12 elements, and, more recently, some have argued for more than four elements. One prominent scholar, for instance, suggested adding politics and public relations, and some have argued for a total of seven elements. We will avoid these definitional discussions and simply adopt the widely used 4 Ps as an approach that gives us a good starting point for understanding marketing.[4] In later chapters, however, we will expand our definition of these elements in order to make the 4 Ps fit the needs of hospitality marketing. For the purposes of this introductory chapter, however, we can accept the following as a starting point. The marketing mix must take into account the following:

- *Products (goods and services)* that consumers need or want;
- Offering products in a *place* so that they are convenient to the guest;
- Setting a *price* that will yield a profit, while providing value to the guest and taking into account the price of competing goods and services;
- Letting prospective guests know of the offering by *promotion;* advertising, direct selling, and other forms of marketing communication are essential.

Marketing as a Social Force

One very broad definition of marketing defines it as "the creation of a satisfied customer." Marketing involves discovering a consumer need and then filling it. An example will make the underlying idea clearer.

Some years ago, the mortgage on the Mayflower Hotel in Plymouth, Michigan, was about to be foreclosed and the hotel was ready to go out of business. Anybody with common sense, people said, could see that the building would eventually be demolished to make way for something more useful. Fortunately for Plymouth—and thousands upon thousands of future guests—a young man two years out of college and possessed of *uncommon* sense saw that broken-down old hotel as an opportunity. Ralph Lorenz managed to persuade the hotel's board of directors to let him take over the property and try to revive it—against, it ought to be said, all the best and wisest advice.

The hotel was in terrible condition. Years of unprofitable operation had left it in sad disrepair. However, it was in an area of large manufacturing plants, and Ralph saw a need at those plants that his hotel could fill. Every plant had a bowling league and he approached company personnel managers, union officials, and bowling league officers with this proposition: "Bring your busloads of bowlers to our hotel for their bowling banquets and I'll give them the biggest T-bone steak they ever saw for one dollar over my cost." Ralph was able to offer that price because he and one waiter—with the help of a couple of high school students—could serve that very simple meal. In addition, he needed the bare minimum of kitchen help to prepare the meal. He, the cook, and the dishwasher cleaned up

A renewed Mayflower Hotel is a vital community institution, largely because its owner, Ralph Lorenz, was a practical marketer with the vision to create value for his customers. (Photo courtesy Mayflower Hotel)

when it was all over—and the hotel cleaned up financially because the bowlers came, hundreds of them, almost every night for several months.

Gradually, Ralph was able reinvest the profits of the bowling banquets to repair the hotel coffee shop and dining room. The Mayflower Coffee Shop became a local gathering spot, and, in time, the hotel's reputation for friendly, fast service attracted people from Detroit and beyond. As successful year followed successful year, the revenue from the food operation was used to refurbish the hotel's guest rooms. An important point in this success story is that Ralph did not do it alone. His friendly, efficient crew of "part-time marketers" were a big part of this success because it was they who provided the service.

Ralph and his hotel became a focal point in Plymouth. As nearby Detroit grew, many lazy little country towns exploded in population but became characterless bedroom communities. Although Plymouth today is unquestionably a suburb of Detroit, it remains a distinctive place—in large part because the Mayflower Hotel has kept alive the small-city community spirit of Plymouth, Michigan.

In the very short run, Ralph recognized a need for low-cost, but bountiful, bowling banquets and used the public space in an old, run-down hotel to fill that need. In the longer run, he recognized the need for a local gathering spot and invested the profits from those bowling banquets to refurbish his hotel so that it could become a town center. In the very long run, he recognized the need for a facility not only to meet the demands for food and lodging but also to provide a focus for the community. The community rewarded his efforts with its patronage.

The story is interesting for us because it embodies the central realities of marketing. Ralph saw a need and, by meeting that need in a new way, he created value for the customer and for the community.

The practice of marketing is not limited to business. The hospitality industry puts all of us in the place of host or hostess, so that our natural concern is for our guest. The guest-centered reasoning that underlies marketing, then, should be perfectly natural to the act of hosting. Marketing, moreover, is equally appropriate to institutional operators—both profit and nonprofit (health care, school food service, college dining, etc.).

Some hospitals have taken to offering gourmet meals, specialized room service, and a whole host of hotel-like amenities. Special services are tailored to particular patient groups. For example, some hospitals offer romantic dinners by candlelight for new parents and specialized services designed for senior citizens. Some also provide concierge service on certain floors, with meals served by white-jacketed waiters—and with prices to fit the service. In nonpatient food service, a hospital's bakery can become a profit center and delicatessens are even being set up in public cafeteria areas. School food service, too, has adapted to its changing funding situation with increased emphasis on marketing to maintain the dollar sales volume necessary to support its staff.

Marketing is an increasingly important management tool in health care. This hospital improves its competitive position by helping new parents to celebrate the arrival of a child with a gourmet dinner served in the hospital room. (Photo courtesy of Marriott Food Services and Management)

In college food service, emphasis on marketing has been so successful that it has actually resulted in sales increases in the face of *declining enrollments*. Certainly, the increasing presence of franchised brand names, such as Taco Bell and KFC, on college campuses is evidence that contract companies *and* institutional operators are responding to what their customers want.

Some would insist that marketing must be connected to profit, and we can agree as long as a broad definition of profit is adopted. A break-even operation sets out to achieve neither a loss nor a surplus of revenue over costs—in other words, it has a zero profit target. Many institutional food service operations are run on this basis. Subsidized operations set out deliberately to achieve a loss on sales, that is, a "negative profit," which is covered by a subsidy. This is true, for instance, in the case of school food service. Both nonprofit and subsidized operations, however, must achieve a level of sales which gives them enough revenue to keep their crew employed and to maintain their services.

Marketing and Society. Before turning to a closer look at the relationship between hospitality services and marketing, we should recognize that marketing is really a central part of our way of life. A free society is one in which—within the limits of the law—people choose for themselves what they want to be and do. The mechanisms of a free society should maximize people's opportunity for choice. This is precisely what marketing does. As we have seen, marketing is based on the sovereignty of the individual consumer.

The reasoning process of marketing is being used today in many noncommercial spheres. Examples of social marketing include public health campaigns in areas such as those aimed at reducing drug abuse, alcoholism, and smoking. Other areas of social concern, such as civil rights and environmental protection, have seen the prominent use of marketing techniques in recent years. Nutrition education and weight control, too, have used the marketing approach.

Marketing cannot solve all our problems, but it is a rational approach to the offering of choices and one that occupies an increasingly central place in contemporary society. Because it takes as given the need to persuade rather than force people to choose, it fits well with our way of life and political system.

WHAT IS SO DIFFERENT ABOUT SERVICES?

Since a major premise of this text is that marketing hospitality services is different from marketing manufactured goods, it is useful to spell out the unique nature of services.

Characteristics of Service

The Service Product. When a manufactured product is purchased, the consumer receives something tangible. When a car or that tube of toothpaste we mentioned earlier is purchased, the customer acquires that product for his or her own use. Although the manufacturer may supply safety warnings and maintenance directions for a product, how the customer uses it is essentially his or her choice. On the other hand, the essence of a service transaction is that what is purchased includes both tangible goods and intangible services. The *intangible* characteristics—hence, the more difficult for the consumer to get a handle on—are often the more important components of a service transaction. A meal in a restaurant may be delicious, but if the room in which it is served is unattractive and dirty, the *experience* is likely to be a failure for many guests. If a guest is provided with a lovely room but only after a long argument about the rate or reservation, the guest's stay is marred from the outset.

If a customer purchases a tube of toothpaste, he or she is not looking for an oblong of goo, but, rather, for the *benefit* of clean teeth and a fresh-tasting mouth. Thus, we should note, there is an intangible component in any transaction. Notice, however, that when you purchase a product, it is a physical thing which you take with you and use yourself. A service, on the other hand, is generally consumed at the time of purchase. It is not a thing which is possessed, however. It is experienced. The product, then, is in large part the performance of the service organization.

Performance Is People Intensive. A service commonly involves people on *both* sides of the transaction. At dinner, there is the waiter or waitress *and* the guest. In a hotel, the clerk and the guest interact. With automation, some personal service is being displaced by machines or electronic devices—as with in-room checkout via the guest room TV screen—but this only makes more important those personal

Employee performance is a critical element in the service transaction. (Photo courtesy Pizza Hut)

contacts that the guest and the hotel's staff *do* make with each other. Employees, then are literally part of the product—and so is the guest.

Because people are involved on both sides, services are less standardized than are products. Two different service personnel, for instance, could do a good—but somewhat different—job in rooming a guest. Highly standardized behavior is often not possible and frequently is not desirable. Service personnel are usually more effective if they are able to be themselves.

No matter how hard an employee tries, if the guest is in a foul humor, the experience probably will not be pleasant for the guest in spite of the employee's best efforts. Managing the service transaction often involves accepting that varying results, depending on the circumstances, are more common than would be the case with that tube of toothpaste we spoke of earlier. This does not mean that quality control is impossible, but it is subject to variation.

Peaks and Valleys. Service organizations tend to encounter surges in demand that alternate with slack periods. Restaurants at meal times are hectic, but business is very slow in between meals; resorts have on-season and off-season periods; commercial hotels experience midweek surges in demand, but often are not busy on the weekend.

Because of the variability in levels of demand—those peaks and valleys—service marketing and service operations management are often concerned with "managing demand." This involves thinking through guest needs and those of the operation in organizations that have severe peaks and valleys, as well as managing the marketing mix to meet the different problems that occur during each of those periods. For example, marketing may conclude that higher prices and stress in advertising on the need for reservations are the best approach to managing during peak periods, whereas special low prices and heavier promotion are what is required to raise occupancy during the offseason. The two extremes in this simplified example manage demand by adjusting elements of the marketing mix to meet changing seasonal conditions.

No Inventory. In manufacturing, products not sold today keep their value in inventory and can be sold later. Obviously, the opportunity to sell a guest room tonight is unique to *this* time period. The value from a room carried vacant tonight can never be realized in a future time period. Similarly, the sale lost when a guest leaves because he or she finds the waiting line in a restaurant too long is lost forever. *Capacity management,* then, is a concern that hospitality marketing must deal with in the face of the extreme perishability of its product.

Unbundling Services. The way service is delivered has changed dramatically in the past generation. The hospitality service industry moved from serving mainly a class market that dealt mostly with a relatively small upper-income group to a mass market. *Self-service,* for instance, involves the guest not only as the recipient of service, but also as an active player. Self-service extends from the buffet to in-room coffee; the result is lowered cost and price, which is popular in the mass market.

In fast food, self-busing is an important labor saver and customers have come to accept it.

Operations are changing the way service is delivered, too, by delegating some service to other organizations or changing the place where the service is consumed. For instance, reservations for individual hotels are now almost entirely managed by somebody other than the individual hotel operator, for example, franchise or referral organizations and travel agents. Similarly, home delivery of food service is now accomplished by independent contractors; the take-out and delivery business, in some ways, makes the consumer's home an extension of the restaurant. This may be changing the image and meaning of restaurants in ways we do not yet fully understand.

Channels of Distribution. Packaged goods make use of channels of distribution made up of brokers, wholesalers, retailers, and other intermediaries. There are channels of distribution of this kind in hospitality. Travel agents and tour brokers play similar roles for many hotels. These arrangements are, however, in the process of rapid change. The global network of reservation systems (discussed in Chapter 9) is increasing the reach of individual properties while vastly increasing in just the past few years the numbers and types of intermediaries with which hotels now deal. These developments provide a key challenge to lodging marketers.

Franchise systems, too, are a form of distribution system—but, instead of distributing goods, they distribute a *format for doing business.* These franchise systems determine the kinds of experiences widely dispersed franchised units provide for guests. Thus, franchise systems distribute the ultimate in intangibles, ideas.

The distinctive characteristics of hospitality services are summarized in Figure 1.1.

The Product: The Guest's Experience

- largely intangible
- involves both goods and services
- guest is purchasing performance of a service

People Intensive

- employees are part of the product
- quality subject to the variability of individual employee and guest
- guest is directly involved in all service transactions

Capacity Management Is Crucial

- variable levels of demand, peaks and valleys
- no inventory; unused capacity is wasted

Unbundling of Services

- several different organizations may be involved in a single service transaction
- channels of distribution increasing in importance and evolving rapidly

Figure 1.1 Distinctive Characteristics of Hospitality Services

THE ENVIRONMENTS OF HOSPITALITY MARKETING

Like any human activity, hospitality marketing takes place in a complex environment. On the one hand, there are broad forces at work, such as population changes and the economic and political climates, which we can refer to as the *macroenvironment* of hospitality marketing. On the other hand, it takes individuals or organizational consumers to make purchase decisions so they, too, are a key environment—the *microenvironment* of hospitality marketing.

The environments of marketing are summarized graphically in Figure 1.2. We will consider the macroenvironment briefly in the next section and defer consideration of the individual consumer, the microenvironment, to the next chapter.

THE MACROENVIRONMENT OF HOSPITALITY

The Demographic Environment

Demographics are concerned with objectively measurable factors in the population, such as trends in population, family income, educational status, and so forth.

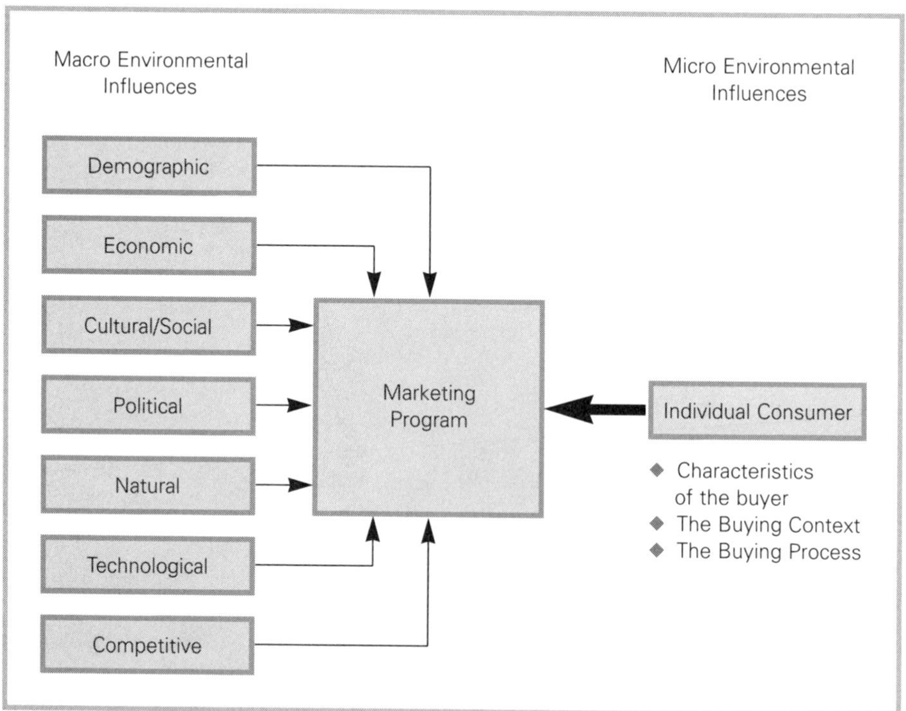

Figure 1.2 Environmental Influences on a Company's Marketing

Changes in these factors result in changes in consumer preferences in the marketplace.

Age. Three changes in the age pattern of North Americans stand out as especially significant. First of all, the number of younger workers (under age 25) has been falling since the end of the 1970s. While most of that change is now over, this age segment supplies a significant part of the hospitality work force, and the shortage of young workers will continue to affect the industry for some time to come. Members of this age group are good customers for QSRs (quick-service restaurants), and the reduction in the size of this segment is a problem which has an impact on fast-food sales. This probably accounts for the increasing efforts of QSRs to serve a more mature clientele—and hold onto some of their customers as they grow a little older.

The demographic fact of greatest significance in the last half of this century has been the baby boom—people born in the wave of births that followed World War II from 1946 to 1964. A second factor affecting hospitality is the entry of the baby boomers into middle age. Today, boomers have entered a time of life when incomes (on average) reach their peak. The growing affluence of middle-aged baby boomers probably accounts for hospitality developments such as the growth of the all-suite hotel and the increasing popularity of upscale casual restaurants.

A third major development related to age is the increase in the older population and the increased importance of retirees as a market. Up to now, this has been a gradual change, driven largely by a declining death rate as people live longer because of improvements in health care. Retirees have plenty of leisure time. A large number of them are both relatively affluent and in good health. Thus, they are a major target for leisure-related industries such as hospitality. The biggest change in the size of the older population, however, lies ahead when, in 2010, the baby boomers begin to reach retirement age. Marketing Environment Note 1.1 highlights the way changes in the demographic and economic environments (in this case, changing business practices) can have an impact on a hospitality firm.

Family Formation and Structure. Changes in the family have already had a major impact. Working wives, for example, have meant an enormous growth in demand for food service. Two-income families can afford to eat out more, and they have less time available to prepare meals and eat at home. On the other hand, a growing number of single-parent families, particularly those that are headed by women, tend to have lower incomes. While they are not as good customers for hospitality in general, they do patronize the lower-priced QSRs.

Later marriage and delay in having children have also had significant impact on the hospitality industry. Couples without children—along with single persons—are food service's most frequent customers. Couples without children can also afford to travel more and to use more expensive accommodations.

Income. Three groups can be regarded as the "income winners," groups that have experienced the greatest gains in inflation-adjusted income. These are

Marketing Environment Note 1.1

A Changing Environment Changes Demand for Marriott's Services

In senior living, demographic trends are creating increased need for quality retirement facilities. The planned acquisition of Forum Group, Inc. in early 1996 will more than double our presence in this fragmented industry, and will provide additional avenues for growth.

Marriott Management Services is benefiting from the trend to outsourcing, as companies increasingly rely on outside suppliers for services not directly related to their core businesses. With only 25 percent of the U.S. food service market now served by outside contractors, we see significant opportunities for new account growth, particularly among hospitals and schools. We also are developing new service offerings that, together with productivity improvements and international expansion, should yield additional sales and profit gains.

Source: *Marriott 1995 Annual Report.*

college-educated people, retirees with investment income, and women with full-time jobs.[5] Educational attainment is the single most reliable indicator of a person's income potential, attitude and spending habits. This is probably because education has such a powerful impact on the jobs for which people qualify.[6]

Retirees are good potential customers because many have private pensions or investments with which to supplement their social security. Although their *income* may not be as high as younger families in peak earning years, many retirees have significant *wealth*—homes and cars paid for, for instance. Moreover, they have raised their families and, hence, have fewer demands on their income. Accordingly, their disposable income is higher than their gross income may indicate.

Working women, on average, do not yet earn as much as men, but their average income has risen from 60 percent of men's in 1980 to 71 percent in 1990. Women aged 25 to 64 have seen their real income increase in all age groups, while men's income has declined in all ages except 45 to 54. From 1980 to 1990, the number of women graduating from college increased three times as fast as the number for men.[7]

Dual-income families, as a group, also stand out, but only if both partners are educated. The average household income of two college-educated spouses was just over $77,000 in 1995, more than triple the average income of a couple who did not finish high school. Thus, while educated couples are relatively affluent, less educated couples may barely be able to keep their heads above water.[8]

The United States has a high degree of economic and social mobility—that is, people changing their socioeconomic status either up or down. The trend during the 1980s was toward more downward mobility than upward mobility. As a result, both higher- and lower-income groups increased in size, while the middle decreased.[9] In fact, this trend has continued into the 1990s. The middle-class share of household income has fallen from 52 to 48 percent in the past 20 years, while the share going to the top 20 percent increased from 44 to 48 percent. At the present time, the income of the top 20 percent of households is roughly equal to the middle 60 percent of households.[10]

The affluent market, defined as households with incomes in 1993 of $100,000 to $250,000 a year, is a relatively small one, about 6 percent of the population, or 9.8 million people. The rich (incomes of $250,000 to $500,000) are only a tenth of that number (one million), and the super rich (over $500,000) are something over half the number of the rich, or 600,000 persons. Although small in number, this is the market for deluxe resorts, luxury hotels, and the most upscale of the fine-dining restaurants. Wealthy people, for instance, are likely to be avid travelers. "Almost 50 percent spend more than 20 nights a year in hotels and they spend $500 to $2,000 per couple per night."[11]

The Economic Environment

Spending on hospitality is discretionary. The recession in the early part of this decade saw the share of household budgets spent on food away from home decline. "When people have to cut back on expenses, eating out and entertainment outside the home are the first things to go," according to Roger Starch Worldwide.[12] Company travel budgets are among the first to suffer in a recession, too. Thus, hospitality industry sales reflect general business conditions and respond to trends in the economy.

Since hospitality firms, particularly in the hotel business, rely on mortgages for funds for new construction, high interest rates can discourage development of new properties and additions to existing facilities. Of course, low interest rates and easy money have often resulted in building booms and then in overcapacity, which makes marketer's challenge even tougher.

The Political Environment

Federal, state, and local government actions affect hospitality, as they do all businesses. Labor laws govern the conditions under which people can work, the minimum wage that must be paid, and, through immigration regulations, even the supply of labor in some markets. Taxes at every level of government affect hospitality, too. For instance, limiting the amount that can be deducted for business meals and business entertainment has hurt many upscale restaurants. The restaurant industry continues to feel pressure for improved nutritional labeling for menus from the federal government and from some state governments, as well. At the local level, some city and county agencies enforce strict standards of menu accuracy.

One of the major activities of both state and national trade associations, such as the National Restaurant Association and the American Hotel and Motel Association, involve government affairs. Both associations are recognized for the effectiveness of their lobbying activity. At the state and local levels, tourism promotion agencies and convention and visitor's bureaus play important roles in building sales for the hospitality industry in their region—and hospitality managers often play key roles as supporters of these efforts.

The Sociocultural Environment

The values commonly held in the community are naturally often reflected in government action. Restrictions on smoking in public places such as restaurants, for instance, have become common. Looking beyond the regulations, however, we can see that the increasingly aggressive posture of nonsmokers represents a broad popular movement not unlike the temperance movement earlier in this century. In response to consumer concerns, many operators provide no-smoking sections even where not required to do so by law. Furthermore, the provision of no-smoking rooms by hotels and motels is a marketing response to the contemporary climate of opinion (i.e., the social environment).

We see similar responses to health concerns in nutrition. The switch from animal to vegetable fat as a frying medium for meat and fish products, the reduction in sodium, and the near-universal adoption of salad as part of the product line in

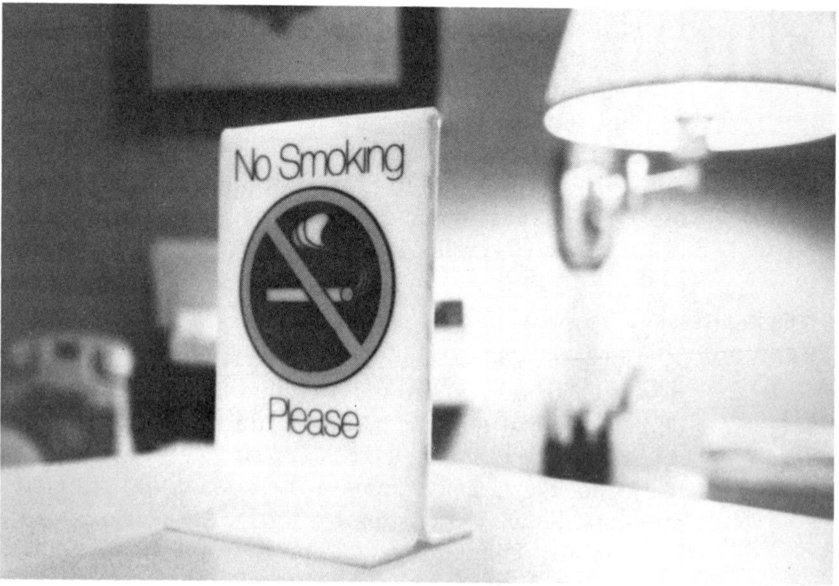

Restrictions on smoking are a response to guest concerns with amenities, such as smoke-free guest rooms in hotels. (Photo courtesy American Cancer Society)

fast food are all examples of marketing responses to the high value that contemporary society places on nutrition and health.

Another important expression of culture in North America is ethnicity. Ethnic specialty restaurants, such as Mexican, Italian, and Chinese restaurants, have typically begun in markets with high concentrations of the particular ethnic group in question. Mexican restaurant chains, for instance, got their start in the U.S. Southwest. Mexican concepts, with initial appeal to Mexican Americans, gradually secured a wider customer base in that regional market before expanding outside it.

Social class is another important influence. Inner-city neighborhoods in large metropolitan areas tend toward the extremes of the social scale: the very well off and the poor. Suburban communities, on the other hand, consist of a largely homogeneous middle-class population. These social realities suggest particular product/service and pricing strategies and also dictate promotional activities. Social classes are generally divided into three major categories: upper, middle, and lower—with two and sometimes even three levels identified within each major grouping.

The Natural Environment

The physical world impinges on hospitality marketing in a number of ways. We will look briefly at two examples, the potential scarcity of energy and of scenic sites. Both indirectly affect our industry, through the marketplace (higher costs) and the legal system (regulation). Ultimately, however, they represent physical realities of the kind that directly affect the hospitality enterprise.

The energy crises of the 1970s and early 1980s provide examples of the relationship of hospitality to the natural environment. The crises had the double impact of reducing demand for hospitality services in some places and increasing costs. On the one hand, energy scarcity meant people traveled less because they were afraid (often quite rightly) that they would not be able to get gas. Furthermore, when they could find gas, its price had risen dramatically. In many areas, regulation in the form of rationing—usually alternate-day availability of gas for odd- and even-numbered license plates—complicated matters further. At the same time, the operating costs of energy for airconditioning, heating, and lighting rose dramatically.

Currently, energy supplies appear adequate, but rising energy costs are predicted based on the limitations of a resource for which demand is increasing. Higher energy prices have already resulted in dramatic changes in tourism patterns, with shorter trips and smaller automobiles becoming predominant. Rising prices, when they come, will probably reinforce these trends.

A similar effect can be seen with scenic areas. The amount of coastline available, the number of mountaintops, and the scenic desert vistas are all limited. This limitation and the increased interest in preserving scenic and wilderness areas have given rise to severe restrictions on land use, thus making scenic resort sites both more costly and sometimes even impossible to obtain. One obvious marketing connection is the availability of appropriate *locations.* Managers and investors

The natural environment offers a limited number of scenic places such as this one. Hospitality operators face increasing difficulty in developing land for commercial uses because of growing environmental concern. (Photo courtesy of Florida Department of Commerce, Division of Tourism)

cannot reverse the current climate of opinion any more than they can make more coastline or mountaintops. What they can and should do is accept the environmental concern as a legitimate expression of contemporary society and work to design projects that will minimize environmental damage and secure public acceptance. Marketing Environment Note 1.2 discusses how the success of a tourism attraction can become a problem—through the attraction's very success.

The Technological Environment

As with so much of the North American economy, one major force for technological innovation is computerization. The greatest impact of computers has been in information flow and analysis. Computerized point-of-sales (POS) systems have revolutionized the analysis of restaurant operating results. The unit manager knows profit results at the end of the day. Furthermore, this information is available immediately to area managers and headquarters staff. This leads us to note a second major technological force, increased ease and speed of communication at reduced cost.

Indeed, the coming together of computer and communications technologies is creating a whole new world of entertainment which is likely to be a major competitor with the hospitality industry as consumers decide whether to go out for entertainment or to stay at home.

Marketing Environment Note 1.2

Tourism and the Environment: The Dangers of Success

An attraction can strangle itself on success. Beachfront resorts that become so crowded that the water is unfit for swimming and the fish unsafe to eat are, regrettably, fairly common all over the world. In some Rocky Mountain alpine meadows, the impact of heightened visitation has been to kill the plants people were coming to see. The tops of several peaks in New York state's Adirondack Mountains are now bare rock because of human activity.

A moment's reflection shows us why this *is* a marketing problem. If success kills the attraction, the tourism business it supports will die along with it. Thus, an enlightened understanding of the ecosystem within which a tourism operation exists is a first essential to preserving "the product." Here are some key concepts for thinking about the tourism environment:

Ecology. The study of how living organisms interact with each other and their surrounding environment.

Ecosystem. Any grouping of plants and animals that interact within a particular physical environment.

Environmental impact assessment. A study that predicts the effects a set of activities will have on the environment and a determination of how to enhance benefits and reduce negative impacts of the proposed activity.

Carrying capacity. The limits to which an area may be used without degradation of its environment. Carrying capacity might be expressed in terms of the number of people that could come through an area—and might specify different numbers depending on infrastructure arrangements (transportation systems, provision for sewage and trash removal, and similar steps to reduce pollution).

There is a second necessity if tourism firms are to use the natural resources of an area "to support economic activity without compromising the environment's carrying capacity" (i.e., its ability to continue to produce economic value). Managers of tourism firms must support those activities which help avoid or reduce the negative impacts of tourism on the attraction. These activities may include such simple steps as ensuring frequent trash removal. More complex and capital-intensive steps may also be needed, however, including construction of roads with adequate carrying capacity, arrangement of mass transportation facilities, or development of adequate sewage treatment facilities.

Respect for the environment has become a popular cultural value. It is also good business.

Source: Adapted from Edward W. Manning and T. David Dougherty, "Sustainable Tourism: Preserving the Golden Goose," *Cornell Hotel and Restaurant Administration Quarterly*, April 1995, pp. 29–42.

In lodging, the computer and communications revolution has created a worldwide means of communicating reservation information. As we will see in later chapters, this is having a major impact on all aspects of hotel marketing.

The Competitive Environment

A concentrated industry is relatively more orderly and predictable in its behavior than one that is fragmented. Within hospitality, only the QSR (i.e., fast food. The terms will be used interchangeably.) segment has reached that kind of stability. McDonald's is clearly the market leader. We see challenges, however, from existing players, such as Taco Bell, and from the introduction of new concepts such as happened with the double drive thru a few years ago. It is reasonable to say that McDonald's has a strong lead, but not one which has been successful in hindering competition from new concepts.

In the casual restaurant segment, the 10 largest chains in 1994 included six that were not even among the 100 largest in 1993.[13] That kind of turnover in market leaders confirms our impression that the marketplace is highly competitive.

In lodging, there is the *appearance* of very large chain dominance. The large franchisor's names appear on literally thousands of properties and create this impression of an industry dominated by a few companies. Behind that appearance, however, is an industry dominated by franchised properties with *many* owners. The real business purpose of each hotel is determined by its owners. Hotels drop brands and pick up others with surprising frequency. The franchise systems are increasingly suppliers of services such as national marketing, reservations, and, to varying degrees, quality control. The point here is that the structure of the industry is *not* that associated with market dominance but, rather, one of extreme competitiveness.[14]

The high degree of competition in both the hotel and the restaurant business affects pricing strategies and, really, all other elements of the marketing mix. The relatively fragmented nature of the industry means that companies will not find a predictable competitive environment; in fact, the reverse is true.

The goods—the physical side of the products that competing hospitality firms bring to the market—are in many ways similar to one another. The key differentiation is service and the real difference is in people, their skill, commitment, and effort. This brings us back to our starting point in this chapter: We must all be "part-time marketers" if the organizations on which our livelihoods depend are to continue successfully.

SUMMARY

The customer is purchasing an experience and, in hospitality service businesses, the employee's attitude and manner, as well as his or her efficiency, are a part of the product. For that reason, we are all part-time marketers. The marketing concept begins with the customers and their needs and wants and delivers products that meet them. Marketing consists of a mix of activities that includes *product, price, place,* and *promotion,* the 4 Ps of marketing. Marketing is a force that is pervasive in our society and is used not only by business firms but by nonprofit organizations and social causes as well.

Service products often have both tangible and intangible facets. From the customer's point of view, the product is an experience in which the people involved are a crucial part. Service firms often experience swings in volume. Because service organizations have no inventory, capacity management is critical. A service often involves more than one service company (e.g., travel agent, reservations service, and hotel).

The hospitality macroenvironments discussed included demographic, economic, political, sociocultural, material, technological, and competitive factors. Each of these has an impact on the way hospitality is marketed. Because the industry has similar physical goods to offer, the real differentiation is in service which makes all of us part-time marketers.

◆ Key Words and Concepts

Goods
Service
Repeat patronage
Part-time marketer
The marketing concept
Product orientation
Sales orientation
The marketing mix
Marketing as a social force
Characteristics of service
Environments of hospitality marketing

◆ Discussion Questions

1. Why is marketing everyone's job?
2. What is meant by "part-time marketer"?
3. What are the three approaches to the market? Why is the marketing approach superior?
4. What are the elements of the marketing mix? Why do you think all four are essential?
5. What are the major characteristics of service? How is the service product different from packaged goods?
6. Why are services so people-intensive? What people are involved?
7. What are the environments of hospitality discussed in this chapter? How do they affect marketing?

Chapter 2

When you have finished reading this chapter, you should be able to

1. Describe the characteristics of buyers
2. Discuss the buying context and consumer behavior
3. Explain the buying process as problem solving
4. Identify hospitality's principal organizational customers
5. Discuss buying centers and the organizational customer

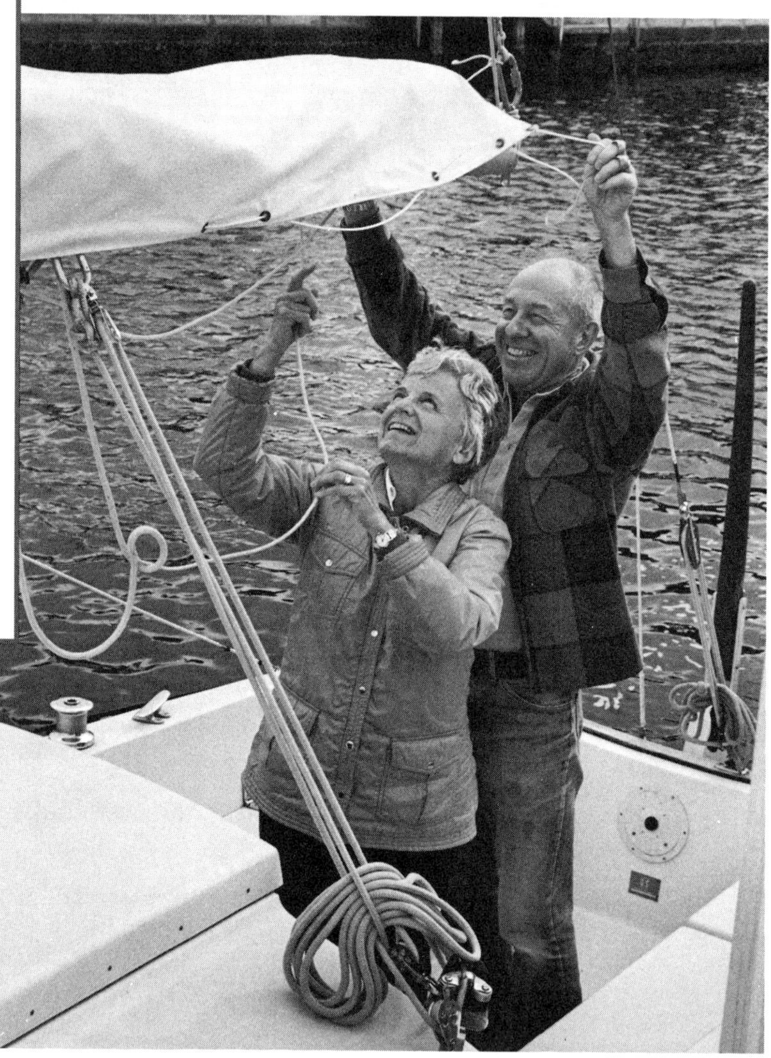

(Photo courtesy Janice Fullman/Picture Cube)

Analyzing Market Opportunities:

Consumer Behavior

Market opportunities relate, essentially, to customers, so in this chapter it is appropriate to consider **consumer behavior** and the factors that affect it. We will look at influences on the individual consumer as part of a model of consumer behavior. We will be concerned with both individual consumers and organizational customers such as companies and institutions.

UNDERSTANDING CONSUMER BEHAVIOR

An understanding of consumer behavior depends on recognizing the importance of the characteristics of the buyer, the buying context, and the buying process. When these are combined with the environmental influences we looked at in Chapter 1, they lay the groundwork for a key marketing concept, segmentation, to which Chapter 3 is devoted.

Characteristics of the Buyer

It is helpful to see the **characteristics of the buyer** from three different perspectives: societal influences, the personal situation of the consumer, and the psychological processes and influences that bear on the individual's behavior.

Societal Influences

The sociocultural aspects of the environment we identified in Chapter 1 have a profound influence on consumers. As well as the macroenvironmental influences identified in Figure 1.2, these include issues such as the ethnic (Irish, Italian, African American, etc.) and regional (Southern, New England, Far West, etc.) background of the consumer. Social class background is another factor that we have already discussed.

Reference Groups

Important influences are also found in **reference groups.** These are units to which individuals belong that influence their values, opinions, and attitudes in a fundamental way. *Primary* reference groups are those such as family, close friends, neighbors, and fellow workers to whom consumers relate on an individual, face to face basis. *Secondary* reference groups include the church people attend, as well as the fraternal and professional groups they join. A third category—sometimes called aspirational—are those groups to which consumers would *like* to belong—or not belong. These groups, for example, include successful sports figures and movie stars or, on the negative side, drunk drivers. Table 2.1 depicts these basic reference groups and indicates some possible marketing applications.

Personal Situation

A consumer's interests are affected by a number of factors that are specific to the individual but may be shared with many others. These factors offer solid grounds for grouping consumers together into viable market segments. Here, however, we will focus on these factors in terms of their impact on the individual.

Table 2.1 Reference Groups Offer Important Marketing Opportunities

Group	Marketing Appeal	Marketing Theme
Primary	Bonds of affection, family loyalty	Give Mom a break—and a treat. Eat dinner out today.
Secondary	Social identity	Dr. X and Dr. Y also belong to our club.
Aspirational	Positive: Glamor	Movie star X dines with us, why don't you?
	Negative: Drunk drivers	Drunk drivers rest in pieces. Try our designated-driver program.

Reference groups influence peoples' values, opinions, and behavior, including their buying preferences and habits. (Photo courtesy Jim Andersen, Woodfin Camp)

Age. One person's intimate cocktail lounge is another's dark smoky den of iniquity. Consumer's interests and needs change as they age. A fast-food favorite for teenagers will likely give many seniors indigestion.

Life Cycle Stage. While **life cycle** stages tend to parallel changes in age, we do best to think of them separately, keyed to social and family responsibilities. The principal life cycle stages and some suggestive consumer considerations related to each are set out in Table 2.2.

To see the significance of life cycle stages, we can consider two segments, the baby boom generation and people over age 65. In 1994, the youngest boomer turned 30 and, in 1996, the oldest boomer turned 50.[1] Thus, this huge generation, accounting for nearly a third of North America's population, is moving squarely into middle age, a period when incomes rise. By the end of the 1990s, the older half of the baby boom will be in their peak earning years, with nearly a quarter of them heading households with incomes of $75,000 or more.[2] In fact, baby boomers account for slightly more than half of all restaurant visits. They are, then, our good customers.

Another key life cycle stage is represented by older Americans—people aged 65 and older. *Fortune* dubbed the upper-income set in this age group "WOOFIES," short for "well-off older folks."[3] Many older people suffer from

Table 2.2 The Life Cycle and Hospitality

Life Cycle Stage	Age	Hospitality Industry Consumer Considerations
Childhood		
Early	5 or less	Problem consumer for parents; need toys and child portions; may require baby-sitter in hotels.
Late	6–12	Important influence on choice of place to eat out. Resort hotels provide recreation programs for subteens.
Teenagers		
Younger	13–15	Becoming an independent consumer but most commonly without significant independent income. Still major influence on dining out; recreation facilities in hotels used independently.
Older	16–19	Independent consumer, often employed part time. High need for social activity.
Young Adulthood		
Young singles	20–24	In labor force or postsecondary education full time—or combine both. Adequate income for small-scale use of hospitality firms such as for dating. Travels with family or on very low budget.
Young marrieds	25–34	Two-income families predominate but family formation expenditures, investments often reduce funds available for travel. Like lively informal dining places. High interest in travel.
Middle Age		
Young middle age	35–50	Incomes rise considerably but children at home or in college require significant continuing support. Highest propensity to eat out, travel.
Advanced middle age	50–65	Incomes at peak though sometimes reduced at early retirement. Very high propensity to travel. Eat out less often than young middle age groups.
Senior Citizens		
Young old	65–75	Fixed but adequate income. Retirement means an affluent leisure class. Generally, healthy, vigorous, and intent on enjoying life. Regular, but less frequent restaurant customer. Some special diet considerations.
Old	75–84	More health problems, often widow or widower living alone; prone to depression; may require nursing home care. Special diet considerations more prevalent.
Very old	85 and over	Most rapidly growing population segment in North America: 1 out of 5 live in nursing homes; 7 out of 10 are women. Frail elderly—but also some alert and very prosperous elderly. Often require special diets, special assistance.

Older couples account for a large percentage of pleasure travel. Determining and catering to their tastes is of growing importance. (Photo courtesy Carnival Cruise Lines)

some of the degenerative effects of aging—impaired hearing, impaired vision, digestive difficulties, loss of teeth, and denture difficulties—but most retirees under age 75 remain active, are relatively prosperous, and have lots of leisure time. This makes them a prime target for hospitality services.

Family Status. Today, the "traditional family" made up of husband and wife in a first marriage with children present is a distinct minority in North America. This is true for several reasons: a high divorce rate; the postponement of marriage and first children; the growing number of couples who decide to have no children; and an increase in the number of people who choose to remain single. One-person households, for example, grew from 18 percent of households in 1970 to 25 percent in 1990. On a *per capita* basis, singles spend more in virtually every category of spending.[4] They are good fast-food customers.

The fastest-growing household type in the 1990s will be married couples with no children at home.[5] Childless married couples can be divided into two categories, those under and those over age 45. Younger couples with no children at home "have plenty of money left over for fun . . . . Their liquor bill is the highest of any married couple type and . . . they spend more on restaurants and take out food than they do on groceries."[6] Couples over 45 without children, on the other hand, are most commonly "empty nesters," families whose children have left home.

Table 2.3 shows the traditional family stages used in marketing analysis and indicates how these are evolving in our rapidly changing society.

Psychographics. Psychographics, or **lifestyle** analysis, examines patterns of *activities, interests, and opinions* (AIO). The task of hospitality marketing is to recognize and fill the needs generated by people's ways of life. Here are some examples:

- The family with a working spouse is a good restaurant and take-out customer at dinner because of the pressures of time and the wife's heavy schedule.
- Families in which both parents are employed in professional capacities often try to combine minivacations with short business trips for one of the spouses. The short vacation and the couple's generally time-stressed way of

Table 2.3 Family Stages

Traditional Stage	Traditional Description	Evolving Reality
Bachelors	Young single people	Will include an increasing number of single—never married or divorced—persons. Some of them will not be particularly young.
Newly marrieds	Young, no children	An increasing number of families are choosing not to have children. Thus, the group of childless couples is growing, but is no longer restricted to newly married.
Full nest I	Married couples with youngest child under 6	An increasing number of families are second families, with remarried parents. Sometimes called mixed families, they may have younger children than would traditionally have been associated with the parents' age.
Full nest II	Young married couples with youngest child 6 and over	
Full nest III	Older married couples with dependent children	An increasing number of these are "boomerang families"—with older children who have left home and then returned.
Empty nest	Older married couples with no children living with them	
Solitary survivors	Older single people	

life, combined with their relatively high income, mean the quality of the experience is often more important than the cost.

- Retired people are more conscious of costs because they are living on fixed incomes, but they have plenty of time, often have considerable wealth, and frequently travel during the off-season.

Each of these sets of preferences—and a myriad of other lifestyle circumstances—offer marketing opportunities for hospitality managers. Lifestyle Note 2.1 offers a somewhat whimsical, but nonetheless revealing, look at psychographic analysis.

Role and Status. A person's position in a group can be thought of as a **role,** and each role implies a status. A manager, for instance, will have a higher status than a plumber. We should note, however, that the plumber may well have a higher income. The manager's status will probably dictate one set of choices with respect to dining out and travel accommodations, whereas the plumber may choose to patronize a quite different set of establishments. Promotional efforts and product design would probably be different if an operation targeted managers or high-income blue-collar workers.

The personal situation of the consumer, then, is influenced and expressed in terms of factors such as age and life cycle stage, family status, life style, and the consumer's role and status in society.

Psychological Influences

The psychological mechanisms we all depend on are important considerations to hospitality marketers. Individual psychology is a complex study, thus, we will confine our attention to just four consumer characteristics: perception, learning, motivation, and personality.

Perception. Let us suppose two people are driving into a congested area full of a variety of retail establishments such as those that surround a shopping center in a typical suburban area. Both people will be surrounded by literally hundreds of stimuli: traffic lights, other cars, pedestrians, road signs, shops, and billboards—to name a few. One of them, however, is driving in a car that is about to run out of gas, whereas the other is an hour overdue for lunch. It is likely that one of them will notice the filling station signs, whereas the other will pay attention to restaurant signs.

We can say that they will experience *selective exposure* and *selective distortion.* The driver must accept exposure to stimuli selectively because the mind cannot deal with *all* the stimuli in the scene simultaneously, and does not need to. Perception will be focused (i.e., distorted) to emphasize restaurant or filling station according to need. Given a large number of restaurants in the area, if the driver is highly cost conscious, he or she will remember the fast food and quickly forget the upscale restaurants. That is, the driver will engage in *selective retention,* holding on to those stimuli (restaurant signs) that most closely fit with his or her

Lifestyle Note 2.1

A Tongue-in-Cheek Look at Psychographics

THE TEENAGE ROOTS OF PSYCHOGRAPHICS

Who says Madison Avenue has the corner on lifestyle segmentation? High school students are the original pigeonholers. At a local high school in upstate New York, *American Demographics* uncovered lifestyles that may be markets of tomorrow.

Greaseballs. At one end of the high school lifestyle spectrum are the Greaseballs, including Farmers and Farmers' Daughters. The boys wear brown jackets from Agway and tractor caps that say "Brooktondale Volunteer Firemen." The girls sport heavy makeup and tight sweaters.

Also in the Greaseball segment are Wrestlers (while other jocks have status, wrestlers do not) and Headbangers. Headbangers wear chains and black concert shirts that say "Twisted Sister"; advanced cases are called Burnouts.

Rah-Rahs. This psychographic segment includes jocks, their girlfriends, and the guys who wish they were jocks. Rah-Rahs are popular conformists with few intellectual or political interests. They used to include Preppies, but this is a disappearing segment, reflecting the elusiveness of teenage fashion.

New Wavers. Also popular, but more involved in current events. New Wavers are fashion conscious in an attention-getting way. They are distinguished by melon and light-green clothing, including color-coordinated socks, all carrying an Esprit label. New Wavers are emulated by Pseudo-Wavers who want to be Wavers but don't quite make it.

Apes. These are the smart kids, the ones who take the advanced placement (A.P.) courses. They are arrogantly articulate and fiercely competitive for 4.0 averages. They are the driving force behind the student newspaper. Although they think of themselves as Achievers, they are known to outsiders as Encyclopedias.

Zobos. Mostly female, Zobos are distinguished by their high political consciousness and studied bag-lady fashion look. Zobos shop in used-clothing stores and eschew high heels. A typical Zobo outfit is a long skirt made from an Indian bedspread, accompanied by high, laced-up hiking boots. Zobos spend a lot of time on worthwhile causes like sponsoring Laotian refugees, and they carry handwoven purses from Guatemala to demonstrate their solidarity with the Third World.

Resistors. Just as VALS has a psychographic category that represents the pinnacle of psychological development—the integrateds—high school students have theirs. Resistors defy psychographic classification or fashion identification, evident in their uniform of T-shirts, sweatshirts, and chinos. Their message is that they are totally unaware of image, being above such trivia.

Source: Adapted from Bickley Townsend, "The Teenage Roots of Psychographics," *American Demographics,* November 26, 1985.

interests. These perceptive processes are important to all areas of marketing because they tell us how consumers see the world—as opposed to what we like to think of as objective reality.

Learning. Consumers respond to internal needs such as hunger and external cues such as the signs to which our driver was attending. When the hungry driver stops for a meal, the choice of restaurant will likely be based on previous experience—on previous learning. If restaurant X and Y are available, and X has generally been a rewarding place to eat, whereas Y has been unpleasant, the prospective diner will have learned through positive (rewarding) and negative (unpleasant) reinforcement. Briefly, a stimulus (hunger) is followed by a response (restaurant choice). Positively reinforced (rewarding) choices are likely to be repeated; that is, they are learned. Negatively reinforced experiences also result in consumer learning: Avoid that place in the future. This example supports the notion that operating quality cannot be separated from marketing: It is so important in obtaining repeat customers.

Motivation. The **hierarchy of needs,** first suggested by Maslow and illustrated in Figure 2.1, indicates that people have many needs that are of varying levels of priority. Physiological needs that relate to issues such as hunger and thirst—bare survival—are first. Once these are satisfied, safety needs can be attended to: those having to do with protection and physical well-being such as shelter and clothing. At the point when survival and relative comfort are assured, Maslow suggests, we can turn our attention outside ourselves to seek to satisfy social needs for affirmation in a sense of belongingness and love. Once we, in effect, are socially comfortable, we turn our attention to higher-level personal needs for esteem, status, and, ultimately, self-fulfillment (the term self-actualization is also used).[7]

In modern society, all of these needs are commonly sought simultaneously, but we are hardly conscious of the lower-level needs because of our higher standard of living. Anyone who has ever handled guest complaints knows that those basic needs are still very "close to the nerve" when not satisfied. Delayed service or a food product not properly prepared generally bring out not a reasoned and balanced complaint but very real anger and frustration. In hospitality, we serve basic needs and reactions related to them can frequently be highly emotional.

Because our customers associate establishments they patronize with people "like us," we also serve social needs. In our more sophisticated recreational activities and service routines, we offer people satisfaction of their personal needs. Calling guests by name and reacting promptly and in a friendly way to the guests' requests confer on them a sense of status, esteem, and self-fulfillment that they seek. The hospitality industry, then, addresses the whole range of human motivation.

Personality. Personality consists of a pattern of characteristics, attitudes, and habits that makes each individual unique. Although we experience our own

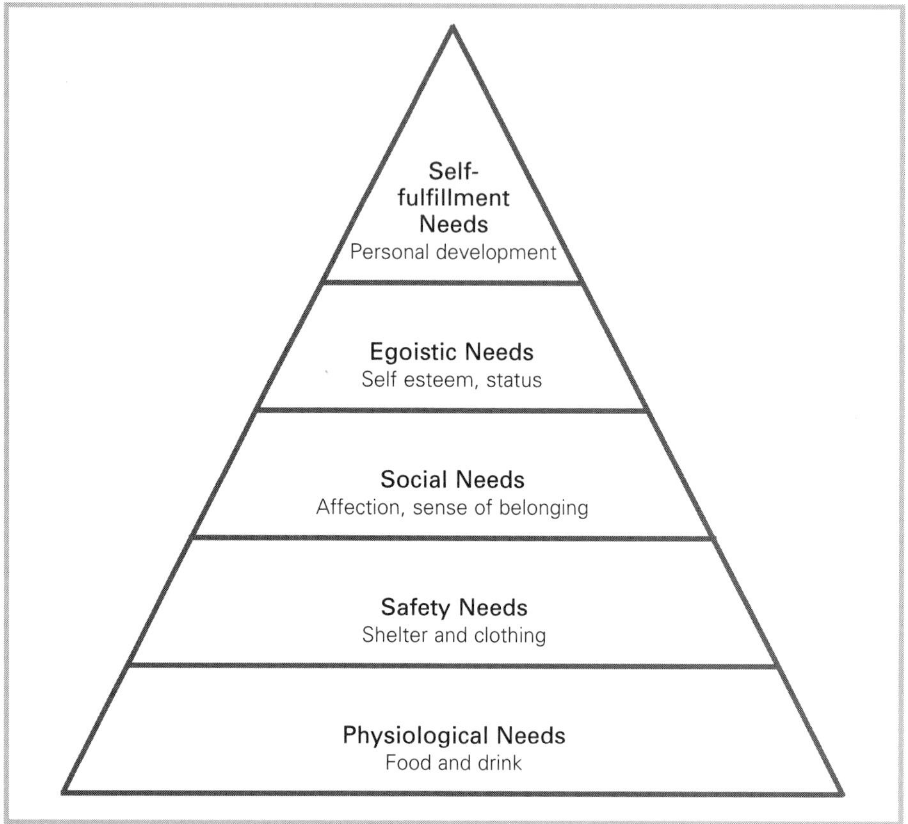

Figure 2.1 Hierarchy of Needs

Source: Abraham, Maslow, *Motivation and Personality* (New York: Harper & Row, 1954).

personality and those of others in terms of the conscious mind, much of the driving force in personality lies at the subconscious level.

One useful way of thinking of personality is in terms of one's **self-concept.**[8] People have an *ideal self-concept* and an *actual self-concept*. The ideal represents what one would like to be, whereas actual human experience usually falls short. Thus, marketing appeals to "be the person you know you should be" can strike a chord by offering opportunities to achieve higher social status or greater relaxation or some other ideal state. In addition, marketers can base appeals on a match of product/service appeal with self-concept. A resort, for instance, might appeal to people thinking of themselves as young, active, and fun loving.

Although people's personalities do affect their buying behavior, the complexity of the human personality is such that this factor is of only general use to most hospitality marketers. It would be difficult, for example, to construct a viable market segment based on personality characteristics.

The Buying Context

The context in which the purchase takes place has a significant impact on consumer behavior. The importance of the purchase, for instance, will influence how much attention the guest will give to analyzing a decision: The choice of a snack in a mall food court will obviously receive less attention than where to have a wedding reception.

The snack is largely a routine kind of decision that requires very little thought. The site of an important business luncheon—or an interesting dinner date—requires, however, at least some limited problem solving. Perhaps a conversation with acquaintances or a call to find out about menu items and prices would be in order. The choice of a resort for a two-week vacation in the Caribbean, on the other hand, would probably involve reviewing brochures and descriptions of various islands, consulting with travel agents, and extensive checking with friends. The amount of information searching, then, varies with the degree of importance of the buying decision.

Another aspect of the buying situation is its complexity. The decision for a family reunion dinner may involve a number of players. The role of initiator might, for instance, be played by a younger member of the family, but that person might not have the high degree of influence older members of the family would have. The buyer may be a grandfather or a rich uncle, but the person or persons who decide whether the event will take place could well be different from the initiator or the buyer. Obviously, in this decision, all the family who attend would be users of the service.

THE BUYING PROCESS: CONSUMER PROBLEM SOLVING

The most constructive way to think about the consumer buying process is as **problem-solving behavior.** Consumers may appear impulsive and sometimes irrational, but they are not *unreasonable*. That is, while *we* may not share their reasons, the purchase behavior *has a reason*—and one that solves the consumers' problem for them. This buying behavior arises to fill the needs, wants, and preferences of the consumer. We do best to try to understand how the consumer sees her or his problem—rather than dismissing it as irrational. In that way, we can understand and anticipate the consumer's problem-solving reasoning. The consumer's purchasing process can best be thought of in terms of the problem solving process as illustrated in Figure 2.2.[9]

Problem Awareness

Consumers do not begin a decision process until they perceive a difference between where they are, what they have, how they feel, and some state in which they would be better off. The problem must be large enough for the consumer to be willing to make some trade-off: to give up something in order to gain some objective. For the marketer, the reasoning is: If the consumer is not aware of a

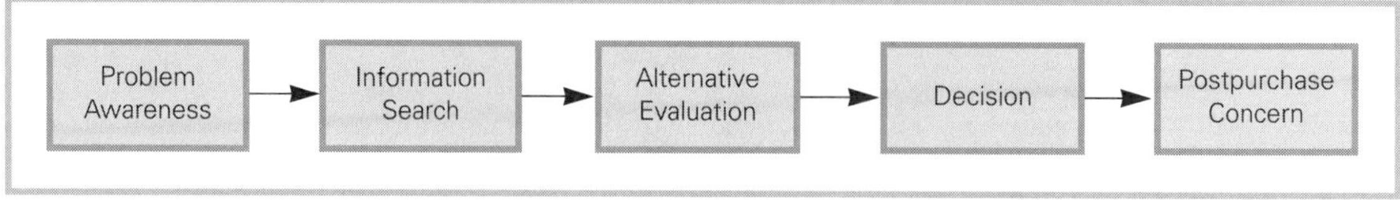

Figure 2.2 Consumer Problem-Solving Process

Source: Leo Renaghan, "Consumer Behavior: The Forgotten Variable in Marketing" *Proceedings, Hospitality Leader's Conference* (Guelph, Ontario: School of Hotel and Food Administration, 1981).

problem, marketing must *help develop awareness.* Other goals might be to heighten the consumer's sense of urgency with regard to a problem and to *inform* the consumer that the marketer's operation represents a solution to a problem.

For instance, a country inn near a big city might decide to play on consumers' concerns about the noise and rush of big-city living and the need to get away from it all. Advertising copy would establish "hectic pace" as a problem that seriously erodes the quality of urban life unless relieved from time to time. It could then offer the tranquility of the inn for a dinner or weekend outing.

Information Search

Once consumers are aware of a problem, they look for solutions to that problem; that is, they seek information. Several factors enter into understanding this stage of consumer behavior: the time and effort a consumer will invest in a search, the kinds of information required, and the sources of information customarily consulted.

The *importance of the decision* to be made is a logical first factor in deciding how much time and effort to invest in a decision. A mother taking her children for a quick lunch while shopping is likely to process the information found on the store signs in front of the nearest fast-food row. When she and her husband decide on a place to celebrate their wedding anniversary, a more careful information search is likely.

A second determinant is *prior experience.* When people go to a distant resort in an area they have never visited before, they will probably consult a travel agent for advice. This example fits a third factor, *perceived risk.* A week in the sun is not just fun, it is expensive. With well over $1,000 at risk, the prospective guest is likely to seek a good deal of information about the decision.

We should note two kinds of risk. *Performance risk* involves the possibility that something will not work. In the resort example, this is the risk that the resort will be poorly run. A different problem is presented by *social risk.* This involves the possibility that the guest will be embarrassed or will be concerned about using the product or service the wrong way. For instance, the resort may be run well enough, but the potential guest may worry that it will be too snooty (or too common) for his or her taste.

Kinds of Information. The factors that consumers consider in making decisions dictate the kind of information they are seeking. Hotel advertising often conveys information about the physical property—number of rooms, names of the food rooms, size of banquet space—that is of no interest to a banker from out of town seeking a good address. The image of the property and the kind of people who patronize it are more important than physical facilities to someone with the banker's buying motive.

The *alternatives* among which the consumer really chooses; called the evoked set, are not all the restaurants in town but (research has shown) usually three to five competitors. The *performance level* that the consumer expects to insist on within the alternatives he or she considers is the final factor in determining the information the consumer seeks. For a quick lunch with the kids, McDonald's reputation for fast, inexpensive, and acceptable food is likely to be enough. The performance level expected for an anniversary dinner will likely be higher, so a much more careful information-seeking process is reasonable.

Sources of Information. According to a National Restaurant Association (NRA) study about information used by consumers in choosing a restaurant, informal sources, such as word-of-mouth recommendations, were substantially more important than formal sources (the firm's advertising, trade association membership, directory listings) to the people who took part in that study. It is worth noting, too, that word-of-mouth advertising, unlike other media, cannot be bought. It can only be earned through superior operating performance. This underlines the close relationship between operating performance and marketing in securing the repeat patronage we referred to earlier.

Alternative Evaluation

Students of consumer behavior have suggested a number of models for the evaluation process. The one we will explore moves from a single criterion for evaluation to a kind of mental weighted average that includes several factors weighted according to their importance.

The natural-foods customer offers an example of a consumer who focuses on a single criterion and who looks to other factors only if the first is satisfied. That consumer needs to be convinced that the food is "natural"; otherwise, no purchase will be made. Another example might be the mother on a shopping tour confronted with a fast-food row: If prices were her major concern, then information on that topic would be what she would use to evaluate her options first, before she turned to matters such as menu selection, flavor, nutrition, and the like.

Guests set minimum standards on a number of criteria: speed of service, facilities for children while waiting, quality of food and service, menu variety, and so forth.

If two restaurants are equal on a single crucial variable, for instance, price, then evaluation may proceed on the second most important variable, perhaps the time needed to drive to the restaurant.

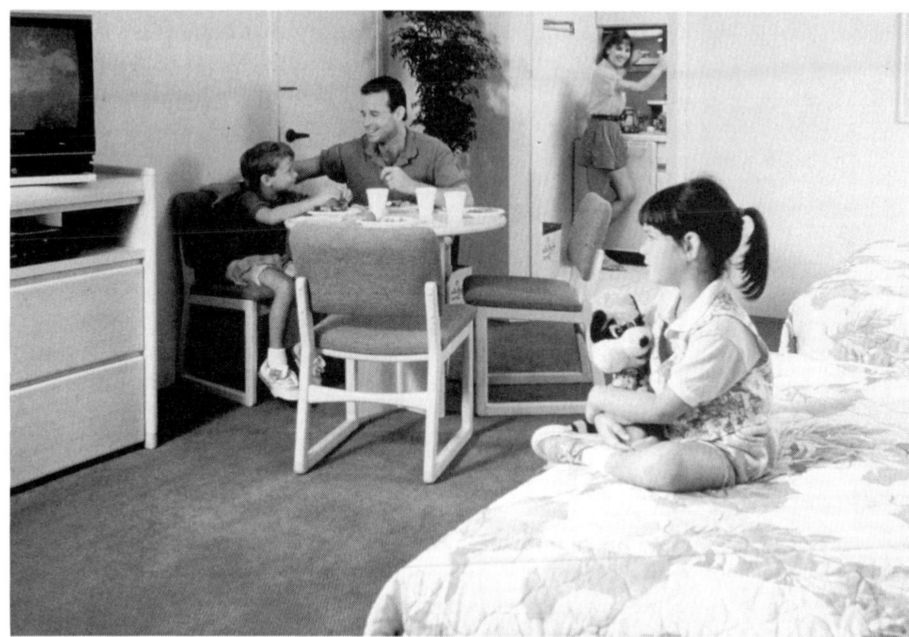

The choice of an expensive resort for a vacation calls for more careful problem solving than the selection of a place to stop for the night. (Photo courtesy of Holiday Inn)

Consumers do not actually *compute* an average to reach a decision, but a similar kind of weighting process takes place. Each decision variable is intuitively weighted by the importance to that consumer of the particular variable and is then summed up for the alternatives being considered. In this model, price may be important but weight could also be given, for instance, to the availability of table service, whether or not there is a playground on the premises, and menu variety.

Decision and Postdecision

After the consumer perceives a problem and seeks information to solve that problem and evaluates the options available, the consumer reaches a decision. Where that decision involves a major purchase, for instance, a two-week trip to a Caribbean island they have never seen before, a couple might well have a number of concerns that were only partly resolved in the buying process. This set of concerns is sometimes referred to as cognitive dissonance. The danger is that, once they have made the purchase decision, these factors will resurface: "Did we make the right decision?" From the marketer's viewpoint, this suggests the need to provide some reassurance in the immediate postpurchase period. Something as simple as a personalized cheerful reservation confirmation could well help that distant couple see their future destination as an accommodating, friendly place.

Table 2.4 summarizes our discussion of consumer problem solving.

Table 2.4 The Purchase Decision: Solving Consumer Problems

Stage	Considerations	Marketing Impact
Awareness		Marketer creates or highlights a problem in the consumer's consciousness
Information Search	*Time and effort* depends on	
	◆ Importance of decision	If important, need for information is greater
	◆ Prior experience	If none—more testimonials or references helpful
	◆ Perceived risk	If high—need reassurance
	Kinds of information	
	Evoked set (alternatives considered)	Who are our direct competitors? What are competitive points of difference?
	Performance levels (consumer expectations)	Beware of overpromising; always deliver as promised
	Sources of information	
	Advertising	Promise only what you can deliver
	Word of mouth	Importance of operation's performance to marketing
Alternative Evaluation	Single criteria	Screening
	Weighted average	The information that enters into the evaluation *for the consumer* needs to be conveyed in the advertising message
Decision		
Postdecision		For major purchases, how can we reinforce the consumer's decision so as to allay any anxiety about that decision?

The Importance of Consumer Expectations in Marketing

One day in class, we were discussing the process of choosing vacation sites and a student volunteered that she had spent a week at a resort that was advertised on a poster we could all see on the classroom bulletin board. The poster showed a beautiful Caribbean beach. Immediately, a second student said she, too, had gone there. I asked the second student how she liked the resort and she said it was a dump and she and her friends had a miserable week. I turned to the first student and she said she and her friends "had a ball."

My first reaction was to be sure they were talking about the same place: They were. What was the difference? The student who *enjoyed* the visit had booked through a travel agent who had *visited* the resort. She was warned: It's really basic, just four walls and a bed with primitive, though clean, sanitary facilities. Her party arrived knowing what to expect and spent all week on the beach, going to the room only to sleep. The other young woman and her friends had only the poster's

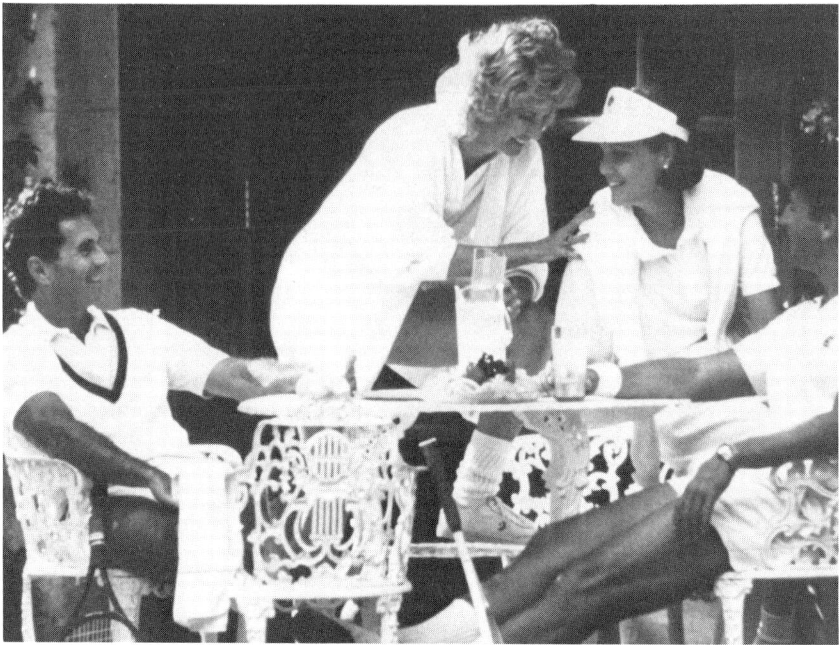

Consumers thinking about a distant resort have concerns about whether facilities and amenities will be acceptable (performance risk) and about how well they will fit in (social risk). (Photo courtesy The Boca Raton Hotel & Club)

glamorous photos and generous description on which to rely. They went expecting a luxury resort and came away feeling cheated.

The Point of the Story: Consumer Expectation. Consumer satisfaction is experienced and the evaluation of that experience is based, in good part, on what the customer expects will happen. The travel agent who briefed the satisfied student did the resort a real favor by clearly indicating how primitive the accommodations were. Because of her successful experience, she was a source of good word-of-mouth advertising. There was no serious gap between what she expected and what she experienced. The gap, however, between the second student's expectations, aroused solely by a glamorous poster, and her experience created an unsuccessful visit and bad word of mouth. A poster that avoided unreasonable expectations, while still conveying the advantages of beaches and good value, might have been more effective in achieving long-term success for the resort.

The consumer behavior, *to the consumer,* is his or her own personal experience. It is evaluated by contrasting experience with expectations. The result of that evaluation is largely an emotional state: satisfaction or dissatisfaction. Two basic points about repeat patronage flow from this. If we make a promise to the consumer, we need to fulfill it. That involves effective operations. Second, in our advertising, we must avoid overpromising and arousing unreasonable expectations if we want to avoid disappointing our guests. The variables at work in consumer marketing are summarized graphically in Figure 2.3.

THE ORGANIZATIONAL CUSTOMER

Probably the largest employer of salespeople in the hospitality industry are contract food service companies, which have combined sales of well over 18.5 billion

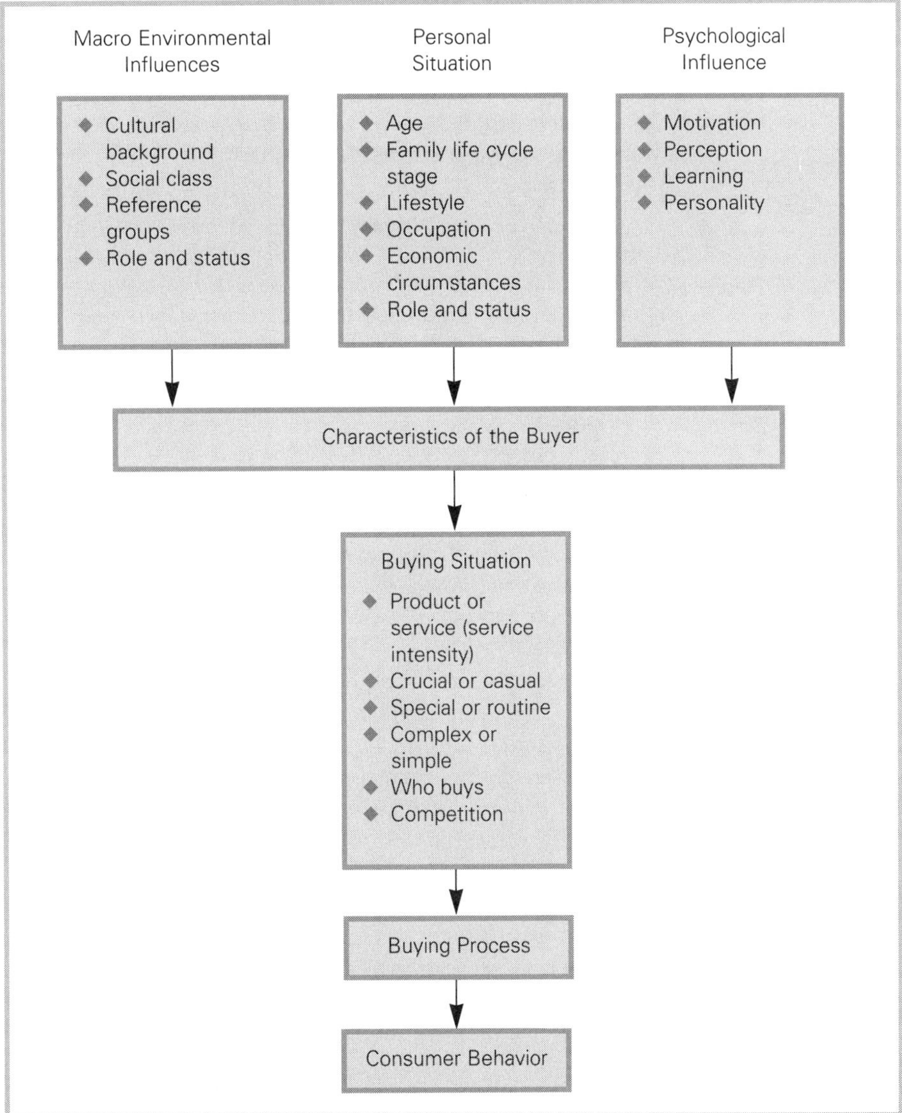

Figure 2.3 Variables in Consumer Marketing

dollars.[10] Their potential market, however, is defined by all institutions, including those operating their own food service, which are, to the contract companies, just customers they have not sold yet. The potential contract market, then, is roughly 50 billion dollars.[11]

In the hotel business, organizational customers are numerous. They include the *corporate market*, both for individuals as well as for meetings. The *association, convention, and trade show market* is another significant group of organizational customers.

Tour wholesalers package vacations for individual travelers, including hotel, transportation, and often food. While there are individual end users involved, from a hotel sales perspective, it is an organizational customer, the tour packaging company, that must be sold. Incentive travel awards are used by companies to motivate sales staff and others to achieve superior performance with the reward of a trip as a bonus for the most successful. In many ways, the incentive houses that arrange these incentive packages are another, more specialized form of wholesaler.

All in all, then, the organizational customer is one we cannot overlook. In Chapter 13, we will consider personal selling which, in hospitality, is almost exclusively directed at organizational customers. For now, however, we will concentrate on understanding organizational customers and their behavior, as we have the individual guest in earlier parts of this chapter.

Organizational Buying Behavior

The organizational customer is conventionally seen as a "rational purchaser" who emphasizes logical considerations such as minimum price or lowest total cost. These "task-oriented" models of buying behavior are not untrue—but neither are they the whole truth. People who make purchasing decisions for companies and institutions are as human as any of us and so can react to nontask motivations such as self-interest and ego needs, as well as uncertainty and risk.[12]

Buying Center. In practice, organizational buying is usually the responsibility of more than one person. Whatever group of persons is involved in the decision, either formally or informally, is referred to as the **buying center.** For instance, when a university chooses a contract company, the buying center will likely involve the dean of student affairs, the person in charge of the university business operations (i.e., the treasurer, comptroller, or vice president for finance). In such a major decision, the university's president would also be involved. Other members of this particular buying center would probably include one or more representatives of the student government, a faculty member, and someone to present the views of staff members (secretaries, lab technicians, etc.). In such a complex decision process, it is important to realize that there are a number of *roles* that the buying center members play. These have been labeled users, influencers, buyers, deciders and gatekeepers.[13]

Users, in our preceding example, would include the student, faculty, and staff members who are all food service customers. The dean of students would certainly

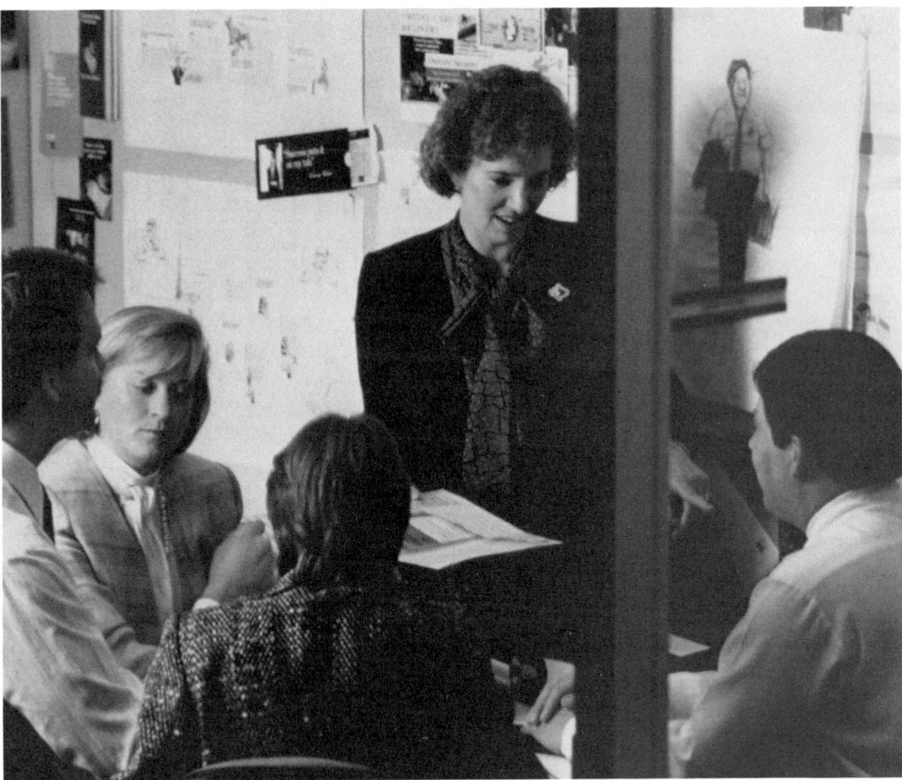

Organizational buying decisions are made by a group of people known as the "buying center." (Photo courtesy Mike Abromson/Woodfin Camp)

be an **influencer,** someone who helps define needs and set selection criteria. The **buyer,** that is, the person with the formal authority to close the purchase, in this case, would probably be the business manager. **Deciders** are the people who have either the formal or the informal power to make the decision. In this case, the decider would probably be the president, perhaps alone or in concert with one or two other senior officials. **Gatekeepers** include people who gather information for the decision process and control its flow such as the purchasing manager and the president's secretary. Table 2.5 offers another example, an office Christmas party. It is interesting to notice, in that example, that it is the gatekeeper who starts the ball rolling.

We noted earlier that there are task-related and nontask-related variables in purchase decisions. Task-related variables

> include environmental variables, organizational variables, interpersonal variables (buying center interactions) and individual variables. These variables are generally considered rational and task related; that is, they are related to a given organizational

Table 2.5 Complexity in the Buying Process: Who Participates in the Organizational Buying Decision?

Buying Decision Role	Participant
Gatekeeper	The manager's secretary raises the question of planning for the Christmas party at a staff meeting in late October. During the period the decision is under consideration, she will maintain and circulate files of proposals and related information.
Influencers	A committee is formed to choose a location and menu. Any person of high informal or formal status not on this committee is likely to be consulted by some member.
Decider	The manager—based on budget, the committee's recommendations, and her or his own judgment—makes the final decision.
Buyer	As the company will pick up the check (and is, therefore, the buyer), the manager must submit final plans for approval to the home office.
User	Everybody has a good time!

> decision . . . . In addition to task related variables, specific significant events and situational factors have been found to influence organizational decision making . . . . Three major types of situational variables are the buy class, risk and power.[14]

Buy Class. The way the buying center will proceed will be affected by which of the following buy class types apply: rebuy, modified rebuy, or new buy. Clark and McCleary studied the way associations chose sites for their annual meeting. In this study, a *rebuy* is a buying situation where

> the buying center is considering a purchase it has made at least once in the past. Because the product and the buying situation are familiar, the tasks are likely to be routine . . . . In a *modified rebuy* the participants have some experience in making the selection. For example they are familiar with specific marketing sets and the procedures for selecting a site but one or more factors have changed. A *new buy* is a buying situation where an association is going through the selection for the first time. That is, the association, or at least the buying center, has never been responsible for a major meeting before and has little relevant experience.[15]

A second situational variable Clark and McCleary cite is risk: Risk can be psychological, functional, physical, or social. Psychological risk is the risk that a poor product choice will harm the customer's ego. Functional risk is the risk that the product will not perform as expected. Physical risk involves risk to the safety of the buyer or product user. Social risk is the risk that the product choice may result in embarrassment.[16]

Finally, there is the matter of influence and power: "The buying center is a group of people who interact to make buying decisions. Some members of the buying center have more influence than others. Their power can derive from various sources and take various forms."[17] Power, for instance, can be based on the power to reward or punish. In addition, a kind of power goes to some people because of the respect in which they are held, to others because of their expertise, and to still others because of the formal position they occupy such as that of a department head. In the case of gatekeepers, power comes from their ability to hold up or pass on information (sometimes selectively) to other buying center members.

In Clark and McCleary's study, most associations' buying centers were made up of five to eight people. Normally, the evoked set (i.e., the range of choices considered) included several sites each year. The typical evoked set was six to eight cities. Clark and McCleary conclude, "Our study showed that situation variables (i.e. those that were not strictly task related, such as buy class, power and risk) are crucial in determining whether a city makes the cut for final consideration. Understanding those variables and how they fit into the purchase process provides a marketing edge."[18]

From the discussion thus far, it is clear that organizational buying decisions are more complex than individual decisions. They are made by a group (buying center) which may or may not be formally appointed and whose membership may change as the buying process unfolds. People play one or more roles (user, influencer, decider, etc.) in the process. Analyzing how the buying center functions—who plays what role—can be crucial to the salesperson making the typical "big-ticket" sale that characterizes organizational purchases. Note that all of the variables at work in the individual purchase decision are at work in each of the buying center's members. This is another way of saying that the broader the acquaintanceship of the sales representative with the members of the buying center, the better the chance of success in influencing the final decision.

SUMMARY

Figure 2.3 summarizes the variables that the marketer must interpret and work with in consumer marketing. The characteristics of the buyer are determined by societal influences, the customer's personal situation, and psychological influences. The buying situation is influenced by the degree of service intensity. The more critical *service* is, the more likely that intangible factors will be crucial. The degree to which the purchasing decision is casual, routine, and simple, as opposed to complex, will affect the consumer's behavior. Finally, the presence and intensity of *competition* for patronage determines the array of choice the consumer faces. All of these factors bear on the individual's buying process: awareness, information search, evaluation, and decision.

The organizational buying decision involves more than one person. The buying center—an often shifting group charged with deciding for an organization—is made up of people who play various roles (users, influencers, deciders, buyers, and gatekeepers). The buying center is affected by both task and nontask variables. Situation (i.e., nontask) variables are often critical to the buying decision.

◆ *Key Words and Concepts*

- Consumer behavior
- Characteristics of the buyer
- Societal influences
- Reference groups
- Life cycle
- Lifestyle
- Role
- Perception
- Learning
- Motivation
- Hierarchy of needs
- Self-concept
- The buying context
- Consumer problem solving
  - Problem-solving behavior
  - Information search
  - Alternative evaluation
- Consumer expectations
- The organizational customer
  - Buying center
  - User
  - Influencer
  - Buyer
  - Decider
  - Gatekeeper
- Buy class
- Rational purchaser

◆ *Discussion Questions*

1. What are the main characteristics of the buyer identified in the text? What is the significance of each?

2. What are the major life cycle stages? How do they affect hospitality purchase behavior?
3. Comment on how a buyer's *perceptions* might bear on a purchase decision. What is meant by "selective exposure"? By "selective retention"?
4. What is the concept of the hierarchy of needs? What parts of the hierarchy are addressed by the hospitality industry?
5. Discuss the impact of the buying context on consumer purchase behavior.
6. How does consumer expectation affect hospitality marketing? What is its importance?
7. How are consumer and organizational buying behavior different?
8. What is a buying center? What are the major roles in the buying center?

Chapter 3

When you have finished reading this chapter, you should be able to

1. Define segmentation and target marketing
2. Explain the advantages of segmentation
3. Discuss the criteria for successful market segmentation
4. Describe the major types of hospitality market segments
5. Explain the importance of psychographic and geodemographic segmentation
6. Identify hospitality's principal organizational segments

(Photo courtesy Bob Perry/Killington Ski Resort)

Analyzing Market Opportunities:

Segmenting and Targeting Markets

SEGMENTING AND TARGETING MARKETS (INTRODUCTION)

The marketer's motto is "Begin with the consumer"—but it was not always so. In the early days of hotel keeping, the industry offered two basic kinds of rooms, less expensive "plain rooms" (rooms without a bath) and rooms *with* a bath. This is a *product-driven* approach. "Here is what we have. Which do you want?" Similarly, early restaurants were fashioned to provide nourishment—with or without the amenities of fine dining. Take your pick!

After World War II, the market for hospitality services underwent a major growth period. Accelerating demand and the arrival of many new customers led to entry into the market of new firms with novel solutions to meet customers' needs. Fast food challenged the old "mom and pop" restaurants; motels challenged hotels. As more competitors entered this growing market, operators needed to gain an advantage over competitors. Gradually, a new consumer-based way of thinking about hospitality came to predominate. This approach *does* begin with consumers, their needs and their wants.

However, the question then arises, "Which customer?" It is impossible to think constructively about millions of *different* customers at the same time. The answer to this dilemma is market **segmentation,** a process of dividing the market into different groups which have common needs and wants:

> A market segment is a group with enough characteristics in common that it will react in a similar way to a marketing appeal.

There are four basic criteria for segmentation. A good segment will be identifiable, measurable, of adequate size, and accessible. Targeting of the hearing impaired by Holiday Inns offers a useful illustration of these points.

1. *Identifiable.* The hearing impaired includes those who are totally and partially deaf and those who have a limited hearing impairment.
2. *Measurable.* The segment should be one for which numerical measures are available. In this case, Holiday Inns learned that the number of persons who were totally deaf was 2 million, with an added 9 million with significant hearing impairment and an estimated 10 million more with some hearing impairment.
3. *Adequate size.* A market of as many as 21 million potential travelers was clearly one of interest. In fact, during the first year that special services for the hearing impaired were offered, the company gained 40,000 to 50,000 room-nights from this segment.
4. *Accessible.* It must be both possible and economically feasible to reach this segment. People feeling like a weekend splurge sounds like a good segment. But how would you find them? On the other hand, there are numerous publications directed at the hearing impaired.

Segmentation, then, is not done for its own sake; instead, it is done to understand consumers.

Target Marketing

Target marketing is the logical action step that follows after segmentation. Having clearly delineated a number of segments, marketers *choose* those segments they can best serve based on what the company's offering is—and on the competitive situation. The segments chosen become *target markets* and the entire marketing mix is shaped to fit those targets.

In this chapter, most of the discussion will be focused on segmentation. You should keep in mind, however, that segmentation is undertaken for the purposes of target marketing, that is, *shaping the marketing mix to meet the needs of a specific segment or segments.* From time to time, our discussion will turn from segmentation to target marketing to make the connection clear.

Why Segment?

The rationale behind segmenting that we have already examined is a good basic starting point. Segmentation gives us a way to understand a marketplace that is diverse and changing. We can, however, be more specific about the advantages to segmenting.

1. Fundamentally, segmentation *ties* the operation and all its marketing activities *to consumers*—not, of course, to all consumers but to some recognizable group or groups of consumers who can be expected to respond in a similar way to a marketing appeal.

The singles bar scene offers a graphic example of a specific market segment that requires a particular marketing mix. (Photo courtesy Howard Drotch/The Image Works)

2. Because a segmented marketing strategy is aimed at specific consumer targets, operators and marketers have *a clear reference group* to use as a benchmark for marketing **decisions.**

3. Segmentation permits choosing those segments that offer the *best profit potential* at a particular time. For instance, a deluxe resort in a warm climate may target wealthy and expense account travelers in the on season, while going after rate-sensitive travelers in the off season.

4. The process of analyzing markets by segment may reveal an unserved segment or at least one that is not as well served as it could be. People being transferred or those attending an extended training program have special needs. They are less interested in on-premise food services, prefer more spacious quarters with adequate working space, and require some opportunity for after-work socializing. Extended-stay properties were developed to target this segment.

Segmenting not only helps us understand what people want in a product, it should also give a good idea of what price they are willing to pay and where they will want to be served. It also offers the opportunity to make more effective use of promotional media by choosing a medium that reaches the markets we are interested in with a message that the target market will listen to. Case History 3.1 describes how the consumer characteristics of a segment were fit together to develop a marketing program.

TYPES OF SEGMENTS

Segments are based on a number of specific variables. We will consider **geographic, demographic, psychographic, attitudinal, benefit, and purchase behavior,** as well as **operational** segments. We should note at the outset, however, that there is no single segmentation approach. In practice, most marketers use combinations of segmenting techniques. That is, a company may combine segmentation based on geography with consideration of demographics and lifestyle. Moreover, several segmentation studies, each employing a different approach, may be used by marketing managers trying to understand just who comprise the segment they are serving. Later in this chapter, we will look at how market analysts combine segmentation techniques.

Geographic Segmentation

One key element in the marketing mix is place. It is essential, in brief, to be "in place." If we want to sell lunch to the busy shopping center customer or a room to the weary traveler at an airport hotel, we need to make that offer *in that place*. Geographic considerations—where our operation is located and where our customers are—seem so obviously important that we might be inclined to skip over them. There are, however, a number of ways of looking at geographic segmentation, and each of them has special applications in hospitality marketing.

Geographic segmentation within North America begins at a regional level—and regional tastes *do* differ. Southerners, for instance, are more inclined to eat biscuits than the rest of the country, while hominy grits are hardly ever offered outside the South.

Political. Another approach to geographic segmentation follows political subdivisions: state, county, and city. In the small convention market, for instance, state-level associations and organizations have annual or even more frequent meetings that involve significant function business, as well as overnight-rooms business.

Census. The U.S. Bureau of the Census divides the country into nine regions shown in Figure 3.1. The census also reports statistics by state. The next smallest unit is a **metropolitan statistical area (MSA).** These are integrated economic units with a population of at least 50,000 which are not part of a larger population concentration. Cities such as Fargo, North Dakota, and Reno, Nevada, are MSAs. Where a city such as New York is part of a larger population grouping, it is referred to as a **primary metropolitan statistical area (PMSA).** PMSAs are then combined in a **consolidated metropolitan statistical areas (CMSA).** Minneapolis and St. Paul, for instance, are each PMSAs and are combined into the CMSA of Minneapolis–St. Paul. CMSAs have a population of at least one million. Since the census is taken only once every 10 years, metropolitan area statistics are less useful as time passes and population increases or decreases within the political boundaries which define census areas.[1]

Case History 3.1 Targeting the Long-Stay Market

Segmentation groups individuals who are alike in important ways. The common characteristics of the group serve as a basis for designing a marketing mix that will serve those guests well—and motivate them to give their business to the company. It is useful to see how one company used its knowledge of a segment to tailor its marketing mix to meet the needs and preferences of a segment of business travelers.

Residence Inns was one of the first to target the long-stay market (which is principally an organizational market). That company used its knowledge of the segment to target its customers and developed a very highly successful sector of the lodging industry.

> ***Product:*** The operation targeted a particular kind of customer: one staying more than a week. Having that customer base as a reference group, the product (all-suite, full kitchen, very limited food services, well lighted, comfortable working area) was developed to meet the customer's particular needs.
>
> ***Price:*** The overnight room rate, in keeping with the all-suite product, is relatively high at a Residence Inn (and for most other long-stay properties), but the price per night is reduced for stays of one week or more—and further reduced for stays of over two weeks.
>
> ***Place:*** A good location for a long-stay property may not be the same as for a transient property. Transient hotels benefit from visibility from the roadway such as is afforded by an interchange location. For long-stay properties, however, it is more important to be located near companies which have visitors who need long-stay properties. For instance, a good location would be one which is near regional or national headquarters of firms that require employees to come in for extended training programs. Visibility from the roadway would be a distinctly secondary consideration.
>
> ***Promotion:*** A long-stay property needs to concentrate a personal sales effort on those particular companies that have programs that require visitors to stay longer than a week. Obviously, roadside signs would be a waste of money in trying to reach this customer.

At the time Residence Inns began operations, the long-stay market was not served extensively by a specially designed lodging facility. The segment has proved to be a fast-growing one and a number of new long-stay chains have been developed.

Census data are by no means limited to large areas such as CMSAs or MSAs. Census figures are broken down into census tracts that cover areas ranging in population size from 2,500 to 8,000 people. An even smaller area, the block group, contains an average of 350 families and roughly approximates a neighborhood area. The block group measurements offer opportunities to target market specific

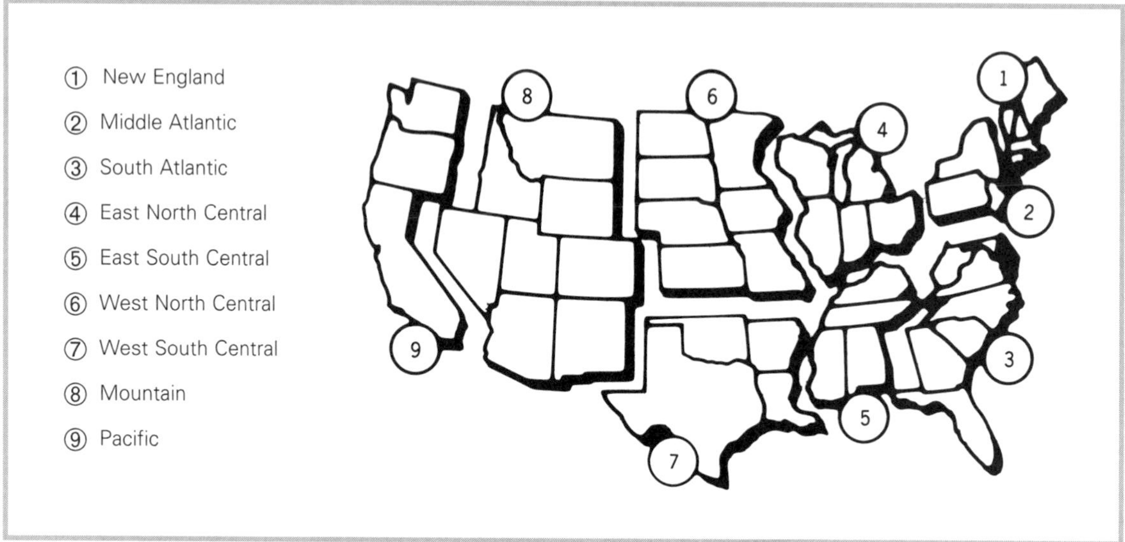

Figure 3.1 U.S. Census Regions
Source: U.S. Bureau of the Census.

neighborhoods and to assess in considerable detail the market of a particular unit at a manageable cost.

Census areas are vital in market research. The U.S. Bureau of the Census collects a great deal of detailed information on families and individuals in each area, and market research service companies offer even more detailed information. As time passes and census data become obsolete, the Bureau of the Census publishes *Population Estimates* which are based on sampling rather than a census. Commercial statistical sources also offer updates.

Postal Zones. Because postal zones are identified by zip code, another small geographic segment operators can use is readily available. Asking customers for their zip codes is also a helpful way of determining which neighborhoods provide a restaurant's customers and a quick way of sorting hotel guest registration data to determine which cities provide most of a hotel's guests.

Trading Area. A more informal geographic area is defined by the patronage of a restaurant or other retail establishment. As noted, asking guests to provide their zip codes gives a ready means to identify the neighborhoods a restaurant serves. This can be done on a periodic basis. A rougher approximation of a *competitive* hotel or restaurant's trading area can be obtained by periodic analysis of the license plates on cars entering the competitor's parking lot.

Media Coverage. Another geographic segment, used in planning television advertising, is the **area of dominant influence (ADI).** The ADI of a major metropolitan center includes any county that views the city's television signals more than half the time. There are over 200 ADIs in the United States that are measured and updated periodically. The ADIs are used not only to plan television marketing but sometimes also in developing the location strategy for restaurants during a chain's expansion. The intent is to choose locations in order to concentrate media purchases in a limited number of ADIs. In addition, ADIs are commonly used by franchisors to set the boundaries for local advertising cooperatives.

Demographic Segmentation

Whereas geographic segmentation looks at *where* people are, demographics looks at a number of aspects of *who* people are. Some common demographic measures are age, gender, family size, family life cycle stage, income, education, and ethnic background. Market Demographics Note 3.1 illustrates the importance of demographic characteristics to food service.

Age. As we have noted in earlier chapters, one of the strongest driving forces in the North American economy in this century has been the baby boom, and the aging of the baby boomers will remain a major force well into the next century. In the immediate postwar years, there was a great surge in marriages and births. The baby boom generation that emerged gave strong impetus to the growth of fast food in the 1950s and 1960s when there were many families with young children. As they became teenagers, baby boomers were themselves customers for fast food. The movement of the baby boomers into the more affluent middle years has been one of the driving forces on the growth of casual dining. As you can see from Table 3.1, average household food service spending rises as the age of the household head increases well into middle age, but then begins to decline after age 55.

Table 3.1 Weekly Expenditure for Food Away from Home by Age of Household Head

Age	Amount Spent per Week
All units reporting	$32.00
Under 25	24.86
25–34	31.75
35–44	38.92
45–54	43.71
55–64	33.48
65–74	20.58
75 and over	13.06

Source: Data derived from *Consumer Expenditure Survey* (Washington, DC: Bureau of Labor Statistics, 1994).

Household Demographics Have an Impact on Restaurant Spending

Household Demographics Have an Impact on Restaurant Spending

Households that spend disproportionately lower and higher amounts on food away from home by demographic characteristics, 1992

Spend a Disporportionately Lower Amount	Spend a Disproportionately Higher Amount
Household income	**Household income**
◆ Less than $30,000	◆ $30,000 or more
Age of household head	**Age of household head**
◆ Under the age of 25	◆ Age 25 to 54
◆ Age 55 and older	
Household size	**Household size**
◆ One person	◆ Two or more persons
Household composition	**Household composition**
◆ Single parents	◆ Husband/wife households with no children
◆ Single person and other households	◆ Husband/wife households with children
Number of earners	**Number of earners**
◆ Single persons who are either employed or unemployed	◆ Households of two or more persons with two or more earners
◆ Households of two or more persons with one or no earner	
Occupation of household head	**Occupation of household head**
◆ Service occupations	◆ Self-employed
◆ Retired	◆ Managers and professionals
	◆ Technical, sales, and clerical workers
Region	**Region**
South	Northwest
	West
Metropolitan Statistical Area (MSA)	**Metropolitan Statistical Area (MSA)**
Philadelphia, Kansas City	New York, Miami
Pittsburgh, Baltimore	Boston, San Francisco
Buffalo, Dallas/Ft. Worth	Chicago, Honolulu
Detroit, San Diego	Minneapolis/St. Paul
Cleveland, Portland	Cincinnati
St. Louis, Seattle	Washington, DC

Source: *Restaurants USA,* August 1994, p. 47.

The needs of affluent baby boomers have had a major impact on casual-dining restaurants. (Photo courtesy of Country Kitchen by Carlson)

We know, too, that people's tastes change in a number of ways. It is not age, alone, that determines preferences but, rather, the benefits sought, for example, quick food, variety, healthfulness, and ease of digestion. Speed is more likely to be important to harried young workers, for instance, whereas digestibility is more commonly a concern of older diners.

Of course, discretionary income is often associated with age. Consumers aged 65 to 75 can travel more and, on average, they do. Still, age alone is not enough to predict travelers' preferences. *Regardless of age,* for instance, upper-income consumers are less likely to patronize economy motels, and there is some evidence that affluent blue-collar workers prefer campers to hotels. Still, in lodging as in food service, knowing the age group of your customers—or which age group you mean to seek out—is a helpful key to market planning all across the marketing mix.

Age-Specific Versus Cohort Effects Age is sometimes an important factor determining behavior. The vitality of youth, the stability of middle age, and the handicaps of the elderly are conventional generalizations that are *age specific.* On the other hand, *when* a person is born can also determine preferences in a way that lasts throughout life. "If a good meal meant meat and potatoes when you were coming of age in 1935, that is what a good meal will mean to a 75 year old today." These lifelong impacts of year of birth are referred to as *cohort effects.* "[But] some eating habits are affected by aging. Later in life, medical conditions such as diabetes and hypertension can dictate food choice and a less tolerant gastrointestinal system can lead to a preference for less food."[2] These needs are age specific. Cohort effects relate to the underlying mindset of an age group (cohort) toward different products and services. Some cohorts commonly referred to today are baby boomers and the younger "Generation X."

Gender. One of the many ways in which women and men are different is in their eating preferences and the amount they need to eat. Men can consume substantially more calories without gaining weight and need more food to maintain their health. Some years ago, Wendy's sought to increase the number of women customers by introducing one of the first QSR[3] salad bars. Taco Bell, on the other hand, sought to increase its share of the *male* eating-out market, introducing the double beef burrito, a heartier menu choice designed to appeal to men's bigger appetites. In these two examples, women were a *target market* for Wendy's, while men were targeted at Taco Bell.

The number of women traveling is growing three times faster than the number of men. Naturally, lodging companies are interested in targeting this fast-growing segment. Research indicates that women business travelers consider security, personal services, and low prices to be more important selection criteria for lodging than do men. In-room amenities of interest to them are hair dryers, and the availability of irons and ironing boards, room service, and bathrobes are also important. Men place greater weight on services and facilities than do women.[4]

Family Size. Table 3.2 shows the importance of singles—*and* of families. Singles are the best *individual* customers of food services, spending an average of $19.86 per week. When compared to other *households,* however, that spending is the

Table 3.2 Weekly Expenditures for Food Away from Home by Size of Household

Size	Household Spending per Week	Per Capita Spending per Week
1 person	$19.86	$19.86
2 persons	33.21	16.60
3 persons	37.54	12.51
4 persons	43.98	11.00
5 or more persons	37.08	[a]

[a]A precise figure for per capita spending is not available for this open-ended category, but it is probably somewhere between $7.10 and $7.40.
Source: Data derived from *Consumer Expenditure Survey* (Washington, DC: Bureau of Labor Statistics, 1994).

lowest on the list because, of course, of the number in the household, just one person. Two-person households do not spend as much per capita ($16.60), but they account for the largest share of away-from-home food expenditures. Families with children, on the other hand, have to make the household's income support more people. Notice that total *household* expenditure on food service continues to rise as the family size increases, up to four persons; after that, not only does per capita spending fall but total household expenditures begin to decline, as well.

Family Life Cycle Stage. In Chapter 2, we discussed the family life cycle stages (see Table 2.3) as an influence bearing on consumers' preferences. Life cycle also offers advantages as a basis for segmentation. Full nest I families, for instance, with their need to adjust financially and in other ways to provide for children, are likely to have different preferences in dining out than are empty-nest families who can afford more expensive choices.

Income. There is a strong positive correlation between food service purchases and income. When incomes rise, people not only spend more in absolute dollars, but also can afford to spend a greater percentage of their food budget on food away from home. Table 3.3 establishes that both the absolute dollar amount spent *and* the proportion of the family's food budget spent on food away from home increase steadily as income rises. Income segmentation—and targeting higher income guests—makes sense because the weekly spending levels at the top and bottom of this scale suggest use of quite different kinds of restaurants.

Table 3.3 Expenditures for Food Away from Home by Income Segment

Annual Household Income	Amount Spent per Week	Percentage of Weekly Food Budget
All households reporting	$33.38	38.4%
Under $5,000	14.75	34.4
$ 5,000– 9,999	11.35	23.0
10,000–14,999	15.23	27.0
15,000–19,999	20.00	29.7
20,000–29,999	26.04	34.1
30,000–39,999	36.62	40.4
40,000–49,999	44.02	41.2
50,000–69,999	50.02	41.5
70,000 +	77.67	49.6

Source: Data derived from *Consumer Expenditure Survey* (Washington, DC: Bureau of Labor Statistics, 1994).

Education. Thus far in North America's recent history, each generation has been better educated than the previous one. Today, by the time they reach their late-20s, almost half of all people will have had some college education, whereas only 20 percent of people in their 60s have had some college. The strong positive correlation between education and income explains, in part, why rising education level, like rising income, is associated with an increase in dining out. The rising level of educational attainment is encouraging for restaurants because it apparently supports a lifestyle that is more dependent on food away from home.

Ethnic Background. By the year 2005, about 28 percent of the U.S. population will be African American, Hispanic, or Asian, up from 22 percent as recently as 1990.[5] Asians and Hispanics are the fastest-growing population groups, with an annual increase of 3.5 percent. Hispanics over the age of 16 numbered 7.6 million in 1990, but are expected to increase to 11 million by 2005, at which time they will nearly equal the African American population's level of 12.4 million.

Chapter 2 noted that ethnic groups generally have distinctive tastes in food—and often in ambience, too. They also respond differently to advertising appeals. Although 80 percent of Hispanics are either fluent in English or able to understand it, nonetheless, advertising in Spanish has a strong appeal. Different cultural values, too, make different kinds of appeals effective.

Demographic Segmentation: Uses and Weaknesses. Demographic variables are important to market segmentation for hospitality marketing. Besides their relevance and usefulness, demographic data are readily available, usually from public sources; hence, they are less expensive to obtain. Demographic variables, moreover, are often related to the way consumers choose hospitality services.

Combining demographic variables heightens their effectiveness. Obviously, not all 30-year-olds behave the same way: Some are rich; others are poor. Families headed by 50-year-olds will vary in their behavior not only according to income but also by family life cycle stage: Full nest III families (see Table 2.3) have more disposable income than those who still have younger children at home or in college. Also, the gender of the customer dictates different tastes in food selection and, often, differences in lodging choice. Any demographic statistic, then, captures only one dimension.

There are weaknesses in demographics as a predictor of consumer behavior. Demographics are unable to deal with individual differences based on factors such as attitudes and values. The wealthy guest is *able* to stay at an expensive hotel but may choose to visit a more economical property when on a family vacation. Middle-aged customers may choose to patronize restaurants with a younger image because they *feel* younger, or want to. Moreover, demographics alone do not provide enough information to determine how to phrase a commercial, that is, what particular buying appeal to use. Demographics are an important starting point for segmentation, but adding the dimension of people's lifestyles gives more depth to the picture.

Most Hispanic people understand English, but advertising in Spanish nevertheless has a strong appeal to them. (Photo courtesy of Pepsi-Cola)

Psychographic Segmentation

A resort may know the average age, family status, and average number of children its guests have, but this does not necessarily indicate what their preferences are—and, hence, how the resort's activity program should be shaped. Are they adventurous, for instance, or do they prefer a resort where they and their young children can be together? Psychographics provide clues that are qualitative in nature.

Psychographics—or lifestyle segmentation—relates to consumer interests, attitudes, beliefs, and values, as well as personality. Psychographics is sometimes referred to as **AIO,** the initials standing for activities, interests, and opinions.

Activities include work-related factors and also social activities, entertainment, sports, and vacation preferences. A consumer's *interests* may be centered on home and family, job or recreation, food or fashion—and, of course, combinations of each. *Opinions* measured may be about products, as well as the special political and economic issues of the day.[6] Segments delineated by AIO research yield insights into factors such as the consumer group's time or price consciousness, their venturesomeness, or their self-confidence. Do they like risk? Buy on impulse? Have an optimistic or pessimistic view of life? Figure 3.2 gives examples of the AIO elements and contrasts AIO with demographics.

One syndicated lifestyle segmentation technique that has attracted attention in food service is the Values and Life Styles (VALS) Program developed by SRI International. VALS2, an updated version,[7] uses the two dimensions of resources and personal orientation to identify adult consumers who have different patterns in their attitudes, behavior, and decision making and to predict their consumer behavior. Figure 3.3 shows the eight segments of VALS2 arranged according to their relationship to resources and personal orientation. VALS2 includes as *resources* not only income but factors such as education, self-confidence, health, intelligence, and energy level. *Personal orientation* refers to the consumer's approach to buying. Individuals who fit best in the first group are more likely to purchase on the basis of beliefs or principles, as opposed to feelings such as desire for approval. Status-oriented consumers, on the other hand, are strongly influenced by the opinions and behaviors of others. The action-oriented group emphasizes activity—social or physical—and seeks variety and risk. Food service companies have used VALS in developing new restaurant concepts and menu offerings, as well as in site selection, design, and in the development and execution of promotional campaigns.[8]

Psychographic segmentation is intended to give a personal dimension to the development of market segments and is often used in combination with demographic characteristics. Segments constructed in this way provide a more detailed description of the consumer.

Activities	Interests	Opinions	Demographics
Work	Family	Themselves	Age
Hobbies	Home	Social issues	Education
Social events	Job	Politics	Income
Vacation	Community	Business	Occupation
Entertainment	Recreation	Economics	Family size
Clubs	Fashion	Education	Dwelling
Community	Food	Products	Geography
Shopping	Media	Future	City size
Sports	Achievements	Culture	Stage in cycle

Figure 3.2 AIO Elements and Demographic Factors Used in Segmentation

Source: Adapted from Joseph T. Plummer, "The Concept and Applications of Life-Style Segmentation," *Journal of Marketing,* January 1974, p. 34.

Activities *can be work related or can involve social activities such as lodge membership. (Photo courtesy Supreme Lodge/Loyal Order of Moose)*

Lifestyles are a function of activities, interests, and opinions (AIO). These dimensions go beyond the objective attributes of demographics and tell marketers about how people live—which, in turn, is linked to buying behavior.

Interests *can range from job to home to food and fashion: here they involve recreation. (Photo courtesy Howard Johnsons)*

Opinions *cover the whole gamut of social, political, and economic issues. (Photo courtesy Republican National Committee)*

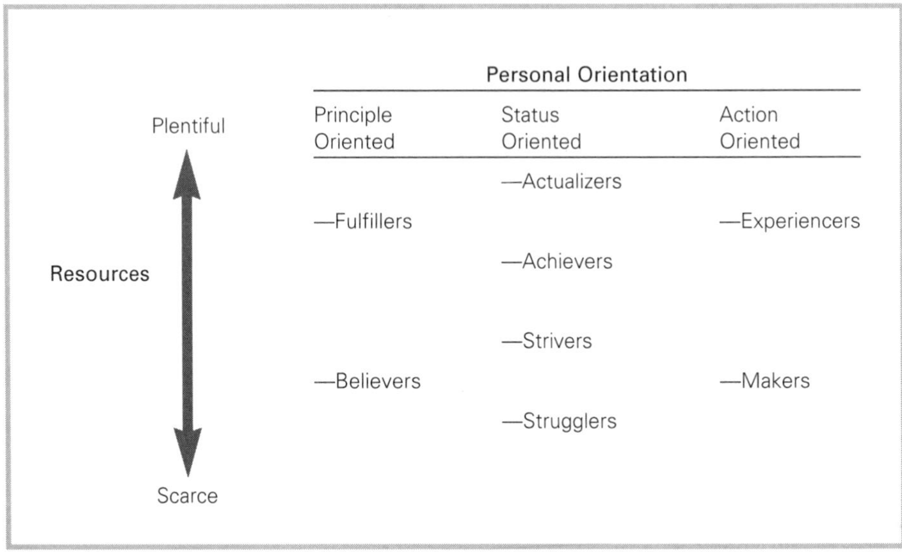

Figure 3.3 VALS2 Psychographic Segments

Source: Adapted from "Values and Lifestyle," SRI International, Menlo Park, CA.

Nutritional Attitude Segmentation

There is no question that people are concerned about health and nutrition. Two-thirds of adults restrict their diets to maintain health, and nearly 80 percent are dieting to lose or maintain their weight at some point during the year. Fat is a number one concern, too, with 71 percent restricting their consumption of high-fat foods. The following percentages of people restrict their diet to avoid having too much of other ingredients: cholesterol, 64 percent; salt, 58 percent; sugar, 52 percent; eggs, 52 percent; and red meat, 51 percent. Consumer behavior is not, however, entirely consistent. This, after all, is an age in which both high-butterfat ice cream and low-fat yogurt have become the basis for food service chains. According to George Rice, consumer preference for "all you can eat" specials has risen substantially, while interest in dieter's specials has fallen. Although diet products are widely used, over half the population are somewhat overweight.

Over one-third of Americans act on their nutritional concerns on a regular basis. National Restaurant Association (NRA) research over a period of years has identified three nutritional attitude segments: committed, unconcerned, and vacillating. The largest of these groups, 37 percent of those surveyed, are the committed patrons, while the rest are more or less evenly divided between unconcerned (32 percent) and vacillating (31 percent). The major demographic characteristics, consumer behavior patterns, and food preferences are summarized in Table 3.4.

Table 3.4 Characteristics of the Three Health and Nutrition Consumer Groups, 1992

	Unconcerned Patrons	Committed Patrons	Vacillating Patrons
Demographic Characteristics	Men 18 to 34 years old Average income Work full time High school graduate/some college education Have children under 18 living in home Live in Southern states	Women 35 to 54 years old Above-average income Married Work part time or not at all College graduate or graduate school education	Over 45 years old Below-average income Widowed No children under 18 in home High school graduate or less education Live in northeastern states
Behavioral Characteristics (Members of all three groups come from all demographic and behavior segments. The characteristics presented here represent those where a-greater proportion than average occurs.)	Patronize fast-food restaurants Order carryout and delivery Not concerned about health Unlikely to order light and healthy menu items Do not diet for health reasons or to lose weight Do not restrict salt, additives, sugar, foods high in cholesterol, or foods high in fat Do not consciously restrict foods consumption of red meat, eggs, and dairy products Do not consciously consume more foods high in fiber and calcium or starchy foods, vegetables and fruits, or beans and peas	Patronize moderately priced table service establishments Are concerned about health Likely to order light and healthy menu items Restrict diet to lose or maintain weight and to control blood cholestorol or maintain health Restrict use of salt, additives, sugar, and foods high in cholesterol and fat Restrict consumption of red meat, eggs, and dairy products Consume foods high in fiber as well as starchy foods Consciously eat more vegetables and fruits	Patronize fast-food restaurants and self-serve cafeteria/buffets Are concerned about health Diet to control high blood pressure and cholesterol Do not consciously restrict red meat Consume foods high in fiber and calcium Consciously eat more beans and peas
Foods Likely to Order in Restaurant (Members of all groups are likely to order any foods covered by the survey. The ones here are foods that group members have a greater likelihood of ordering compared to all consumers. Foods are shown in descending order based on the difference in mean score between the group and total consumers.)	Regular soft drink Fried chicken French fries Rich desserts Hamburger Fried fish or seafood Steak or roast beef Premium ice cream Mexican dishes Latin American dishes French dishes Italian dishes	Calorie-controlled entree Vegetarian pizza Low-fat frozen yogurt Low-fat, low-calorie fruit dessert Vegetables seasoned with herbs, lemon Reduced-calorie salad dressing Whole-grain muffins Diet soft drink Food cooked without salt Raw vegetable appetizer Caffeine-free coffee Main-dish salad with vegetables and grains	Steak or roast beef Fried chicken Caffeine-free soft drink Premium ice cream Food cooked without salt Hamburger Fried Whole-grain muffins Reduced-calorie salad dressing French fries

Source: National Restaurant Association, *Nutrition and Restaurants: A Consumer Perspective,* 1993.

Benefit Segmentation

A powerful segmentation technique can be derived from patterns in buying decisions that consumers have shown in the past. For instance, we can question consumers to determine what *benefits* they sought in a particular buying decision and then construct segments according to the benefit sought. In restaurants, some seek mainly convenience and speed, others nutrition or flavor, still others an adventurous experience.

Purchase Behavior Segmentation

Two common ways of segmenting by behavior relate to actual purchase behavior. They are user status and user frequency. *User status* divides consumers into nonusers, first-time users, and repeat users. One approach, for instance, might be to distinguish trial users from nonusers and mount campaigns based on different kinds of appeals to the two segments. An increasingly common approach is to single out our *present customers* as a priority segment.

User frequency is usually divided into light, medium, and heavy users. Pizza delivery operations, for instance, often target principally the heavy users who account for as much as 80 percent of their business. Hotels and restaurants, like airlines, have come to recognize and target heavy users, offering them bonuses and discounts for repeat patronage.

For hotels, an important behavioral segmentation tool involves the travelers' purposes. Guests are commonly divided into business, convention, and pleasure travelers, each of whom have somewhat different facility requirements, rate sensitivities, and interests.

Operational Segmentation

Just *when* and *how* consumers use an operation could well be considered a part of behavioral segmentation. It is both distinctive and important enough, however, to deserve separate treatment here.

In restaurants, the meal occasion offers important insights into consumers' needs and preferences. Typical meal occasions are breakfast, lunch, early-evening dinner, and late-evening dinner. Snack occasions are midmorning, midafternoon, late evening, and early morning. McDonald's has used *meal occasion expansion* as a major business builder, first with breakfast and later with chicken nuggets in its snack meal occasions. McDonald's success suggests the power of this form of segmentation.

Another operational distinction is seen in seasonal variations in resorts and weekday–weekend differences in hotels. The weekend customer is more likely to be a pleasure traveler, whereas the weekday guest is most frequently a business person. Off-season guests are often seeking bargain rates and, consequently, are likely to be price sensitive on other purchases in the property. In-season guests, because they are paying top rates, can be expected to be very demanding in the matter of service quality. Eat-in and take-out restaurant customers have differing require-

The service needs of the delivery market set them apart as a specific operational segment. (Photo courtesy Domino's Pizza Inc.)

ments in regard to packaging, delays in service, and (in some cases) price. These distinctions are useful bases for planning the operation, as well as for planning the deployment of the elements of the marketing mix.

Combining Operational Segments. We can fine-tune operational segments by measuring, in effect, segments within segments.[9] The result is a segmentation matrix that permits us to focus on particular markets in planning product, pricing, and promotion.

The first step in building the segmentation matrix is to identify the operation's eater occasions or "day parts." Using a fast-food example, we can begin with eight eater occasions—four for meals and four for snacks. Next, we identify *where the food is eaten.* We will use the following possibilities in this example: food eaten in the restaurant, food taken out, and food delivered. As you can see, at this point we have 24 possible subsegments. Because different consumer needs are often met by meals away from home on weekdays and weekends, we can finish the matrix by recognizing those two week-parts, giving us 48 operational subsegments as shown in Figure 3.4.

The fact that a certain number of segments is possible is not the key. Rather, primary resources should be concentrated on those segments that can provide the greatest return. Rice[10] suggests that a fast-food chain such as Wendy's might

Part of week	Where food is eaten	Meal occasion / Snack occasion	Breakfast (Meal)	Midmorning (Snack)	Lunch (Meal)	Midafternoon (Snack)	Early evening dinner (Meal)	Late evening (Snack)	Late evening dinner (Meal)	Early morning (Snack)
	In restaurant									
Weekday	Taken out									
Weekday	Delivered									
Weekend	In restaurant									
Weekend	Taken out									
Weekend	Delivered									

Figure 3.4 Segmentation Matrix Based on Day Part, Location of Food Consumption, and Week Part

establish eight segments as key. These are listed in order of potential importance in Table 3.5.

Priority must vary with the size of the opportunity posed by a particular segment and the operation's ability to exploit competitive points of difference in a specific segment.

Combining Consumer Segments: Geodemographic Segmentation

Geodemographic segmentation is based on the theory that birds of a feather flock together. That is, neighborhoods will be made up overwhelmingly of people with similar demographic and lifestyle characteristics. Using the block-group level of census data, neighborhoods are studied in detail.[11]

Block groups are made up of about 350 households, and their boundaries are defined by the actual city streets so that they approximate real neighborhoods. Geodemographic information is especially powerful because it provides objective, measurable demographic information in combination with a lifestyle picture of the *people* involved.

The process of building a geodemographic segmentation system begins with an analysis of census data to identify key factors around which the population can

Table 3.5 Segmentation Example Based on Occasion and Eating Site

1.	Breakfast | Eat-in | Weekday
2.	Breakfast | Take-out | Weekday
3.	Breakfast | Eat-in | Weekend
4.	Breakfast | Take-out | Weekend
5.	Lunch | Eat-in | Weekday
6.	Lunch | Take-out | Weekday
7.	Lunch | Eat-in | Weekend
8.	Lunch | Take-out | Weekend
9.	Dinner | Eat-in | Weekday
10.	Dinner | Eat-in | Weekend
11.	Snacks | Eat-in | Weekday
12.	Snacks | Take-out | Weekday

Source: Adapted from George D. Rice, "Target Marketing: The Art of Segmentation," *Proceedings, Chain Operators Exchange, 1983* (Chicago: International Foodservice Manufacturers Association, 1983).

be clustered. The analysis includes demographic data such as age, income, and household size. However, it goes well beyond these. The analysis also takes into account information such as educational attainment and occupation of residents, home ownership rates, and family types, as well as consumer attitudes, product preferences, and media use.[12] Information from commercially available databases are combined with the census data to achieve the final segmentation system.

Interestingly, the approach to developing these systems is based on the experience of the biological sciences, where researchers had to "merge hundreds of plant and animal species into categories that made sense."[13] Geodemographic segmentation systems "are not perfectly accurate, but they are not meant to be. Their purpose is to predict consumer behavior—thereby giving users a competitive edge."[14]

There are four major neighborhood-based cluster systems commercially available. ACORN uses 40 residential clusters, ranging from the "Top One Percent" to "Distressed Neighborhoods." CLUSTER-PLUS 2000 has 60 neighborhood cluster designations, each of which can be further divided into 8 subclusters. MICROVISION 50 has 50 clusters with descriptive titles like "Upper Crust" and "Urban Singles."

PRIZM, one of the oldest lifestyle cluster systems, has recently updated its clusters, expanding them from 43 to 62 segments arranged in 15 social groups. The 15 *groupings* reflect two sets of variables, degree of urbanization (ranging from rural to urban) and income. Figure 3.5a contains a list of the segment names, arranged by social group designation (T1, R1, S1, etc.). Figure 3.5b also shows how the groups range in terms of levels of urbanization and income.

PRIZM[15] uses not only the census data but a network of more than 1,600 local sources of demographic data and these sources are also used in periodic updates. In order to measure the degree of urbanization, PRIZM divides the United States into 900,000 geographic cells.

While PRIZM uses a large number of variables in its demographic analysis, they can be grouped into five categories:

Social rank (income, employment, education, etc.)

Household composition (age, sex, family type, dependency ratios, etc.)

Mobility (length of residency by owner or renter, auto ownership, etc.)

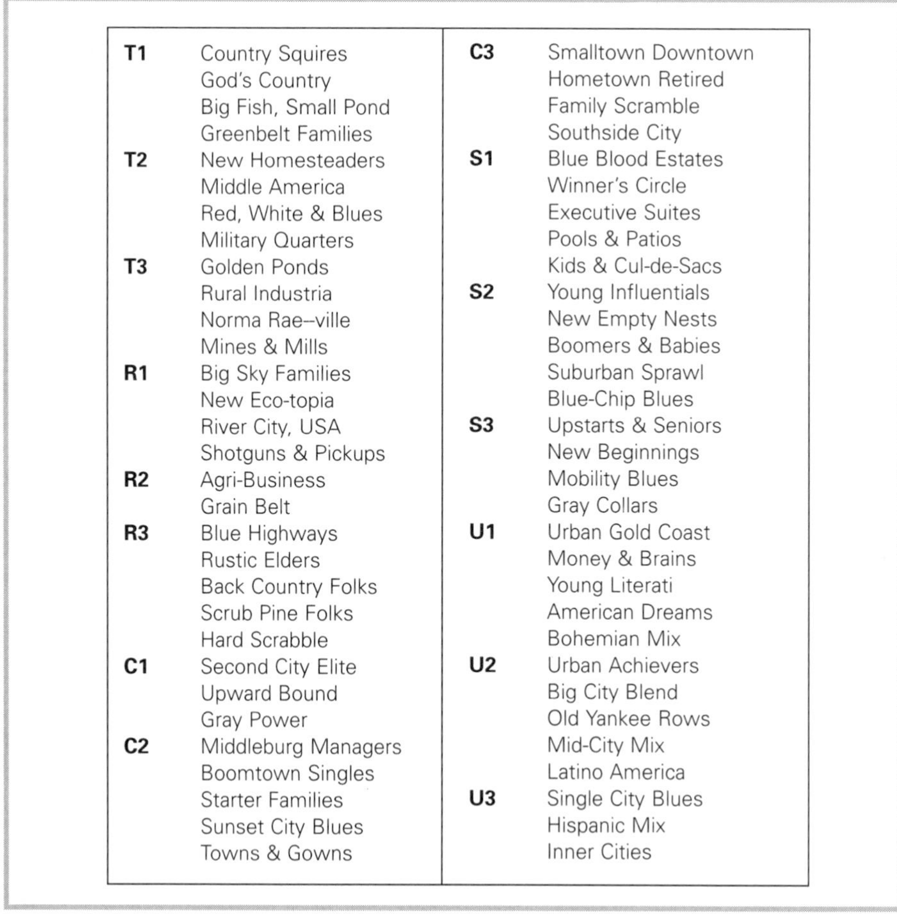

T1	Country Squires	**C3**	Smalltown Downtown
	God's Country		Hometown Retired
	Big Fish, Small Pond		Family Scramble
	Greenbelt Families		Southside City
T2	New Homesteaders	**S1**	Blue Blood Estates
	Middle America		Winner's Circle
	Red, White & Blues		Executive Suites
	Military Quarters		Pools & Patios
T3	Golden Ponds		Kids & Cul-de-Sacs
	Rural Industria	**S2**	Young Influentials
	Norma Rae–ville		New Empty Nests
	Mines & Mills		Boomers & Babies
R1	Big Sky Families		Suburban Sprawl
	New Eco-topia		Blue-Chip Blues
	River City, USA	**S3**	Upstarts & Seniors
	Shotguns & Pickups		New Beginnings
R2	Agri-Business		Mobility Blues
	Grain Belt		Gray Collars
R3	Blue Highways	**U1**	Urban Gold Coast
	Rustic Elders		Money & Brains
	Back Country Folks		Young Literati
	Scrub Pine Folks		American Dreams
	Hard Scrabble		Bohemian Mix
C1	Second City Elite	**U2**	Urban Achievers
	Upward Bound		Big City Blend
	Gray Power		Old Yankee Rows
C2	Middleburg Managers		Mid-City Mix
	Boomtown Singles		Latino America
	Starter Families	**U3**	Single City Blues
	Sunset City Blues		Hispanic Mix
	Towns & Gowns		Inner Cities

Figure 3.5*a* Fifteen PRIZM Social Groups Are Made Up of 62 Clusters

Source: PRIZM Lifestyle Segmentation (New York: Claritas).

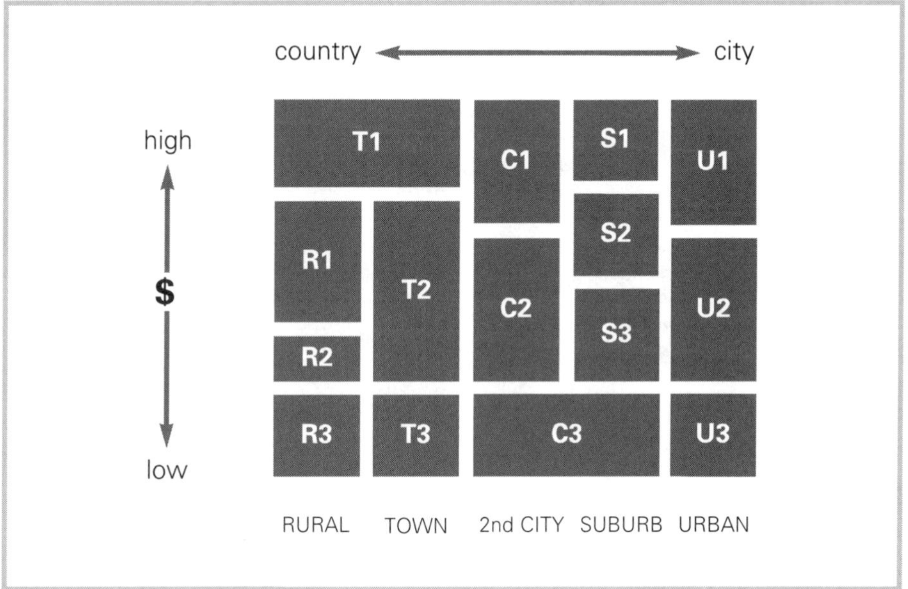

Figure 3.5*b* PRIZM Social Groups Are Classified: From Rural to Urban and by Income from Low to High

Source: *PRIZM Lifestyle Segmentation* (New York: Claritas).

Ethnicity (race, foreign birth, ancestry, language, etc.)

Urbanization (population and housing density: urban, suburban, small city, town, rural, etc.)

Figure 3.6 shows how the PRIZM clusters are put together, working from data sources (census, geography, and consumer behavior data) to data analysis to the clusters themselves.

Geodemographic segmentation has two major uses which are particularly important to restaurants. Restaurant chains often rely on the population within a small radius for the bulk of their patronage. The geodemographic information can help, therefore, in location analysis and selection. Another use is in direct mail—where block groups whose lifestyles fit those of the restaurant's target market can be selected for mailing. Geodemographic segmentation is also used as a basis for planning other forms of advertising. For instance, similar to direct mail, newspaper advertising supplements can be inserted into zip-code-zoned editions of newspapers.[16]

SEGMENTING ORGANIZATIONAL MARKETS

The logic of segmentation applies to organizational markets, too. We should consider briefly two areas of hospitality marketing where the target is an organizational customer and its "buying center" (see Chapter 2). Hotels commonly sell

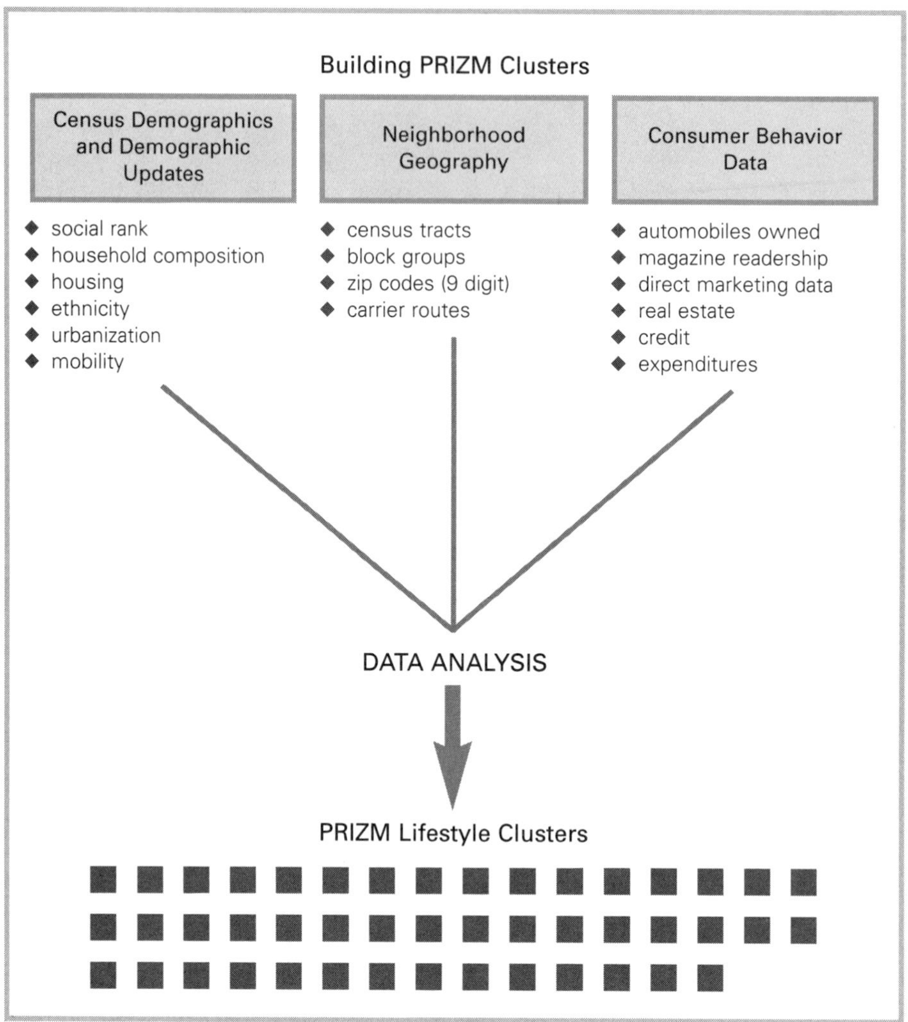

Figure 3.6 Building PRIZM Clusters

Source: *PRIZM Lifestyle Segmentation* (New York: Claritas).

not only to individual customers but also to other organizations. Contract food service companies sell their services exclusively to the client institution but must also satisfy the individual guests.

Lodging's Organizational Customer Segments

Business Travelers. Lodging companies, of course, sell to individuals, but a major part of the marketing effort to reach individual travel *business* customers may involve marketing to the local organizational affiliates of that customer. Local business travel generators might include companies that have headquarters in a particular city or companies that have a significant number of people visiting them. Professional organizations (such as accounting firms) and businesses that have people on the road working are also a significant source of business. An important question, here, is who the *buyer* is, as opposed to the customer. If the local secretary makes the reservation, then secretaries become a significant factor, even though they may never stay in the hotel themselves. The same is true of the travel manager or meeting planner for a business or professional organization in a distant city. Individual business travelers are a vital segment for most hotels, but they are often sold through their organizational affiliation. Business travelers can be further segmented in a number of ways such as by travel budget size or frequency of visit. A chain of hotels may segment organizations by size and number of room-nights generated, targeting those that provide a large volume of business by offering special rates and services.

Group Markets

Different group business segments[17] have quite different needs and characteristics. Several such segments are identified in Table 3.6 and some possible means for targeting them are summarized there, as well. We will consider each briefly.

Table 3.6 Targeting Lodging Organizational Market Segments

Segment	Target by
Individual Business Travelers	Contacting local or distant referral source Special rates for high-use organizations
Group Markets	
Corporate meetings	
Large	Special facilities
Small	
Function (management, sales, training)	
Business and professional	
Associations	
Large	Convention hotel facilities for large conventions and trade shows
Small	Small meeting rooms
Travel and tour[a]	Special pricing to wholesalers Sales calls on tour packagers
Other Organizational Markets	
Airline crews	Contract price, quiet rooms
Government	Special rates
SMERF	Special rates

[a] Includes incentive houses.

Corporate Meetings. Organizational customers with meeting requirements can be subdivided further by size of meeting. Another useful segmentation basis is the level of dollar spending per participant, since a Four Seasons business group is probably not the same as a Budget Host meeting customer. The meeting market can also be segmented by function into management meetings (ranging from an annual retreat for senior executives to a meeting of unit managers), sales meetings, and training classes.

Business and Professional Associations. Another major organizational segment is business and professional associations. This segment generates individual rooms business and meetings, but a distinctive characteristic is their requirement for conventions and trade shows. The large convention market is a specialized segment that is served by convention hotels. We should note, however, that there are smaller organizations and state conventions which can be served by the typical full service property. Trade shows generally require the specialized facilities which have been developed for them by convention hotels and civic convention centers.

Group Tour and Travel. Travel wholesalers often purchase blocks of rooms over a substantial period of time and then resell them as a part of a packaged tour. These rooms are normally purchased at a considerable discount and, for this reason, are often considered a low-profit-margin sale. With the amount of discounting that has been prevalent in lodging, along with the "fringe" benefits for individual guests such as free services and frequent travel awards, some in the industry are

Business travelers have distinctive needs and preferences. (Photo courtesy of Holiday Inn)

Business and industry accounts have needs ranging from executive dining rooms like this one to cafeterias and even fast food.

Good relations with client institution's buying center require a smooth working relationship with student customers.

Most schools operate under tight federal guidelines.

Health care is characterized by a highly professionalized environment.

Organizational customers in instititional food service can be segmented by the particular needs of the *client institution.* (Photos courtesy of ARAMARK)

Leisure services operate in specialized facilities, and very large crowds create a need for very high volume operations.

now seeing this segment in a more favorable light. While there *is* a discount from rack rate, it is a known quantity and there are no other special costs, nor is credit and collection generally a problem with this market.[18] Thus, the cost of doing business is significantly reduced.

Incentive Travel. Organizations commonly offer special incentives—a week in San Juan, Las Vegas, or New York, for instance—for employees who exceed their performance targets or win sales contests. "Incentive houses" are firms that arrange travel packages for this purpose.

Airline Crews. In cities with a major airport, airline crews offer a significant volume of business. Rooms are generally sold on contract at a fixed rate for an extended period of time. Airline crews, like other segments, have special needs. They may require the room for a relatively short period of time and may need to sleep while everyone else is at work or at play—and so need quiet rooms. The discount offered in the airline contract makes this an unattractive segment when business is good, but the guaranteed volume makes it attractive when occupancies are low.

Government. Government agencies generally reimburse their employees at a fixed rate per day called a *per diem,* making this a very rate conscious segment. "Government rates" are often well below most other special rates, which makes this segment similar in terms of price to the airline crew segment. Another similarity is that many government agencies centralize their travel arrangements. Accordingly, the buyer may be a travel manager, much like the purchasing person from an airline company that contracts for rooms.

SMERF. This acronym stands for social, military, education, religious, and fraternal organizations. The SMERF rates are notoriously low and so the organizations in this segment are accommodated in off-seasons at the favorable rates, but their business is not generally sought after during high or shoulder seasons—at least, not at the special rates.

Contract Food Service: Organizational Segments

Contract food service companies have two kinds of customers to be concerned with. The guest, as in any food service operation, must be served satisfactorily and in a cost-effective way. This is a consumer market. The other customer, the client, is an organizational customer. The four largest organizational segments served by contract companies are business and industry, colleges and universities, schools, and health care facilities.[19] Figure 3.7 shows the major segments and the basis on which they may be further subdivided.

Several other smaller segments deserve brief consideration as well. First, however, we should note that all elements of the market can be segmented according to their *susceptibility to the use of contract companies.* As a rule, the least susceptible

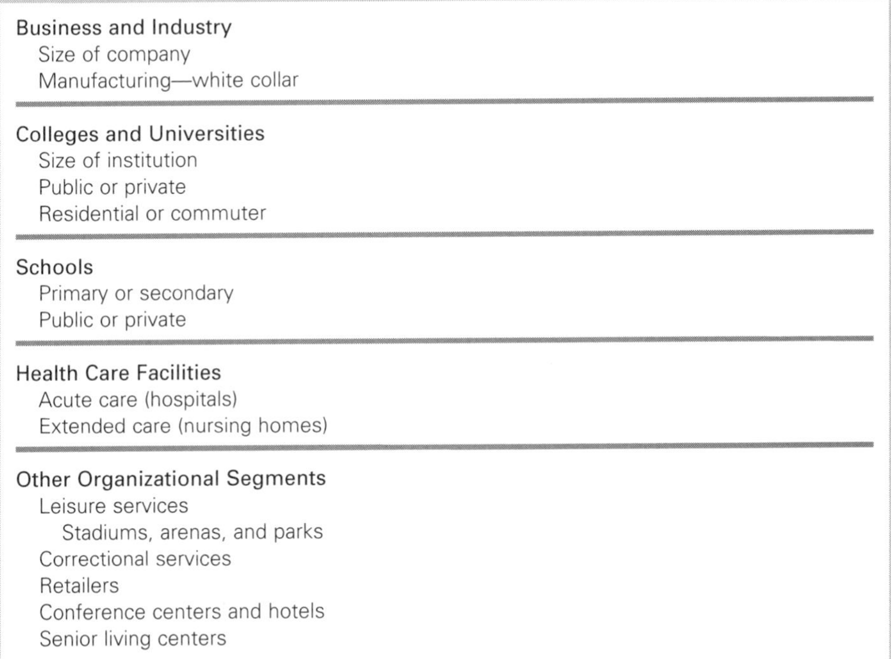

Business and Industry
- Size of company
- Manufacturing—white collar

Colleges and Universities
- Size of institution
- Public or private
- Residential or commuter

Schools
- Primary or secondary
- Public or private

Health Care Facilities
- Acute care (hospitals)
- Extended care (nursing homes)

Other Organizational Segments
- Leisure services
  - Stadiums, arenas, and parks
- Correctional services
- Retailers
- Conference centers and hotels
- Senior living centers

Figure 3.7 Contract Food Service Companies' Organizational Segments and Basis for Further Subdivision

are institutions that have never been served by a contract company. The sales approach here must often overcome a reluctance on the part of the client's buying center to give up control of an important element of their institution. Where an institution has worked with a contract company, the sale is generally a competitive one—that is, "our" company versus other suppliers.[20]

Another overall segmentation variable is between fee operations, where the cost of the operation is assumed by the client, and an account in which the contract company has full profit-and-loss responsibility. In the latter, the client is not as concerned with costs since the contractor bears them. The fee account clients are, however, very cost sensitive.

Business and Industry. "B&I," as this segment is often called, can be further segmented by size. The very large account, say 3,000 to 5,000 employees, has quite different characteristics as a customer than does a 1,000-employee firm. Below 300 employees, the account will likely have to be serviced by vending. Another way in which this market can be divided is between manufacturing plants and offices and other white-collar operations.

Colleges and Universities. The large/small division applies to this segment, too. Generally, very large institutions operate their own food service and so are not as likely prospects. Another division is between public and private institutions. Residence and commuter institutions also have quite different characteristics as prospects and as customers.

Schools. The public–private dimension divides schools into subsegments. The sale in a private school is usually to a small buying center at the school, while the sale in a public school is usually to a large central administration at the school district level. Another major divider is between primary schools (kindergarten through grade 8) and secondary schools (grades 9 through 12). The *consumer* in the secondary school is a substantially different customer than the consumer in a primary school, and this gives the client a quite different set of concerns.

Health Care Facilities. A primary distinction in this segment is between acute care (hospitals) and extended care (nursing homes). In the latter, the emphasis is on palliative care and helping the resident to enjoy life. In acute-care settings, however, the pressure to move the patient out of the (very expensive) hospital as soon as possible translates into pressure on the dietary department to educate patients to any new diet requirements and help them become accustomed to them as quickly as possible.

Other Institutional Segments. Leisure services can be divided into sports and entertainment (stadiums and arenas), convention centers, and national and state parks. Correctional facilities are a fast-growing segment and a number of specialized companies have sprung up to serve them. Another growth area for contract companies is retailing, with supermarkets seeking the service-intensive experience of institutional food service companies to run their food service operations. Contract companies also manage food service in training and conference centers and in some hotels.

SUMMARY

In order to relate to millions of consumers, we need to segment markets into groups who have some common aspects from a marketing perspective. Target marketing involves manipulating the elements of the marketing mix so that a particular (target) market will be appealed to. The principal segment types discussed are geographic, demographic, psychographic, nutritional attitude, operational, and geodemographic. Organizational marketing can also benefit from segmenting. Lodging's organizational markets are business travelers, business groups, associations, travel and tour groups, incentive travel, airline crews, government, and a catch-all group called SMERF. Contract food service company markets are generally segmented into business and industry, colleges and universities, schools, health care facilities, and other institutional segments such as leisure services, correctional facilities, and retailing.

◆ Key Words and Concepts

Segmentation
Target marketing
Types of segments
  Geographic
  Demographic
  Psychographic
  Attitudinal
  Benefit
  Purchase behavior
  Operational
Geographic segmentation
Metropolitan statistical area (MSA)
Primary metropolitan statistical area (PMSA)
Consolidated metropolitan statistical area (CMSA)
Area of dominant influence (ADI)
Demographic segmentation
Psychographic segmentation (AIO)
Nutritional attitude segmentation
Benefit segmentation
Purchase behavior segmentation
Operational segmentation
Geodemographic segmentation
Organizational segments
  In lodging
  In food service

◆ Discussion Questions

1. What are the four basic criteria for segmentation? Why is segmentation helpful to marketers?
2. What is meant by "target marketing"? Give an example from your *own* community of a firm that targets a particular market.
3. What are the principal variables on which segmentation is based? Give an example of each, showing how it could be used to shape a marketing program.
4. What is meant by the word "psychographic"? From your own experience give two or three examples of psychographic segments.
5. What appeals would a hotel need to make to attract the various organizational customer segments discussed in the chapter?

Chapter 4

When you have finished reading this chapter, you should be able to

1. Describe the major sources of information used in making marketing decisions
2. Identify common hospitality research concerns
3. Give examples of marketing research in action
4. Describe the marketing reseach process
5. Explain the function of exploratory research
6. Discuss the value of database marketing

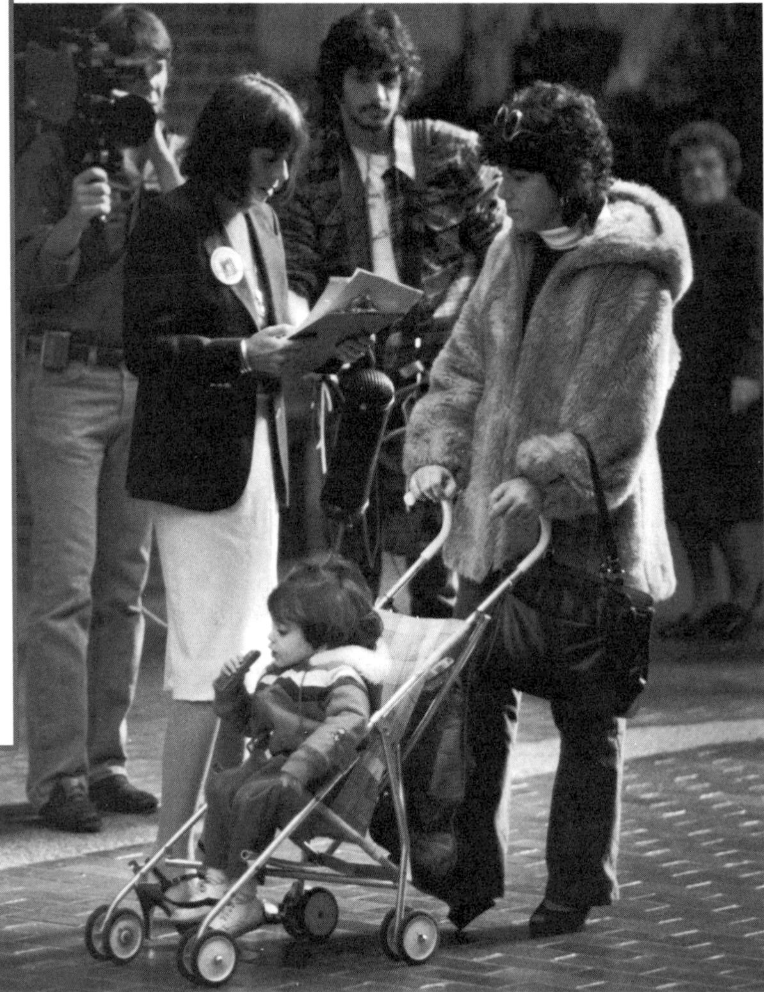

(Photo courtesy Ellis Herwig/Stock Boston)

Marketing Information and Marketing Research

In the last two chapters, we have looked at some general approaches to analyzing the consumer, including models of consumer behavior and approaches to segmenting markets. In this chapter, we move to a concern with analyzing consumers for the purposes of making specific marketing decisions.

FACT-BASED DECISION MAKING

As the level of competition in the hospitality industry continues to increase, total spending on marketing continues to rise. These large dollar expenditures are hardly something operators can afford to gamble with. As we move away from the unit level to chain marketing activities, the level of expenditure moves to the astronomical, with McDonald's alone spending two billion dollars a year on marketing.

To make marketing dollars have the maximum impact, marketers want solid, fact-based information to make their marketing decisions.

Marketers use many kinds of information, but we can discuss the most common sources under three headings: marketing information systems, market research, and customer information.

MARKETING INFORMATION SYSTEMS

A wide variety of raw data flows into an organization. Some information comes from the routine operation of a hotel or restaurant. On the other hand, because facts are a necessary basis for action, businesses also *seek out* information they need from readily available public sources—and sometimes from perfectly legal observation of a competitor's activities. Some marketing decisions, finally, are based on complex mathematical models of business situations. We will consider each briefly.

Internal Company Sources

Many of the routine *operational* reports generated in hotels and restaurants are useful sources of *marketing* information. The hotel's property management system, for instance, contains data on the percentage of double occupancy for each night of the week. After comparing this ratio to industry or company averages, a hotel manager might decide that the reason the property's average rate was not as high as it should be was low double occupancy. Efforts to promote more family business might result.

Reservation data are routinely used to make marketing, as well as operating, decisions. For instance, reservation turndown data may reveal an opportunity to construct a new property or an addition to the property. For instance, Sheraton's decision to build a $750 million property in Las Vegas was based, in significant part, on the Sheraton reservation system turning down 140,000 room-nights per year.[1] Analysis of reservation requests by room type should provide useful information on what kind of rooms should be built.

Point-of-sale (POS) systems have revolutionized information availability in food service. Sales information can be provided in great detail: by item sold, by restaurant unit, by time of day, by region, and so on. Properly programmed and monitored POS systems can indicate the degree of success for special deals; assess the popularity of new products; and even track sales of individual servers. At the end of the shift, for instance, the manager could determine how many bottles of

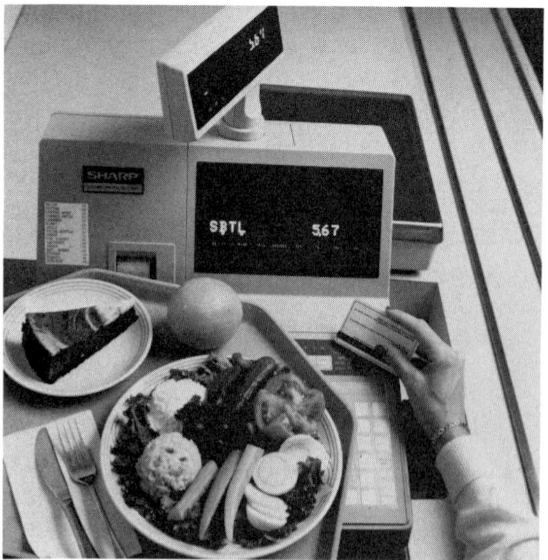

Modern point-of-sale cash register systems automatically provide reports that are—or can be—rich in marketing information. (Photo courtesy Marriott Food and Services Management)

wine were sold on a special offer, how many orders of a new menu item had been sold, and (in some systems) how many of each had been sold by each server. Moreover, at area, region, or chain headquarters, the same kinds of information can be available by unit, area, or on a companywide basis.

A management information system design takes into account the information that is available in a company. Reports that abstract information from several sources on some periodic basis can be assembled by the company's comptroller or the market research department or—at the property level—by an operations analyst. Moreover, company records can serve as the basis for special studies aimed at identifying trends or solving particular problems. (Note that the reports we have been discussing involve guest behavior in aggregate terms—total sales, for instance, rather than individual sales. The last part of this chapter, however, deals with the power of tracking sales to individual customers.)

Marketing Intelligence

Company executives require information that will help them keep current with what is happening in their environment. This includes not only the economy but also such diverse areas as labor market conditions, legislative and regulatory developments, and other pertinent events such as public health developments. All of this information is available from public sources, but keeping abreast of it—environmental scanning, as it is called—takes time and effort. Too often, "everyone" is supposed to undertake this work, but, since it is assigned to no one, results are erratic.

Management also needs information on the company's specific competitive environment. *Competitor intelligence* can be collected on a routine basis by using a clipping service to monitor the local and trade press. Hotel sales staffs commonly visit their competitors to monitor the announcement boards in the competitors' lobbies in order to determine what group functions are being held there. Reports on this kind of information are of interest not only to local salespeople but also to the national sales staff. Many companies require their executives to shop their food service competitors on a regular basis. Brief written reports of those visits, which often include sample menus, can provide headquarters people with an insight into competitive conditions in local markets.

An activity as simple as counting cars in a competitor's parking lot can yield valuable information, as can an analysis of a roadside hotel's clientele based on examining license plates to determine what states people come from. Most hotels know the occupancy and average rate of the neighboring properties through the informal exchange of information (and just plain gossip) between night auditors and other front-office staff. Indeed, occupancy information is sometimes exchanged by hotels on an hourly basis to facilitate placing overflow.

Econometric Modeling

Operations research models attempt to simulate aspects of the real world. Some companies, for instance, use macroeconomic models as a basis for forecasting long-term demand. The most widely used form of modeling in the hospitality industry is probably related to restaurant locations. Models have been constructed that are used to assess the likely sales volume and profit of a particular location; which is helpful in making place decisions. The same model can also be used to project the sales an existing unit should be achieving, based on model variables such as population numbers, income of surrounding area, and automobile and pedestrian traffic. Current operating results can be compared with the modeled results as a part of assessing whether an operation is doing as well as it should. If the model output indicates subpar results, that should stimulate a review of menu pricing and the level of promotional spending, as well as a review of the quality of the operation.

Marketing Information Systems (MIS)

The flow of marketing information should be organized in a way that provides both marketing and operations executives at all levels of the organization with the information they need to take appropriate competitive action. Ideally, unit level marketing information, such as competitive shopping reports, should be relayed in summary form to higher levels in the organization on a regular basis. In addition, information gathered by headquarters that is relevant to regional and unit marketing and line managers should be summarized and dispatched for their use. The danger in the busy world of an operations-dominated company is that there will be pockets of information which are not fully exploited because they are known only by those directly involved with collecting and analyzing the information. While the design and operation of an MIS are beyond the scope of this text, we can specify the key sources of information. These include the information we have just discussed, information internal to the company, such as sales analyses and marketing intelligence reports, as well as findings from any market modeling that the company undertakes. In addition, the MIS should disseminate the results of market research to which we now turn.

MARKETING RESEARCH

Marketing research responds to specific needs for information with specialized studies. Marketing research uses both secondary data (i.e., information assembled by others for some general purpose) and primary data (i.e., original data collected for a specific study). Since "secondary research can often save the time and expense of conducting original research,"[2] we should begin our discussion of research there.

Secondary Research

"Secondary research is finding information that is derived from original research. . . . It is finding the answers to questions people have already asked and applying them to your own problems."[3] There is a huge body of information that is readily available from government sources, civic bodies, associations, and trade sources at little or no cost.

Government Sources. The *Statistical Abstract of the United States* is a compilation of statistical data on the economy, population, and social and political structure of the United States. It contains summary data and, through its footnotes, provides reference to other, more detailed sources. Data on banking activity—sometimes used as an indicator of the level and direction of economic activity in a community—are published in the *Federal Reserve Bulletin*.

Current Population Reports. These reports, published by the U.S. Bureau of the Census, provide updated information on special topics on an annual basis. The Census Bureau also publishes periodic studies on a wide range of population-related topics. The *Census of Population* is taken every 10 years. It provides information on population by geographic region, including a detailed breakdown of the demographics of each region, showing factors such as distribution of the population by sex, marital status, age, race and ethnicity, family size, and employment and income statistics. The *Census of Housing* is published every 10 years and provides data on areas and types of building, as well as their size, condition, rentals, and average value. Other census reports, available every 5 years, survey retail and wholesale trade, service industries, manufacturers, mineral industries, transportation, agriculture, and state and local governments.

Data are also published by state agencies, providing information on tourism at the state level that often is available from the state Tourism Promotion Bureau. This office may also have information on regions of a state and large cities related to travel patterns and spending behavior of tourists.

Regional-, county-, and city-planning agencies, as well as traffic engineering offices, are useful sources of information on traffic patterns. They can furnish maps indicating traffic counts for major streets. These agencies are also a good source of information on planned changes in the roadway system, which is so important in location decisions.

Civic Bodies and Associations. The local Chamber of Commerce generally has a statistical profile and description of the community's economy, including information classified by types of activity (manufacturing, service, etc.). A list of large employers is usually available from the same source. It indicates the employers' location and number of employees, and describes their business. This is helpful in developing an understanding of the detail of the economic life of a city, and it can also help in developing a prospect list. The local Convention and Visitor's Bureau usually publishes statistics on visitors to the community and may be able to provide a forecast of future visitation and lists of conventions booked in the next few years.

Trade Sources. The trade press provides a great deal of information on competing companies and trade practice. *Restaurants & Institutions* publishes an annual study, *The Institutions 400,* which surveys the 400 largest hospitality firms and institutions. *Hotels* magazine publishes a similar study each year of worldwide hotel chains. The *Hotel and Travel Index* lists most hotel properties for each city, as does the *American Hotel and Motel Red Book.* Accounting and consulting firms that have specialized practices in hospitality publish annual studies that provide information on city, regional, and national occupancies, as well as operating statistics, as does Smith Travel Research, whose figures sometimes serve as the basis for the accounting companies' publications. The National Restaurant Association (NRA) research department publishes an annual profile of the food service business in its magazine *Restaurants USA* and a study of service restaurant operating results, as well as a number of original market research reports on issues of importance to food service marketing. State and national trade group meetings that provide provocative and well-informed information programs are another major source.

Assessing Secondary Research. Secondary data have the advantage of being readily and immediately available. They are especially useful in the early stages of a research effort when the problem is being identified and when background information is being assembled. On the other hand, secondary data almost never address the specific question that the researcher wants to ask. Categories into which data are assembled often do not fit the researcher's needs. In some cases, such as Chamber of Commerce or trade association data, the possibility of bias in reported statistics cannot be overlooked. Secondary data, then, are generally useful, but alone they usually are not enough for an in-depth study.

Another potential problem with secondary data is that there is so much of it, and busy managers, particularly in smaller companies and independents, may not have the time to sort through all the material. There are, however, professionals who, for a relatively modest fee, will conduct an information search. Many belong to the Association of Independent Information Professionals.

Syndicated Studies

There are numerous market research studies that are commercially available. One of the most widely known is CREST, which is the acronym for "Consumer Reports and Eating-Out Share Trends." CREST provides reports on purchases of food prepared away from home based on consumer diaries provided by a panel of 13,000 participating households. Summary information from CREST is published monthly in *Restaurants USA,* a publication of the National Restaurant Association. Many restaurant chains subscribe to CREST's special studies, which provide information on their market share and trends in their restaurant segment and geographic region. The geodemographic lifestyle studies of neighborhoods, such as those done by PRIZM, which were discussed in Chapter 3 (pages 68 to 72), are useful in conjunction with a restaurant trading area study to determine good geographic target markets for direct mail and other promotions. Another major contract research firm is Technomic, Inc., which publishes studies of chain restaurant size and market penetration, as well as studies of emerging trends in food service and a monthly digest of food service news, *Technomic Foodservice Digest,* which is cited frequently in this text. In the hotel business, Smith Travel Research offers studies of market share and operational performance of hotels.

PRIMARY RESEARCH

Primary research is the most specific way of gathering information about a marketing problem. Primary research requires the development of a specific research question, a research design to answer that question, as well as the collection and analysis of original data. We will begin by discussing some consumer applications of primary research in the hospitality industry and then examine, in more detail, the research process.

COMMON HOSPITALITY MARKET RESEARCH CONCERNS

Some of the most common areas of concern include customer identification, product research, promotional reactions, and tracking studies. Each of these will be discussed briefly in the following sections.

Who Is Our Customer?

One way to begin to identify a restaurant's customer base is with a trading area study. Such a study deals with the question of who the restaurant's customers are in strictly geographic terms. In such a study, an employee can be designated to ask customers where they have just come from and where they live. These data yield two kinds of valuable information. They should help provide a picture of the geographic draw of the restaurant. In addition, they will give information on what proportion of customers—by meal period—come to the unit from work and from home. It may be useful to consider "from home" and "from work" as two

State travel agencies collect information on travelers who visit information centers in order to help identify who the customer is.

somewhat different segments. Each location can then be plotted on a street map of the area. (An alternative to finding out the address of customers—something they may not want to tell a stranger—is to ask them for their zip code.)

When a sufficient number of responses have been received (one hundred to two hundred), the area that encompasses the majority of sites reported can be marked on a map. This tells operators more than just who their customers are in locational terms and activity. It also indicates any markets underreported that *should* be significant sources of business, suggesting areas for heightened marketing effort.[4]

The NRA has developed a questionnaire for independent restaurants to survey their customers in somewhat greater depth. The questionnaire highlights characteristics that consumer research indicates are important to restaurant customers. The NRA questionnaire, which is shown in Figure 4.1, also provides information on where customers come from and what some of their key demographic characteristics are.

Product Research: What Does the Customer Want?

Under the general topic of product and service research, we can look at customers' purchase behavior, that is, what products and services they buy, whether they like a sample product, and what they think they would like in a proposed product.

Usage studies can provide a basis for segmentation, with the market divided into heavy, medium, and light users. User categories can be established by a survey of a sample of the population from which the operation's customers are drawn. This type of survey might report characteristics such as age, sex, income level, place of residence, and the like. An estimate—though one of much less precision than afforded by a properly conducted survey—could also be drawn from simple observation of an operation. In fact, we hear that kind of judgment being drawn frequently: "Most of the people who come in here are . . . ."

The Marriott Corporation has been a pioneer in using market research to design hotel facilities. Using a technique called conjoint analysis, Marriott studied responses to questions on what consumers would like to see in a hotel room before designing the guest facilities in its new Courtyard properties. People were given a list of features a room might have, together with a price list that specified a cost for each feature. They were also given play money. The respondents were told to "buy" the list of features they thought represented the best value for them until they had used up all their money. Varying the values attached to each feature provided information on the relative importance of attributes to customers. Marriott was able to measure the relative importance of the features against all other possible features by studying the preference ordering and combinations of features chosen. The Courtyard properties have been extremely successful. Another use of market research in guest room design is discussed in Field Practice Note 4.1.

A wide variety of product decisions are studied by market researchers. *Taste panels* sample actual products to determine whether there is a noticeable difference between products. A common method is the triangle test in which two like and

We would appreciate it if you would take a few minutes to complete the following questionnaire so that we can find out more about our customers.

1. Which of the following best describes where you were just prior to coming to this restaurant? (Check one.)

(4) ________ 1 At work
________ 2 At home
________ 3 Shopping
________ 4 Social or recreational activity
________ 5 Travel or vacation
________ 6 Other, please specify ________________

2. Which of the following best describes where you will go immediately after you leave this restauring? (Check one.)

(5) ________ 1 Work
________ 2 Home
________ 3 Shopping
________ 4 Social or recreational activity
________ 5 Travel or vacation
________ 6 Other, please specify ________________

3. Excluding this restaurant, what is your favorite restaurant for dinner? (Please give full name of restaurant.)

____

4. Please compare this restaurant with the favorite dinner restaurant you have mentioned for each of the categories listed below. (Check under the appropriate word how you feel this restaurant compares with your favorite one.)

Characteristics	*Much Better*	*Better*	*Same*	*Worse*	*Much Worse*
(6) Service	❑	❑	❑	❑	❑
(7) Cleanliness	❑	❑	❑	❑	❑
(8) Quality of food	❑	❑	❑	❑	❑
(9) Menu variety offered	❑	❑	❑	❑	❑
(10) Employee friendliness	❑	❑	❑	❑	❑
(11) Atmosphere	❑	❑	❑	❑	❑
(12) Convenience of location	❑	❑	❑	❑	❑
(13) Value for the price	❑	❑	❑	❑	❑

5. How many people are in your party today?

(14) ________ 1 One ________ 4 Four
________ 2 Two ________ 5 Five
________ 3 Three ________ 6 Six or more

6. How often do you eat at this restaurant?

(15) ________ 1 More than once a week
________ 2 About once a week
________ 3 About every 2 to 3 weeks
________ 4 About once a month
________ 5 About once every 2 to 3 months
________ 6 Less than once every 3 months
________ 7 First visit

Figure 4.1 National Restaurant Association Customer Attitude Questionnaire

Source: Market Research for Restaurants.

7. Who chose this restaurant for today's meal?
(16) ________ 1 Myself
________ 2 Another family member
________ 3 Coworker
________ 4 Friend
________ 5 Other, please specify

The last few questions are just for classification purposes. All answers will be confidential.

8. How old are you?
(17) ________ (1) 18 to 24 ________ (4) 45 to 54
________ (2) 25 to 34 ________ (5) 55 to 64
________ (3) 35 to 44 ________ (6) 65 or older

9. Are you a male or female?
(18) ________ 1 Male ________ 2 Female

10. How many members are there in your household?
(19) ________ 1 One person ________ 4 Four persons
________ 2 Two persons ________ 5 Five or more persons
________ 3 Three persons

11. How many wage earners are there in your household?
(20) ________ 1 One ________ 2 Two ________ 3 Three or more

12. What is the best description of your occupation?
(21) ________ 1 Sales ________ 7 Management/administration
________ 2 Clerical ________ 8 Service worker
________ 3 Farmer/rancher ________ 9 Housewife
________ 4 Self-employed ________ 10 Retired
________ 5 Professional/technical ________ 11 Student
________ 6 Government ________ 12 Other, please specify

16. What is your approximate household income:
(22) ________ 1 Under $10,000 ________ 4 $20,000 to $24,999
________ 2 $10,000 to $14,000 ________ 5 $25,000 to $29,999
________ 3 $15,000 to $19,999 ________ 6 $30,000 and over

Figure 4.1 *Continued*

one unlike unidentified samples are given to a panel of tasters under controlled conditions. Respondents are asked to match the two like samples. If a large number of errors in matching are made, this suggests there is no noticeable difference between the two products.

A danger in decisions based on this kind of product testing is that, over a *series* of product changes, the *total* change is not measured, only the incremental change each time the product is altered. Although the differences between A and B, B and C, C and D, and D and E in Figure 4.2 may not by detectable, their cumulative effect from A to E could be quite noticeable.[5] The cumulative result of the changes, then, could be a problem, even if the steps along the way were very small.

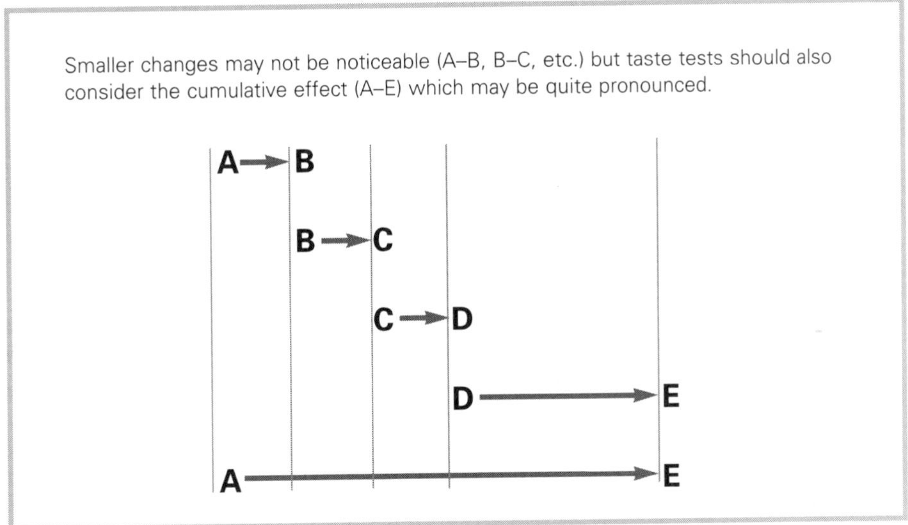
Smaller changes may not be noticeable (A–B, B–C, etc.) but taste tests should also consider the cumulative effect (A–E) which may be quite pronounced.
A → B
B → C
C → D
D → E
A → E

Figure 4.2 Incremental Change Can Be Overlooked in Taste Tests

Other product-oriented research includes concept screening—using a discussion group called a focus group (discussed later in the chapter); concept testing based on consumer interviews; and test marketing, in which a product is tried out in a test market.

The Marriott Courtyard guest room was designed on the basis of extensive market research. (Photo courtesy Marriott Corp.)

Field Practice Note 4.1

"The Room That Works": Market Research in Hotel Room Design

Marriott Hotels is a leader in the application of market research to lodging product design. The very successful Courtyard by Marriott guest room was designed based on consumer research. More recently, Marriott formed an alliance with AT&T and Steelcase, a furniture manufacturer, to study the needs of contemporary business travelers. The research process that resulted provides a good example of market research as an exploratory process that begins very broadly and, as results are available, gradually becomes more specific until it reaches a conclusion.

The situation facing the business traveler was summed up by Marriott's Director of Market Research, Daniel Bretl:

> There is an overwhelming need for people to get more done at all times. With globalization and increased technology, people are traveling more

"The Room That Works" is a room designed by market research for a particular target market. (Photo courtesy of Marriott International)

Reactions to Promotional Programs.

Advertising ideas are often tested early in the design stage to determine their likely acceptance by consumers before production expenses are incurred. This practice—called copy testing—is particularly common with television advertising.

Much of the research we have described so far has been *survey research,* that is, research based on questions asked consumers about their opinions, preferences, than ever. With corporate downsizing, they have to get more done.

This created a need for a room that would accommodate the special requirements of busy business travelers.

The first step in the research process was a review of secondary research, that is, existing research from Marriott and Steelcase as well as information from industry sources such as the trade press. As a result of reviewing this information, Marriott added a number of questions regarding traveler needs to a tracking study it regularly conducted.

Using the information assembled to this point, a research agenda was prepared for a series of focus groups and six focus groups were conducted—in Atlanta, Chicago, and San Francisco. With the results from this qualitative research in hand, three room prototypes were developed for field testing.

In the field test, the prototype rooms were installed in Marriott hotels. Guests occupied these rooms *without being aware* the rooms were part of a field test.

The field test provided the basis for preparing two more room prototypes which were constructed and then examined by business travelers. These travelers were asked to evaluate the two rooms in comparison with each other and a standard Marriott room to determine which was the most likely to generate incremental visits to Marriott hotels.

"The Room That Works" incorporates features the target market, business travelers, sought. Specifically, the new room design features:

- A large console table and mobile writing desk (so guests can move the table to the window and work from natural light if they wish)
- Two power outlets and a modem jack mounted in the console top
- A movable task light
- A fully adjustable ergonomic chair

Marriott hotels committed to converting a minimum of 20 percent of its full-service guest rooms to "The Room That Works" by the end of 1996. The rooms will be available to guests without additional charge.

Source: This note is based on information supplied to me by Daniel J. Bretl who was Marriott's Director of Market Research at the time this research was conducted. He is now Senior Director of Strategic Alliances at Marriott.

or behavior. Another basic approach to market research—and one commonly used in copy testing—involves experimental research. Two kinds of experiments are used: laboratory and field. In a laboratory setting,

> the investigator creates a situation with the exact conditions he wants to have and in which he controls some and manipulates other variables . . . . [In contrast,] a field experiment is a research study in a realistic situation in which one or more

> independent variables are manipulated by the experimenter under as carefully controlled conditions as the situation will permit.[6]

In either case, the experimental design is chosen because it is thought to give a clear link between cause and effect and is often referred to as causal research.[7]

In a laboratory experiment assessing a television commercial, for instance, an audience is recruited and shown programming selected by the investigator, including the commercial that is the subject for evaluation. All the variables, including not only viewing content but also audience composition and audience attention, are under the control of the researcher. Audience members all provide feedback in the same way, as required by the investigator.

Another route to achieving the same purpose—a field experiment—might be to show the commercial on cable television to a selected number of homes or to all homes in a test city on cable or broadcast television. In the laboratory setting, the studio audience will certainly sit through the program. In the field setting, some viewers will not have turned on; others will use the commercial break to take a "flush break," wash the dishes, or do their homework.

The laboratory setting provides tighter control, costs less, speeds data collection, and provides greater confidentiality of the research findings. The laboratory design also incurs the risk that people, realizing they are being observed, will react differently, often by trying to please the experimenter. The field test offers less control of the situation, but, because of that, it has greater realism. Also, in a field test, because a large sample group is exposed to the commercial, it may be possible to track actual purchase behavior and infer a cause-and-effect relationship. Experimentally oriented research, either field or laboratory, lends itself well to advertising evaluation.

One authority[8] offers the following list of researchable topics with respect to advertising evaluation—called copy testing:

Persuasiveness	Will buy or want to?
Communications	Hear the main point?
Recall	Break through the clutter?
Self-involvement	Does this sound like me?
Credibility	Believe it or not?
Clarity	Understand it or not?
Tastefulness	Does it offend?
Stimulation	Exciting or dull?

What is not measurable are the creativity and technical execution. A commercial that will be a real hit cannot be identified by research.

In addition to theater and on-air evaluation, advertising can be evaluated through questionnaires administered in person (usually in malls), by mail, and by telephone. Nontelevision ads are also evaluated by methods analogous to those just described.

Tracking Studies

A **tracking study** follows consumers' reactions over a period of time, rather than at a single point in time. A common method for conducting such a study is a telephone survey based on a random sample in the market area. A first study is conducted to establish a basis for comparison in later studies. Subsequent studies track changes in consumer behavior and attitude. Although the subjects to be studied vary from company to company, the topics listed in Figure 4.3 provide a good illustration of the contents of such a study.

A typical study for a restaurant might include the following kinds of information. A *customer profile* would contrast the demographics of heavy and light users for that restaurant and the restaurant's principal competitors. A tracking study would also track awareness. *Restaurant awareness* is measured at three different levels. The first level is "top of mind"—that is, the first restaurant mentioned. The second level of awareness is "unaided recall": Is the restaurant mentioned without prompting? Finally, the lowest level of awareness is "aided recall": "Have you ever heard of Pinfeather's restaurant?" Demographics for each level of awareness would be reported in the study.

Study of *restaurant trial* takes us a step further to determine the percentage and demographics of those who have tried the restaurant and each of its principal competitors. *Restaurant frequency and occasion* analyzes how often, on average, customers have visited the restaurant in the past month and for which meals. This can lead to a measurement and comparison of *meal occasion share* for the restaurant and its competitors and a demographic profile of strong and weak market segments, by meal.

Restaurant customer profile

Restaurant awareness

Restaurant trial

Restaurant frequency and occasions

Advertising awareness and recall

Restaurant attitude and image

Restaurant preference by type of occasion

Preferred product/service characteristics

- Salad bar
- Drive-thru

Figure 4.3 Contents of a Tracking Study

The survey might also be concerned with the restaurant's advertising, measuring both *awareness and recall* of advertising. Advertising awareness is measured in terms of aided and unaided recall of advertising. Once the awareness level is established, the respondent can be asked what ideas or topics were mentioned in the advertising for the restaurant and its competitors. This helps establish what was communicated by the ad or commercial. Questions in this section also measure which advertising *medium* has the best recall.

Attitude toward the restaurant and its *image* are measured by asking the respondent to rate the restaurant, on a scale of 1 to 5 or 1 to 7, against its competitors on a list of attributes. One possible list of attributes is:

Quality of food	Convenient location
Good-tasting hamburger	Variety of menu
Buns	Cleanliness
French fries	Quick service
Other products (by name)	Decor
Friendly service	Seating arrangements
Value for money	Atmosphere

The results of these attribute ratings provide a basis for analyzing the strengths and weaknesses of the restaurant and its principal competitors.

In the next set of questions, restaurant usage can be looked at in more detail, using such questions as

Thinking about A, B, C, and D (list of four restaurants in the study), which do you prefer most when:

1. You eat lunch alone?
2. You eat lunch or evening meal alone?
3. You eat lunch with friends?
4. You order food to go at the drive-thru window?
5. You eat out with your children?
6. You eat dinner or the evening meal with friends?

The final set of questions addresses key product and service features. The intent is to see which features are positively related to increasing the likelihood of customer trial or customer repeat business. Questions are also asked to determine the impact of possible new services on trial and loyalty.

Regional comparisons can also be made for each of the subject matter areas just discussed. This kind of information indicates which geographic regions are areas of strength and to what degree. It will also identify regions where more marketing effort is needed.

Market research before and after an advertising or promotional campaign helps measure the impact of that campaign on factors such as awareness, attitude, trial, and frequency of visit. A series of studies, beginning with a baseline study before any special promotion has taken place, provides the insights needed to assess the company's ongoing marketing program. Moreover, it will serve as a basis for preparing future marketing and advertising programs.

THE RESEARCH PROCESS

The **research process** has been likened to a funnel, an idea illustrated in Figure 4.4. It begins in the broadest possible way by developing an understanding and definition of the problem. In this stage, the research is basically exploratory. As the research progresses, it becomes more specific and pointed. Field Practice Note 4.1 illustrates the process of moving from the very general to the more specific in a research process until a specific product design decision is reached.

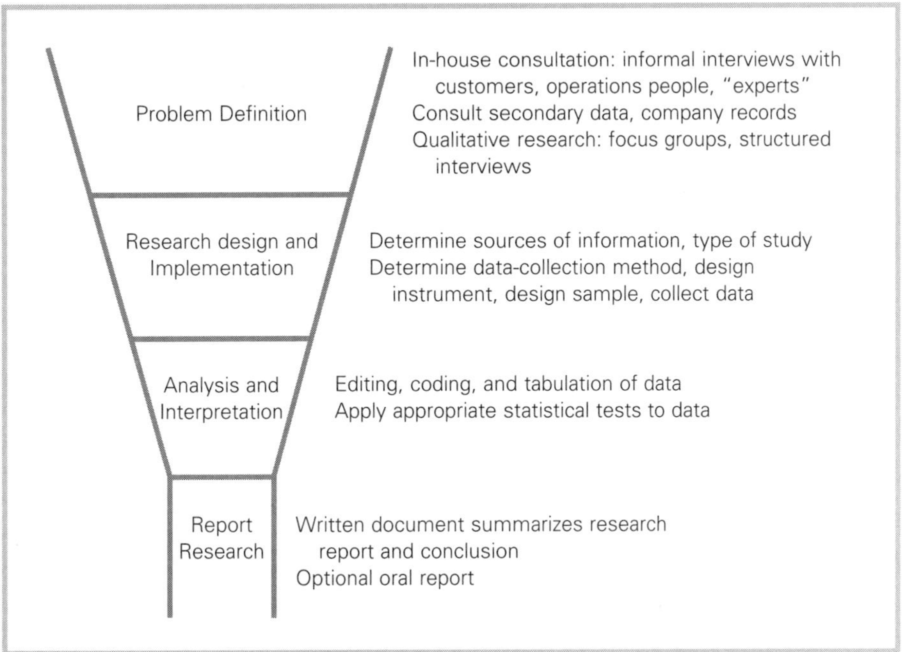

Figure 4.4 The Research Process

Source: Kenneth G. Hardy, University of Western Ontario.

Exploratory Research

The major emphasis in **exploratory research** is on gaining insight, uncovering ideas, and finding possible explanations—not on getting *the* answer.[9] An exploratory study is used for some or all of these purposes:

1. To establish more specifically the nature of the problem so that it can be more fully researched.
2. To establish priorities for future research.
3. To improve understanding of the practical problems ahead in a proposed research project.
4. To improve general understanding of a problem area or to clarify the concepts that are applied to it.

At the exploratory stage, there may be a veritable laundry list of possible problems. If sales are off, for instance, marketing may suggest the problem is poor food or service; operations may point to superior marketing by competitors—perhaps to couponing or some other promotional activity; store managers may express concern that prices are too high. Top management may wonder if it is general economic conditions that are at the root of the problem. Exploratory research would seek to reduce all these possibilities to a manageable list that could then be studied through conventional, quantifiable research techniques.

Let us look briefly at several major tools of exploratory research: the literature search, examination of in-house information, key-informant survey, and the use of qualitative research techniques such as the depth interview and focus groups. A *literature search* involves reviewing the trade and business and professional press, as well as appropriate published statistical sources—the secondary research we discussed—and appropriate syndicated studies. Included here might be a search of the company's own records such as sales records, quality control reports, customer comment files, and the like.

A *key-informant survey* involves interviewing people who are likely to have some insight into the problem: operating managers; sales staff, including waitresses and waiters and desk clerks; other operations people; managers; suppliers; and consultants. In some situations, *analysis of selected cases* may prove useful. For instance, units with the best and worst results might be studied in depth and contrasted.

Finally, *qualitative research techniques,* such as depth interviews and focused group discussions, can be used to develop better insight into the problem. **Depth interviews** begin by posing a general topic to the person being interviewed. The interviewer's task is to encourage the respondent to talk freely on the subject. Beyond the opening question, the interview is basically unstructured; however, the interviewer will probe to be sure he or she understands what is being said. The point of the technique is for the interviewer to develop an in-depth understanding of what the interviewee's point of view is. The technique requires a highly skilled interviewer. For the researcher, interviews of this kind can identify issues that serve as a basis in formulating a more refined research instrument later in the research process.

Focused group discussions (commonly referred to as **focus groups**) usually involve between 8 and 12 participants and a trained group discussion leader. The focus group is somewhat more directive than a depth interview, in that the leader uses a topic outline to guide discussion so that all the topics under study are covered. The leader's role is crucial. She or he must balance openness and an accepting attitude with the need to keep the discussion on the subject and to cover all of the topics specified. The leader is also expected to encourage the interaction between group members and to avoid either a series of monologs or one member dominating the group.

Focus groups are often observed through one-way mirrors while they are being conducted. Sessions are tape-recorded and they are also often videotaped. The record of the discussion and the impressions of observers, as well as the group leader, are helpful in subsequent analysis.

One danger with focus groups is that they are so lively that they seize the imagination. This can be particularly true with operations executives accustomed to operating on intuition. They experience a personal insight into a situation as a result of listening to—and becoming emotionally involved in—the group's discussion. One group of researchers, for instance, listened to a group of senior citizens discussing food choices and restaurant preferences in the first of a series of focus groups. They discussed the health aspects of that topic in a very lively way, making them seem a really key issue. A second and third group, however, found that aspect of the topic completely uninteresting. This experience is a good illustration of the fact that the groups are *not* representative and the results of focus groups are, therefore, *not projectable.*

Follow-up research is often needed to clarify the preliminary hypotheses the focus group generates. Like personal interviews, however, focus groups are useful in developing a research agenda and often provide a useful background in the development of research instruments such as questionnaires.

Research Design and Implementation

Once the purpose of the research and the nature of the problem have been determined, the design decisions remaining involve the type of research, the source of the respondents, and the data collection form and method. We will now survey these briefly in summary form.

Type of Research. The choice of laboratory or field research, as we noted earlier, involves deciding about trade-offs between precise control and lower costs, as opposed to achieving a greater degree of reality. One laboratory test that is very commonly used in the hospitality industry is the taste panel. Another example of a laboratory test we have already discussed is the uses of market research by Marriott in designing the rooms for its Courtyard properties and "The Room That Works." Test marketing of a new product, on the other hand, represents an

The "experts" in this respondent group were children who helped a hotel develop its children's menu. (Photo courtesy Spencer Grant/Photo Researchers)

example of field research, as do surveys such as the trading area and customer attitude studies referred to earlier.

Source of Respondents—Sample Design. One possibility is to go out and interview everybody who is or might be a customer. This might be done, for instance, in a private club—but for "political" reasons (to avoid offending any member who otherwise might not have been consulted), not for information purposes. Generally, a census—as the polling just described is called—is too expensive and time consuming. Instead, a representative sample of the population in question is used. It may be desirable that some proportion of the sample have a particular characteristic such as patronage of a specific operation. This would be a quota sample. Stratified proportionate sampling might be used where a number of key-customer groups (or customers in certain regions) needed to be surveyed in proportion to their total numbers.

In sampling, it is critically important to be sure that the sample is drawn from an appropriate group. A large food service company, for instance, was considering entry into the pizza business. Its researcher used a sample that was drawn from the general population, but the company's target market was frequent users, defined as 18- to 26-year-olds. The result was a program built, in large part, on information that related to the entire population but which did not really fit the target market.

Use of random sampling is desirable, but it is also expensive in time and money. In place of a random sample, sometimes researchers use a *convenience* sample, drawn from readily available respondents such as employees or—in a course—classmates. In making such a decision, the researcher runs the risk of some error, but, depending on the importance of the decision, this may be tolerable, in the face of the cost of a true random sample. Researchers are always faced with the question of whether the value of the information is equal to or greater than the cost of obtaining it.

In some cases, particularly where a large budget is available (and costs are spread over many units of a chain), researchers may choose to use a consumer panel such as those maintained by market research firms such as CREST. These panels are carefully matched with target populations and, consequently, are said to offer a high degree of reliability.

Data-Collection Methods. At this stage, the researcher is faced with three basic choices. First, will the study use observation of the consumer's (or experimental subject's) behavior or will a questionnaire be used? Second, will data collection be structured or unstructured? An unstructured approach may involve observation

Field research must be based on carefully developed procedures and must use trained workers who should be under expert supervision. (Photo courtesy Ellis Herwig/Stock Boston)

of consumer's choices or it may involve the use of unstructured interviews. Unstructured research techniques are more common in the earlier problem identification stage of research. At later stages, the data they yield are difficult to quantify objectively—and, hence, to generalize on. They are also expensive to collect because they require highly skilled interviewers. Furthermore, they tend to be time-consuming to obtain.

Finally, will the research be openly identified or will it be disguised? Most researchers identify their organization and the purpose of the study. Sometimes, however, the purpose of the research may be disguised in order to avoid a tendency on the part of respondents to give answers that try to please the researcher.

The work of the researcher in determining the data collection method involves, first of all, specifying the detailed information needs based on the research question. Next, the data collection instrument (e.g., a questionnaire) must be designed. Here, special attention must be given to the wording of the questions to avoid word choices that might influence the subject. A response scale must also be selected; the most common scale is the kind that ranges from "like" to "dislike" or "strongly agree" to "strongly disagree." A scale—commonly one of five to seven points—is used to capture the range of possible responses. Different words (appropriate to the research design) can be used to designate the points on the scale or a numerical scale may be used. The results are displayed as shown in the following extract from a hotel's market study. In this study, as you will note, a five-point scale denoted by words (rather than numbers) was used.

	Excellent	Good	Very Good	Fair	Poor	Don't Know
1. Quality of meeting rooms	24.8%	24.0%	21.7%	11.2%	18.3%	8.7%
2. Value for money of meeting room facilities	22.8	18.3	21.9	12.1	11.8	13.1
3. Quality of guest room accommodation	22.8	35.7	23.1	8.7	0.8	8.9

The means of communication with respondents must also be specified. The three most common techniques are mail, phone, and personal interview. Mail generally has the lowest cost, but it is the least flexible and often achieves a poor response rate. The phone interview is somewhat more expensive, but it is also more flexible. The length of the questionnaire, however, has to be limited to the time you can hold somebody on the phone. Personal interviews use interviewers in malls or on the street to interview passersby. Training and supervision of the interviewers is costly, difficult, and time-consuming. On the other hand, personal interviewing is flexible and permits face-to-face assessment of the respondent's reaction.

Data collection requires the research manager to develop field procedures, train research workers to follow them, and oversee the research to be sure that the way in which the data are being collected does not bias the responses. Completed questionnaires must be checked to be sure that prescribed procedures are followed. Where interviewers are used, the manager must be sure research workers are following the questionnaire pattern as specified in the field instructions and training, recording answers legibly, and generally following instructions. As necessary, feedback on problems is given to interviewers and incorrectly obtained information is deleted so that it will not be included in the analysis.

Analysis and Interpretation. The completed responses are tabulated and the results are summarized and analyzed. Simple tabulation of responses gives the percentage of responses to each question such as that shown in the preceding tabulation of ratings of hotel meeting and guest room facilities. A cross-tabulation from that hotel survey shows responses divided between respondents who have used the hotel for conferences and those who have not. The question: "What is the most important factor in choice of hotel?"

	Used Property for Meetings and Conferences					
	Yes		No		Total	
Most Important Factor in Choice of Hotel	Number	Percentage	Number	Percentage	Number	Percentage
Location of hotel	28	40.0	32	40.0	60	40.0
Contact person	0	0	3	3.8	3	2.0
Good conference service	9	12.8	8	10.0	17	11.3
Good meeting room facilities	10	14.3	9	11.2	19	12.7
Good guest room accommodation	0	0	2	2.5	2	1.3
Hotel facilities	15	21.4	16	20.0	31	20.7
Other	8	11.4	10	12.5	18	12.0

Reaching Conclusions. In the final analysis, conclusions must be drawn from the information collected. At this point, judgment, experience, and common sense must come into play, because the meaning of the statistical report is usually not self-evident. Statistics, then, can help in reaching conclusions, but market research that will tell you exactly what to do just does not exist. The research process is summarized graphically in Figure 4.5. Market research, to some, is a dry and abstract subject—and yet it plays a vital role in operating hospitality businesses. Case History 4.1, the story of a company turnaround based on market research, provides an example of this liveliness.

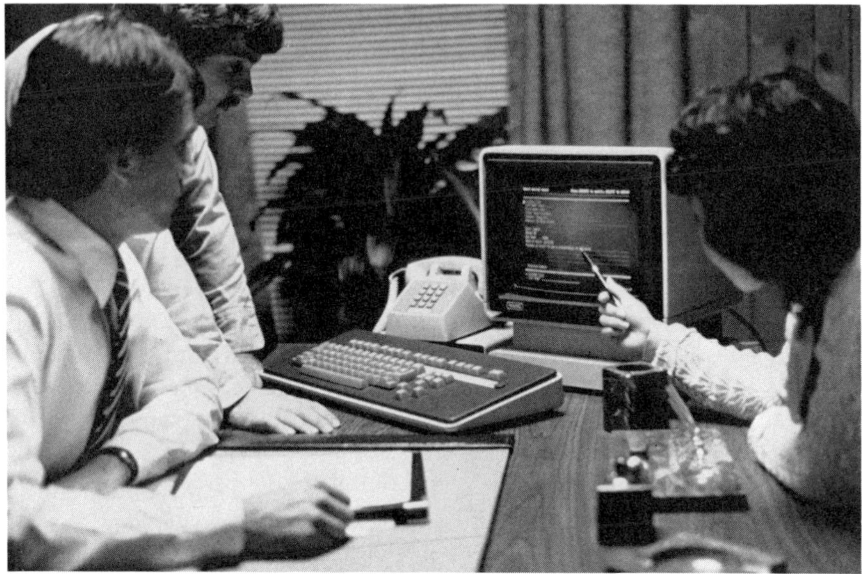

The final analysis of the research data requires experienced, informed judgment. There is no such thing as market research that will tell you what to do. (Photo courtesy Wang Laboratories)

CUSTOMER INFORMATION: MINING THE GUEST DATABASE

The process of using the guest database for marketing purposes is referred to as **database marketing (DBM).** That is, it implies *action* related to product, price, aspects of place, as well as promotion, based on information extracted from a guest database. We will be further concerned with these topics in other chapters. In this chapter, however, we will emphasize the *information* side of the story of database marketing, but, from time to time, some of the actions which flow from having a database will also bear brief discussion. (Database marketing is also discussed in Chapter 14.)

Tracking Guest Transactions

The basic principle on which DBM rests is that it is even more powerful than other means of segmentation such as demographics. One expert put it this way:

> In a hierarchy of value, what someone has done is much more insightful than who someone is. I can't really tell very much about whether you are likely to come to my restaurant and what you are likely to eat from knowing your income or your age. But I can tell a lot if I have the detailed information on a few meals you've had.[10]

The process starts when an operation begins to keep track of who its customers are. A hotel, for instance, will log each visit by a customer in its guest history file. Guest history files, incidentally, have long been a feature of luxury hotel

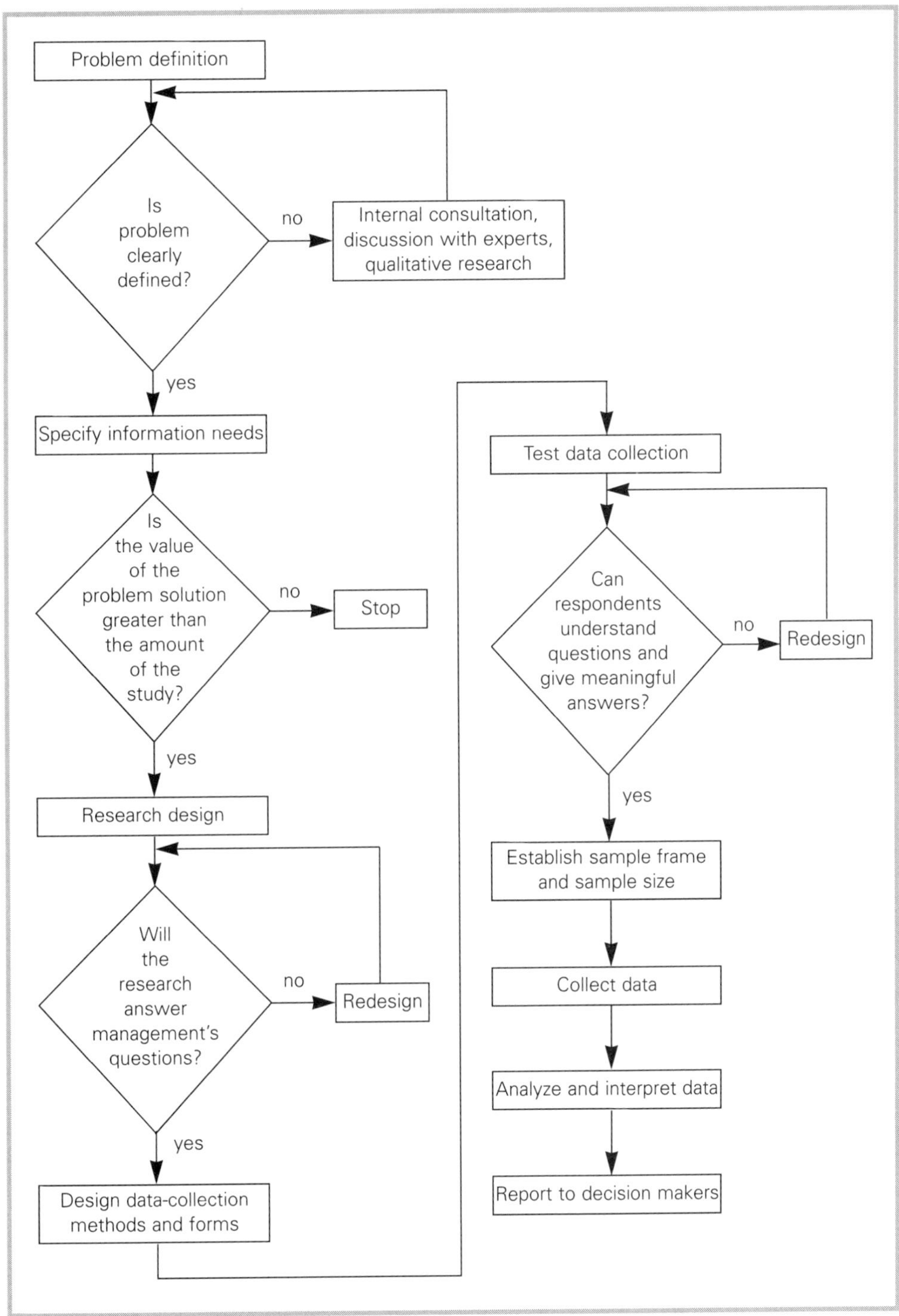

Figure 4.5 The Marketing Research Process

Source: Adapted from Burke Marketing Institute, Cincinnati, Ohio.

Case History 4.1 Marketing Research Lays Ground for Turnaround at Round Table Pizza?

When Round Table Pizza undertook a self-assessment, it had 100 stores, all concentrated in California. Marketing research revealed that Round Table was last in brand and advertising awareness. Round Table was, in effect, an undifferentiated and unmarketed brand. The reseach also revealed widespread consumer skepticism about pizza chains and the quality of their product in a market where independents had over 50 percent share.

The company set out to position Round Table as the premier pizza restaurant. To achieve this goal, it determined through marketing research what consumers wanted and shaped its operation to meet those expectations. Then, the promise its advertising communicated reflected reality in its operations:

1. Dough: rolled in the restaurant twice daily, never frozen. (Commercial: "We don't thaw pizza, we make it.")
2. Cheese: grated fresh daily in restaurant "with fresh, not frozen, whole milk—not skim—mozzarella."
3. Sauce: "Prepared fresh in our stores with our own secret spice formula—not pre-canned at some distant packing plant."

Round Table Pizza's amusing commercials were successful, in large part, because Round Table's management knew what customers wanted to hear. (Photo courtesy Round Table Franchise Corporation)

operations. In the 1930s, the guest history file in Chicago's Palmer House—all filed on 3 by 5 inch cards by hand—filled a room the size of the lobby of a modern Holiday Inn. What *is* new is the vastly increased power to track customers inexpensively that is conferred by the modern computer.

The information about who an operation's customers are and what their preferences are can be used to build customer loyalty:

Frozen, dehydrated, and precooked were not part of the Round Table concept.

The results (see the following table) can be summed up by the fact that Round Table within five years had moved to number 1 in market share in the Pacific states. Round Table focused on consumers, found out what they wanted, gave it to them, and told them what it was doing. It all began with determining what the consumer wanted.

Attitude and Usage—Unaided Measurements

	Advertising Awareness		Best Quality
	After Repositioning	Before Repositioning	After Repositioning
Round Table	45%	16%	54%
Major Competition			
Chain *A*	19%	47%	14%
Chain *B*	11	23	8
Chain *C*	14	30	6
Chain *D*	11	—	3
All other chains	14	—	10

Source: Scott Bergen, "Pizza . . . a Fresh Experience," *Proceedings, Chain Operators Exchange, 1985* (Chicago: International Foodservice Manufacturers Association, 1985).

A customer's loyalty can be won by small gestures. The Ritz-Carlton Hotel chain uses high tech to remember your previous requests and thoughtfully provide them for you again, anywhere in the world. If you stay at the Ritz in San Francisco, you may call room service, ask for white wine, and request an ice cube in it. A month or a year later, you stay at the Ritz in Amelia Island, Florida and you call room service and ask for white wine. Ice will be brought with it, since that's the way you like it.[11]

Starting the process of tracking customer transactions is more straightforward for hotels because they begin the transaction with the guest's registration. Restaurants, however, have found ways to accumulate this information as well.

One of the major ways of gaining information for guest tracking is **frequency programs.** As soon as a diner signs up for a frequent-diner card, her or his name, address, and usually some demographic information are available to be logged into the restaurant's database. The inducement to sign up for the frequent guest card is that there is some reward for frequent patronage. Rewards can be divided into two categories, "hard" and "soft." Hard rewards have actual monetary value: discounts, a free bottle of wine, or a free meal or—in hotels—a free night's stay. Soft rewards include such benefits as special reservation handling, personal recognition, and other perks.[12]

Database marketing need not be aimed solely at a company's present customer base. It can also be expanded to a program of marketing to others who are similar to the present customer base. Using demographic and geodemographic databases now available on disk from information suppliers, together with software designed to be used to manipulate the data, it is possible to locate other potential customers who are similar to an operation's present customers. These people are logical target markets for promotions.

Relationship Marketing

Database marketing is sometimes referred to as **relationship marketing.** This is because, as we have seen, once an organization has a database that captures who its guests are, and what their preferences are, the organization can use that information to build and enhance relationships with its customers. Because the goal of these kinds of programs is to encourage more frequent patronage by present customers, they are sometimes referred to as *loyalty marketing.*

The word *relationship* in everyday use implies something personal such as a friendship or partnership. A personal relationship analogous to this—such as recognizing and treating frequent guests on a personal basis—is sometimes the goal of a relationship marketing program. Often, however, relationship marketing refers to an impersonal relationship such as sending coupons to guests based on the preferences apparent in their purchases on previous visits. "Relationship," in such cases, means something more like convenience[13] than the conventional, everyday meaning of relationship alluded to previously.

The advantages of DBM have been summed up by Francese and Renaghan:

> First, it builds the loyalty of existing customers. Second, it expands your market share through identification and acquisition of potential customers . . . . Third, it provides a basis for revenue stream analysis . . . and finally, it reduces marketing costs over the long run by allowing you to target the use of your marketing budget more precisely.[14]

Using the Database Marketing Program

A customer database is raw information which must be sorted, most commonly into one of two large categories. Francese and Renaghan call these categories operational data (e.g., customer name, title, company name, home and work address, and method of payment) and marketing information (e.g., source of reservation, prior use, frequency of visit, responses to promotion, and special preferences).[15]

Francese and Renaghan point out that, in most businesses, 20 percent of the customers generate 80 percent of the business, so it is clearly in an operation's interest to know which of its customers are frequent patrons. It is also useful to know what their average spending is. With time, the database may suggest division of customers based not only on frequency but on the dollar value of their patronage. Extra good customers may warrant special rewards and recognition. Some airlines, for instance, will see to it that extra frequent travelers are never bumped from crowded flights and accord them special consideration when lines are long or flights are canceled.

Identification of an operation's best customers is based on the "RFM principle; that is, recency, frequency and munificence. Your best customers are those who have purchased recently, purchase frequently and deliver the greatest monetary expenditure."[16]

Once a database of frequent customers is established, it is possible, as noted earlier, to supplement these data with information from secondary sources:

> Many hotel companies overlay an on line data-base with information from credit card or transportation companies. Secondary overlays are available from geodemographic and psychographic information firms. In combination, the data from these external sources provide invaluable enhancement to your own in-house records."[17]

Building a database marketing system is expensive, and operations must allow roughly two years to achieve a working system.[18] Adopting a data-based approach to marketing is a long-term commitment and, since roughly 18 percent of the U.S. population moves each year, continuing effort to keep the database current is required.

Beyond having a readily accessible database on which to base marketing efforts, analysis of guest history information can provide help to hotels in planning their yield management implementation. If the guest history includes the date the reservation is made as well as the date of arrival, analysis of that information in the aggregate can give reservation lead time (by season). This information is useful in assessing the current reservation backlog. Assume, for instance, the high season at a resort starts on June 15, and the normal lead time is 60 days. If reservations are weak during the latter half of April, it may be time to open up lower-rate categories as well as to launch special promotional efforts—aimed, no doubt, at people who have been visitors in the past but have not reserved for this year.

In conventional mass marketing, the most powerful tools are reducing price or increasing promotion. Both, however, reduce the margin of profit on sales. DBM, on the other hand, builds patronage by offering customers what we know they want—and communicating with them on the basis of some degree of familiarity. Most fundamentally, DBM is based on the notion that it is not a product or service that ultimately gives value to a business but, rather, the customers of the business and their continuing patronage.[19]

SUMMARY

With rising marketing expenditures, fact-based decision making, supported by marketing information systems and market research, has become the order of the day. Marketing information comes from internal company sources, such as sales analyses, and from marketing intelligence drawn from a variety of external sources, including competitor site visits. Marketing research relies on secondary data (published sources) and syndicated studies, as well as primary research based on data collected for that purpose. Common topics for market research include customer identification, product research, promotion evaluation research, and tracking studies. The research process starts with problem identification, often based on exploratory and qualitative research techniques. As the research question becomes clear, the research design process moves on to consider the type of research to be used, the sample design, and data collection methods. The last stage is data analysis and interpretation (see Figure 4.5).

Increasingly, research is being concentrated on getting to know more about a company's own customers by tracking guest transactions, often through frequent-customer programs. Operators seek to establish a relationship, either personal or impersonal, with regular guests and to reward guest loyalty.

◆ *Key Words and Concepts*

Fact-based decision making
Marketing information systems
Internal company sources
Marketing intelligence
Econometric modeling
Secondary research
Syndicated studies
Primary research
Product research
Copy testing
Laboratory research design
Field research
Tracking study
Research process (Figure 4.5)
Exploratory research
Depth interviews
Focus groups
Research design
Database marketing (DBM)
Frequency programs
Relationship marketing

◆ *Discussion Questions*

1. What are the major sources of marketing information? What information do you think is vital at the unit level? At the headquarters level?
2. How is marketing intelligence gathered?
3. What are the principal sources of secondary research? What are the advantages and disadvantages of secondary research?

4. What are some common topics of market research reports? How do you think they could be used?
5. What is the purpose of exploratory research? What are some of the techniques involved?
6. What are the steps in the research process? (See Figure 4.5.)
7. What is the purpose of tracking guest transactions? How is it accomplished?
8. What is meant by "relationship marketing"?

Chapter 5

When you have finished reading this chapter, you should be able to

1. Discuss the significance of the strategic triangle
2. Contrast a strategy of opportunism with that of strategic foresight
3. Differentiate strategy from tactics
4. Identify and discuss the building blocks of strategy
5. Define competitive structure using Porter's five forces model
6. Explain the relationship of SBUs to portfolio management
7. Indicate what is meant by "generic strategies"
8. Describe four strategies for growth
9. Describe the logic of positioning and its role in marketing

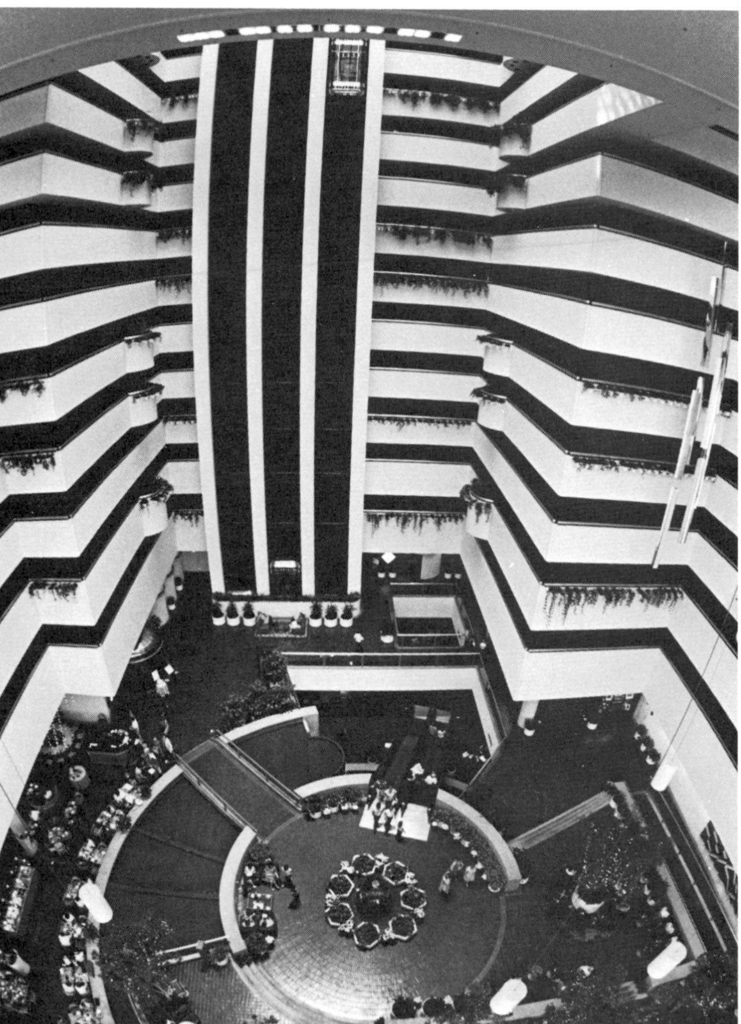

(Photo courtesy Peter Menzel/Stock Boston)

Marketing Strategy

The word **strategy** comes from the Greek word, *strategos,* meaning, very roughly, a general. The word, then, comes to business from the world of warfare. In warfare, strategy is the science or art of using all the resources available to achieve the objective of winning the war.

"Corporate warfare" needs to be put in quotes because—happily—there are real limits on the warriors. Nobody is killed; the physical violence of war is missing. On the other hand, the reality of the competitive marketplace is one of socially regulated and sanctioned economic struggle.

STRATEGY IN BUSINESS AND IN MARKETING

Business or economic strategy "results from a matching of opportunity and corporate capability at an acceptable level of risk."[1] More specifically:

> Corporate strategy is the pattern of decisions in a company that (1) shapes and reveals its objectives, purposes, or goals; (2) produces the principal policies and plans for achieving those goals; and (3) defines the business the company intends to be in and the kind of economic and human organization it intends to be.[2]

Our principal concern is with marketing, but it is somewhat artificial to speak of marketing strategy in isolation from other strategic variables. For instance, a marketing strategy that took as its goal the doubling of market share in a specific market would be dependent on the financial and operational resources required to achieve such a goal. Although we will focus largely on marketing, our discussion will accept that the strategy of the firm is a unity that involves other issues as well:

> Marketing strategy is the analysis of alternative opportunities and risks to the firm, informed by external (i.e. environmental) and internal information which leads management to choose a particular set of goals related to markets, customers and product offerings. The object of marketing strategy is to pose the goals that will direct marketing actions.[3]

Strategy, as this definition suggests, is about goals and about the premises on which subsequent plans and actions will be based.

The Strategic Triangle

The elements of the strategic situation are summarized in Figure 5.1. The figure identifies what Kenichi Ohmae calls the **strategic triangle** of customer, corporation, and competitors. The value of a firm's offer is significant in relation to the value offered by the competition. A better value, based on lower price, better

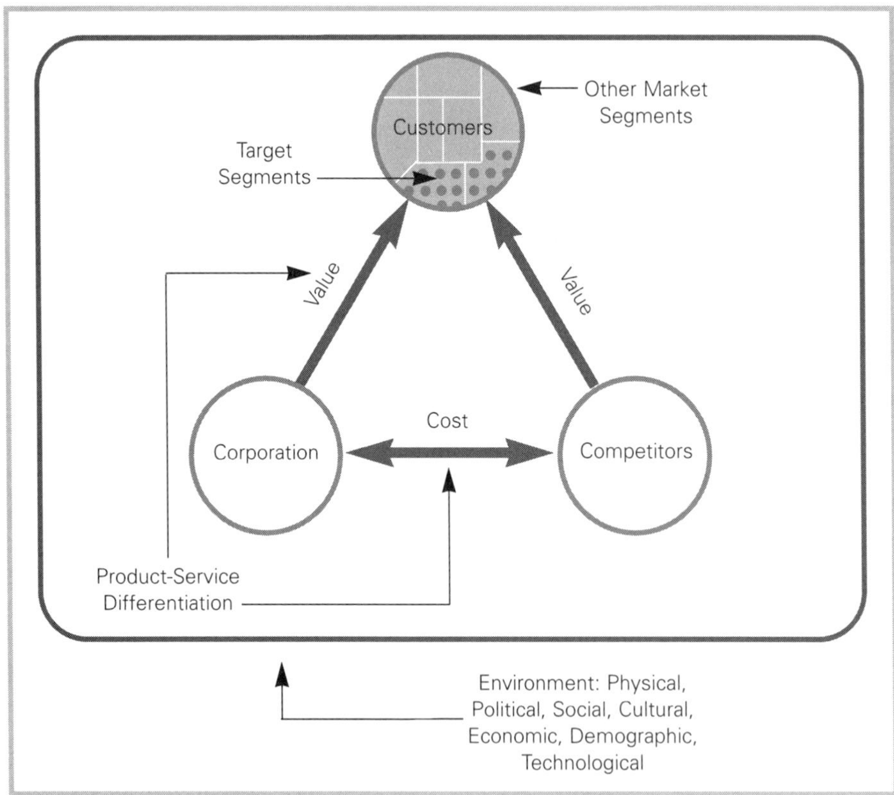

Figure 5.1 The Strategic Triangle

Source: Adapted from Kenichi Ohmae, *The Mind of the Strategist* (New York: Penguin Books, 1982), p. 92.

product, or both, will give an advantage in consumer acceptance to one or the other of the players. The firm's profit is determined by its level of sales and costs which must be measured, too, against that of the competition. This is a struggle in which the winner is the one who achieves the greatest market power as measured by long-run profit.

The environment in which the struggle takes place constrains the players with physical realities, social and cultural preferences, economic scarcities and benefits, as well as the regulation by government and the possibilities offered by technology.

What distinguishes strategy "from all other kinds of business planning is, in a word, competitive advantage. Without competitors, there would be no need for strategy."[4] The goal of the strategist is to gain sustainable competitive advantage.

Strategic planning has been attacked as an empty process to keep corporate staff busy, as a "waste of time and money," and as "an academic, ill-defined activity with little or no bottom line impact."[5] Lawless and Hart suggest that applications of planning by food service firms may be on less firm ground than those for manufacturing firms. The food service industry is highly fragmented. This makes less certain the economies of scale and the accumulation of operating experience, which so often underlie long-range planning in other industries. To a significant degree, it can be argued, the same is true of the hotel business.

Indeed, the practice in much of the hospitality industry has shifted from a five-year time span for corporate planning to periods of two or three years.[6] Marketing plans, which are discussed in the next chapter, generally look ahead only for one year. One astute observer of the industry, however, reports that recently there have been a number of planning efforts to look further out:

> What is the value and what should drive the need for long range planning? Our answer is that the intensified need is caused by the fact that the rules under which business is conducted are changing more rapidly, customers are more demanding and the pace of technological change has accelerated. To address these issues, management must think longer term because there are likely to be strategies that, if required, cannot be accomplished in today's short term reactive mode.[7]

The case for strategic planning rests largely on the growing complexity of the marketplace and the central importance of marketing. It is no longer enough to run a good operation. To survive and prosper, an organization must battle for a share of the consumers' attention, in competition with many others who are seeking that same attention. To project a consistent image of who they are and what their business stands for, operators need the clarity of purpose that strategic planning confers. The problem of the multiunit organization to achieve a clear strategic direction is more difficult than for smaller organizations where the intuition of the owner may be adequate. The larger organization is complex. It must coordinate multiple operations and promotions, as well as factors such as operating quality and appropriate pricing—in many local markets. Strategic planning should confer the important advantage of clarity of purpose and a solid understanding of the market and the competition.

Strategic Opportunism or Strategic Foresight?

Strategic opportunism refers to a commitment to respond to current opportunities and problems in today's marketplace.

The case for strategic opportunism is fairly straightforward. In the dynamic environment in which we live, it can be argued that it is chancy at best to undertake an effort based on any distant future target. In any case, "Unless a business is structured to have strategic advantages in the present, it is unlikely to ever be strategically successful in the future."[8] Strategic opportunism calls for strategic flexibility and an ability to quickly respond to strategic opportunities as they emerge. This is a strategic approach many independents and smaller chains are comfortable with, emphasizing an organization that can adapt quickly to focus on new opportunities as they emerge.

The danger, of course, is that this approach will lead to an organization that is going off in all directions at once as it responds to rapidly changing circumstances. This could result in a firm dissipating its energies on too many projects.

Strategic Foresight (Vision). Taking a longer-term view certainly poses the risk of making a long-term judgment, wagering time and money on it, and being proved wrong. In a strategic move, involving major investments, the cost of such an error could be severe. On the other hand, letting a competitor "get to the future first"[9] could condemn a firm to playing catch-up ball permanently.

Strategic foresight can only result from careful and reflective study of the customer and of the industry, grounded in real experience. (The reason for preferring here the term "foresight" over the term more widely used in business, "vision," is the connotation of the word "vision" as a "single blinding flash of insight,"[10] as opposed to an understanding of the future based on careful study, experimentation, and reflection.)

Strategic foresight seeks to answer three critical questions:

1. What type of new customer benefit should an organization seek to provide in five, ten, or fifteen years?

2. What new corporate competencies will be needed to provide these benefits?

3. How must we change the way we serve the customer to offer these benefits in a cost-effective way?[11]

The corporate competency referred to previously "can be thought of as a bundle of skills and technologies." Essential, or "core," competencies represent the "sum of all learning," both individual skills and technical mastery in the organization. The notion of core competency emphasizes the importance of people and what they know as well as organizational culture, as opposed to more conventionally conceived financial assets.

Case History 5.1 offers an opportunity to consider the contrast between the two views of strategy, opportunism and foresight, taken from the contemporary lodging industry. One group of companies has grown by seizing current opportunities for fast growth through conversion franchising. On the other hand, other companies have chosen to develop a core competency of superior operations. The issue posed in the case involves not only the companies' growth strategies and franchising strategies but their definition of who their customer is.

Strategy and Tactics

The distinction between strategy and tactics is a relative one. In general, strategy is concerned with long-term issues that involve basic commitments that affect all or a very substantial portion of the organization. Strategy is more concerned with goals and objectives than with means. Although strategy usually draws on research, it is also likely to involve judgments that require the personal experience, talent, and intuition of senior executives. **Tactics** are concerned with the day-to-day actions that implement strategy and respond to minor changes in the marketplace. The distinction between strategic and operational or tactical planning is highlighted in Table 5.1.

Certainly, strategic goal setting is the work of top management. The modern organization is typically divided into the three levels shown in Figure 5.2.[12] At the very top, a small management group is responsible for the organization's relations with those outside the organization: the customers, the financial community, the government, and so forth. This is the level of strategic planning. Below this is a larger group concerned with the internal organization of the firm's resources and the administration of the company in the light of policy set by the senior group. This is the group responsible for the development of operational plans. Last are those concerned with carrying out the work of the company's operations.

Table 5.1 Basic Definitions

	Definition	
Term	Strategic Planning	Tactical Operational Planning
Time horizon	2 to 20 years	1 day to 24 months
Purpose	What business to be in Broad allocation of resources	Succeeding in chosen business Short-term trade-offs in resource allocation
Nature of process	Less formalized and more flexible	More formalized and structured allocations
Specificity	Tentative, broad-ranging nonroutine issues	Specific, timed actions, expenditures, and controls—often concerning routine issues
Who does it	Inputs from few senior corporate and operating managers	Inputs from large number of operating managers

Source: Adapted from M. R. Pearce, University of Western Ontario.

Case History 5.1 Strategic Perspective: Foresight or Opportunism?

The Marriott Corporation has been in the hotel business since the 1950s. Initially, it operated only Marriott Hotels, which were typically four-star properties. While the company experimented with franchising, it generally operated properties it owned or for which it had a management contract. Beginning in 1983, however, as brand segmentation became more popular, the company entered the mid-market and limited-service segments with its Courtyard and Fairfield properties. It also entered the extended-stay market with the acquisition of Residence Inns.

Developing Long-Term Competencies

Marriott is generally recognized as one of the finest *operators* of hotels in the United States. In each of the segments it serves, its brands command a premium price and generally enjoy relatively higher occupancies than many of its competitors. Marriott's core competence, we might say, is operations, that is, running hotels in a way which guests find satisfying. While Marriott has franchised some properties, it is known for its very high—some might say rigid—standards which have limited its franchising activity. It has done some conversion franchising (franchising existing properties built for another franchising brand), but most of its properties are newly built to fit a common company design. In fact, some might say that Marriott, with its extensive experience in the lodging industry, has not expanded as quickly as it could have and that market dominance has gone to other firms that were prepared to adopt a more flexible approach to franchising.

CONVERSION FRANCHISING: OPPORTUNITY KNOCKS

In the 1970s and 1980s, the number of hotel brands proliferated as franchising became established and the number of properties rose. In the mid-1980s, the practice of conversion franchising became common. During this period, a number of franchising companies were also put up for sale by their owners. Here was an opportunity that called forth a strategic response from companies such as Hospitality Franchise Services (HFS) and Choice Hotels International.

Each of these companies acquired several franchise brands[1] and offered one or another of them, depending on a property's qualifications, to franchisees who were seeking to change brands or to independents who wanted the advantage of a brand name and a reservation system. By growing the number of brands they offered and aggressively pursuing conversion prospects, these companies have become the largest lodging groups in the world. Indeed, in 1995, with 435,000 rooms and 4,400 properties under license, HFS had become the world's largest hotel group. Choice, though smaller in *number of rooms* than long-time market leader Holiday Inns, was number two in *number of properties* with 3,476 hotels under license. Marriott, by way of contrast, had just over 186,000 rooms and 898 properties.[2]

HFS and Choice do not own or operate hotels. "We're not in the hotel business," the president of HFS said. "We're in the franchising business. We provide services to our customers and our customers are our franchisees."[3]

In fact, HFS has recently acquired a franchising company, Century 21, which is in the real estate business. HFS sees itself as likely to acquire "franchise rights to other non-hotel businesses."[4]

The relative sizes of the largest U.S.-based hotel organizations are shown in the table below:

The interesting question is, which of these formulas will prove the most successful over the *long term*? Marriott has contented itself with gradual, controlled growth, thereby achieving an enviable reputation for superior operations with guests. HFS and Choice, on the other hand, have multiple brands in many markets and at least one brand suitable for almost every market and very wide geographic penetration.

NOTES

1. It should be noted that one of Choice's original brands was the well-established Quality brand and three others, Clarion, Comfort Inns and Sleep Inns, were developed by the company rather than purchased. The company did, however, acquire the Roadway, Park Inns, Econolodge and Friendship brands. The company has merged the Roadway and Friendship brands under the Roadway name. More recently, Hospitality Franchise Systems has begun the development of a limited-service brand, Wingate.
2. *Hotel and Motel Management,* September 18, 1995, pp. 34–35.
3. *Hotel and Motel Management,* July 5, 1995, p. 8.
4. Ibid.

Size of U.S.-Based Hotel Organizations* 1995

Name of Company	Number of Properties	Number of Rooms
Hospitality Franchise Systems (HFS)	4,400	435,000
Choice Hotels International	3,476	299,881
Best Western International	3,476	276,659
Holiday Inn Worldwide	2,031	365,309
Marriott Hotels Resorts & Suites	898	186,656
*The two largest non–U.S.-based chains are		
Accor (France)	2,205	252,887
Forte PLC (United Kingdom)	954	98,450

Data: From Hotel and Motel Management, September 18, 1995, p. 35.

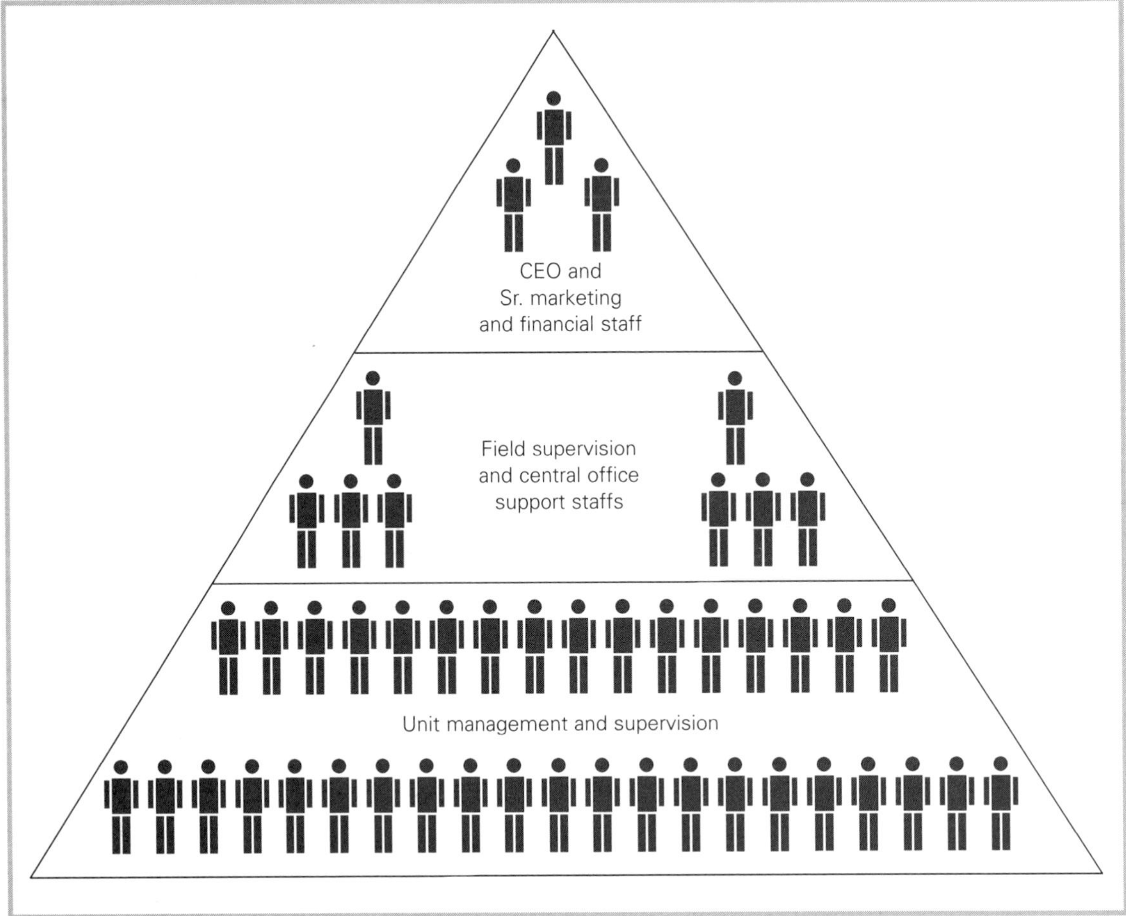

Figure 5.2 Responsibilities in Modern Organizations

Source: Thomas F. Powers, "Hospitality Management Development," *Cornell Hotel and Restaurant Administration Quarterly,* February 1980, p. 40.

Managers and supervisors are generally not responsible for drawing up strategies, but they often have information that is important to their sound development. Moreover, they are the people who will implement the strategy and their support can be crucial to the strategy's ultimate success. For these reasons, the fullest possible consultation is healthy whenever it can be carried out without broadcasting information which would be useful to competitors.

THE BUILDING BLOCKS OF STRATEGY

Strategy is built on five broad considerations: the customer, the competitive structure of the market or industry, the competitive position of the firm, market opportunities, and company resources. In addition, if the business unit is a subsidiary of another company, its strategy will need to fit the parent's overall strategy. Finally, the personal values of key personnel and the need to meet the firm's objectives relative to society and its legal framework will have an impact on the strategy formulation process. We will consider each of these.

The Customer

The first and most fundamental strategic building block is and understanding of the **customer.** For most of this century—and before—hotels and restaurants followed traditional designs in their menus, systems of operation, and facilities. Today, however, we see an industry that is based on segmentation, that is, on the consumer. An almost bewildering variety of restaurants has emerged, each targeting a relatively distinct set of market segments. This variety can be seen not only in food type but also in ambience, service type and intensity, and price.

The hotel business, too, has increasingly adopted a segmentation strategy. Marriott, for instance, speaks of "upstairs" and "downstairs" guests in every price segment.[13] Upstairs-oriented guests want guest room comfort and amenities emphasized, but they are relatively indifferent to supporting facilities such as multiple dining rooms, cocktail lounges, and meeting and banquet facilities. These customers want luxury at a modest price. Courtyard by Marriott meets the needs of such consumers, with large and luxurious rooms accompanied by pleasant,

Strategy is determined, first of all, by customer need and wants. (Photo courtesy of Taco Bell)

but limited, food service and support facilities. Marriott's Fairfield Inns targets an upstairs segment that is more price conscious and requiries even less service.

The downstairs guests, in contrast, do require the more elaborate facilities and services and they are prepared to pay for them. Marriott's upscale hotels meet their needs. Similar segmentation is reflected, too, in the growth of clearly differentiated product groupings developed by other chains aimed at different segments of the market. Examples are rapidly growing all-suite hotels, budget properties, and superluxury chains.

Segmentation, you will recall, is not just demographic and psychographic. It can also be occasion oriented: by time of day, meal occasion, social function for restaurants, and purpose of trip for hotels—and who is paying. The same persons are a different operator's customers, depending on what they are doing. The executive in a hurry or with a family of young children can be a QSR customer, although he or she may normally patronize more upscale establishments. The need to segment off-season (summer in the Caribbean) and down-time customers (early-bird specials for people who are willing to eat between 3:30 and 5:30 P.M.) adds another dimension of complexity. Growing cost pressures, as the industry matures, make the need to maintain high utilization and occupancy rates even more important.

The bedrock on which a hospitality operation's strategic plan is built is the customer. The job of identifying his or her needs and wants has become more complex and changes with each passing day. Consumer research, once almost unheard of for most of the industry, has become so common as to have spurred the growth of a subindustry of research firms specializing in hospitality market research.

Competitive Structure

A second determinant of strategy is the industry's **competitive structure.** The five factors affecting industry competitive structure have been described by Porter.

Porter's Five Forces Model. Michael Porter, in his study of competitive strategy, identifies five forces that together determine the intensity of competition or, as it is sometimes called, the competitive structure of an industry:

1. Intensity of competition among the firms that now make up the industry.
2. Ease of entry.
3. Threat of substitute product or service.
4. Bargaining power of customers.
5. Bargaining power of suppliers.[14]

Intensity of Present Competition Much of the economy of North America is characterized by large firm size and some degree of oligopolistic competition (a

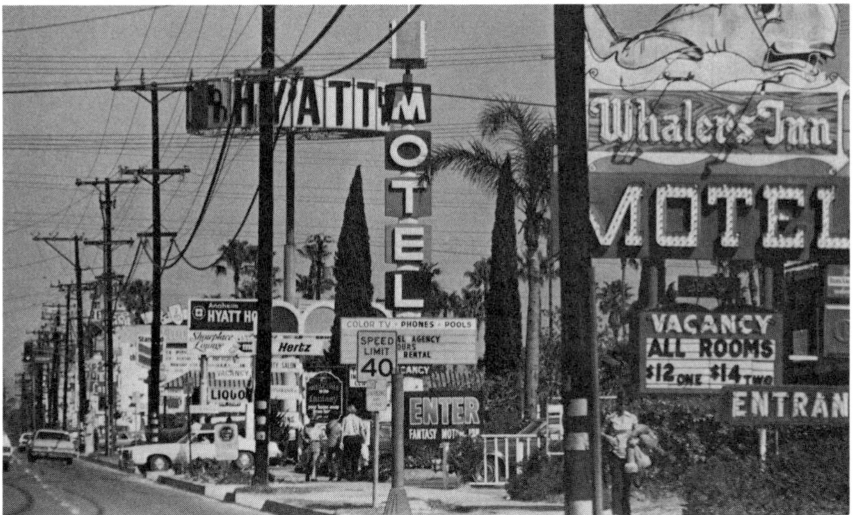

Competition in the hospitality industry is intense. (Photo courtesy Jan Lukas/Photo Researchers)

market dominated by a few large companies). These large firms have been characterized as "the center" of the economy. In contrast, a much more competitive situation is found at the periphery of the economy in service industries such as hospitality. Porter speaks of an industry such as ours as fragmented, "that is, an industry in which no firm has a significant market share and can strongly influence the outcome."[15] The absence of a market leader and the presence of wild cards, in the form of small firms whose behavior is entirely unpredictable, make outcomes beyond a very short period of time unpredictable. Added to these factors is the presence of considerable overcapacity in both lodging and food service. When there is supply in excess of demand, the effect is always to heighten competition.

Ease of Entry Many industries have barriers to entry such as, in automobiles, the huge investment required to get into auto manufacturing and the need for a national dealer and service network. While national advertising by companies such as McDonald's makes the formation of national chains difficult, this barrier is more than offset by the fact that McDonald's and other leaders face successful regional chains in every market and these regionals can expand on a market-by-market basis as they seek national stature. Regional chains and QSRs offering other products not only compete but encourage new entrants into the market through franchising.

Franchising makes it possible, at the level of the individual unit, for people without any training or experience to invest in hotels or restaurants. Franchise chains have led the expansion of both businesses. Instead of a bar to entry, hospitality has—in franchise chains—an actual *inducement to entry.* Ideally, every franchise wants to be represented in every viable market. The inducement to entry is especially strong in lodging, because each company wants not only the destination

Both established franchise brands and new brands, such as Wingate, offer people with capital a ready means to enter into the hospitality industry. Franchise systems contribute an inducement to market entry. (Photo courtesy of Wingate Inns)

volume at each location but also the origination volume; that is, they want travelers from that city as customers for their reservation network.

Threat of Substitution Just as the threat of entry is great, there are also lots of potential substitutes for the services hospitality firms offer. This raises the competitive level further. For instance, the most frequently used accommodation for travelers is staying with friends and relatives. Recreational vehicles and second homes are also serious competitors for leisure travelers. Increasingly, business travelers can replace a trip with a phone call or a meeting with a video conference.

There are clearly plenty of nonrestaurant sources for food service. The largest of these is the home. A restaurant's greatest competition at the noon meal is the "brown bag." The dynamics of the home entertainment center, with its videocassette player, computer games, and stereo system, all backed up by the camaraderie of the backyard barbeque and the convenience of the increasingly ubiquitous microwave oven, is perhaps the greatest competitive threat restaurants face. The supermarket, with its well-stocked freezer compartment, growing delicatessen department, and convenience foods of all kinds, is making every effort to serve those interests. The home entertainment center and its stay-at-home potential also competes as a pastime with travel and hotel stays.

Bargaining Power of Customers In some industries, one or a very few large buyers maintain some order, that is, predictability, within the industry. The hospitality industry, however, fits the competitive model ("many buyers, many sellers").

The fact that no customer can dictate the behavior of hospitality firms removes another possible element of predictability.

Bargaining Power of Suppliers As with customers, there is no one supplier of goods or services that is large enough to dominate and thus exert an ordering influence.

Impact of Competitive Structure on Strategy On each of Porter's five points for weighing competitive structure, we find the hospitality industry at the competitive end of the scale. This has two major impacts on strategy. The first is that, in the face of extreme competition, any innovation that is successful will quickly be copied. When Marriott's Courtyard concept proved successful a few years ago, for instance, competing companies quickly brought out concepts so similar that they were referred to in the trade press as "Courtyard Clones." While the innovation has a head start, then, any innovation will soon be matched and its effectiveness diminished accordingly.

A second conclusion involves stability and predictability. In a market that is so fragmented and competitive, there is a greater degree of uncertainty and, hence, a higher risk for investors than in less fragmented industries.

The Relative Competitive Position of the Firm

We will consider three possible positions for a firm: the market leader, the major follower, and the guerilla. The kinds of strategic options a firm can choose are dictated, to a considerable degree, by how a firm fits into one of these three categories. As will soon become clear, however, this frame of analysis is more useful at the present time in examining food service than lodging.

The Leader. McDonald's is the market leader in fast foods and especially so in the hamburger chain market. Burger King is second and Wendy's, Hardee's and KFC are principal followers. Until the mid-1980s, Holiday Inns was the market leader in lodging, but it is impossible, in today's turbulent lodging market, to identify clearly which firm will emerge as the leader. Lodging, then, is in a competitive free-for-all, out of which someday a market leader may emerge.

The market leader's strategy is fundamentally defensive. As the largest firm, a leader has a dominant market share and the leader's goal is to retain its share. A defensive posture, however, is not a passive one. McDonald's, for instance, is a very aggressive competitor and will increase its share whenever the opportunity presents itself. A few years ago, Burger King launched a new, reformulated Whopper as part of an effort to increase its market share. To block that move, McDonald's introduced a sandwich product called the McDLT. The McDLT was actually the more successful of the two, perhaps because consumers found a "new" product more interesting than a reformulated one. In any case, McDonald's successfully stole Burger King's thunder. Though it later actually discontinued the McDLT, McDonald's gained a modest amount of market share during what was supposed to be a Burger King offensive.

One further point about the McDLT is that it undoubtedly also took sales from other of its own products, a process referred to as *cannibalization*. The leader must sometimes cannibalize its own products in order to maintain its leadership, as McDonald's did against the reformulated Whopper.

The Major Follower. The major followers must take the offensive and attack the leader. At first glance, it does not make sense that the smaller firm would attack a larger one, but a moment's reflection will show you why that is true: *That is where the sales are*. As hard as it is to take business from the larger firm, it can be expected that the smaller firm will fight even harder to defend its smaller market because the loss of the same dollar amount will constitute a much larger percentage of the smaller firm's sales than it would for the market leader with its larger sales.

The Guerilla. Guerilla warfare is the strategy that suits a company that is small relative to the giant players in the market, the leader and the principal followers. In most large markets, this is the strategy best suited to the independent and regional chains.

The first rule of guerilla warfare is to find a segment of the market that is small enough to take and hold. Some health-oriented restaurants, for instance, have established a strong enough reputation with their market segment that they are relatively secure. Others rely on luxury and special preparation techniques such as a barbeque process. The luxury operation is generally a stronghold of the independent.

The guerilla is a smaller, more flexible organization. It can—and must—be able to react quickly to changing market conditions. If there seems to be a market opportunity, the smaller company can decide to pursue it without elaborate staff work, communicate that decision quickly, and begin to implement it almost immediately.

This flexibility is especially important in regional markets. Large chains hesitate to add a regional item to their product line because it will dilute their national image. On the other hand, local operators can build on a product with strong local appeal. In this way, they can attack the leader on the basis of the leader's very success and market size—and resulting inflexibility in responding. Regional chains that featured biscuits were given a good head start in carving a market niche for themselves in the southern United States by the hesitancy of the larger chains to add a product regionally that they could not sell in the rest of their units nationally.

Niche Marketing. The strategy we have called guerilla warfare is sometimes spoken of in terms of mastery of a particular market niche. The word *niche* offers another powerful analogy for marketing strategy. In ecology, a niche is the smallest unit of physical space occupied by an organism. In nature, some species develop particular characteristics that permit them to survive and dominate in one small area. In hospitality marketing, this translates, for instance, into the small indepen-

A neighborhood bar offers a good example of niche marketing: dominating a market small enough that it doesn't attract additional competition. (Photo courtesy Peter Menzel/Stock Boston)

dent hotel that serves a local market that is too small to attract a second competitor—as long as the first one does a good job. To give a different example, a successful neighborhood bar may occupy and dominate a two- or three-square-block niche. A key to niche marketing is to find a unique segment that is small enough *not* to attract competition, yet large enough to support a unit serving it profitably.

Relative Competitive Position and Strategy. To illustrate the concept of competitive position, we have used the national market for fast-food hamburger chains. The concepts that underlie our discussion, however, have broad applicability and can be extended on the basis of your own experience in the market you know best. At the local market level, however, there may not always *be* a true market leader, in the sense of one company having a dominant market share, because there are so many players among whom a given local market can be divided.

Our discussion of relative competitive position underlines the crucial importance of competition to thinking about marketing. It is *not* enough to be customer oriented:

> Today every company is customer oriented. Knowing what the customer wants isn't too helpful if a dozen other companies are already serving the same customer's wants. [Beyond being customer oriented,] a company must be competition oriented.[16]

Market Opportunity

Competitive conditions change, creating opportunities where none existed earlier. The growth of limited-service lodging offers an interesting example.

Until the early 1980s, it was always taken for granted that a hotel had to have a restaurant to provide good service to its guests. During the period following

World War II, however, the number and variety of restaurants increased rapidly. The hotel restaurant was no longer the only place a visitor felt safe in eating. Rather, there were now many well-established restaurant brands familiar to the guest from which a visitor could choose. Seeing this, La Quinta Inns[17] developed a property that eliminated both the investment and the operating cost of food service, while offering guest rooms that were comparable to the then-dominant Holiday Inns. A restaurant was always available nearby. Because of lower investment and operating cost, La Quinta was able to offer these first-class guest room facilities at a rate 20 percent below the competition. La Quinta's early success blazed a trail a number of firms, such as Fairfield Inns and Hampton Inns, have followed. One of the keys to the success of all-suites, as well, has been their elimination or deemphasis of food service. The growth in the number of restaurants, then, created a market opportunity that has proved almost revolutionary in lodging. Furthermore, those firms that established an early lead in seizing this market opportunity have managed to maintain a significant portion of their lead in consumer preference in their particular target markets.

Company Resources. A final major determinant of strategy is the company's resource base. The most obvious resource requirement for undertaking a strategy is financial. A firm that expands too fast for its capital base generally experiences serious difficulty or goes under. Human resources, however, are crucial as well. Human resources refer especially to the people the company must have on board with expertise in marketing and operations.

One of the difficulties a regional chain faces if it chooses to expand beyond the region of its initial success is the need to compete in the media for the attention of prospective customers in the new territory who are *not* familiar with the chain's concept and operation. It is a quite different order of difficulty to sell a new concept (or one new to the territory) than it is to maintain an image already established. Sufficient depth in operations is also critical if new units are to be staffed with managers and new employees trained so that quality and cost control standards can be met in the new units.

Other Factors Determining Strategy

Subsidiary Status. The overall strategy of the parent company has an obvious bearing on that of a subsidiary. For instance, the subsidiary would not usually expect to enter a line of business in direct competition with another subsidiary. The hurdle rates (expected return on investment) of the parent will affect the acquisitions and divestments a company undertakes. A change in management style at senior levels of the parent company may have profound effects on marketing, operating, and personnel strategies in subsidiaries.

Personal Values. The values that guide the personal conduct of top management will have a major impact on strategy formulation.[18] The executive who is impressed by General George Patton's motto, *"L'audace, toujours l'audace!"* ("Audacity,

The evolution in the appearance of McDonald's restaurant units in response to public concern regarding "visual pollution" indicates both a responsiveness to society's concerns and a healthy self-interest. (Photos courtesy McDonald's Corp.)

always audacity!") will probably put more emphasis on boldness than a manager who is an admirer of British General Bernard Montgomery's caution and conservatism. Isadore Sharp's almost fanatical committment to high-quality operations has had a profound impact on the development of Four Seasons Hotels.

Obligation to Society. There is a self-interested market-based response to public opinion that is characteristic of companies' public behaviors. The evolution of McDonald's exterior appearance offers an interesting example. The original golden arches and McDonald's restaurant exterior were regarded by many architectural critics, city planners, and civic leaders as garish, a form of visual pollution. This, in turn, led to difficulty in obtaining zoning regulations favorable to McDonald's. Thus, the more modest and restrained golden arches evolved, as did the attractive brick building with its signature mansard roof, in order to meet these public objections—and deal with their practical impact on growth.[19]

This example contains the key elements of the public policy of the sensible corporation: a responsiveness to society's concerns and a healthy self-interest. Frequently, companies undertake a long-run, strategic commitment to public-spirited efforts such as participation in programs for training the unemployed or a major charitable effort. We should not be surprised that, in virtually all cases, the corporation expects to do well by doing good and that benefit to the corporate image is an inherent part of the planning of such ventures. It is unrealistic to expect the corporation to be run as a charitable enterprise, but it is also unrealistic for a company to ignore the public interest.

CORPORATE STRATEGIC PLANNING

Top management is responsible for translating its understanding of demand (i.e., customers), competition, industry structure, and the company's own strengths and weaknesses into a strategic plan. This means (1) the identification of the company's purpose for being—that is, its mission; (2) the fundamental organization of its efforts into major divisions; and (3) the determination of how corporate resources will be invested in these units.

The Corporate Mission: Business Purpose

Peter Drucker, an economism and management consultant, has said that the basic purpose of a business is "to create a customer." That is, a business must shape itself to respond to consumer needs. In order to do that, Drucker says, managers must constantly ask themselves these questions:

Who is the customer?

What is value to the customer?

What will our business be?

What *should* our business be?

These are the questions that underlie the formation of a business mission statement such as the following from a unit of the Carlson Companies:

> Country Inns and Suites by Carlson is a growth oriented global franchisor of mid-market lodging properties that provides franchisees with unsurpassed service and support. We will be the value leader in the segments in which we compete as measured by the growth rate in our systemwide annual revenue and the satisfaction of our key stake holders.

Investment Decisions

The most fundamental question any business must consider in assessing its future is whether to invest, maintain the present position, or reduce that position. Figure 5.3 frames this decision on how to deploy the firm's resources. One option is to invest. If the answer is yes, the question is whether to do more of what the firm is already doing or to expand into related or different businesses. Later in this chapter, we will look at this decision in more detail.

A very common decision is to "hold"—that is, to continue in the same business. Here, too, further decisions are required. Should we maintain the business as is? This implies a more aggressive investment program to maintain the business at its current level. On the other hand, a decision to "harvest" calls for operating without any investment except that necessary to remain in business. A hotel company five years away from a franchise renewal deadline, for instance, might decide not to seek renewal of the franchise. Under these circumstances, it might decide to harvest the property by spending only the funds necessary to enable continuing operation and to take out all profits rather than reinvest them. The decision to harvest normally implies a future decision to divest, that is, to sell the asset.

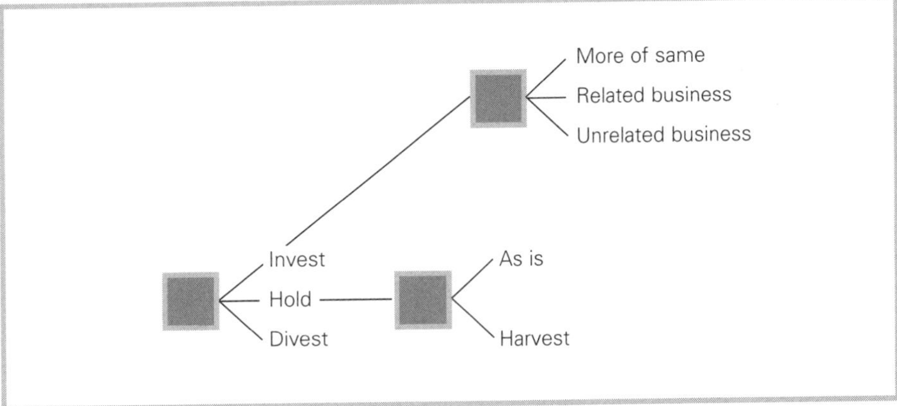

Figure 5.3 Deployment of Resources

Source: Kenneth G. Hardy, University of Western Ontario.

Corporate Organization: Strategic Business Units

Because large companies are commonly engaged in several different businesses, many companies recognize different centers of business, which are referred to as **strategic business units (SBUs).** Ideally, an SBU is a single business unit or collection of related businesses and has a mission distinct from other SBUs, as well as its own target market or markets and distinctive group of competitors. An SBU has control over its own resources and its plan is independent of other SBUs. As an example, Taco Bell, one of PepsiCo's SBUs, in addition to its own operations, acquires and operates other fast-food companies such as Hot 'n Now. Taco Bell, as a business, is distinct from PepsiCo's other restaurant companies, KFC and Pizza Hut.

Portfolio Management. With several different centers of business activity in its SBUs, the issue of how to allocate resources among SBUs must be resolved. One way of viewing the relative merits of a company's SBUs is summarized in Figure 5.4, in which the attractiveness of a business unit is seen as a function of the attractiveness of the market in which it is located and the relative position of the unit in that market. A unit's position can be delineated as lying in one of the nine cells

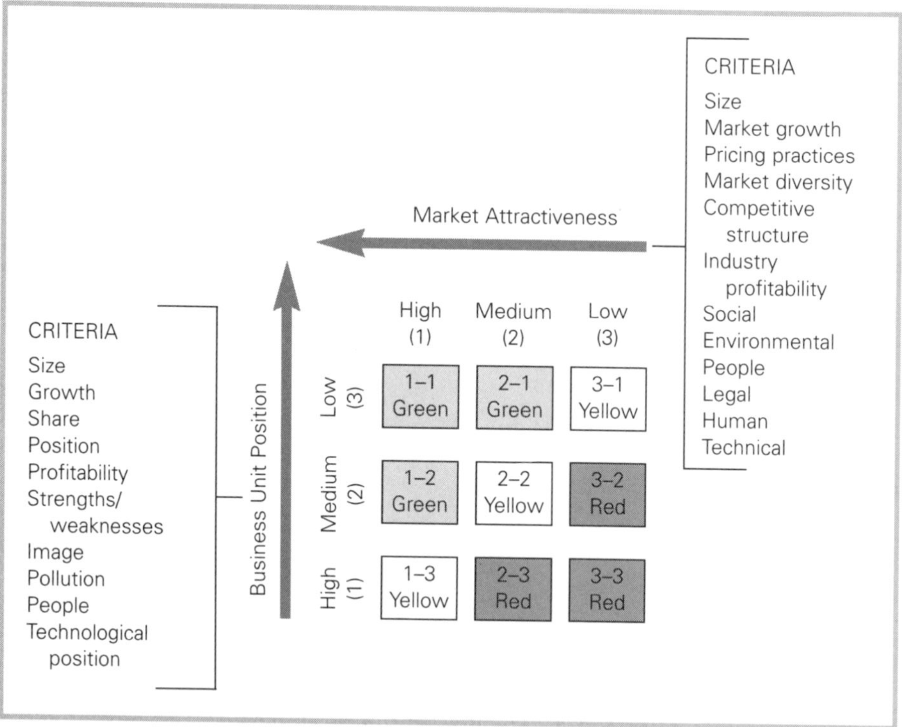

Figure 5.4 Company Position/Market Attractiveness Matrix

shown, with a high number attached to attractiveness and strength and a low number given to the reverse. Thus, a 1–1 situation is most attractive and warrants investment, as do other green cells. A 2–2 is right in the middle (as are the yellow cells 3–1 and 1–3) and justifies holding but with caution. A 3–3 is a worst case and probably warrants divestiture, whereas a 3–2 or 2–3 suggests harvesting or divestiture.[20]

Another way of summarizing the prospects for a business unit is the Boston Consulting Group's growth/share matrix, depicted in Figure 5.5. The assumption underlying this model is that the two key variables that sum up the prospects for a business unit are its growth and market share relative to the largest company in the market and that these two factors can be used to reflect policy. The four cells can be characterized as stars, broncos (also called question marks), cash cows, and dogs. In the upper left corner are stars, units that have a high market share (which usually means they are profitable) and good growth prospects. These are the

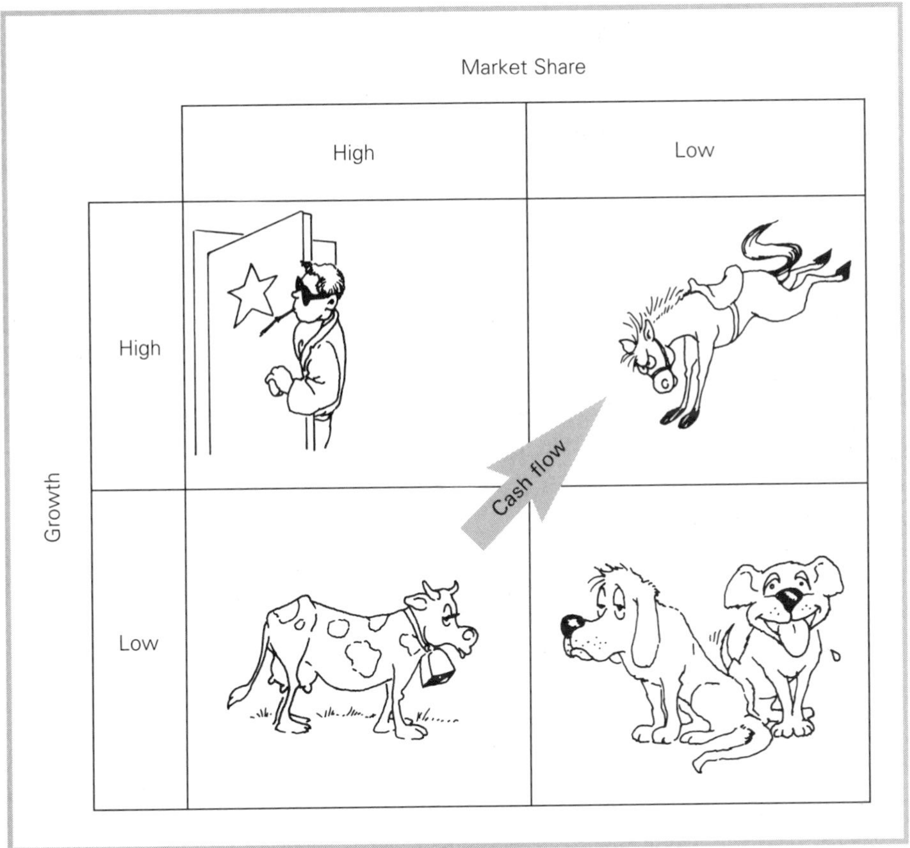

Figure 5.5 The Growth/Share Matrix: Stars, Broncos, Cash Cows, and Dogs

winners. Generally, they generate enough profits to fund their own growth or, perhaps, require modest cash inflows to grow fast enough to take advantage of their business opportunities.

In the upper-right corner are the broncos, where growth opportunities are high, but market share is low. A bronco will, ideally, receive enough investment to become a star, but, at the moment, it requires considerable cash investment to grow fast enough to attain optimum market share.

A cash cow, found in the lower-left corner, is a well-established business with a high market share but limited growth prospects. Such, for instance, is the situation of a hotel that has high occupancy but that cannot expand in size. The funds from this successful property will be used to fund the company's new properties. Thus, the indication in the diagram of the ideal cash flow from cow to bronco represents the desired pattern of investment in growth. An SBU that is a cash cow is "milked" to supply the investment need of a fast-growing bronco.

Finally, in the lower-right corner is the unit with low market share and low growth. Although this is conventionally shown as a rather sad-faced dog, we have shown two dogs—one of whom is a cheerful-looking fellow. This represents the reality that harvesting, as well as divestment, is an option and that harvesting can still be a profitable activity. When their property comes up for refranchising, many owners of franchised hotels, for instance, choose not to make the major investment in upgrading the property. Instead, they affiliate with a lower-cost brand or they operate as an independent—for instance, on low-rate business or as an overflow house for nearby, newer hotels that have higher occupancies.

It is worth noting how a unit's position might affect its marketing program. Stars are winners but require aggressive marketing to maintain their position in a growing market. Cows, on the other hand, require maintenance marketing but they are already dominant in their market. They need to be alert, however, for the bronco who is out to take the leadership away from them. Broncos need a high level of investment if they are to break out of their low-market-share position. While dogs require some promotional expenditure, they are most likely to rely on reduced prices or discounting.

Generic Strategies

Michael Porter, in his study of competitive strategies, suggests that "at the broadest level we can identify three internally consistent generic strategies (which can be used singly or in combination) for creating a defendable position and out performing competitors in an industry"[21]—that is, for creating a sustainable competitive advantage. These strategies are: overall cost leadership, differentiation, and focus. They are illustrated in Figure 5.6.

Strategy 1. *Overall cost leadership* is harder to obtain in the hospitality industry because the need to serve the customer in many convenient places limits plant economies of scale, which are a common basis of cost leadership. Scale economies are available, however, in advertising and, probably to a lesser degree, in food

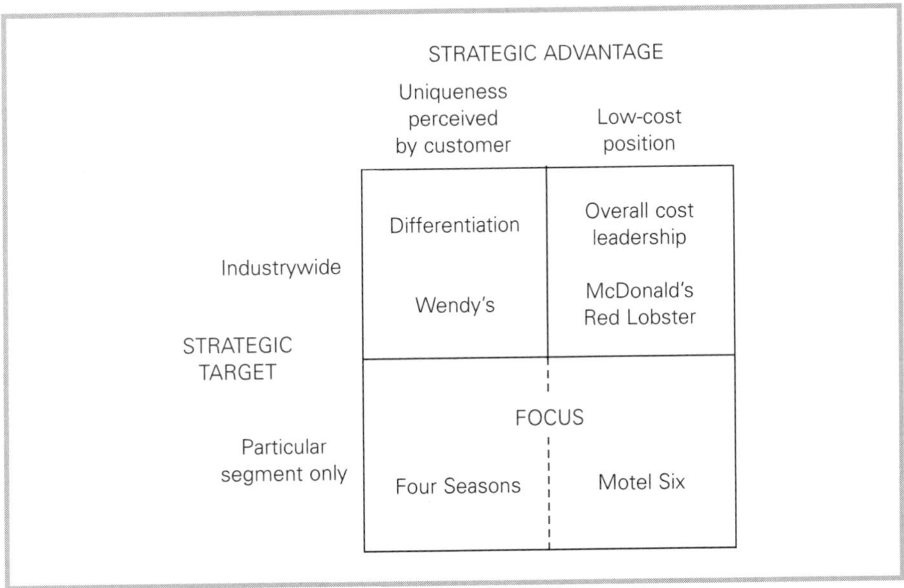

Figure 5.6 Three Generic Strategies

Source: Adapted from Michael Porter, *Competitive Strategy* (New York: Free Press, 1980), p. 39.

purchasing to such giants as McDonald's. In addition, McDonald's can achieve economies from the sheer accumulation of operating experience in thousands of units in many regional and national markets. Porter refers to this accumulation of experience as the learning-curve effect.

Where a specialized food product, such as seafood, is the basis of a menu, purchasing economies are more likely. Red Lobster, for instance, is able to "maintain a cost advantage over its competitors through volume purchasing and a vertically integrated supply chain."[22]

Strategy 2. *Differentiation,* as a strategy, relies on "differentiating the product or service offering of the firm, creating something that is perceived *industry wide* as being unique."[23] Within the fast-food hamburger market, Wendy's successfully established itself in its initial format by differentiating itself from other hamburger chains along several dimensions: product and ambience, as well as slightly upgraded service (no self-busing). These differences supported a significantly higher price and made Wendy's a high-profit, high-growth chain in a market some considered saturated at the time.

Strategy 3. *Focus* refers to a very tight segmentation strategy, "serving a particular target very well."[24] In the luxury market, this strategy works well for Four Seasons, in conjunction with relatively higher prices. It also works in the extremely price-sensitive segment for the North American economy lodging leader, Motel Six.

Synergy is the goal of Carlson Companies colocation of the three branded units shown here: County Inns and Suites, Country Kitchen, and Italianis. (Photo courtesy of Carlson Country Hospitality)

To these three basic strategic approaches, we should add preemption and synergy.[25] A *preemptive strategy* is one which brings a new product, technique, or technology to a market in a way which is difficult for competitors to copy. We have already noted that there is a tendency for competitors to match any innovations. (While La Quinta developed the limited-service hotel concept, for instance, it was unable to dominate that segment.) It is true, nonetheless, that an innovator can gain and often maintain a significant advantage by being the first to implement a concept on a broad scale. While there are many "Courtyard Clones," Marriott's Courtyard is still the best known, clearly identifiable chain operating in its particular segment. In fact, one means of preemption is to become the "industry standard." Holiday Inns, in the 1960s and 1970s, had many imitators—but they were *seen* as imitators and the term "Holiday Inn room" became an industry standard—as did the mix of services that company offered.

Companies that seek to use *synergy* as a strategy work to gain from shared abilities in several divisions of a firm. Perhaps the leading practitioner of this in the hospitality industry is the Carlson Hospitality Group. Carlson Travel Group has 9,000 reservation terminals in 4,000 locations in 125 countries. Carlson Hospitality Group operates or franchises over 1,000 hotels with over 150,000 rooms. Carlson also franchises two restaurant concepts, Country Kitchen by Carlson and T.G.I. Friday's, which fit in well with many of its hotels. As the company says in one of its publications:

> Propelled by the synergistic relationship between hospitality service, travel agencies, and marketing, Carlson companies brings to the world marketplace a network of companies poised for global leadership in the 21st century.[26]

Strategies for Growth

Growth is generally a desired goal of multiunit organizations—and often of independent operators. There are four strategies that a company can employ in order to grow. These are presented graphically in Figure 5.7. We will briefly discuss the salient characteristics of each strategy.

Market Penetration. The object of **market penetration** is to improve sales of existing products in existing markets. This can be as simple as a program to increase sales through suggestive selling—wine with the meal, desserts or liqueurs after dinner, and the like. In lodging, inducing guests to stay three days instead of two fits this definition. This is the lowest-risk growth strategy—but, if a firm is already successful in its operations, it probably also offers the lowest rewards.

Product Development. There is a somewhat riskier strategy than market penetration, new **product development.** This is riskier because of its cost and because that cost may be lost if the product fails. A new product may be as "new" as a bacon cheeseburger (i.e., a modification of an existing product) or it may be a genuinely "new" product for the segment, as were the salad bar and baked potato for fast food. When successful, as with McDonald's introduction of breakfast to the quick-service restaurant segment, product development can bring major advantage to the firm. Nevertheless, the discouraging fact is that the vast majority of new products fail.

	Existing products/services	New products/services
Existing markets	Market penetration	Product development
New markets	Market development	Diversification

Figure 5.7 Growth Options

Source: H. Igor Ansoff, "Strategies for Diversification," *Harvard Business Review,* September–October 1957.

Market Development. Another equally risky approach is **market development.** It has greater risk than market penetration because, in seeking to enter new markets with existing products, it risks the loss of market development expenditures. The most common market development activity is that of new geographic markets. In hospitality, franchising is the major tool to facilitate this kind of market development. Franchising uses the franchisee's investment capital and shifts most of the risk to the franchisee, thus solving two of the major problems of expansion. The franchisee, as owner, is expected to provide highly motivated management; this solves another hindrance to rapid expansion, the need to provide a rapidly growing management network.

One mode of market development that is currently getting attention from U.S. firms is expansion into other countries. This expansion is discussed in Global Marketing Note 5.1.

An alternative to geographic expansion is to seek to serve additional market segments in the present territory. Commonly, this involves the development of a different marketing mix to attract new market segments. To supplement the weekday business traveler, special pricing attracts local families to a hotel on the weekend. Companies might achieve similar goals by advertising in different, specially targeted media. A hotel seeking convention business for the first time, for instance, might begin advertising in *Conventions and Meetings Magazine*.

Diversification

When new products are introduced in new markets, **diversification** occurs. The combination of new products and new markets is the highest-risk strategy. Although Aramark's entry into areas such as contract cleaning and periodical distribution was built on existing strengths in that company, nevertheless, they represented new products in new markets at their introduction.

Illustrative of the risk of diversification is the string of unsuccessful acquisitions by Holiday Inns some years ago that were subsequently divested. The company attempted to enter the prefabricated construction business, transportation (with a busline), and the freestanding restaurant business, but it left all of them because return on investment was unsatisfactory.

FUNCTIONAL STRATEGIES

Functional strategies are concerned with how a company will implement its overall strategy. Functional strategies are, however, long-term approaches to tactical marketing activities, not tactical plans. The most fundamental of these is the company's *positioning strategy*. Positioning is concerned with how the *company* will relate to the other two key elements of the strategic triangle, *customer* and *competition*. The long-term approaches to using the elements of the marketing mix are derived from the positioning strategy. Thus, positioning determines the product, price, place, and promotion strategies.

Positioning Strategy

Positioning refers to the "process of establishing and maintaining a distinctive place in the market for an organization and/or its individual product offerings. It links market analysis and competitive analysis to internal corporate analysis."[27] Figure 5.8 summarizes these linkages. Position is developed on the basis of external and internal analyses. *External analysis* involves a careful study of *customers* and *competitors,* while *internal analysis* focuses on the company's *objectives* and *capabilities.* Figure 5.8 also depicts, in the simplest terms, a *process* of analysis that is explored in the following discussion of customer and competitor analyses.

Customer Analysis. By analyzing the market, strategic planners can determine how the population should be divided into segments that makes sense for the product(s) in question. A hotel company might begin with segmentation based on the use of the hotel to the traveler: individual business, individual leisure, corporate group, association members. These groups might be further divided into demographic segments, with income levels, employment classification, and age playing key roles. From this process, management chooses a target market or markets. An economy chain on a highway route to Florida might choose to target middle-income retirees, while an upscale resort property might target middle-aged, higher-income executives and professional people and their families. An upscale restaurant might choose a similar target market—but it would probably be drawn principally from some local geographic area, rather than the larger geographic target market appropriate to lodging.

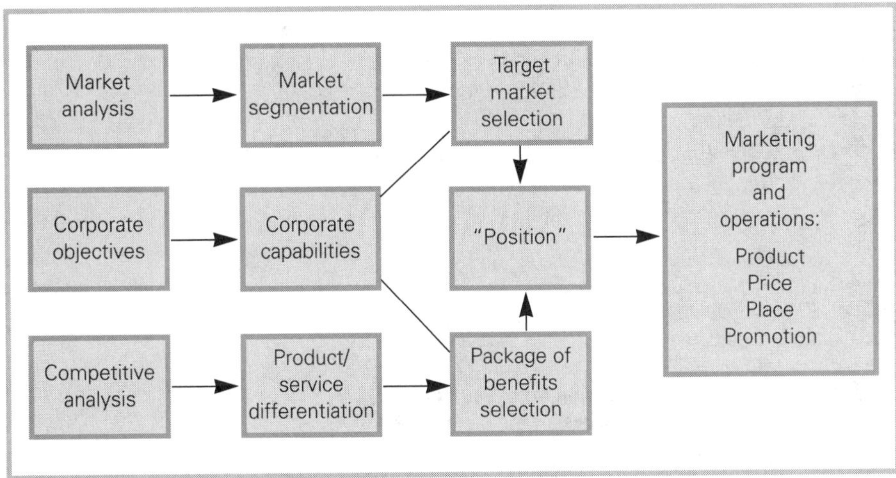

Figure 5.8 Forces at Work in Defining Market Position

Source: Michael Pearce, University of Western Ontario.

Global Marketing Note 5.1

International Expansion in Food Service

Most of the major areas in the world—Asia, Eastern and Western Europe, and South America—are experiencing real economic growth and leading North American companies are moving aggressively into these markets. There are approximately 160 food service companies operating internationally. The 100 largest U.S. chains were operating more than 16 percent of their units outside the United States at the end of 1994.

Far and away the most aggressive in its plans is McDonald's, which already has 2,500 units and $11 billion in sales overseas. McDonald's had plans to add 800 to 1,000 units in 1995. According to James Catalupo, president of McDonald's International, there are 27 customers for every McDonald's unit in the United States but a potential for 970 globally outside of the United States. Nearly 43 percent of McDonald's systemwide sales come from nondomestic units. Also in expansion mode is Wendy's which plans to double or even triple its international presence by 1998.

While QSRs dominate today, casual chains are following in their trail. T.G.I. Friday's vice president for international business put it this way:

> Fast food has had incredible success introducing American Foodservice to international markets. And, we're following in their footsteps. They helped create a huge demand for American service and Americana, and introducing casual dining into those markets is a natural progression from fast food's international success. For us it's a wide open market.

Planet Hollywood's international growth is accelerating rapidly. The company operates nine international units, six of which were opened in 1995.

FOUR REGIONS TO WATCH

Asia Pacific Rim

With 1995 projected gross domestic product growth ranging from 1 percent in Japan to 11 percent in China, this region is clearly the hottest international market. T.G.I. Friday's set a systemwide sales record when one of its units in South Korea had sales of over $52,500 in a single day. T.G.I. Friday's is also building in Beijing and Tianzin, China. Breslers Ice Cream and Yogurt has a master franchise agreement covering five Chinese provinces and the city of Shanghai. Other companies expanding in China, according to *Restaurants and Institutions,* include Subway, Pizza Hut, Pizza Inn, and Church's. (McDonald's and KFC are already established in China.)

In Southeast Asia, Baskin-Robbins became the first U.S. QSR to open in Vietnam. Metromedia has a four-unit deal in South Korea, while Long John Silver's will expand from Singapore to Bangkok, Thailand. Domino's anticipates a $60 million market for pizza in Thailand and has plans for 75 stores there.

Mexico and Latin America

In spite of monetary difficulties in Mexico, Wendy's is attracted by the soft real estate prices and the healthy long-term outlook for that country. T.G.I. Friday's and KFC have plans to continue expansion in

Chile, while Pizza Hut, Pizza Inn, Arby's, and Domino's all have plans for growth in Brazil.

Eastern Europe

A huge market potential in the former Iron Curtain countries is attractive, but operators are finding the legal climate uncertain and operating costs often high. Still companies such as McDonald's, Burger King, Domino's, and Baskin-Robbins appear committed to continue to grow in this area.

Western Europe

U.S. chains already have a significant presence here, but expansion continues with, for instance, McDonald's adding 50 units in Great Britain in 1995, bringing the company's total to over 600. T.G.I. Friday's recently opened in Paris and has plans to add nearly 200 units by the end of the decade.

Top International Food Service Growth Companies

	1995					
Chain	Total	Canada	Europe	Asia	Latin America	Middle East
McDonald's	5,513	720	2,130	2,187	445	39
KFC	4,207	835	433	2,173	357	409
Pizza Hut	2,989	531	940	913	451	154
Baskin-Robbins	1,428	211	707	97	274	139
Burger King	1,375	207	625	254	272	17
Subway	1,037	823	17	118	66	13
Dunkin' Donuts	964	232	527	165	34	6
Domino's	722	165	125	206	196	30
Wendy's	432	187	18	142	60	25
Arby's	168	113	3	7	36	9
Taco Bell	139	76	7	7	40	9
Hardee's	69	0	0	38	4	27
Sbarro	53	8	16	6	15	8
T.G.I Friday's	44	0	21	18	5	0

Source: *Restaurants and Institutions,* July 1, 1995, p. 146.

Competitive Analysis and Differentiation. A study of the competition needs to take into account initially all the competitors in the market but then focus more closely on direct competitors. The object of this analysis is to achieve a successful differentiation from its competitors. For instance, a white-tablecloth restaurant should be aware of quick-service restaurants and family restaurants in its market area since they offer indirect competition. It should, however, focus special attention on other upscale operations since these are the ones from which it must differentiate itself. Differentiation requires the operator to determine, "How will we be different—and better—than competitors X, Y, and Z?"

Suppose a steak restaurant, "Chez Nous," faces three competitors in its trading area which have good food at reasonable prices. One of these restaurants offers a very basic salad bar and has only mediocre service. The other two offer fuller salad bar selections and have acceptable, but not particularly friendly, service. To differentiate itself, Chez Nous might choose to offer a more elaborate salad bar coupled with a dessert bar. Chez Nous might also decide to bring in a service training company (unless it had the capability in house) to plan an upgrade in service and to develop a training program for servers to deliver really sparkling personal service. The resulting "package of benefits" would need to include good food as a minimum way of meeting the local standards and prices would need to be competitive, too. The *competitive difference,* however, would be greater choice in salads and desserts and the ability of the customers to make their own selection and portion decisions for dessert. In addition, Chez Nous would provide efficient and personally pleasant service.

Internal Analysis Chez Nous' ambitious program suggests it has a *corporate goal* of being the market leader in its area. It could not, however, carry out its ambitious service training plans unless it had the *corporate resources* required. Among these would be sufficient revenue (or cash reserves) to cover the cost of this service training program—and the vigorous committed of management to carry on the new service program once it was established.

Position Chez Nous is now ready to develop a positioning statement which gives concrete expression to its strategy:

> Chez Nous serves a market of middle-aged business and professional people and their families who live in the northwest quadrant of city X. We provide fine steaks and the fullest choice in surrounding courses and the most personalized and friendly service in our market area.

From this positioning statement, the marketing program—that is, specification of product, price, place, and promotion—can be spelled out. Each element of the marketing mix will be designed to suit the needs of Chez Nous' target market and to meet and, on some variables, exceed the competition.

There will be strategic, as well as tactical, elements in planning the deployment of the marketing program. Thus, it is useful to include in a list of functional strategies product strategy, pricing strategy, place strategy, and promotional strategy.

A Final Word on Implementation. The finest, most intelligent strategy in the world is just so much paper and verbiage unless the resources and determination exist to carry it out. Implementing a strategy depends on not just the owners or top management but the commitment the company's leadership are able to secure from the people who serve the guest, prepare the food—or make the beds, and see to the cleanliness and sanitation in the operation. Thus, the success of any strategy is dependent on its implementation by operations.

STRATEGY IN THE SMALL FIRM

The meaning and implementation of strategic planning in the small firm—typically a single unit or family-run property—is different from that for the large multiunit firm. Strategy is equally important, but the approach to it is generally and, quite rightly, less formal.

The mission statement is a key point on which many small firms flounder because they operate as they "always have," serving "their customers what they like." This works fine until something changes such as the population base (through aging or migration) or new competition appears. When changes begin, the unplanned business is left wondering what happened as profitability slips away. Responses to unexpected developments are likely to be unplanned. Consider, however, a mission statement that says:

> We provide our guests with a needed opportunity to relax, to feel important, to be waited on and to experience luxury. We serve hearty steaks and roast beef to the middle-class population in the area XYZ. We are the "favorite restaurant" of our clientele and are committed to maintaining and enhancing that position.

Assume that this mission statement reflects accurate observation of the operation, rather than just wishing. If business begins to slow, the mission statement provides a basis for study before action. Logical questions, based on the mission statement, are these:

1. Is business poor because our strategy is no longer working?
   a. Is the middle-class population we rely on dwindling?
   b. Has our product mix (steaks and roast beef) lost its appeal?
   c. Has new competition replaced us as the "favorite restaurant" in our market area?
   d. Has the way we are communicating with our clientele become ineffective?
   e. Is our market definition incorrect or too narrow?

or

2. Is business poor because of temporary, local, or broader economic trends?

These are questions of fact that can be researched without enormous expense in either funds or time. An action plan can then be directed at specific defined problems. The mission statement, then, is the premise for the business and the keystone for the rest of its planning.

We should note that many small businesses have an excellent sense of mission and strategy which is based on the owner's experience. The strategy may not be reduced to a formal written document, but it *is* carefully thought out and verbalized to employees and guests. One of the reasons for writing down statements of this kind, however, is that it facilitates communication. Moreover, a written statement can be examined—even criticized—when the time comes to question current practice.

Certainly, the building blocks for strategy are fundamentally the same for small firms as those discussed earlier in this chapter. The implications for strategy of market position (i.e., market leader, follower, etc.) are also useful ways to reason about strategic direction in a local market. On the other hand, unless the small firm is set on a pattern of rapid growth, the portfolio reasoning we explored earlier seems to have limited applicability, though an analogous reasoning process might be applied to revenue centers instead of SBUs.

SUMMARY

Strategy is concerned with goals and serves as the premise for subsequent plans and actions. Strategy must take, as its starting point, the strategic triangle of customer, corporation, and competition. Two different approaches to strategy are *opportunism,* which is based on current opportunities, and *foresight,* which takes a longer-term view. Strategy, which is long term, very general, and flexible, can be contrasted with tactics, which are short term, structured, and specific. Strategy is the work of top managers, while tactics are the work of midlevel and unit managers.

Strategy is premised on five major building blocks: the customer (segmentation), competitive structure, the firm's competitive position, market opportunities, and company resources. Strategic decisions are also affected by the subsidiary status of an SBU, the personal values of owners and senior executives, and the company's obligations to society. Decisions to allocate resources through growth, maintenance, or reduction of a business's scope, as well as deciding which SBUs to grow, which to "milk," and which to harvest or divest, are all strategic decisions. Generic strategies discussed were cost leadership, differentiation, and focus, as well as preemption and synergy. There are four growth strategies: market penetration, product development, market development, and diversification.

Functional strategies include positioning and long-term decisions related to the implementation of the elements of the marketing mix. Positioning should be based on three factors: (1) an analysis of customers, leading to target market selection; (2) an analysis of competitors, leading to development of a differentiation strategy and package of benefits selection; and (3) an internal analysis of corporate objectives and capabilities. While strategy may be applied differently in the small firm, the principles that undergird strategy formulation have general applicability.

◆ Key Words and Concepts

Strategy
Strategic triangle
Strategic opportunism
Strategic foresight
Tactics
Building blocks of strategy
- Customer
- Competitive structure
- Five forces model
- Relative competitive position
- Market opportunity
- Company resources
- Other factors
  - Subsidiary status
  - Personal values
  - Obligation to society

Strategic business units (SBUs)
Investment decisions
- Deployment of resources
- Portfolio management

Generic strategies
Market penetration
Product development
Market development
Diversification
Functional strategies
Positioning

◆ Discussion Questions

1. What are the elements of the strategic triangle? How do value and cost relate between a corporation and its competitors to determine success.?
2. Why is competition such an important reason for the development of business strategy?
3. Contrast strategic opportunism and strategic foresight. Which seems the most likely to succeed to you?
4. What are the roles of different levels of management in strategy formulation?
5. What are the building blocks for strategy formulation? How do you assess the importance of each?
6. Using the framework of that model, how do you size up the competitive climate of the hospitality industry?
7. The text offers several examples of applications of strategy. Choose three of them and apply them to business situations with which you are familiar.
8. What is the relationship of positioning to the marketing program? On what is positioning based?

Chapter 6

When you have finished reading this chapter, you should be able to

1. Explain the importance of marketing planning
2. Describe the analysis used for marketing planning
3. Discuss the contents of a typical marketing plan
4. Explain tensions between marketing and operations
5. Define internal marketing
6. List four common bases for organizing the headquarters marketing unit
7. Discuss common means of monitoring the marketing function

(Photo courtesy Susan Greenwood/Gamma Liaison)

Marketing Planning and Management

WHY PLAN?

Given the competitive conditions in the hospitality industry, we may better ask, first of all, "Why would anybody *not* plan?" The rational case for a need to plan is easy to make—but, then, in busy operations, a similar case can be made for a number of other activities. Sufficient staff to do all of the work that managers *should* do, however, may be hard to come by. Busy operators may find it easy to push off marketing planning to some time in the future: "When I have more time."

Even in some large companies in the hospitality industry, marketing planning may get only lip service or be seen as something the advertising manager does. This low priority for planning activities in some firms can result from the dominance of line-operations people which is common in hospitality organizations. Much of the discomfort with marketing planning that operations people experience relates to their own experience of more concrete work requirements.

Marketing planning is frustrating. That is so because it is done in the face of so much uncertainty. When a building is designed, we all expect it will come out looking pretty much like the architect said it would. In a similar vein, operations people know that if they put a cost-control program in place, once it is working right they can expect operating costs to come out within the cost percentage limits set. With a marketing plan, the only thing one can be absolutely certain of is that things will not go the way expected.

Large parts of the plan may come out as projected, but unforeseen—and uncontrollable—events often require changes: The economy may go soft;

unexpected competition may arise; bad weather may ruin a month's results. Moreover, the impact of marketing expenditures is difficult to assess. For instance, if sales improved, was it because of the promotion—or good weather or a rising economy or other outside factors? Furthermore, if the short-run effects of marketing are often hard to assess, the long-term impact of marketing activities is difficult, if not impossible, to measure with any precision. For those unaccustomed to marketing planning, the need to measure results in the face of these uncertainties can make marketing planning look like an impractical waste of time, a thing to be avoided or delegated to somebody else. *Operators* often prefer to follow their short-run instincts and their sense of the market.

The problem, of course, is that this leaves the firm in a reactive mode, putting its competitors, in a very real sense, in control of its marketing planning! Has hotel X begun a salesperson's club? Then we had better have one, too. Is hotel Y offering free cocktails? Maybe we should, too. Has restaurant Z raised its advertising budget dramatically? Well, how much should we be spending?

The short-run orientation puts the operation in the position of not knowing—really—where it is going. Yet the need for marketing expenditures, even if only reactive ones, does not go away. As a result, increasing sums are spent just to meet the competition, and the opportunity to plan for long-run impact is largely abdicated. Furthermore, market opportunities that could have been anticipated rush by in the hurly-burly of everyday concerns. In fact, the future is always uncertain and that is especially true in the fragmented hospitality industry. Having a plan in place gives operators a solid point of departure from which to *alter* plans when conditions change unexpectedly.

Although the long-run effects of a marketing program are difficult to measure with precision, a moment's reflection on the power of advertised trademarks in hospitality will offer incontrovertible proof that there *is* such a thing as long-run effects. Ronald McDonald is said to be second only to Santa Claus in name recognition among children. The face of Colonel Sanders looks out on Tiananmen Square in Beijing, as well as on Times Square in New York City. The names Hilton and Holiday Inns conjure universal images for travelers. Without coherent marketing strategies, these outcomes would not have happened.

The case for marketing planning, then, rests squarely on the importance of the marketing activities, the increasing level of competition, growing marketing budgets, the need to achieve a competitive advantage—and the need to know where we are going so we can tell if we get there.

MARKETING PLANNING

In this section, we will discuss the contents of a **marketing plan** in a general way. In the next section, we will look at a specific property level marketing plan and extracts from that document. The order in which a marketing plan is presented varies from company to company, but a logical point of departure in preparing a marketing plan is the business **mission statement.** The mission statement establishes what business the company is in, what its products are, and in what markets

The success of American hospitality firms worldwide is testimony to the impact of marketing and marketing planning. (Photo courtesy Marcia Weinstein)

it chooses to compete. Reference to the mission statement ties the marketing plan to the overall strategy of the firm. We will discuss the analyses that underlie marketing planning and then look at excerpts from a property level marketing plan to develop a more concrete feel for its contents.

SWOT Analysis

The acronym SWOT stands for strengths, weaknesses, opportunities, and threats. Another way to sum these up is internal and external analyses. The acronym SWOT is a useful aid to memory—but it has things backwards. The customer, who *always* comes first, is normally considered under opportunities (and sometimes threats), and this text is committed to the motto, "Begin with the Customer." Accordingly, we will consider external factors first (opportunities and threats), and then internal factors (strengths and weaknesses).

External Analyses. A discussion of the general environment within which a firm is operating helps set the stage for the marketing plan. This covers topics such as economic, social, and technological trends, as well as the governmental and regulatory climate. This is likely to be a smaller section in an individual property's marketing plan, where attention will be concentrated on the immediate surrounding area (city, metropolitan area, or even just a portion of one of these).

A *market analysis* is concerned with the size and growth trends in a market. An individual hotel, for instance, would specify the total market size in units available, rooms rented, and dollar room sales, for the last year as a part of its plan. In addition, the plan would establish what kind of growth trend there has been in the market.

Customer Analysis **Customer Analysis** is the vital foundation on which any business is built. Significant customer segments should be identified. Where customers come from, what kind of organization they work for, demographic and lifestyle information are all appropriate. In addition, the uses customers have for the product we sell often determine what the customers' needs are. For instance, for a restaurant, who are its customers: family entertainment, businesspeople on a lunch break, travelers passing through, and so forth. If price is important, as it is to most hospitality customers, the kind of price expectations customers have should be clear.

Competitor Analysis **Competitor analysis** will list the competition, identify direct and indirect competitors, and evaluate direct competitors in some depth, focusing on *their* strengths and weaknesses, where they have competitive advantages, and where we have the advantage. In an individual property, considerable specific information on competitive operations is available from suppliers, employees, visits to competing properties, and identification of who competitors' customers are by, for instance, examining their function board. This section should discuss new unit construction by competitors or give progress reports on construction in progress, including additions or remodeling, by competitors.

Opportunities and Threats The discussion of environment, market, customer, and competitor is intended to identify the possibilities for growth and the dangers that lie ahead during the planning period. A sample summary of opportunities and threats at the property level is shown in Figure 6.1.

Internal Analyses. The **strengths and weaknesses** of the organization need to be examined in a candid fashion. For instance, the quality of product (rooms, food, beverages, etc.), service, and facilities should be reviewed. Internal analysis should include a review of performance data and trends. In chain organizations, this may include portfolio analysis (see Chapter 5) of the principal SBUs.

Strengths and Weaknesses. It is always appropriate to recognize strengths and to develop ways to capitalize on them, but there are particular advantages, especially in the individual unit, to recognizing weaknesses in a unit level marketing plan. The plan is a document that will be seen at senior levels in an organization and the annual marketing plan is a good place to communicate the needs of the unit to headquarters in a constructive way.

Goals, Strategies, and Tactics

The goals of the organization and strategies to meet them are supported by the foregoing analyses and by reference to the mission statement. Since a marketing plan generally covers one year, considerable emphasis in the plan should be given

Opportunities		Hurdles/Risks	
1. Market growth	X	1. Erosion of market share	X
2. Location strengthening	X	2. Reduction of ROI	X
3. Room renovation/upgrade	X	3. Market obsolesence	___
4. Leisure area renovation/upgrade	X	4. Location obsolesence	___
5. Rest/bar renovation/upgrade	X	5. Product obsolesence	___
6. Meeting/banquet renovation/upgrade	X	6. Political environment	___
7. Major renovation	X	7. Economic climate	___
8. Repositioning	___	8. License renewal	X
9. Price/value strategy	___	9. Labor climate	___
10. Advertising/sales strategy	X	10. Excess supply	X
11. Recruitment/training	X	11. Lease constraints	___
12. New promotions	___	12. Lease expiry/renewal	___
13. New development opportunity	___	13. ________________	___
14. ________________	___	14. ________________	___
15. ________________	___	15. ________________	___
16. ________________	___	16. ________________	___
17. ________________	___	17. ________________	___
18. ________________	___	18. ________________	___
19. ________________	___	19. ________________	___
20. ________________	___	20. ________________	___

Figure 6.1 Summary of Opportunities and Risks for a Hotel Chain

to tactics, that is, what to do in the coming year. While the examples we are working with in this chapter are principally from the unit level, Field Practice Note 6.1 gives an alternative view of planning with a statement of a broad-gauged plan from a large company.

MARKETING PLAN CONTENTS

While the order of presentation may vary, a marketing plan will generally contain the elements identified in Figure 6.2. This figure is the table of contents for the annual marketing plan we will be examining in this section.

It is interesting to compare Figure 6.2 with Figure 6.3, which is the table of contents for a marketing plan for a national restaurant chain. While the latter is more detailed, the general topics covered are virtually the same.

In the following sections, we will examine extracts from an actual hotel's marketing plan. The hotel, the Travel Inn, was affiliated with a national franchise chain. The property had become somewhat rundown over the years, and the general manager, John Swinton, was concerned that it was losing its competitiveness.

Executive Summary
Mission Statement
External Analysis
  Summary of current market situation
  Analysis of present customer base
  Assessment of the competition and comparison of property's market share performance with that of other properties
Internal Analysis
  Strengths and weaknesses
  Assessment of facilities
Goals and Targets
Sales Forecast
Strategy

Figure 6.2 Contents of a Property Level Analysis

Executive Summary

The executive summary is an overview of the entire document and should not be confused with the introduction. It summarizes the analysis, presents *key* facts, and summarizes the plan's recommendations.

> This property has slipped from third position to fifth within its marketplace. To maintain volume, a rate repositioning was undertaken. In spite of this, our net operating profit dropped from $380,000 two years ago to $190,000 in the past year. We anticipate a profit of $70,000 during the coming year.
>
> Without major changes to our physical plant, our performance is unlikely to improve and could worsen to the point where the property loses money.
>
> Accordingly, we propose, for future years, major capital improvements to the plant.

Current Market Situation

The property's present and recent past performance is reviewed with a comment on any trends. The following discussion summarizes a detailed statistical summary, which is not reproduced here.

> Historical trends show falling occupancy and the impact of a recent rate reduction on revenue—after several years of rising rates. Total room revenues have declined for two years. Although food and beverage sales rose last year, combined food and beverage revenues are off this year because of a 5.3 percent

Field Practice Note 6.1

Goals—and Plans to Reach Them: Extracts from "Achieving Global Dominance"

McDonald's is not satisfied with today's global leadership position. We want to increase the existing gaps between us and our competitors in every market around the world. We define our competition broadly—quickservice eating establishments, takeouts, pizza parlors, coffee shops, street vendors, convenience food store, delis, supermarket freezers and microwave ovens. The strategies to increase our competitive lead are *Execution, Convenience, and Value.*

EXECUTION

Operational Excellence
A combination of strict standards, proven operating procedures, and thousands of dedicated employees, franchisees and suppliers throughout the world provide McDonald's with distinct advantages in cultivating a customer base which is satisfied and loyal. Our excellence strategy leverages these operational strengths.

Nothing Less Than 100%
McDonald's will settle for nothing less than 100% customer satisfaction. We are committed to providing a 100% McDonald's experience on every visit, for every customer, in every market. Our Execution Strategy identifies seven initiatives that will provide a 100% experience: Hot and tasty food, fast service, food safety, accurate orders, friendliness, employee satisfaction and merchandising.

CONVENIENCE

Optimized Market Penetration
McDonald's wants to have a presence wherever people live, work, shop, play or gather. Our Convenience Strategy is to monitor the changing lifestyles of consumers and intercept them at every turn. As we expand customer convenience, we gain market share.

Targeting the World
On any day, McDonald's serves less than one-half of one percent of the world's population. This means that more than 99.5% of this population, or over 5 billion people, represent our target market.

VALUE

Lower Costs, Higher Sales and Profits
The Value Strategy utilizes McDonald's economies of scale to minimize costs per transaction, maximize value, and grow sales and profits. We strive to operate low cost restaurants and to gain a margin advantage over competitors. This allows us to deliver value to our customers.

Beyond Value Pricing
Lower costs allow us to provide value to customers, maximizing transactions, sales and profitability. For us, value is more than low prices and special offers. It is taste, service and all other experiences that make customers think of McDonald's as a better value than our competitors.

Source: *McDonald's Corporation 1994 Annual Report,* pp. 7–11.

> decline in beverage sales that is, in large part, attributable to lower occupancy. The monthly statistical summary shows that occupancy has fallen compared to the previous year in each of the last nine months and is projected to fall for the rest of the year. Room revenue also began to fall when the lower rates went into effect. Beverage results have also been unfavorable for the past five months.

This section of the report might also include comparative occupancy and rate information and data on additional room construction in the market (as well as any withdrawals of rooms from operations).

This section also includes an assessment of the local economic outlook. This assessment lists major employers and comments on any prospective new plant openings, major construction projects, or other significant factors in the local market that will increase or decrease employment and travel in the area. Any developments affecting area transportation, such as airport additions or highway improvements, should also be cited.

It is appropriate to present a brief history of the area here and describe the culture and traditions of the surrounding area, as well as the community's political climate. Population statistics and changing demographics should also be summarized. This section may also include a discussion of tourism, including major tourism attractions, their attendance records, and any pertinent trend data or new developments. This information is needed by senior managers outside the property who review the plan. It is also a helpful review and summary of significant factors for the local management team.

Customer Base

This section of the report presents guest profiles for major operating departments. The Travel Inn's customers are discussed below.

> Rooms — Of the corporate business we receive, a large percentage comes from companies that receive our special local corporate rate. There has been a definite improvement in our sports-rate business over the past six months. We can foresee it becoming even stronger, because many of our guests are families. The directory-rate business, predominantly pleasure travelers, continues to make up a relatively small part of our business.
>
> Function/Meetings — We continue to receive considerable repeat business made up of small meetings from local companies.
>
> Arbitration Services provides plenty of regular meetings but little food business.
>
> Several monthly association dinner/meetings and weekly Rotary luncheon/meetings are held, in addition to weddings and Christmas parties.
>
> Owing to inadequate meeting and recreational facilities, the hotel receives a minimum of conventions.

Food & Beverage	Throughout the week the average luncheon customers in Maggies are local businessmen and those who are using our meeting rooms. Dinner customers are primarily in-house guests, usually businesspeople. Weekend business is predominantly local families with young children who take advantage of the "all-you-can-eat" specialty nights—very value-conscious people. The average lounge customer is between the ages of 20 and 30 years, single, and semiskilled. Owing to the Dinner Club, many of our regular customers are value-conscious business executives.

Competitor Analysis

All direct and indirect rooms competition and direct food and beverage competition should be listed. Direct competitors should be described in considerable detail, including their facilities and service level. The following is an example of material presented on one of the Travel Inn's direct competitors.

Hotel name	Hotel Goodhost
Address	750 Main Street
Phone	(519) 824-9999
General manager	Mr. Jim Walpole
Director of sales	Mr. Ralph Fornicola
Sales staff	Ms. Celia Montreau
Number of rooms	165
Location	Route 226, off Exit 2 onto 6
Public facilities	2 dining rooms, with full beverage service
	Lounge
	Cafeteria
Recreational facilities	Heated outdoor pool

1. GENERAL

   10 meeting rooms—maximum 500 theater-style

2. ADVANTAGES AND STRENGTHS

   Equipped to serve paraplegics

   City center

Additional information likely to be contained in this section includes a rate structure summary to indicate any special rate plans. Where possible, market research studies yielding ***competitive data*** should also be included or summarized here. The section on food and beverage competition should contain not only an operational description but also a comparison of menu price levels of the major competitors.

This section is also a good place to analyze market share. In Table 6.1, the property's fair market share (the percentage of market sales gained by the property compared to its percentage of market capacity) is presented and analyzed. This material was summarized in the marketing plan as follows:

> We earned slightly more than our fair share of market sales. (See last two columns of Table 6.1). Properties B and C however, did somewhat better on this score than we did.

It is also useful to compare room sales by market segment with those of the competition. Table 6.2 makes this comparison. The report summarized the results found there as follows:

> Our corporate individual business is our strongest segment. We outperform all of our competitors there on total rooms sold although competitor C has a slightly higher proportion of its business from that source.
>
> While we outperform the local industry average on corporate groups, competitor A sells more rooms in that market and competitor B has a higher proportion of its sales from this source than we do.
>
> We are the local leader in the convention segment but that is a relatively small part of our business.
>
> Our tourist business is a weak spot and we trail the market. Our Sports Tour segment is a small but strong segment for us with only competitor B outperforming us by 30 room nights over the year.

Table 6.1 Marketing Plan: Percentage of Market Share Compared to Percentage of Capacity

Property	Number of Rooms	Room Nights Available	Occupancy, %	Room Nights Sold	Total Room Nights Sold, %	Property's Capacity, %
Travel Inn	220	80,300	71.1	57,158	26.7	26.5
Property A	250	91,250	66.4	60,555	28.3	30.1
Property B	200	73,000	72.7	53,114	24.8	24.1
Property C	160	58,400	74.0	43,228	20.2	19.3
TOTAL	830	302,950	70.6	214,055	100.0	100.0

Note: Market share is computed by comparing the room nights sold by a property with the total room nights sold in competitive properties. Share earned may then be compared with the property's percentage of capacity (i.e., number of rooms available as a percentage of total rooms available).

Table 6.2 Marketing Plan: Rooms Occupied by Major Market Segment (Annual)

	Travel Inn		Competitor A		Competitor B		Competitor C		Total	
Market Segment	Rooms	%	Rooms	%	Rooms	%	Rooms	%	Rooms	%
Corporate—individual	26,181	47.8	28,294	46.7	23,857	44.9	20,931	48.4	99,263	46.4
Corporate—group	13,682	23.9	14,122	23.3	12,914	24.3	8,858	20.5	49,576	23.2
Conventions	9,114	15.9	8,014	13.2	7,022	13.2	2,910	6.7	27,060	12.6
Individual pleasure travelers (tourists)	7,009	12.2	9,110	15.0	8,119	15.3	10,118	23.4	34,356	16.0
Tour groups	1,172	2.0	1,015	1.7	1,202	2.3	411	1.0	3,800	1.8
TOTAL	57,158		60,555		53,114		43,228		214,055	

Strengths and Weaknesses

The report presented the following analysis of strengths and weaknesses.

Strengths

Major hotel affiliation (reservation system and all support service).

Location on Highway 8 close to Highway 401.

Next door to region's largest shopping complex.

Good local reputation, especially for Maggies entertainment lounge.

Good base of employees in terms of friendliness, attitude, and dedication.

Excellent landscape facilities.
Free parking.

Good affiliation with Rotary Club.

Good local reputation of value-for-money concept in food department.

Weaknesses

Aging property.

Lack of recreational facilities, especially in winter months.

Living rooms of suites are too small.

Entertainment lounge interferes with dining room.

Entertainment lounge might deter hotel and dining room guests.

Insufficient parking in front of hotel on weekend nights.

Inadequate outdoor lighting.

Exterior appearance of hotel is not inviting.

Lack of professionalism in some departments.

Some department heads have held positions for too long.

- Executive Summary
- Introduction
- Market Assessment
  - Restaurant Market Overview
  - Consumer Attitudes
  - Competitive Environment
  - Business Performance
  - Mission Statement
- Marketing Objectives and Strategies for the Year Ahead
- Positioning Statement
- Action Plan
  - Advertising
    - Role of Advertising
    - Advertising Objectives
    - Advertising Strategy
    - Creative
      - Creative Objectives
      - Creative Strategy
      - Rationale
    - Media
      - Media Objectives
      - Media Strategy
      - National Tactics—Timing
  - Promotions
    - Role of Promotions
    - Promotion Objectives
    - Promotion Strategies
  - National Marketing Calendar
  - Local Store Marketing Objectives
  - Public Relations Objectives
  - Pricing
  - Product Development Priorities
  - Unit Expansion Program
  - New Territories Program
  - Research
    - National Consumer Research Commission
    - Syndicated Research Participation
    - Image Research
    - Consumer Perception
    - Facilities
    - New Product Intelligence
    - Media Trends
    - Competition: Media Spending and Creative Execution
    - Storyboard Testing
- Franchise Marketing Support System
  - Structure
  - Key Marketing Responsibilities
    - The Franchisor
    - Planning
    - Advertising
      - Creative
      - Media Plans and Buys
      - Research
      - Promotion
  - Franchise Support
      - Regional Co-ops
      - Local Franchisees
- Budget

Figure 6.3 Contents of a Marketing Plan for a National Restaurant Chain

Physical Plant

The case for upgrading the Travel Inn is strongly implied in the negative review of physical facilities.

Public Areas Building Exterior (signage, landscaping, parking, etc.)

A low, common, nondescript, L-shaped building consisting of two stories. The poolside area is beautifully landscaped, very attractive, plenty of flowers. However, the back and east side of the building are rather unattractive, boring. (The back of the hotel is also facing an unattractive vacant field and the back of a roadside hotel.) The front of the building is mainly a large parking area. The small sign on the building can be seen from Highway 8. The main sign faces Fairway Road; it can also be seen from Highway 8 and it is dated.

The two entrance signs from King Street and Fairway Road are very small and hard to see.

Hotel Entrances (main, F&B, meeting, etc.)

Canopy is dated; lobby is small and shows signs of wear; inadequate signage in lobby, no coat check area for banquet hall; no outside entrance to Maggies; entrance to banquet hall unattractive.

Main Lobby/Foyer Areas (including front desk related)

As mentioned previously, lobby is small and shows signs of wear. The dining room and lounge entrance as well as the entrance to the banquet hall are directly off the main lobby and at night when functions are taking place it is usually very congested in this area. The noise level from the entertainment lounge and from the banquet hall when functions are taking place makes it very difficult at times to carry on proper conversation at the front desk with hotel guests. Front-desk area is in need of upgrading. The reception and cashiers area needs to be revinyled. The key rack has to be replaced.

Service

The plan summarizes the hotel's service as follows:

> We have a loyal base of long-time employees who have good rapport with our guests and particularly with regular guests. On the other hand, their professional manner often leaves a great deal to be desired. While this is a matter the executive staff constantly strives to improve, we have a very small complement of managers. None of us is adequately trained as trainers and our other duties leave us little time for a concerted training program.

Goals and Targets

Goals and targets offer an opportunity to unit management to communicate their aspirations for their unit to senior management. One of the goals for this unit, remodeling the property, requires strong corporate support. The second goal, improving training capabilities to upgrade service professionalism, can be undertaken with resources available to the manager with the approval of the district director. It is interesting to note that both of these marketing plan goals involve the product element of the marketing mix and require action by *operations people,* rather than marketing staff.

Forecasts

To look ahead, it is not enough just to say what should be achieved and what marketing activities will be undertaken. Managers must analyze the impact these activities *should* have and, based on that analysis, prepare a forecast of sales, costs, and profits. At the property level, this should be done on a market-segment-by-market-segment basis.

In a national organization, either of two approaches to forecasting are possible: top down and bottom up. A top-down forecast is prepared by the central office, generally using computerized modeling. This is probably the most efficient approach in terms of time utilization, but involvement at lower organizational units comes only after the fact. A bottom-up approach begins with unit forecasts which are built into district forecasts which are ultimately incorporated into a company plan. This approach ensures "ownership" of the financial goals at all levels of the organization which generally secures more support for the plan from the people involved. Each organizational level has accepted responsibility for its own forecast.

Duration and Frequency of Forecasts. The longer the period a forecast covers, the more general its conclusions must be. In an industry changing as rapidly as hospitality is, it is difficult to forecast more than a year ahead. Longer-range studies are, however, sometimes undertaken by the top management of a firm as a part of the firm's strategic planning.

As suggested previously, the marketing plan is generally prepared for a period of one year. Within the plan, there will likely be quarterly or monthly action plans. Normally, a marketing plan is revised on a quarterly basis—or more frequently if market conditions dictate. A marketing plan, then, is a living document which is regularly reexamined and updated.

Tactics

While John Swinton hopes his property will be remodeled soon, his marketing plan would be incomplete without a program for the short-term future. The following summary is followed by a detailed discussion (not reproduced here) of the major points:

Plan of Action: Summary for the Year Ahead

The year will be fiercely competitive in regard to market share and rate. Major strategies in this marketplace can be summarized:

1. Corporate
   a. Additional bonus-point program based on three return visits
   b. Beefed-up Executive's Club program
   c. President's letter
2. Groups—continuing solicitation by sales
3. Competitive rate structure coupled with the City Action Package
   a. Complementary weekend for every five reservations
   b. Increase profile through "Travel Agent of the Month" program

4. Regional market
   a. Two-year stopover contracts
   b. Competitive and effective rate program
5. Contract buys
   a. Cruise lines
   b. Airline crew
6. Triple S program (succinctly executed sales solicitation in all markets)
7. Advertising program
   a. Regional market
   b. Travel agents
   c. Summer program
   d. Consistent awareness campaign—all markets

Month-by-month plans for each operated department complete the Travel Inn's marketing plan. Samples from the Rooms and the Food and Beverage Departments are shown in Figures 6.4 and 6.5.

A final section (not reproduced here) is a budget for all activities to be carried out at the property level. This would include areas such as any special local marketing efforts.

ORGANIZING AND MANAGING THE MARKETING FUNCTION

In Chapter 1, the point was made that everyone was involved in marketing in a hospitality firm because operations has the responsibility for servicing the sale and most of the responsibility for gaining repeat customers. Here, we will look at the impact this arrangement has on the organization of marketing in hospitality companies. In the next chapter, we will explore this issue further and find reasons to call operations people "part-time marketers."

Marketing responsibilities in hospitality are distributed throughout the organization. In this section, we review the division of the marketing function's responsibilities between marketing and operations staffs, some of the possible conflicts between marketing and operations, and how these can be resolved. The basis for organizing the headquarters level marketing unit and the means for evaluating and controlling marketing activities in multiunit organizations are also reviewed.

Hospitality, like other service industries, initially took its model for organization largely from the manufacturing and packaged-goods industries that were predominant in the economy before the service industries came to their present prominence. In most manufactured-goods companies, the marketing department is able to control virtually all of the marketing function. The nature of the service transaction, however, makes this specialization impractical in hospitality.[1] Accordingly, there are special problems in managing hospitality marketing that call

MONTHLY SALES ACTIVITY PLAN
ROOMS

MONTH OF May

MONTH OBJECTIVES	BENEFITTING AREA	TARGETS
1. Maintain strong directory-rate business	rooms, food, and beverage	2,985 rooms nights 1st quarter
2. Attract summer sports-rate business	rooms, food, and beverage	210 room nights June–Aug.
3. Maintain local corp. business	rooms	425 room nights May–July

ACTIVITY	BY WHOM*	COMMENTS	MATERIALS REQUIRED	BUDGET	ACTUAL
1A. Design print & mail theater package (room, dinner, theater) to AAA clubs in N.Y. & Michigan tourists info. centers			brochures	360	
B. Design and print rack-rate brochure			brochures	150	
2. Design and print sports-rate brochure and distribute to baseball, soccer, and track & field coaches			rack brochures	350	
			mileage	50	
3A. 40 sales calls for month, follow-up and service for all calls on companies receiving LCR			mileage	60	
B. Establish "Most Valuable Patron" program					
C. Establish "Wednesday Night Cocktail Hour" with manager			invitations	100	
			TOTAL	$	$

*BY WHOM: Objectives should reflect where region or corporate support is required.

Figure 6.4 Monthly Rooms Action Plan

for a different organizational arrangement than that found in manufactured goods. Patterns of organization that respond to these problems are becoming more common in hospitality businesses.

In hospitality, the employee—his or her attitude and behavior—is a part of the experience the customer purchases. Certainly, the physical product—food, guest room, and the like—is important, but an unpleasant interaction with an employee can ruin the guest's experience. Marketing is responsible for promotional activity which can help to secure trial from new customers and remind old customers to return. The real job of gaining repeat sales, however, is in the hands of the operations staff and managers. In fact, advertising an operation that is poorly run will, in all likelihood, actually decrease sales as more and more customers are driven from the door by poor experiences. People are twice as likely to talk about a bad experience and, on average, talk to about 10 other persons. As these disillusioned

MONTHLY SALES ACTIVITY PLAN
FOOD & BEVERAGE

MONTH OF May

MONTH OBJECTIVES	BENEFITTING AREA	TARGETS
Implement "Kids Eat Free" promotion	Breakfast	To achieve dining room budget
Implement sponsor training program (breakfast, lunch)	Lunch Dinner	To achieve 600 card sales for year (Dinner Club)
To continue selling Dinner Club cards	Lunch	
Implement Mother's Day promotion		300 covers

ACTIVITY	BY WHOM*	COMMENTS	MATERIALS REQUIRED	BUDGET	ACTUAL
Ensure flyers/posters in place			flyers lobby signage posters	400	
Establish system to monitor number of persons taking advantage of this promotion					
Select sponsor trainer, update task list, and implement training program	Reg. Train.			600	
Continue mail/telephone solicitations for Dinner Club card sales; sell cards in dining room			tent cards, applications follow-up letters	500	
			TOTAL	$	$

*BY WHOM: Objectives should reflect where region or corporate support is required.

Figure 6.5 Monthly Food and Beverage Action Plan

customers spread the word, the danger is that bad word of mouth will have a serious negative impact on business.[2]

Clearly, then, operations is the key to an important part of success in marketing because all customer service activity is under the control of operations personnel.

This division of the marketing function into components carried out by a marketing department and others under the control of operations[3] leads us to an important general conclusion. Concern for marketing has to begin with the firm's top management and senior operating executives as well as its marketing executives. Otherwise, the marketing department's promotional activities will lack the operating support they need to be effective.

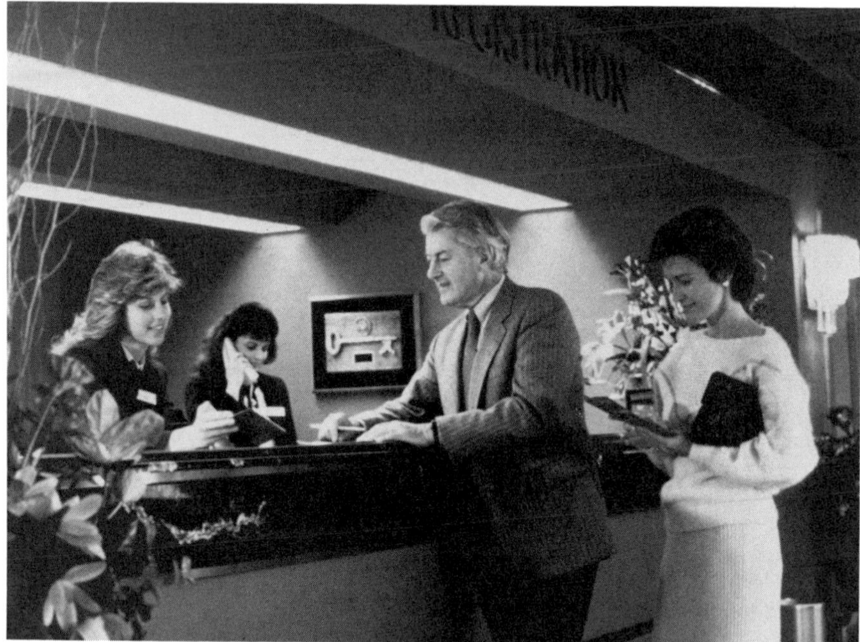

The success of the interaction between guest and staff at the time of purchase and then, later, during service is an important key to gaining repeat patronage. (Photo courtesy Marriott Corporation)

The Marketing Department in Multiunit Companies

Marketing as an organizational unit in hospitality has received increasing recognition and status in recent years. Most chain organizations have a marketing executive at the vice-presidential level. As we just noted, however, the organizational unit with formal responsibility for marketing does not have direct responsibility for the buyer/seller interaction. Marketing usually has responsibility for advertising, public relations, and the design of promotional programs and the supporting media, as well as for market research.

The increasing use of market research, as promotional expenditures rise, extends marketing executives' interests into domains that have traditionally been those of operations. Research asks questions about customer satisfaction. These questions involve matters such as products offered, services received, prices charged, issues regarding quality, and location convenience. Moreover, research serves as one important basis for strategic planning and product development, whether these report to operations, to marketing, or directly to the head of the company. We have a situation, then, where operations has responsibility for service activities that are a part of the marketing function, though not of the marketing department. Marketing has involvement in assessing functions that have historically been the province of operations. The potential for "turf" disputes is obvious.

Conflicts Between Marketing and Operations Departments

Because of the necessary crossing of organizational lines entailed by marketing's broadening domain, there are several points at which a potential for organizational conflict is built into the hospitality firm. First, there is friction between the operations and marketing *points of view.* Service is a continuous process of human interaction between server and guest. Controlling that process requires aggressive operations management. "Because of the ways in which they are evaluated, operations managers tend to be concerned with improving efficiency and keeping down costs, whereas marketers look for opportunities to increase sales."[4] There is a conflict, then, between operations' goals of cost control and marketing's interest in maximizing revenue through new marketing products and services.

Operations also has a *vested interest in the status quo.* Operations managers deal with a thousand problems—more or less—every day. They come from unexpected events arising from employee and guest behavior, as well as such factors as equipment malfunction, poor weather, competitive action, and the like. As long as

The need to control a complex process and maintain an efficient operation gives managers a strong interest in a stable framework while marketers are more likely to press for change. (Photo courtesy of ARAMARK)

operations managers can cope with the myriad problems from the point of view of a stable *framework,* they are inclined to feel comfortable—experience will serve them. When services are changed, however, or new products introduced that require adjustments in the operating system, the stability of the order they have imposed on events is threatened. Resistance to change in operating procedures, the most common experience in any organizational setting, is especially a problem in hospitality operations.

Lovelock points also to a difference in *time horizons.* Marketing executives may be aware of competitive activity and motivated by it to feel a sense of urgency to respond to the competition. They may also be more conscious of the promise made in the company's advertising and promotion and concerned with prompt adjustments in operating priorities to match competitive activities.

Operations executives, on the other hand, are more aware of the thousand little problems of which an operation is made up. With greater experience of the difficulty of implementing change in an operating setting and of achieving quality in the revised operation, operations people are likely to seek more lead time for detailed planning at the unit level, staff training, and system testing.

These three areas of tension—concern with cost versus market, resistance to operating change versus an inclination toward innovation, and differing time horizons—thus become more important as the place and the need for marketing grow in significance in hospitality. Figure 6.6 illustrates a graphic view of these contrasting points of view.

Resolving Conflict

The present distinction between marketing as a central-office function and operations as something that happens at the unit level needs to be broken down, and this is already happening. Some large firms are moving marketing staff and significant marketing decision-making power to the regional level, in order to establish

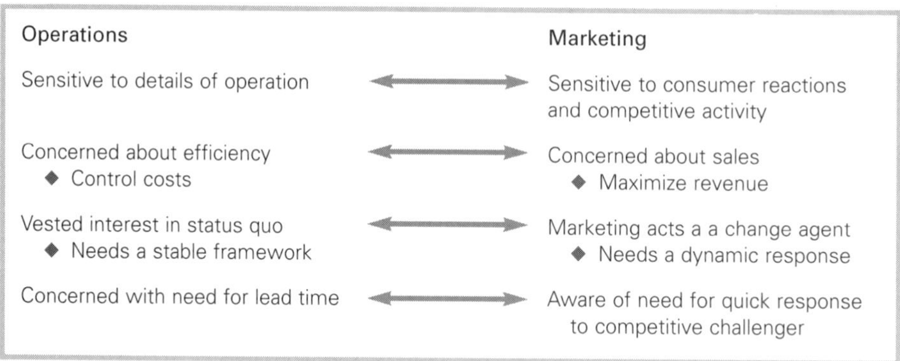

Figure 6.6 Two Contrasting Views of the World: Operations and Marketing

Internal communication programs of all kinds are an important part of efforts to motivate operations employees. (Photo courtesy Marriott Food and Services Management)

a clearer linkage between operations and marketing. In franchise organizations, the local advertising co-op is likely to be responsive to unit operating realities.

The danger, however, is that moving marketing down the organizational line will result in too great a subordination of marketing to the status quo point of view of operations executives. Another step required, therefore, is that operations executives obtain the training necessary to gain a broader view of the organization's functioning, including marketing. This requires training not *just* in marketing as a separate subject but in marketing as a part of an interdisciplinary approach to management.[5]

Similarly, marketing people need to be trained so that they are aware of the operating realities. This means, at a minimum, a significant cross-training effort for marketing people that involves working assignments for a significant period of time in operations or, better still, the promotion of operations people with specialized training in marketing into marketing positions.

Closer involvement of operations and marketing in joint committees and task forces, as well as increased informal working contact between operations and marketing, will undoubtedly help each side in the marketing-operations equation see and understand the problems of the other. Until, however, marketing understands operations and operations sees marketing as part of its necessary competence, the conflict between the two points of view will continue to present costly problems.

Internal Marketing

Internal marketing involves identifying the company's internal customers, its employees, and realizing there is a need to take a marketing approach to securing their support in fulfilling the company's mission. This involves seeing the company's jobs as products which bear a price in time, effort, and inconvenience for the employee–customer. To secure their support, management must package jobs and their rewards in a way which fits the needs of its customers. Berry defines internal marketing in this way:

> Internal marketing means applying the philosophy and practice of marketing to people that serve the external customer so that (1) the best possible people can be employed and (2) they will do the best possible work. More specifically, internal marketing is viewing employees as internal customers, viewing jobs as internal products, and endeavouring to design these products to better meet the needs of these customers.[6]

The topic of internal marketing will be discussed in more detail in the next chapter.

ORGANIZING THE HEADQUARTERS MARKETING UNIT

The bases for departmentalization of the headquarters marketing unit vary according to the needs of companies. The four most common are functional, geographic, market, and product.

Functional

The marketing unit may be organized around basic marketing *activities* such as advertising, market research, and sales, as illustrated in Figure 6.7. This is a common organization in smaller companies.

Geographic

With the increasing emphasis on local marketing as competitive conditions change from market to market, organizations are establishing regional marketing departments. These commonly report to the director of operations for the region in

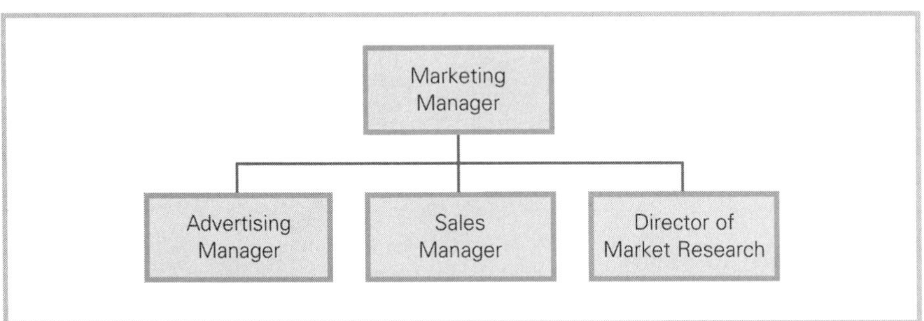

Figure 6.7 Marketing Department: Geographic Organization

question, with the senior marketing officer and her or his staff exercising staff supervision, that is, reviewing activities and results and advising regional people, as illustrated in Figure 6.8. The central office also provides the general marketing plan within which local marketing plans are prepared. Local plans are subject to review by top-level marketing officials.

Market or Customer Group

Particularly at the hotel property level, some marketing activities are organized by customer group with one salesperson handling (perhaps) the convention and tour market, another handling corporate accounts. This organizational format is illustrated in Figure 6.9. Contract food service companies, too, are often organized by customer group: business and industry, colleges and universities, schools, and health care facilities being the largest customer groups.

Product

Product managers have not been common in hospitality, probably because it is difficult to see how two different items on the same menu can be marketed separately. Dunkin' Donuts, however, had success with the appointment of product managers, even where the product in question did not have a separate advertising

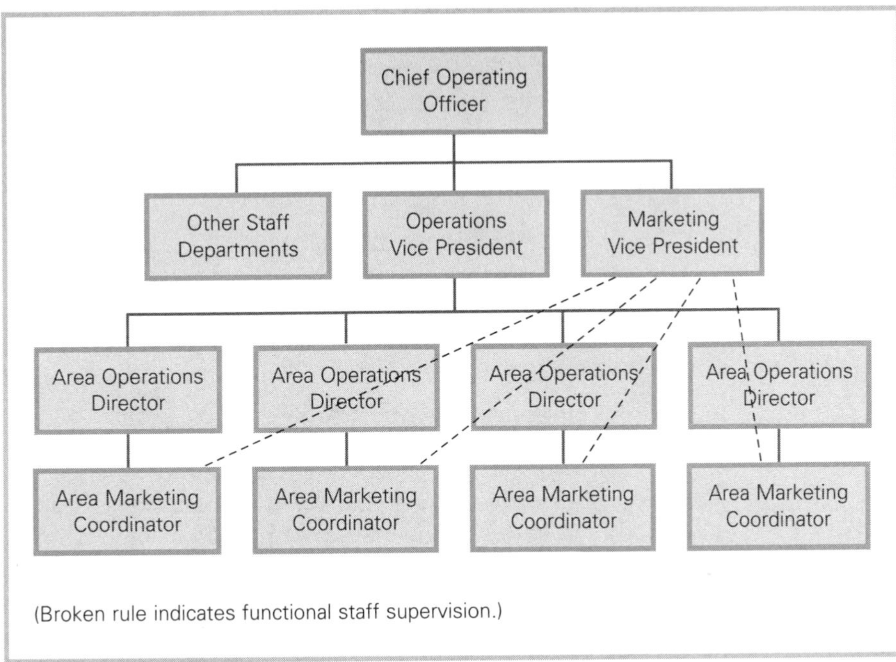

Figure 6.8 Marketing Department: Functional Organization

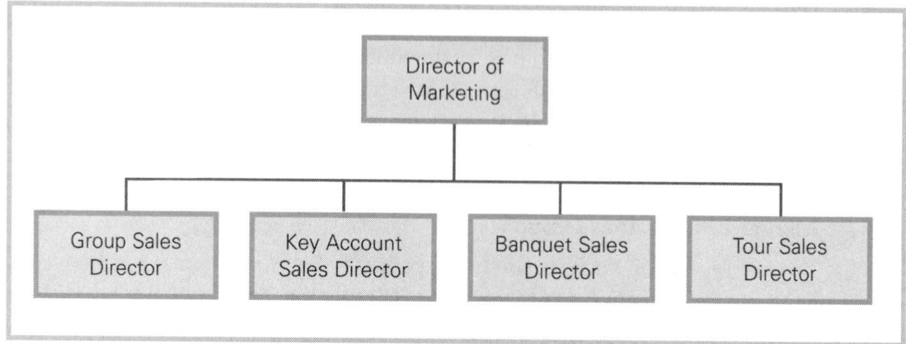

Figure 6.9 Marketing Organization: Specific Markets

budget. This was the case, for instance, with coffee. The product manager for coffee, facing a declining customer base as a result of growing health concerns, determined that the heavy coffee drinker could be encouraged to spend more if a larger "economy size" cup was offered to take-out customers. The Big One (as the new product was called) helped improve overall profits by approximately 12 percent, with no investment and no incremental labor.[7] This innovation, as coffee drinkers well know, has since been widely copied.

Often, a combination of organizational categories is used. Some restaurant companies have their headquarters marketing group organized functionally, but they also use regional marketing managers. Contract food service companies often have geographically designated sales territories but divide the work within territory by customer type (e.g., college, health care, business and industry).

CONTROL: MONITORING THE MARKETING FUNCTION

Performance Standards

At the point when marketing results are being reviewed, the marketing plan can serve as a performance standard. A number of bases can be used to quantify results. Several are discussed below.

Market Share. The proportion of the total market's business gained by the company in the period under review can be contrasted with similar results in previous periods and with the share attained by major competitors. Syndicated research, such as the CREST[8] studies, can provide data on food service **market share.** Smith Travel Research provides such information for hotels. Independent operators can also make reasonable estimates of their market share based on observation of competitors' operations. Hotels often estimate data for other properties or exchange local information among a group of operators in a market. It is generally useful, as noted earlier, to break down market share data so as to see how the operation's share is holding up by *market segment*.

Monitoring market share is especially important if the market is changing rapidly. If new operations are opening, share is likely to be endangered and falling share numbers may suggest a revision of the marketing plan to increase promotional expenditures or even a fundamental rethinking of menu strategy or remodeling of the physical plant.

Sales Analysis. A detailed **sales analysis** is often revealing. For instance, a hotel's food and beverage sales were on budget and ahead of last year. Detailed analysis, however, revealed that its large, popularly priced restaurant's sales were well ahead for lunch but that dinner sales were falling behind. Moreover, a small supper club in the hotel was performing poorly and well below last year's sales level. Further analysis suggested that the luncheon increase was probably due to a combination of increased activity in the area (a new office building had been completed and occupied recently) and a substantial luncheon menu redesign. The new luncheon menu format had decreased service times by featuring more ready-to-serve dishes, thus enabling a faster chair turn.

In this situation, the overall numbers could be read to be reassuring—but detailed analysis suggests real cause for concern regarding the evening meal and a need to rethink the entire marketing program for the dinner business in a fundamental way.

Profit Analysis. It is not enough just to reach sales targets. In the same hotel just discussed, the bar was performing at the planned sales level, but profits had deteriorated significantly. Investigation revealed that the bartender had built up a steady clientele of regulars through overpouring and providing occasional drinks on the house. This probably meant increased tips for the bartender (and also suggested the bartender was pocketing some of the receipts). The practice supported good sales performance, but the house was not making any money from all this sales volume.

Marketing Audit. Monitoring the ongoing operation against sales and profit targets is an essential activity, but it is sometimes not enough. When it is determined that a fundamental reexamination of the entire marketing function is appropriate, a marketing audit should be undertaken. A **marketing audit** questions the basic premises of the marketing activities—their goals and policies—and reviews the way the marketing activity is organized and executed, as well as the effectiveness of the people who are carrying it out. A marketing audit is especially useful in a changing market because a marketing audit not only examines past performance and current activities but looks to the future allocation of resources. Because it is intended to question all aspects of marketing, it should be conducted by an independent party either inside or—more likely—outside the firm.

SUMMARY

Marketing planning is a difficult and frustrating task because of the uncertainty it must face. Major elements of the marketing plan consider external and internal factors that are critical to marketing. Marketing plan contents are shown in Figures 6.2 and 6.3 for a unit level and national chain plan, respectively.

The points of view of marketing and operations are contrasted in Figure 6.6. Operations tends to be detail oriented and concerned with costs and stability, while marketing is consumer and competitor oriented and concerned with sales. The basis for organizing the headquarters marketing unit organization is discussed. The bases for monitoring the performance of the marketing function include market share, sales analysis, and profit analysis. The most searching review of all aspects of marketing is embodied in the marketing audit.

◆ *Key Words and Concepts*

Marketing plan
Mission statement
Customer analysis
Competitor analysis
Strengths and weaknesses
Point of view of operations people
Point of view of marketing people
Internal marketing
Performance standards
- Market share
- Sales analysis
- Profit analysis

Marketing audit

◆ *Discussion Questions*

1. Why are many people not anxious to be involved in marketing planning? Why is such planning important?
2. What elements are considered in an analysis of external factors affecting marketing? In an analysis of internal factors?

3. What is a mission statement? Why is it important?
4. What are the main elements of a marketing plan?
5. What are the major differences in points of view between operations and marketing?

Chapter 7

When you have finished reading this chapter, you should be able to

1. Describe the characteristics of services
2. Explain how and why services are complex
3. Discuss the dimensions of service quality
4. Identify the limits and purposes of zero-defect goals
5. Describe the critical aspects of service operations management
6. Explain the importance of capacity management to service organizations

(Photo courtesy Patrick Ward/Stock Boston)

Hospitality Service Operations and Marketing

One of the real dangers hospitality companies face is that their product will become a commodity. After all, how much *real* difference is there between the physical aspects and menu of the various categories of restaurants or different brands of hotels? If they *are* all pretty much the same, the danger is they will be treated like other commodities, where the general quality grade (choice beef, #1 fancy vegetables) and price are the only buyer considerations. Under these circumstances, profit margins are thin and the opportunity for differentiation is minimal.

In hospitality, the great opportunity for differentiation is **service.** When the guest interacts with the hospitality firm's operation—its people, facilities, and systems—that is a "moment of truth," a time when the guest matches his or her experience with the promise of performance the firm has made. In this chapter, we return to a theme set out in earlier chapters: Everybody who works in hospitality is an active participant in his or her company's marketing because operations and marketing are so closely tied together.

The quality of service is vital to a company's operational and financial success. In this chapter, we will look at just what services are, what service quality is, and how quality is controlled in a service operation. Managing service operations, we will find, is dependent on selling employees on their work—that is, *internal* marketing—and developing a service culture. Finally, because there is no inventory in service organizations for unsold products, we will need to consider how capacity utilization is achieved.

HOSPITALITY SERVICES

With the increase in automation in hospitality, it is important to note that service is rendered not only by **people** but by electronic and mechanical **devices** and by complex **systems** maintained by hospitality companies. For instance, in-room television checkout, vending machines, and reservation systems all provide service with minimal human involvement. Thus, the following definition of service encompasses all kinds of service encounters:

> A service is an intangible activity that takes place between the guest and a service organization's service employees, physical resources, or systems—or some combination of those—which are provided as solutions to customer problems.[1]

From the guest's point of view, the **service is an experience,** the sum total of everything that happens to him or her in connection with a transaction or series of transactions.

Characteristics of a Service Transaction

The service transaction is an *interaction* between the guest and some aspect of the service organization. In this interaction, the *consumer participates in the production process.* The service transaction is intangible, an activity or a series of activities, rather than a thing. Service is highly perishable: An unsold airline seat or an unsold guest room cannot be sold at a later time. Since services are produced and consumed at the same time, there is no way to build an inventory. The inability to store excess production in inventory makes issues of capacity utilization critical to services management and marketing. Ultimately, the product purchased is the guest's experience. Employee behavior, in all its nuances, is a major component of service, which, again, emphasizes the link between operations and marketing. These characteristics are summarized in Figure 7.1.

An Interaction—Guest and Server*

An Experience

Intangible to varying degrees

An Activity (or Series of Activities) rather than an object

Customer Part of Production Process

Perishable—No Inventory

Employee Behavior a part of the product

*Human, electronic or mechanical device, or corporate system

Figure 7.1 Characteristics of a Service

THE SERVICE PRODUCT

We have just said that, from the guest's point of view, the product purchased is an experience. From the organization's point of view, however, the **service product** is a deliberately orchestrated *event*. The best way to think of the service product is as a continuum blending both intangible interaction and physical good. Service products vary from an extreme of almost all tangible goods such as a vended sandwich, to almost entirely intangible service interactions such as a travel agent's booking services. Indeed, there are very few products which are purely good or service.[2]

Three Overlapping Service Systems

As we have already said, the service product is a complex phenomenon made up of everything that happens to the guest. Figure 7.2 gives an overview of this complexity. The hospitality product, as experienced by the guest, is made up of three

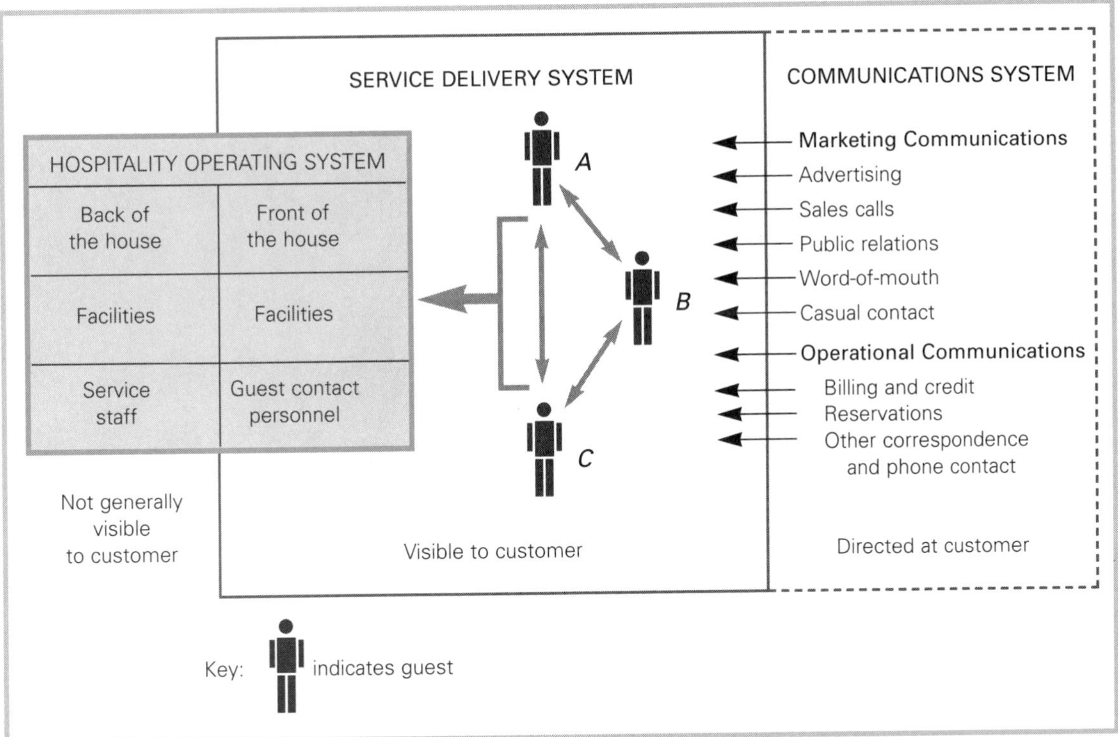

Figure 7.2 Three Overlapping Hospitality Systems: Operating, Delivery, and Communications

Source: Adapted from Christopher H. Lovelock, *Services Marketing*, 2nd ed. (Englewood Cliffs, NJ: Prentice-Hall, 1991).

overlapping systems.[3] Significantly, only a small portion of these systems is under the direct control of marketing; most are under the direction of operations.

The **service delivery system** includes front-of-the-house facilities—dining rooms, lobbies, front desks, and guest rooms—as well as front-of-the-house personnel who are (or should be) trained for guest contact. Significantly, however, other guests are also a part of the service delivery system; that is, guests affect each other's experience of the operation. The guest, then, is in a way a part of the product. A low-priced bus tour (or noisy conventioneers) bursting into the lobby of an upscale hotel may change the view of the regular clientele of the hotel as to what kind of place they are staying in—and the value of that stay. The fact that the guest is part of the product has serious implications in selecting appropriate target markets.

The **hospitality operating system** is where the work gets done for the guest. As Figure 7.2 suggests, part of the hospitality operating system is physically located in the portion of the service delivery system visible to the guest. The front of the house is deliberately designed, physically and organizationally, to achieve an appropriate impression, while providing important functional services. The back of the house provides the utilitarian production activities essential to the delivery of service such as housekeeping, food production, engineering, and the like.

A chance contact with back-of-the-house personnel may alter the guest's view of the operation—for better or worse. (Photo courtesy of Best Western International)

The intent is that the back of the house is kept out of sight of the guest—but the operating reality is that guests do step into service corridors, interact with maids and housemen, or wander into the kitchen, in error or as part of exploring the operation. "Back stage" has a special authenticity for guests. They know that the front of the house is "on stage" and that the impression there is a planned one. For that reason, experience in the back of the house sometimes is viewed by guests as providing clues as to what things are "really like" in an operation. Cleanliness and order in the back of the house and friendly, courteous employees are important to an orderly operation—and they can also have an impact on the guest's perception of the operation.

The **communications system** includes deliberate planned marketing communications such as advertising, promotion, and public relations. Operational communications, however, like back-of-the-house operations, sometimes give guests a sense of "how things really work." The impact of the courtesy of a good front office can be destroyed by rude credit communications, inept reservations staff, or even by an unanswered letter.

SERVICE QUALITY

"Quality," experts agree, "is whatever the customer says it is and the quality of a particular product or service is whatever the customer perceives it to be."[4] As you can see, the emphasis is on the customer and on **perceived quality.** There are, undoubtedly, "objective" measures of service that can be reduced to numbers such as service times, errors in orders, length of waiting time, and the like. These are "proxies" (i.e., indirect measures) that are useful in tracking service quality. The product, however, is, ultimately, the customer's experience and the *subjective* quality of that experience is the final determinant of quality. What the guest *perceives* as quality is the ultimate test of success or failure in service operations.

Quality Dimensions: Technical and Interpersonal

Quality can be conceptualized broadly along the two critical dimensions shown in Figure 7.3. The first of these is **technical:** Did things go right? (Was the food hot? The reservation in order? The room clean?) The second is the more difficult dimension of **interpersonal** quality. (Was the server friendly? Did service staff go out of their way to be helpful? Did I feel welcome or out of place?)

Technical quality issues are relatively objective, that is, measurable. Technical quality, however, is generally the minimum expected of a hospitality operation. Technical (and facility) innovations are frequently subject to duplication by competitors. Moreover, as Grönroos points out, "Even when an excellent solution is achieved, the firm may be unsuccessful, if the excellence in technical quality is counteracted by badly managed buyer-seller interactions."[5] Of course, we should note that all the charm in the world will not make up for bad food or a lost reservation. Interpersonal success without technical competence is also unsatisfactory. Each dimension is critical.

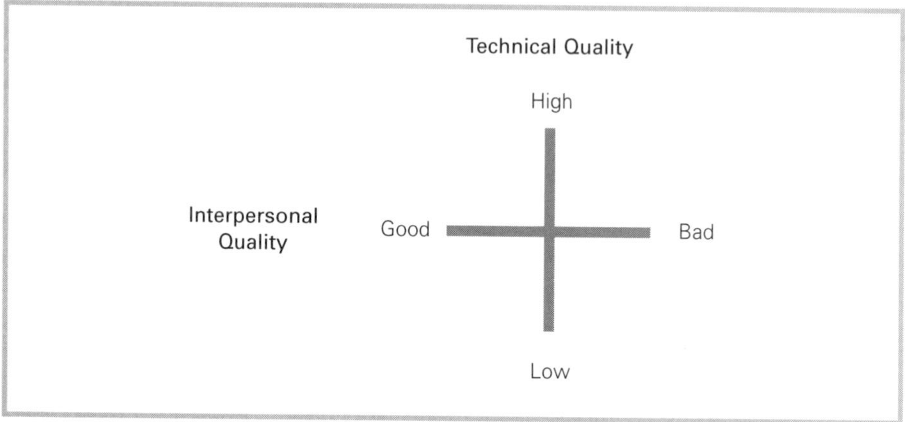

Figure 7.3 Critical Dimensions of Quality in the Service Experience

Measuring Service Quality

Research on measuring service quality and customer satisfaction yielded five significant **aspects of service** that are important to consumers. These are:

Tangibles	Physical facilities, equipment, and appearance of personnel
Reliability	Ability to perform the promised service dependably and accurately
Responsiveness	Willingness to help customers and provide prompt service
Assurance	Knowledge and courtesy of employees and their ability to inspire trust and confidence
Empathy	Caring, individualized attention the firm provides its customers[6]

As you can see, only the first of these characteristics is a strictly technical one. The second can reflect technical and interpersonal dimensions. The last three all clearly relate to interpersonal aspects of the service encounter. It is difficult to overstate the importance of people in service.

Service Quality Gaps

The same researchers studied service failures. They wanted to know what the causes of the service failures were. What they found were four specific gaps between what actually took place and what should have taken place. These are summarized briefly here.[7] The fifth gap shown is basically a summary of all the other four possible difficulties.

The people responsible for greeting the public on behalf of an organization must develop a "public personality." (Photo courtesy of Intercontinental Hotels, Cairo, Egypt)

Misunderstanding	There is a gap between management's understanding of consumer wants and what consumers actually want.
Communication	Management has a correct understanding of customer preferences, but these are not translated properly into service quality specifications.
Performance	Adequate service standards are set but not met in practice by the organization.
Overpromising	Marketing communication promises performance that is not met.

Expectations The service experience is not, for whatever reason, consistent with the customer's expectation.

Reflecting on these five pitfalls suggests five positive policy conclusions for service operations and marketing:

1. The importance of understanding what value is to the consumer is clear.
2. *Understanding alone is not enough.* Management must translate its knowledge into policies and procedures and thus communicate its understanding to the rest of the organization.
3. Moreover, it is not enough for everyone to agree on good, solidly researched service standards: *performance is critical.* That is what the guest will experience.
4. An organization must deliver what it promises and avoid overpromising in its promotion.
5. The expectations aroused by all forms of communication including word of mouth must be met by the operation.

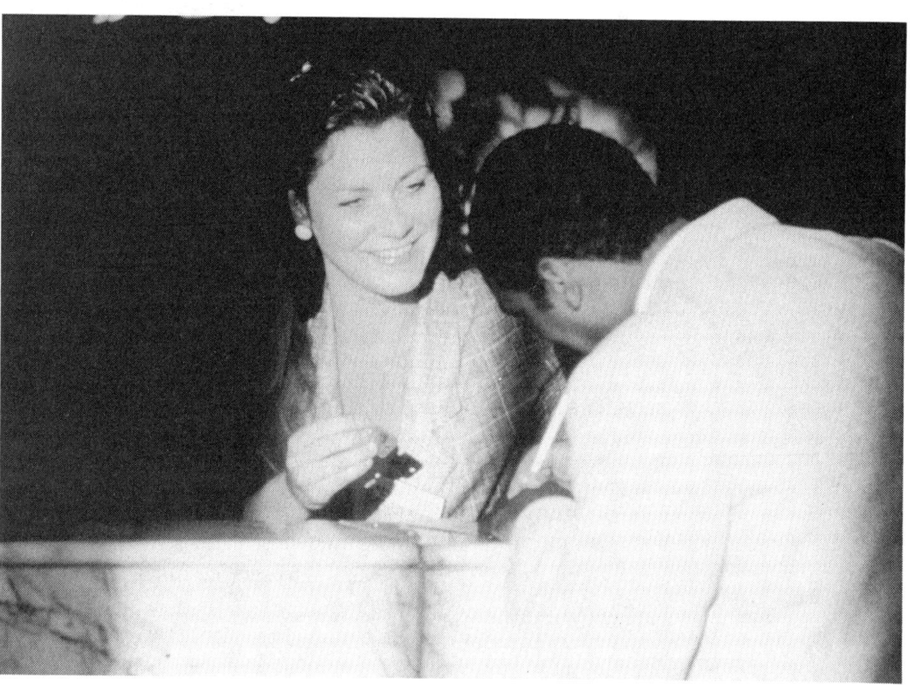

Much of the success of the service system depends on qualified, motivated employees. (Photo courtesy of Holiday Inns Worldwide)

SERVICE QUALITY CONTROL AND THE ZERO-DEFECT GOAL

In product manufacturing, the goal of quality control is to reduce defects to a minimum. In the final analysis, a strong product quality control program can not only reduce defects but ensure that defective products are removed from inventory for reworking or discard. In hospitality services, however, there are no rejects, just unhappy customers. Because a "defect" is an event that happens to somebody, there is no way to call it back. Under these circumstances, the argument for a **zero-defect** standard is compelling.

On the other hand:

> The fact is that in services, no matter how rigorous the procedures and employee training or how advanced the technology, zero defects is an unattainable goal. Unlike manufacturers that can adjust inputs and machinery until products are perfectly uniform, service companies cannot escape variation. Factors like weather and the customers themselves are beyond a company's control.[8]

Setting a zero-defect target, although an unattainable goal in any absolute sense, *does* help to set an organization's sights on minimizing service problems. Moreover, guests are demanding but they are not usually unreasonable. The standards an operation must reach are based on guest expectations. Delay or even a moment's inattention in a luxury operation are an annoyance at best and a potentially serious defect in operating quality. On the other hand, waiting lines are a part of life at a theme park and most people understand if the service interchange is sometimes a bit hurried. Nobody expects the Ritz at Disneyland.

While guest expectations set reasonable bounds on what a failure is, service failures are a serious problem because they reduce the likelihood of repeat patronage and of good word of mouth. Thus, programmatic efforts to reduce quality problems are essential to success in a service operation. Field Practice Note 7.1 summarizes one company's quality management program.

The Cost of Quality

Reducing defects dramatically may seem an expensive undertaking. There are good reasons to believe, however, that improving quality will actually *reduce* costs. The costs of correcting people's errors, estimated at 35 percent of operating costs, are a serious burden.[9] Avoiding these errors could generate significant savings. Moreover, the planning necessary to reduce or eliminate errors and that required to control costs are closely parallel.

There are three major costs of service defects. They are: lost customers, the cost of attracting new customers, and bad word-of-mouth advertising. We will look at the cost of lost business first:

Field Practice Note 7.1

Quality at the Ritz

The Ritz-Carlton Hotel Company has undertaken a program to continually raise its quality level.[1] The Ritz is the only hospitality firm to win the Malcolm Baldridge National Quality Award. The Ritz-Carlton's total quality management (TQM) program has several elements. The program begins with an absolute commitment on the part of the senior management to the development and implementation of TQM. This is not only a policy commitment but involves a commitment of roughly one-fourth of the senior executives' time. Following from this top management commitment is a commitment on the part of the unit level managers and of the employees they work with.

The *standards* of the program—called "Gold Standards" at Ritz-Carlton—are spelled out in objective detail. New employees receive a two-day orientation that emphasizes the corporation's service culture and so Ritz-Carlton standards become an integral part of the organization's value structure and corporate culture.

Detailed *planning* begins with property level teams setting objectives and devising action plans to meet them which are then reviewed by a corporate steering committee. Quality results are tracked daily in *quality production reports* derived from each area of the hotel. Hallmarks of the TQM program are a focus on customer satisfaction and an organizational structure in which employees are empowered to solve guests' problems.

[1]The following discussion is based on Charles G. Partlow, "How Ritz-Carlton Applies TQM," *Cornell Hotel and Restaurant Administration Quarterly,* August 1993, pp. 97–104.

> At Club Med, one lost customer costs the company at least \$2,400: a loyal guest visits the resorts an average of four times after the initial visit and spends roughly \$1,000 each time. The contribution margin is 60 percent. So when a Club Med customer doesn't return, the company loses 60 percent of \$4,000, or \$2,400. It also has to replace the customer through expensive marketing efforts.[10]

Moreover, the cost of gaining a new customer is estimated at roughly six times the cost required to retain an existing one. Finally, there is the matter of word of mouth. Customers are much more likely to complain to their friends and acquaintances than to the company. One study suggests that people with a complaint talk to roughly 10 other people about that complaint.[11] Since recommendations by others play a key role in consumers' decisions about which hospitality operation to patronize, the impact of "disrecommendations," is certainly a significant cost, though one that never shows up clearly on a company's financial statement.

Given the costs we can impute to service errors—and the savings that avoiding those errors will bring—we can say, as one quality control expert put it, "Quality is free."[12]

Enlisting the Customer in Quality Control

Christopher Hart makes a compelling case for involving the customer in quality control programs. Paradoxically, the medium for achieving this end is customer complaints. When a customer complains, management gains valuable information on where failure points in the service system are. Accordingly, efforts to secure customer feedback and to retain customers in the event of a problem go hand in hand. Service guarantees and other programs to secure customer feedback can have a positive impact on both service standards and customer retention.

Guarantees. Hart argues that the way services are generally structured, customers have little incentive to complain. Services are intangible and so it is hard to frame a complaint. Moreover, the customer may not know what an appropriate standard is and so may not be sure a complaint is valid. (How long *should* you wait for an order to be served?) Finally, it is not clear to whom the guest should complain—nor what good it will do the guest to take the trouble to do so. A

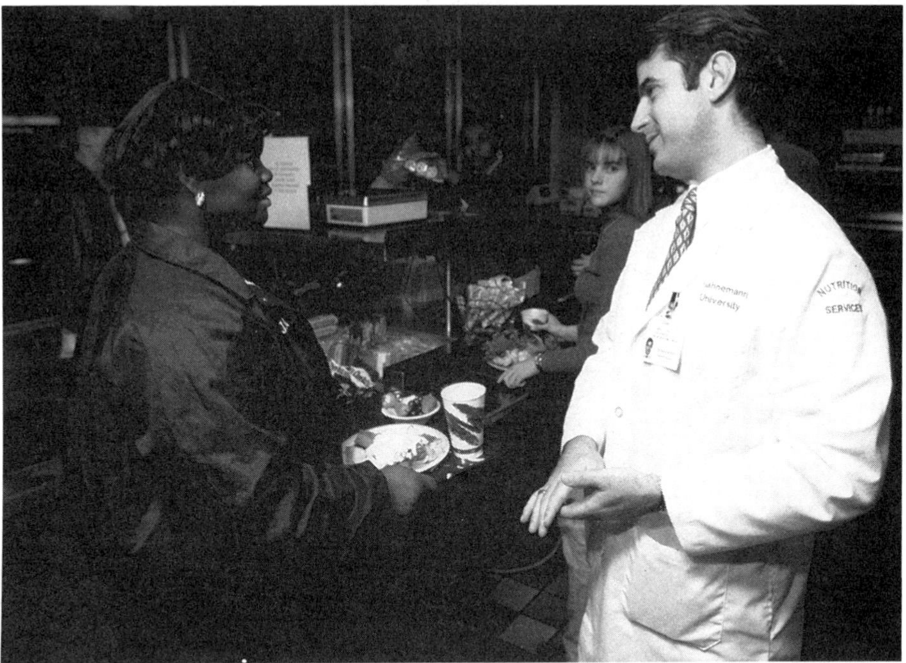

A customer complaint represents an opportunity to gain valuable information. (Photo courtesy of ARAMARK)

guarantee, however, attacks these problems by "giving the consumer an incentive and a vehicle for bringing their grievances to management's attention."[13]

Promus Company (franchisors of Hampton Inns, Embassy Suites, and Homewood Suites) pioneered the guarantee to their guests of "one hundred percent satisfaction." In each of its hotels, the guest is promised high-quality accommodation, friendly and efficient service, and clean, comfortable surroundings. The company's assurance that "If you are not completely satisfied, we don't expect you to pay" has enhanced that firm's reputation with the target markets it serves. From the point of view of quality control, however, it is equally powerful because it forces managers to understand why they fail and to focus on the customer's definition of quality. A guarantee will, moreover, set clear performance standards and generate reliable data. Claims against the guarantee can help identify failure points in a chainwide hospitality system—and, equally, in each individual unit. Complaints provide data for steps ranging from system redesign to training program planning.

Hart suggests that a good service guarantee program should have five characteristics:

1. *An unconditional guarantee.* The object is to satisfy the customer, not argue with them so all elements that the company can control should be covered without any "ifs, ands, or buts."

2. *Easy to understand.* The guarantee "should be written in simple, concise language that pinpoints the promise" . . . . "Five minute" lunch service rather than "prompt" service creates clear expectations.

3. *Meaningful.* A guarantee should cover the aspects of a service transaction that are important to the customer and should provide a significant payout if the promise is not kept.

4. *Easy to invoke.* The guarantee should not present the customer with any complications nor should the reaction to the complaint make the guest feel guilty about speaking up.

5. *Easy to collect.* The procedure for collecting "should be easy and, equally important, quick."[14]

Other means to secure customer complaints—and thus enhance the chances of *keeping the customer*—include the use of 800 numbers to encourage people to report problems by making it easy to do so—and cost free. *Asking*—at the front desk or the cashier's counter "How was everything?" is a more direct way to solicit complaints. People who will not take the trouble to fill out a form or dial a number may share their problems with a sympathetic staff member when asked to do

Hampton's unconditional guarantee pleases guests, and complaints that stem from it provide valuable management information. (Photo courtesy of Hampton Inns)

so. Finally, questionnaires administered to periodic samples of guests as well as the ubiquitous "comment form" help obtain information and identify guests an organization is in danger of losing.

The reaction to complaints should be prompt and, wherever possible, should involve remedying the problem the guest has experienced, even if the company is not at fault. Once the guest has left, some companies make it a practice to answer complaints by phone. This prompt personal attention is appreciated by the guest and the person dealing with the complaint has an opportunity to work with the guest to determine what amends will be appropriate. Finally, the organization's ability to respond can be multiplied manyfold if it empowers its employees to remedy the guest's problem on the spot.[15]

MANAGING SERVICE OPERATIONS

As Figure 7.4 shows, the hospitality marketing cycle begins with promotional activities which stimulate interest in the company's offering. If inquiries about the service (reservation requests, for instance) are handled properly, a favorable purchase decision is likely—but the success of the initial contact with the operation is critical to moving to the next phase. Then, when the guest arrives, a pleasant exchange helps keep the guest's patronage—and an unpleasant one can spoil the guest's experience. The same is true during the balance of the guest's visit to the operation. Successful encounters enhance the experience and build repeat business. Unsuccessful ones risk losing a guest's valuable repeat patronage. The cost of securing a new customer has been estimated to be six times that of retaining a regular customer.[16] A regular customer, then, is a significant asset. To get at the importance of operations employees to the success of the service company's marketing program, Christian Grönroos has dubbed people working in operations "part-time marketers." Others refer to service organization employees as "service

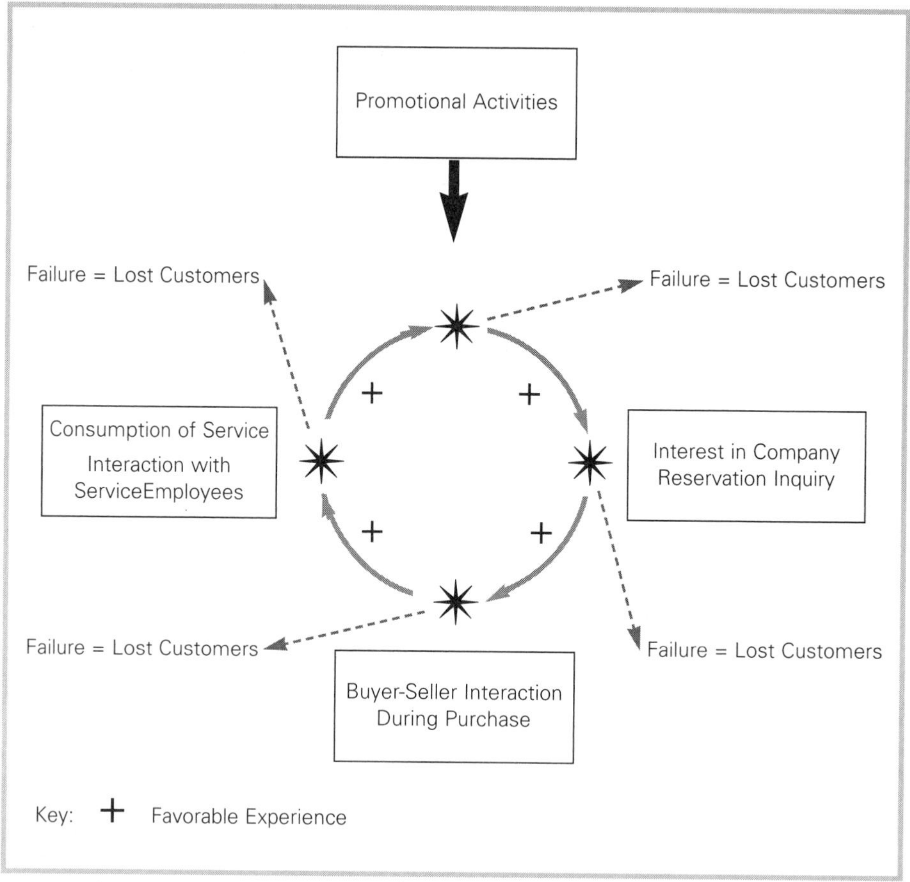

Figure 7.4 The Hospitality Marketing Cycle: Marketing and Operations. At each stage, customers are gained or lost on the basis of their evaluation of their experience.

Source: Adapted from Christian Grönroos, "The Marketing and Need Adaptation Circle," *Long Range Planning*, April 1980, p. 37.

ambassadors,"[17] to denote the importance of their guest relations role no matter what their duties. Operations and only operations can build a strong base of repeat customers.

Internal Marketing

Given the importance of people to an operation's success, it is no surprise to learn that plans aimed at maintaining employee morale and effectiveness have been carefully developed. These are often called **internal marketing** programs.

A program of communications is used in successful companies to market the company and its goals to prospective employees. That is, managers must think of themselves as having "jobs for sale" and develop a marketing strategy to "sell" those jobs in their labor market. Once an employee is on board, it is important to gain and keep his or her support for the company's programs. Field Practice Note 7.2 discusses the elements of a typical internal marketing program. Internal marketing was also discussed in Chapter 6.

Service-Oriented Operations Management

To succeed in a service business such as the very competitive hospitality industry, successful customer-oriented service is a necessity. In this section, we will examine other requirements of an operating strategy to deliver service the customer will come back for.

Selection. Some years ago, I was interviewing some operations executives at Disney World and I asked them how they trained their people to be so friendly. I was somewhat surprised when the reply came, "We don't." The managers went on to say that they took care of friendliness by aggressively screening people who were applying as "cast members," as Disney calls its employees. One Marriott official observed, "We can train people to do any task, but getting people with a friendly attitude starts with recruitment and hiring."[18] Careful selection, then, is critical to successful service-oriented operations.

At Four Seasons, a key employment criterion is whether the employee will be somebody present employees would like to work with. Several interviews are the rule and, before a final hiring decision is made, the prospect will be interviewed by a senior executive, generally the executive assistant manager (and sometimes the general manager). This is effective not only in assessing the employee but in communicating to the employee a sense of the importance of the job and of what the company's values are.

Orientation and Training. Grönroos[19] identifies three keys to developing effective service employees:

1. Developing an understanding of the entire organization and how it functions in a market-oriented manner.

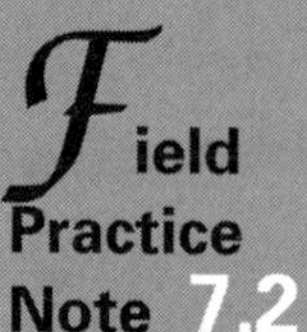

Field Practice Note 7.2

Internal Marketing

MARKETING JOBS

Defining a customer is always the first step in any marketing program, so a "marketing program for jobs" needs to begin with an understanding of the local hospitality labor market, how it can be segmented, the needs and preferences of appropriate segments of potential employees, what level and kinds of benefits will interest them, and how the company can best communicate with prospective employees about the opportunities the company has to offer.

EMPLOYEE RECRUITMENT

As an example, consider a restaurant whose luncheon volume is growing so rapidly that it is having trouble attracting enough service personnel. A logical segment to fill this particular need is mothers of young children. While many of these mothers may be working full time, a significant number drop out of the regular work force while their children are young. Once children are enrolled in kindergarten or in school, many are interested in working—if the hours fit their family obligations. Having identified an attractive segment, the next step is to design an "internal product," a job that fits their needs. This probably involves limited hours of work and flexible scheduling, as well as the customary considerations of pay and fringe benefits. The offering of this "internal product" can probably be communicated to this segment through notices on bulletin boards in grocery stores and possibly through the PTA in local schools and kindergartens. Newspaper advertising might be used—but it is not as targeted to the segment selected and generally requires a major applicant screening process which can be time consuming, given the large number of responses newspaper advertising yields.

Of course, there are many such segments. College and university students are often a good segment for evening hours and weekend jobs. They, too, need flexibility in scheduling. The offer of employment opportunities can be communicated through placement offices and student newspapers.

One of the most powerful recruiting tools, and one used by many companies, is to recruit through the present employees, perhaps by offering prizes or cash awards for each recruit who joins the company and stays for some specific period. This provides some screening—people do not normally recommend somebody they do not want to work with—and it heightens the likelihood of attracting an employee who will be compatible with the present work force.

MARKET RESEARCH AND COMMUNICATION

The attitudes and job satisfaction of a company's present employees are commonly the subject of market research. Efforts to communicate the company's values are facilitated by a service culture, by recognition and reward programs such as awards for outstanding service and long-term service, and through company newsletters, magazines, and other in-house communication programs.

Skill training at the unit level, one of the most important tasks for entry-level managers, is a key marketing step, as well as a necessary operational one. (Photo courtesy of Arby's)

2. Developing skills related to the specific tasks associated with the job.
3. Developing communication and service skills.

One of the most costly and dysfunctional practices we have in some parts of the hospitality industry is to hire new employees, hand them an apron or a bellman's uniform, show them to their place, and say, "Here's where you'll be working. If you have any questions, ask John or Mary." Successful companies follow a more deliberate process of investing in employees, instead of just hiring a "warm body." This involves a program of orientation, training and retraining, and motivation.

An orientation to the entire company, such as the two-day classroom program provided at the Ritz-Carlton, is imparted during an employee's early days on the job. Classroom work is often supplemented by videotaped messages about the company, its history and its values. Skill training is usually accomplished through on-the-job training supplemented by videotapes and written training materials. Skill training generally relies on an experienced employee who has been *trained as a coach.* It is important that a reasonable degree of mastery be attained before the employee actually performs the duties of a position independently. Very often, people carry a light station for the first few days after initial training or work along with a more experienced employee, sometimes wearing a badge that identifies them as a trainee.

Developing communication skills (how to deal with guests) calls for a different training process than does technical skill training (how to prepare or serve a meal). One of the most effective training techniques in developing guest relations skills has proved to be role playing, in which one or more members of the training class handle a typical service situation. Following the role play, the class discusses each player's performance. Communication skills are especially important to guest contact service workers but, because back-of-the-house employees often come in contact with guests, they should also be sensitized to the need to treat guests in a courteous and friendly manner.

Most organizations that have a commitment to training see it as not just something for new employees. These companies generally encourage (and often pay for) educational programs for their employees, provide cross-training opportunities, and offer training to move up in the organization. Moreover, they provide for periodic *retraining* on critical skills and to reinforce the company's service culture.

Motivating Continuing Performance: A Service Culture

Corporate Culture. **Corporate culture** is really the shared values of an organization. A corporate culture provides a company with an internal climate of beliefs, goals, and norms of behavior. More formally, corporate culture may be defined as

> the pattern of shared values and beliefs that give members of an organization meaning, and provides them with the rules of behavior in the organization.[20]

Service Culture. The corporate culture is, among other things, a powerful communication tool for "nurturing a **service culture** that will shape employee behavior more effectively than rules and regulations can."[21] That is, a service culture provides the rewards and encouragement necessary to motivate employees to go out of their way to perform superior service.

Davidow and Uttal contrast the impact of service culture on two retailing organizations, Nordstrom and Macy's. At Nordstrom:

> Service is an attitude, a kind of caring on the part of everybody in the store . . . . Macy's, once the undisputed king of California retailers, seeing that Nordstrom always won when they faced off in the same shopping malls, decided to "Nordstromize" itself. [In order to do so] it put sales clerks on commission, deepened inventories, adopted a more liberal returns policy, started talking up service, and hired people away from Nordstrom to train employees in the mysteries of coddling customers . . . .
>
> The Macy's effort was a flop . . . . All of Macy's efforts to mimic Nordstrom couldn't overcome Macy's leadership culture and organization, ... [Macy's] strongly centralized, strictly hierarchical [culture] . . . kept front line workers from doing their jobs. [At Macy's] at every level, people care most about what their bosses think, and they manage by dictating to their inferiors.[22]

The problem highlighted at Macy's reflects the attitude prevalent in many hotel and restaurant companies. Some years ago, an international chain of franchised hotels faced changing market conditions. For years, the company operated very successfully, largely on the basis of the power of its franchise and the franchisor's reservation system. The key to its success was offering generally similar upper-midpriced hotels, maintaining standard procedures, and controlling expenses. The company, like Macy's, was a top-down organization, and operating procedures were spelled out in great detail.

Over a period of years, however, competition increased both in numbers of competitors and in the power of the brands (and reservation systems) the company competed against. The company's market position was no longer preeminent, and management realized that it had to rebuild market share on a property-by-property basis in many local markets depending on local market conditions. This, in turn, required the company to decentralize its organization and put more responsibility on local managers and their teams to achieve the service mix appropriate to their particular market. While the company was eventually successful, it took several years, massive restructuring, and a shift in its brand strategy to bring it off successfully.

One of the most difficult initial problems was a rule-bound culture in which the job of managers and their subordinates was to do what they were told. When they were suddenly asked to turn themselves into problem solvers, many failed in that new role in which they had no previous experience. Development or redevelopment of a culture is not subject to a "quick fix." Rather, it is a labor of many years. Field Practice Note 7.3 describes the evolution in the company culture at Omni Hotels.

Empowerment. **Empowerment** organizes work quite differently than does the typical rule-oriented culture in which management, the boss, or the owner determines what is to be done and when and how. An organization that empowers workers still has rules—but gives employees the power to change or break these rules, within some limits, to *solve the guest's problem*. The shift is from a boss-oriented culture to a customer-oriented culture.

For instance, at Hampton Inns (and an increasing number of Hampton's competitors), *any employee* has the authority to do whatever is necessary to satisfy a disgruntled guest, up to and including complimenting a guest's room for the night.

Our discussion of empowerment should not leave you with an impression of a permissive organization. While rules tend to become guidelines in empowered employees' hands, modern hospitality operations still must plan the flow of operations and set standards of performance. A key to this rationalization of the service process is service procedures.

Service Encounters: The Role of Procedure

Anyone who has worked in a well-run hospitality organization is familiar with well-worked-out, detailed procedures. These are designed to handle all recurring tasks such as taking an order, serving each course, and presenting the bill in a food service operation. In hotels, reservations, check-in, and checkout are key procedures. Procedures in hospitality services may be likened to the machinery in a production line.[23] An orderly arrangement ensures efficiency; disorder leads to chaos.

Field Practice Note 7.3

Omni Invests in a "Sales Culture"

Omni Hotels has announced a new training program that will create a "sales culture" throughout the entire chain. That sales effort is keyed to providing excellent service to guests.

Omni spent $600,000 developing the training program, according to CEO Jerry Best. Although the program is targeted at sales personnel, all employees will experience the ongoing development program. "This is not just a one-time event," said Best. "Part of the consideration in creating this training program is that we need to create a powerful sales culture in each hotel and throughout the company. The sales culture must equip sales associates with information, tools, encouragement, and daily support to become the best in the industry."

The training program involves three tracks: the Self-Directed Development Plan, Professional Selling Skills, and the Sales Leadership Foundation. The self-directed portion of the training program provides for continuous development of employees in sales and marketing. F&B, rooms operation, finance, and human resources. A mentor, called a "champion," will monitor, guide, and grade each employee. Best said this will be a grueling process, but it will result in superior employees.

Three principles undergird the program. (1) All sales must be a balance between profitability and customer satisfaction and loyalty. (2) In a sales-oriented culture, all associates must work together to ensure a customer-friendly environment. (3) All GMs must be intimately involved in the training process to ensure support once the sales associates return from initial training.—*G.W.*

Source: Cornell Hotel and Restaurant Administration Quarterly, April 1995, p. 16.

Operating procedures need to focus on production line aspects of the work to achieve operational efficiency, but they also need to be planned as a service encounter with the guest's experience in mind. Encounters with the organization are the main source of information the guests have about the operation, and they are likely to generalize about the operation from the limited number of encounters they have. One authority has written, "When superior service firms are examined, a consistent pattern is evident. One sees a pronounced emphasis on controllable details, continuous investments in training, a concern with the customer's view, and a reward system that places value on service quality."[24] Poor performance, she says, is usually associated with an inward-looking organization preoccupied with its own activities. These operations view guests as an interruption to be tolerated only because they are necessary to provide the transaction. Such organizations give a low priority to guests' feelings in the transaction and a high one to the production side of their work.

Personal encounters include such variety that "scripting" is difficult, if not impossible. Careful selection of procedures and personnel can go a long way toward reducing problems in personal service. (Photo courtesy of Catherine Ursillo/Photo Researchers)

Shostock argues that service encounters need to be deliberately designed to achieve guest satisfaction. She distinguishes three levels of encounter:

1. *Remote encounters* involve no human interaction. An example would be in-room checkout via the guest room television.
2. *Indirect personal encounters* involve verbal interaction—usually by phone—but no personal contact.
3. *Direct personal contact* involves face-to-face interaction.

Remote encounters have increased rapidly in hospitality over the past few years. Hotel guests, for instance, can check out via their room television—or examine and verify their account status. Fast-food customers have begun to place their own orders via touch screens. Hospitality firms that are successful have spent considerable resources perfecting these systems. As this evolution continues, hospitality firms need to be prepared to make major investments in adequate hardware and software to ensure an acceptable experience for guests, as well as an efficient operation for the organization.

With indirect encounters, as in a reservation service, it is often appropriate to actually script the employee's most common encounters. There is, as Shostock puts it, "a world of difference between well and poorly crafted verbal dialogs."[25] Experience with WATS line reservation services suggests that this need is just as pressing in hospitality as it is elsewhere.

Direct person-to-person interactions are the most difficult to control. Consistent successful personal service encounters are based on carefully developed procedures, adequate training, properly selected employees, and rewards keyed to performance.

Procedures are not intended to make people act like machines, but careful design of all the elements where the guest encounters the operating system is a necessity if the guest is to feel welcomed and served. If success in the hotel business, as Ellsworth Statler once said, is attributable to "location, location and location," then success in managing service encounters comes from "detail, detail, detail."[26]

SERVICE OPERATIONS AND CAPACITY MANAGEMENT

We need, now, to turn our attention to a different aspect of service operations and marketing. Earlier in this chapter, we mentioned that one of the characteristics of services was that production and consumption of the service are simultaneous. Today's unused rooms have no value tomorrow. For this reason, there is no inventory of "yesterday's guest rooms." Service organizations produce *a capacity which must be utilized effectively*—or wasted. Capacity utilization is crucial to the profitability of service organizations.

Measuring capacity utilization involves measures of occupancy. This, essentially, means being sure that all facilities (rooms or tables) are fully used. *Fully used,* however, should mean more than physical occupancy. It should mean achieving the *most profitable use* of facilities. A hotel may have high occupancy but a low average rate and, thus, earn less than another property with a lower occupancy that does a better job of selling the higher-rate rooms. *Utilization,* then, refers to *revenue* as well as *occupancy.*

One way of measuring the level of profitability in capacity utilization in a hotel is to compute the room sales efficiency (RSE) rate. The RSE is formed by dividing the actual room sales by the total dollar sales that could have been achieved had all rooms been rented at their maximum (i.e., rack) rate. For example, if occupancy were 75 percent and the average room rate for the period was 85 percent of the full rate, then the RSE would be 0.75 × 0.85, or approximately 64 percent.[27] The RSE reflects the degree of discounting that a hotel is engaging in and, in effect, whether it is "buying" occupancy with low rates.

In food service, measures of profitable utilization of capacity involve statistics, such as *average check per guest* and *seat turn.* Seat turn is calculated by dividing the number of guests served by the number of seats available. It is a measure of "occupancy," that is, of the utilization of physical capacity. The average check is computed by dividing total sales for the period by the number of guests served in the time period. Average check serves the same function as the average rate in the hotel business in measuring sales per guest against targeted sales. A food sales efficiency (FSE) could be estimated by establishing what a reasonable goal for seat turn for a meal should be and multiplying it by the budgeted average check for that meal. If a coffee shop with 200 seats expected to achieve a seat turn of 2.0 at lunch and and average check of $5.00, then ideal sales would be $2,000 and sales of $1,800 would have an efficiency rating of 90 percent.

Managing Demand

Economists speak of supply matching demand at a given price level. Marketers, however, need to think in terms of **managing demand,** particularly in a business as volatile as hospitality. Peaks and valleys are generally predictable: Resorts have on seasons, shoulder seasons, and off-seasons. Food service demand peaks three times a day at breakfast, lunch, and dinner. One of the marketer's jobs is to try to create demand during low-volume periods. Moreover, marketing and operations need to work together to avoid overstimulating demand during high-volume periods, as well as to develop means for managing excess demand.

The general rule is *full pricing during high periods of demand* to maximize revenue and reduced pricing to minimize or avoid idle capacity during low periods of demand. In most hospitality operations, marginal revenue (i.e., the balance left after covering variable costs) accounts for a large part of the sales dollar—in lodging somewhere between 80 and 90 percent and around 50 percent in food service.[28] Most operations, therefore, have considerable room to discount the regular price. The need—in some operations—to retain skilled staff is another inducement to price reduction to maintain sales volume during slow periods.

One way to approach filling low-demand periods is by market segmentation. Groups known to be rate sensitive, for instance, are encouraged to hold their conventions during an off-season. Convention sales personnel concentrate on such groups during these periods. The author, a college professor, goes to a convention every August when the rest of the world is on vacation. And, more than half the time, the meeting is in the southern United States where it is hot as blue blazes. Needless to say, the rates are at a minimum, a consideration of interest to college professors, school and college athletic teams, and many other groups who have limited or no expense accounts. On the other hand, in peak seasons, sales staff do well to concentrate on more well-heeled market segments.

In transient hotels, weekend business has, as a rule, been very slow. Some properties, however, have built their weekends into relatively high occupancy periods by offering a dramatic reduction in weekend rates aimed at family weekend travelers, attracting a whole new market. All-suite hotels, learning from this experience, generally have two sets of rates—weekday and weekend to fit the differing needs of business and family travel segments. To cite another example, experience has shown that, in markets where there are a lot of senior citizens, early-bird specials and other offers of reduced prices for eating before 6:00 P.M. will bring in diners, in what is otherwise a slack late-afternoon period.

Special products and special events can also be used to attract off-peak customers. Restaurants use promotional specials—wine tastings, exotic menus, and similar attractions—to bring people in on the slower early days of the week. Perhaps the best known example of using a product to build off-peak demand is

Conventions are solicited by some properties for an off-season period, and some hotels offer special convention rates in slow periods as a means of offsetting low demand. (Photo courtesy Allan Carey, The Image Works)

McDonald's initial use of McNuggets. McNuggets was originally designed as a snack food to draw people in during low-volume day parts.

Inventorying Demand

While capacity cannot be inventoried, many means of persuading customers to tolerate waiting lines or to make modest changes in their plans have been successfully developed.

An everyday means of "inventorying customers" is the waiting line. The experience of waiting can be managed so as to minimize the perceived time lag for the guest. Maister[29] describes a hotel that received numerous complaints about slow elevator service. Unfortunately, nothing could be done about elevator carrying capacity, but management did install mirrors in the elevator waiting areas. This let the guests check their appearance while they were waiting. Although elevator performance had not changed, complaints fell, apparently because guests had a way to pass the time.

In other cases, more active entertainment is provided. Ski resorts, for instance, train staff to provide entertainment to guests when lines get too long at ski lifts. Staff may get everybody started singing, joke with each other and those in line, and even perform skits. None of these techniques makes the lines move faster, but they do make the time pass more quickly and pleasantly. At Disney World, waiting line areas are decorated in a way to give people something to watch—and they are often visited by human-sized animals, small oompah bands, and other diverting sights.

People wait more patiently in lines where they have a lot of action to occupy their time. (Photo courtesy of Arthur Glauberman, Photo Researchers)

Maister suggests that people wait more patiently when they have something to do, when they have both a good idea of how long they will be waiting and why they are waiting, and if they are made to feel part of a group, perhaps through interaction with others. Preprocess waits—that is, waiting to start—are less acceptable to guests, and so operators may give guests the menu to study while they are in line at a restaurant to encourage a sense that the process *has* started. Especially annoying are postprocess waits—for instance, waiting for the bill—as well as waiting that is unexplained or a waiting line system that seems unfair. Inventorying guests, then, requires planning that takes the guests' feelings into account.

Another way of inventorying customers is to try to shift their request to a place or time when their need *can* be met. Hotel reservation systems, for instance, are generally set up so that, if a reservation request at one property cannot be met, a reservation at a nearby property will be offered. For an example of a similar tactic in food service, see Field Practice Note 7.4.

Strategies for Manpower Utilization

If there are a lot of employees on duty and few customers, costs will be excessive, driving up prices. If there is a large crowd of customers but few staff to serve them, service will be slow and, depending on customer expectation, may be judged to be unacceptable. One way to handle this problem, which we have already considered, is demand management.

Field Practice Note 7.4

Inventorying Dining Room Demand

In food service, peak demand sometimes cannot be met, but a reservation system that shifts demand to *slightly* earlier or later times helps spread demand over a longer period of time. A restaurant, for instance, that experiences very heavy demand on holidays such as Easter or Mother's Day plans its reservations in advance. On the basis of past experience, the restaurant estimates a table turn on holidays at one and a quarter hours and one and a half hours for large tables. Each waitress or waiter station has three to five tables. A seating chart (see the accompanying figure) keyed to the time it takes to dine is developed.

Seating is planned to ensure that the tables in each station are occupied by parties arriving at least 10 minutes apart. The result is a seating chart with a series of arrival times specified. When a party calls for reservation, the host or hostess can respond to a request for a table for four at noon with a suggestion of a reservation time of 11:45 or 12:15. Indeed, if the whole noon hour is sold out, an attempt is made to sell a later time. Not everyone is willing to have his or her timing switched in this fashion, but a significant numer are.[1]

[1] The reservation system described here was developed by Ralph Lorenz at the Mayflower Hotel. There are many similar systems.

A Pattern for Selling Time

Seating Chart Shows Four Server Stations and Approximate Guest Arrival Times; Staggering Arrivals Ensures Server Capacity Is Not Overloaded →

On the other hand, the problem of an imbalance between servers and the need for service is an operational problem, of manpower planning—and quality management. Earl Sasser has suggested two basic approaches to manpower planning: chase demand, which calls for low customer contact, and level capacity, which calls for a much higher level of customer contact.[30]

Chase Demand. The term **chase demand** implies that, during high-volume periods, the staff can barely keep up with demand and does so only with waiting lines. Operations such as fast-food units and amusement parks are planned on the basis of highly variable demand, with peaks at, or above, normal operating capacity. Because a theme park's attendance may be 20,000 one day and 5,000 the next, staffing must be flexible and related to demand. Similarly, during the lunch rush, a busy fast-food operation may have long lines that staff is barely able to cope with as it attempts to catch up with demand.

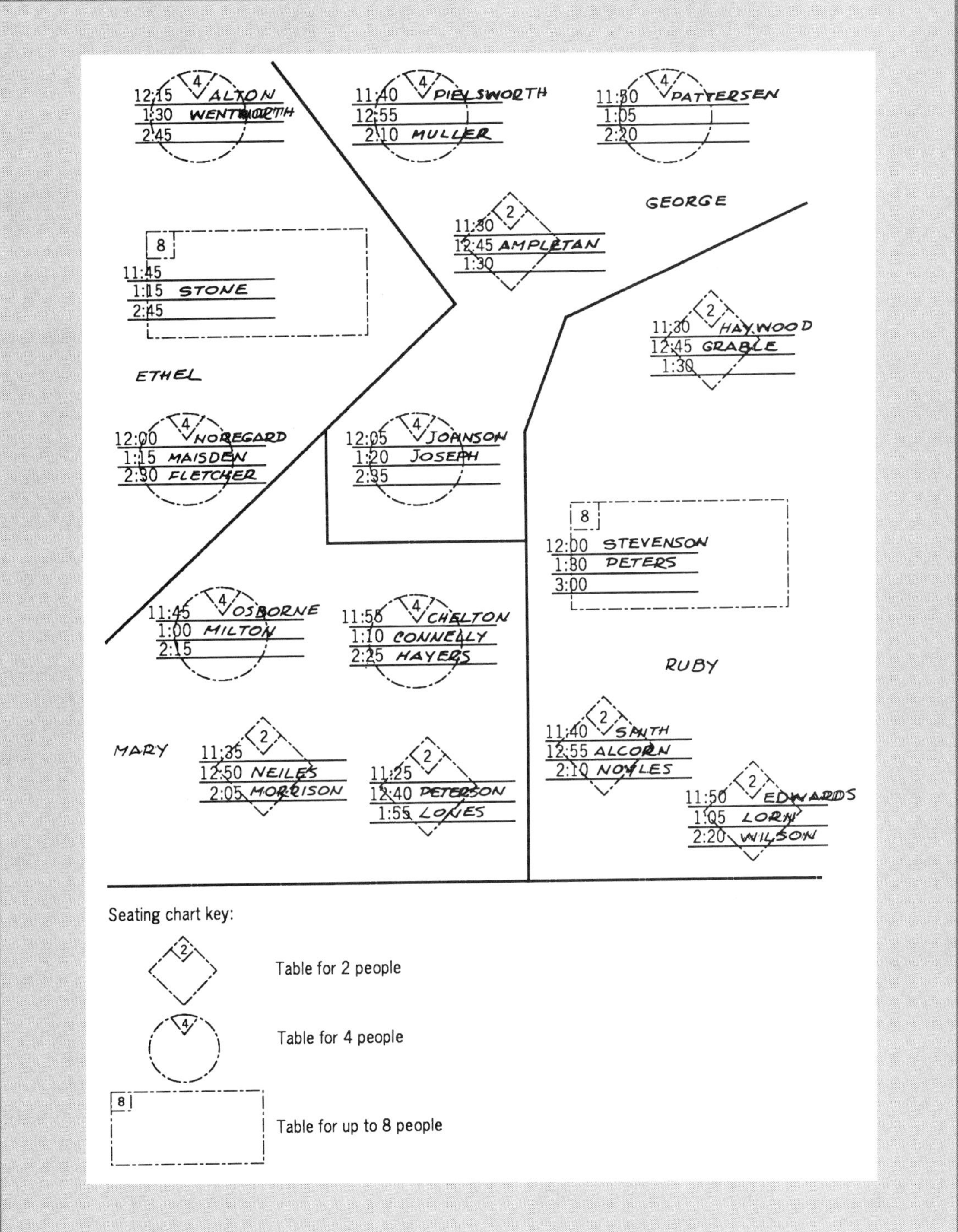
4
12:15 ALTON
1:30 WENTWORTH
2:45
4
11:40 PIELSWORTH
12:55
2:10 MULLER
4
11:50 PATTERSEN
1:05
2:20
GEORGE
2
11:30
12:45 AMPLETAN
1:30
8
11:45
1:15 STONE
2:45
2
11:30 HAYWOOD
12:45 GRABLE
1:30
ETHEL
4
12:00 NOREGARD
1:15 MAISDEN
2:30 FLETCHER
4
12:05 JOHNSON
1:20 JOSEPH
2:35
8
12:00 STEVENSON
1:30 PETERS
3:00
4
11:45 OSBORNE
1:00 MILTON
2:15
4
11:55 CHELTON
1:10 CONNELLY
2:25 HAYERS
RUBY
MARY
2
11:35
12:50 NEILES
2:05 MORRISON
2
11:25
12:40 PETERSON
1:55 LONES
2
11:40 SMITH
12:55 ALCORN
2:10 NOYLES
2
11:50 EDWARDS
1:05 LORN
2:20 WILSON
Seating chart key:
2
Table for 2 people
4
Table for 4 people
8
Table for up to 8 people

Operations that staff on a "chase demand" basis need flexible staffing in order to cope with high (and low) volume fluctuations. (Photo courtesy of Pizza Hut)

The staffing strategy of a chase demand operation uses unskilled employees to do jobs that are highly routinized and leaves little or no discretion to the workers. Pay is minimal; job pressures are severe (noise, heat, and hassle, for instance). Training time requirements in this kind of operation are at minimum and pay rates are low. Nevertheless, hiring costs are high because of labor turnover. The assumption is that customers will accept, or at least tolerate, the kind of service that results. They may do so because of relatively low prices—as in fast food—or because they accept crowds as one of the hazards of a particular recreation pastime—as with theme parks. The service they experience, that is, roughly matches their expectations.

Level Staffing. Patrons of upscale service operations such as fine-dining restaurants or luxury hotels demand highly expert service. Such service can only come from skilled employees. The training cost to replace such employees is high: In many markets, even a suitable trainee, much less a fully trained replacement, is very hard to find. Under these circumstances, major layoffs during slow periods are not a good idea. As a result, staffing in such operations aims to provide year-round employment for core staff members.

The strategic decisions of what kind of business we are in, at either of these two extremes—or somewhere on the spectrum in between—is a *marketing* strategy decision, though its implementation is usually carried out by operations. A wrong call on this decision in planning the operation can lead to (1) service nightmares—guests with higher expectations of service than the system in place can possibly manage or (2) cost nightmares—more staff and cost than an operation can carry at reasonable sales volume levels.

The Industrialization of Service

Leavitt has written of the "industrialization of service" in hospitality and other service industries. He likens McDonald's to "a machine" which uses unskilled labor to produce "a fairly sophisticated reliable product at great speed and low cost."[31] What is noticeable in the 20 years since the notion of the industrialization of service was first discussed is that it has been accepted in lower-priced operations, such as fast food or economy motels, but usually only in the back of the house in more upscale operations. When it comes to luxury, there seems to be—so far—no real substitute for personal service.

SUMMARY

The chapter begins with a discussion of the characteristics of service (Figure 7.1). The service product's complexity is seen in three overlapping systems in a service operation. Service quality has technical and interpersonal dimensions. Aspects of service that are important to consumers are identified, as are service quality gaps. A zero-defect goal in service operations helps an organization set high-quality goals, but the actual cost of a high-quality operation may be less than the cost of failure in terms of lost customers. Customers should be encouraged to complain by guarantees and other means, so efforts can be made to keep their business and to provide information on service failures.

Service-oriented operations management is dependent on internal marketing, careful selection, orientation, training, and motivation of employees. A key to motivation is a companywide service culture. One aspect of a service culture is empowerment of employees to solve guests' problems, but successful service also relies on carefully developed service procedures.

Since there is no inventory in services, capacity utilization is critical. Approaches to this problem include managing demand and inventorying demand. Two strategies are available for adjusting staffing to guest demand: chase demand and level staffing.

◆ *Key Words and Concepts*

Service
- By people
  - Devices
  - Systems

Intangibility
Service as experience
Characteristics of service
Service product

Three overlapping systems
- Service delivery system
- Hospitality operating system
- Communications system

Perceived quality

Quality dimensions
- Technical
- Interpersonal

Aspects of service
- Tangibles
- Reliability
- Responsiveness
- Assurance
- Empathy

Service quality gaps
- Misunderstanding
- Communication
- Performance
- Overpromising
- Expectations

Zero defects

Cost of quality

Complaints and quality control

Internal marketing

Corporate culture

Service culture

Empowerment

Operating procedures

Capacity management

Managing demand

Inventorying demand

Chase demand

Level staffing

◆ Discussion Questions

1. What are the characteristics of service? What impact do they have on operations?
2. What aspects of service are important to customers? What gaps occur in service?
3. What are the limitations of a zero-defect quality control program? What are its uses?
4. Is quality free? Why?
5. What is meant by "internal marketing"?
6. What corporate culture is appropriate to a service organization?

7. What is meant by "empowerment"? How does it relate to the role of procedure in service?

8. What is the impact of the absence of inventory from service? How is it managed?

9. What strategic issues are particular to the hospitality industry?

Chapter 8

When you have finished reading this chapter, you should be able to

1. Discuss the character of the hospitality product
2. Describe the main elements of the hospitality service offering
3. Explain the role of the environment of the service transaction
4. List the elements of the restaurant concept
5. Identify who the customers are for chain concepts
6. Discuss the role of branding in hospitality marketing
7. Explain the product life cycle and its limitations
8. Identify the responses to product maturity
9. Analyze the importance of new products in hospitality marketing

(Photo courtesy Steve Weinrebe/Picture Cube)

The Hospitality Product

THE HOSPITALITY MARKETING MIX

In the next six chapters, we will be discussing the elements of the **marketing mix,** product, price, place, and promotion. In this chapter, our focus will be on the *hospitality product,* but, before we begin a detailed discussion of any element of the mix, it is important to understand why the mix itself is a necessary concept. It is important to recognize that the marketing mix is, like a recipe, a blending of ingredients to achieve a designed effect.[1]

Some operators in hospitality see their product as *the* variable to concentrate on. Others feel that the key to success is to *get out and sell.* These points of view, the product and sales orientations examined in Chapter 1, are not so much wrong as only partly right. It *is* necessary to get the goods and services right; it *is* necessary to make the offer of the product known to consumers; but neither of these can stand alone and even both of them together are not enough. Price and the place of the offering must be considered, too. The key to understanding the concept of the marketing mix is the same as that for most other marketing concepts: the consumer. We recognize that the entire mix is necessary because all the variables in the mix are important to the guest.

Certainly, the quality of the product and service is a central consideration. Accordingly, in this chapter, we begin our discussion of the marketing mix with the mix element, product.

HOSPITALITY PRODUCT CONCEPTS

Some of the concepts related to hospitality products, like life cycle and the role of new products, are generally similar to the same ideas in product marketing. We will begin, however, with concepts which are more or less unique in their application to hospitality and to services.

Product as Intangible Experience

A customer purchases a frozen dinner, takes it home, prepares it according to directions, and eats it. If the power goes out and it takes forever to prepare the food—or if the meal is interrupted by noise from the neighbors or phone calls—or if the customer just does not feel at his or her best and has a headache, the last people the purchaser will blame for an unpleasant meal is the grocer or manufacturer. If the food does not taste the way one expects it to, one complains; otherwise, the product is okay. That is not the way it works in the service transaction, where goods and services are combined, as in hospitality.

What we have for sale in a restaurant is an *experience*—not just the physical goods that make up a meal—and we will be judged on the basis of *performance*, rather than just the food itself. Important aspects of the product are intangible. The manner and expertness of service, as well as the quality of the food, are essen-

The total experience of a service transaction clearly includes more than the tangible product and encompasses the entire experience. (Photo courtesy of Resorts International Casino Hotel, Atlantic City)

tial. Other experiential factors will enter into a guest's evaluation. The other guests, for instance, are a part of the dining experience. If a boisterous party at the next table ruins an evening's meal, the guest may be angry at that party. However, in declining to return to the restaurant, the guest is, in effect, holding the operation responsible for the behavior of its clientele. The other guests are, in a very real way, a part of the service experience offered by the restaurant, as is every other factor that enters into the guest's experience. This is one of the reasons that target marketing is so important in hospitality. Guests become part of the product.

All of the interactions between the guest and the hospitality system bear on the quality of the experience. For years, one of the major exasperations for hotel guests has been long checkout lines. Video checkout from the guest room has been adopted because it improves the hotel's performance in the customer's eyes. The hotel was not changed physically, but this service improvement enhances the product, the guest's experience.

Goods and Services. As we develop the idea of the product element of the marketing mix, it will be important to keep the complexity of the offering in mind. We will generally use the word *product* for the sake of simplicity, but as long as the subject is the hospitality industry, we should remember that the product is made up of both goods and services that are inextricably mixed.

THE SERVICE OFFERING

The hospitality service product is a bundle of features and benefits.[2] The **service offering** has three elements: (1) a *core* benefit, (2) essential *facilitating* services, and (3) competitive *supporting* services. Each of these is discussed and illustrated in the following sections.

The Core Benefit

The **core benefit** is the generic function the service product provides the guest. For the operation, it is "the reason for being in the market."[3] To illustrate, a hotel's core benefit is a night's lodging. For a resort, it would be both lodging and some combination of entertainment and relaxation. A restaurant's core benefit is the provision of nourishment and a social experience.

Facilitating Services

Facilitating services are services that are absolutely essential to the operation. If the facilitating services are lacking, delivering the core benefit is impossible. In a hotel, for instance, the absence of a front desk or housekeeping would make the hotel's operation impossible. In a restaurant, a kitchen provides a facilitating service; without it, the operation would shut down. For a resort, provision for entertainment would be an essential facilitating service—as would the basic hotel services referred to previously. While facilitating services are essential, they may also be arranged in such a way that they are also used to differentiate the operation from others. For instance, a restaurant might have not just a kitchen but one that provides exceptional cuisine—or perhaps an open kitchen with display cooking.

Often, facilitating *goods* are not just helpful, they are necessary. Clearly, in a restaurant, the provision of raw foodstuffs is essential. Linen and appropriate furnishings are necessary to a hotel. In most hotels, a parking lot for travelers arriving by car is essential. All of these, however, are goods and services that facilitate providing the core benefit the guest seeks.

Supporting Services

Supporting services are not essential to providing the core benefit, but they are essential to *marketing* the operation. Supporting services are used to differentiate the operation from its competitors. For instance, a restaurant is not a necessary component of a hotel, but the presence of a restaurant *is* used to differentiate one property from another. To take one company as an example, Marriott Hotels all

A short transaction time and speed of service are essential features of the drive-thru restaurant. (Photo courtesy of USA Cafes)

offer a variety of food service in each property, while the company's Fairfield Inns do not. Somewhere in between is Courtyard by Marriott, which offers limited food service. Food service (or its absence), then, differentiates each of the Marriott hotel products from each other—and from other lodging products.

One of the most powerful supporting services in lodging is reservation services. The convenience, courtesy, and availability of a hotel chain's reservation service is important in differentiating one chain from another. (Simply availability of a reservation service, however, may really no longer be a powerful differentiator since reservation services have become so common.)

Yet another supporting service offered by most hotel chains and an increasing number of restaurants is membership in a frequent-traveler or frequent-diner club. This service is intended to bind the customer to the operation. Supporting *goods* (membership cards, for instance) are required to maintain the frequency club services, as are other supporting goods such as reservation confirmation correspondence.

The basic service offering to the guest, then, includes a *core* benefit, that is, the generic product (lodging, nourishment). The core benefit, however, requires *facilitating* services to make delivery of the core benefit possible (front desks, housekeeping). *Supporting* services are necessary to the *marketing* of the product because they differentiate the product offering from those of competitors (for instance, a hotel or restaurant frequency club). Figure 8.1 shows the three levels of the basic service offering in a hotel.

PHYSICAL ENVIRONMENT: MANAGING THE EVIDENCE

If the service product is an experience, then, clearly, the environment in which it takes place is a key part of the product. In a special way, the physical setting is a *representation* of the experience on offer. The perception of the product is "shaped to a large extent by things that consumers can comprehend with their five senses—tangible things. But a service itself cannot be tangible, so reliance must be placed on *peripheral* cues."[4] Guests take an appearance of luxury or crisp efficiency in an operation as representing the reality they are experiencing. Anyone who has ever walked into a disorderly restaurant or a worn and frayed lobby will recall that the reverse is also true.

Our discussion will follow roughly the line of the guest's experience. We will look first at the appearance of the exterior, then at the interior.

First Impressions: The Exterior

A family is riding down a road. Everybody is hungry and ready to stop. A brightly lighted shopping area appears—signs and stores abound. Where will the family stop? In just a moment a decision is made. Perhaps it will be a bright red or blue Bob Evans Farms. Maybe the Golden Arch will beckon with its familiar mansard roof. Perhaps there is a strong vote for fish, and Long John Silver's nautical theme strikes the eye. The chances are that the visual appearance of the operation selected will be a strong element in the decision:

> If a physical plant has been designed successfully, the customer should be able to tell what is happening inside the building simply by viewing its exterior. The physical structure should reflect the intangible service elements that are part of the total offering. Trader Vic's, for example, looks like not only a restaurant but also a *Polynesian* restaurant. A hotel designed by John Portman is not only a hotel but also a specific type of environment.[5]

The building's exterior design and the landscaping of the exterior must be complementary to the image intended. Clean parking lots imply an efficient operation, perhaps even the cleanliness of the kitchen. Even trash receptacles are designed to blend with the building design.

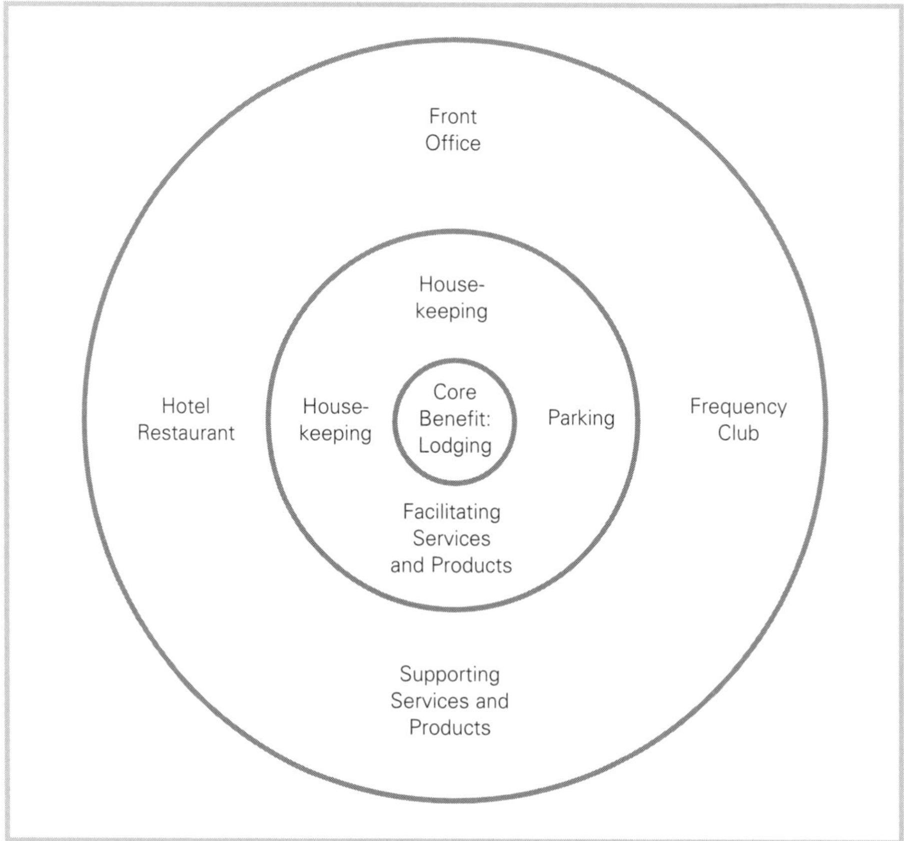

Figure 8.1 Three Elements of the Basic Service Offering in a Hotel

Source: Adapted from Christian Grönroos, *Service Management and Marketing* (Lexington, MA: Lexington Books, 1990).

The exterior appearance of the Hyatt Regency in Dallas tells us to expect an upscale, contemporary experience. (Photo courtesy of Hyatt Hotels)

Lasting Impressions: The Interior

The place in which service is rendered, what Lovelock calls the "physical support" or the "service delivery system," is, in many ways, a stage setting.[6] To create the desired impression—to give the desired cues about the nature of the service which is to take place there—the design of the interior sets out to achieve certain desired effects, called **atmospherics.** Atmospherics have been defined as

> the conscious designing of space to create certain effects on buyers. More specifically, atmospherics is the effort to design buying environments to produce specific emotional effects in the buyer that enhance his purchase probability.[7]

Atmospherics have three functions in marketing an environment.[8] First, atmospherics are an *attention-creating* mechanism. Color, noise, and motion can be used to make an operation stand out. Second, atmospherics send a *message* about the quality of experience offered. Finally, atmospherics impact the guest's feelings, creating a sense of excitement or serenity, for instance. Atmospherics go beyond mere visual appearance. In fact, they impact four of the five senses:

Sight. Designers create a visual effect with color, brightness or dimness, size, and shape.

Sound. The sound of water in a fountain or of soft (or brash or loud) music says a great deal to the guests about where they are and how they are supposed to feel.

Smell. No-smoking rooms offer an odor-free environment to the hotel guest. Some restaurants arrange to pipe the odor of baking bread into guest areas. Others exhaust the scent of barbeque at their entrance.

Touch. Luxurious linen napkins and tablecloths are the hallmark of the white-tablecloth restaurant. Extra-thick bath towels and deep-pile carpets support the feel of luxury in an elegant hotel.

Manipulating the Environment

The setting of the service interaction provides important cues that are (or should be) deliberately introduced by the operation's design.

Restaurant designer Regina S. Baraban suggests four different measurements of distance:[9]

Public distance	12 feet and beyond
Social distance	4 feet to 12 feet
Personal distance	18 inches to 4 feet
Intimate distance	contact to 18 inches

The way people perceive their surroundings falls into two main categories. *Distance receptors*—the eyes, the ears, and the nose—examine faraway objects and sensations. *Immediate receptors*—the skin, the membranes, and the muscles—are used to examine the world of touch. Table 8.1 shows how environmental cues may be manipulated to achieve particular environmental effects.

Hospitality operating experience clearly indicates the importance of keeping decor current. The time to obsolescence of a design in food service, according to one authority, has fallen from a 5- to 7-year life to a 3- to 5-year life.[10] In the hotel business, decor packages for franchisees are under constant review and are a major subject of negotiation at franchise renewal time. In food service operations, experience suggests that, although menu and service style are the foundation on which the rest of the restaurant is initially planned, decor changes have a heavy impact on revitalization programs. One authority even asserts that where menu and service have not been changed but where atmosphere has, through remodeling, there is a change in the guest's perception of the dining experience. By contrast, this expert reports, where food and service have been changed but where there has been no remodeling, little change is found in consumer perception.[11]

Supporting Cues. Decor is clearly the dominant theme in the message an operation's atmosphere sends the guest. Other measures to support that effort, however, include uniforms, tabletop appointments, and graphics. Uniforms that support a certain theme are used in many steakhouses; wraparound menus in the French style support a bistro that seeks to capture the feel of the Left Bank. Tabletops—from china and glassware to salt and pepper shakers to silverware may be used to support a starkly modern theme, for instance, or recap baroque luxury. Graphics integrate wall designs, directional signs, and the operation's logo to create a unified impact.

Table 8.1 Achieving Atmospheric Effects

Designed Effect	
To Create a Sense of Privacy	*To Encourage Turnover*
◆ Use high-backed booth instead of banquette to reduce visual distraction. ◆ Reduce lighting to limit visual contact. ◆ Use sound-absorbing material for acoustic control. ◆ Background music can help to diffuse other noise. ◆ Lower ceiling over perimeter seating. ◆ Use varying levels in large room to define smaller areas. ◆ Source of illumination between customers (candles) will draw them together. ◆ Muted, subtle colors create a restful effect.	◆ Use banquette or table seating. ◆ Permit high noise levels by using reflective surfaces. ◆ Use smooth, hard surfaces for seating and tabletops. ◆ Warmer room creates sense of crowding, encourages turnover. ◆ Brightly lit architectural surfaces tend to move people. ◆ Bold, primary colors encourage turnover.
To Direct Movement	*To Create Sense of Movement/Excitement*
◆ Use columns, pillars, spindles on top of booths or other vertical elements to exaggerate movement and encourage specific circulation patterns. ◆ Use different patterned floor covering for aisle areas.	◆ Use vertical element to break up appearance of large room that otherwise might look like a sea of tables and chairs. ◆ Raise light level. ◆ Permit higher sound level.

Source: Adapted from Regina S. Baraban, "The Psychology of Design," *Proceedings, Chain Operators Exchange, 1984* (Chicago: International Foodservice Manufacturers Association, 1984.

Atmospherics. Atmospherics provide a summary visual statement of the experience offered by the operation. Atmospherics offer the first visible—and often auditory and tactile—cues that the guest experiences. Atmospherics reinforce the experience of food and service (or rest and leisure in a hotel room) during the guest's visit, lingering as memories, often long after the menu items selected have been forgotten.

THE CONCEPT AS PRODUCT

We have referred to hospitality operations, such as KFC or Courtyard by Marriott, as "concepts." We need, now, to explore in more depth the meaning of concepts in the realm of hospitality and to look at **concepts as products.** A hospitality concept is the total offering to the guest. From the guest's point of view, the concept is an **experience,** but, from the point of view of the company deploying a concept, it is an **operating system.** This operating system and its benefits are offered to individual guests in order that they may purchase the service experience offered. In quite another way, the concept is offered to prospective franchisees as a business opportunity which they may gain the right to operate for their own benefit.

The atmospherics in a restaurant provide guests with important clues as to the kind of experience available there. (Photo courtesy L'Hotel, Toronto)

If the *franchise product* is to be successful, it must provide a successful business operating format, a substantial marketing program, and the field supervision necessary to success. One industry expert summarized the difference between an idea and a concept in this way:

> It's easy to have an idea. Ideas are cheap and plentiful. It's tough, however, to have an idea defined as a good idea by the marketplace. It's tough to conceive, to make and to market at a profit a product that people want . . . . Products, broadly conceived, are benefits offered to consumers.[12]

A concept, then, is one that can be sold to guests at a profit because its core benefit is of value to them.

The Restaurant Concept

A restaurant concept, as it is offered to the guest, can be broken into five elements:[13]

1. *Menu.* The range can be from a single item (ice cream or donuts) to a full selection.

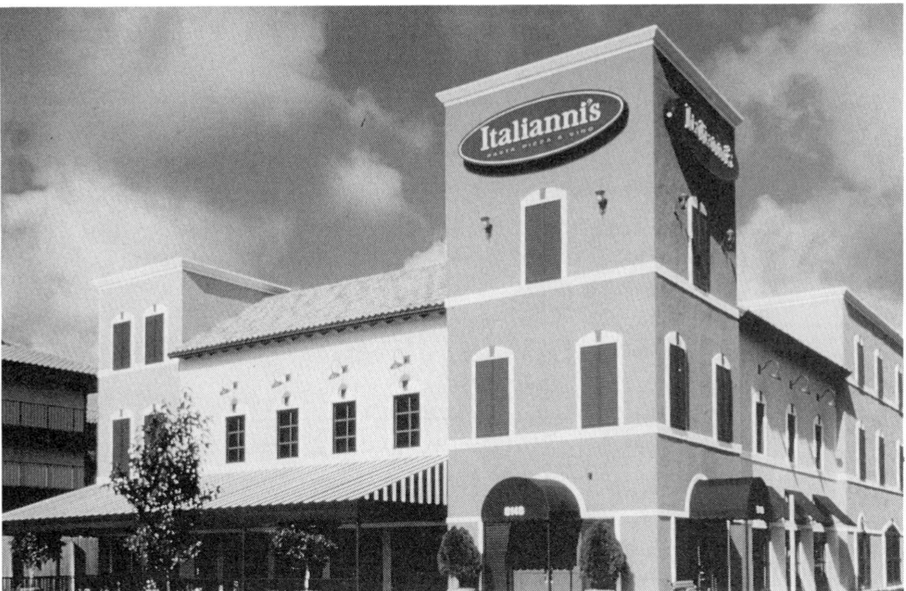

Italianni's, Carlson Hospitality's new restaurant concept, can function as a part of a motor hotel or, as in the picture above, as a freestanding restaurant. (Photo courtesy of Carlson Hospitality International)

2. *Food production strategy.* Some operations rely almost completely on prefabricated items (ready-to-cook hamburger patties, french fries, other convenience foods), whereas others prepare everything from scratch on the premises—and there is a wide variety of combinations in between these two extremes.
3. *Service.* A whole range of service choices—both formal and informal as well as self-service systems, are used.
4. *Pricing.* The range is from an ice cream cone for under a dollar to a dinner valued—with wines—in the hundreds of dollars.
5. *Decor/ambience/environment.* Such elements as decor, ambience, and environment include the clean, functional fast-food restaurant, as well as the plush luxury operation—and the casual but comfortable varieties in between. Some operations have a noisy roadhouse atmosphere that targets younger consumers, whereas others offer quiet dining designed to appeal to patrons in their middle or later years.

The range of possibilities in concept variability is suggested in Table 8.2. The opportunity to vary one or two elements gives operators a chance to tailor their unit to the particular needs of their target audience. The continuing success of new concepts attests to the guest's eagerness to try new specialty restaurants in their

Table 8.2 Concept Variability

Menu	+	Food Production Strategy	+	Service	+	Price	+	Decor/Ambience/ Environment	=	Concept
Basic hamburger	+	Portion and finish fabricated product	+	Self/drive-thru	+	Low	+	Basic	=	Wendy's
Upscale hamburger	+	Fabricated on premises (ground beef)	+	Self	+	Mid	+	Casual	=	Fuddrucker's
Gourmet pizza	+	On premises	+	Full	+	High	+	Chic	=	Spagos
Varied	+	From scratch—all fresh	+	Casual Waitress/waiter	+	High	+	Trendy	=	T.G.I. Friday's
Individualized; limited choice; changes frequently	+	From scratch on premises	+	Formal	+	Very high	+	Individualized, usually formal or ethnic	=	Haute Cuisine (Cote Basque)

Source: Adapted from Ronald N. Paul, "Emerging Concepts: Picking the Winners," *Proceedings, Chain Operators Exchange, 1984* (Chicago: International Foodservice Manufacturers Association, 1984).

search for diversity. Signature items, foods that are interesting and eye-catching, can play an important role in setting a concept apart from others. They give the operation a hook to hang its concept on. Food bars—breakfast, salad, and dessert bars—have been successfully introduced by operations as signature products that help the operation to develop an image of bounteousness, choice, and plenty.

The Restaurant Chain Concept

The restaurant chain has two kinds of customers. To the guest, the chain restaurant offers a menu implying a style of food and service that fits the concept, as well as reasonably consistent prices and generally a standardized decor. In brief, the guest is offered an experience but one that is available in many places and is consistent from place to place.

The restaurant chain's other customer group is made up of investors. Investors may wish to buy a franchise (or they may be involved as lenders or investors in the company's stock). Investors are interested in the company's operating system and its chances for financial success. The operating system elements that make up the chain's offering to investors are summarized in Table 8.3.

Hotel Concepts

Perhaps because the concepts in use in lodging are fewer in number and less varied than in the restaurant business, the notion of concept, while important, has not

In fine dining establishments, service is elaborate and highly expert.

Table 8.3 Operating System Elements That Make Up a Chain

System Elements	Includes
Franchise store policy	Number of units, geographic distribution, density; ability and willingness of present franchise owners to accept change and to expand number of units and take on new areas.
Company-oriented policy	Number, distribution, and density of units; quality and depth of personnel; ability to expand profitably.
Distribution and supply	Uniformity provided by quality; acceptability of food costs relative to prices; control systems for unit operations; ability to expand logistical support base.
Human resource development training	Training and development and systems for personnel at all levels (i.e., hourly, supervisory, management), including upgrading and retraining of current employees.
Real estate ownership policy	Own and lease real estate to franchise versus franchisee ownership of real estate.

Source: Adapted from *George D. Rice,* "The Art of Segmentation," *Proceedings, Chain Operators Exchange, 1983* (Chicago: International Foodservice Manufacturers Association, 1983).

Basic full-service properties are being challenged by limited-service properties such as this Holiday Inn Express. (Photo courtesy Holiday Inn Worldwide)

taken as firm a foothold in lodging as in food service. Lodging concepts can be divided into two main groups, full service and limited service. Each of these are further divided by price and service levels. The mainstay concept for many years was the *basic full-service property.* This kind of property, however, has seen its costs escalate until its rates, in most locations, no longer represent a bargain. Full-service properties positioned above this level include an upscale segment occupied by chains such as Hilton Hotels, Marriott Hotels, and Sheraton Hotels, as well as a deluxe segment which includes the Four Seasons and the Ritz-Carlton.

The basic full-service property is gradually being displaced by *limited-service* concepts that offer little or no food service and few of the traditional hotel services such as a bell staff. Fairfield Inns and Courtyard by Marriott, as well as Hampton Inns, are well-known brands in this group. Holiday Inn, which until recently has typified the waning basic full-service hotel, has developed its own limited service concept, Holiday Inn Express. Holiday Inn is also developing more highly targeted subbrands in the midmarket and has established a separate identify for its more upscale Crowne Plaza brand. The basic full-service property, however, remains a mainstay in many small to midsized cities, where it continues to be the premier property. *All-suite* properties are offered at all levels of price and service.[14]

BRANDING

Branding is seen as a *product* characteristic because the brand is associated in the consumer's mind with the product it represents. While a brand image often results,

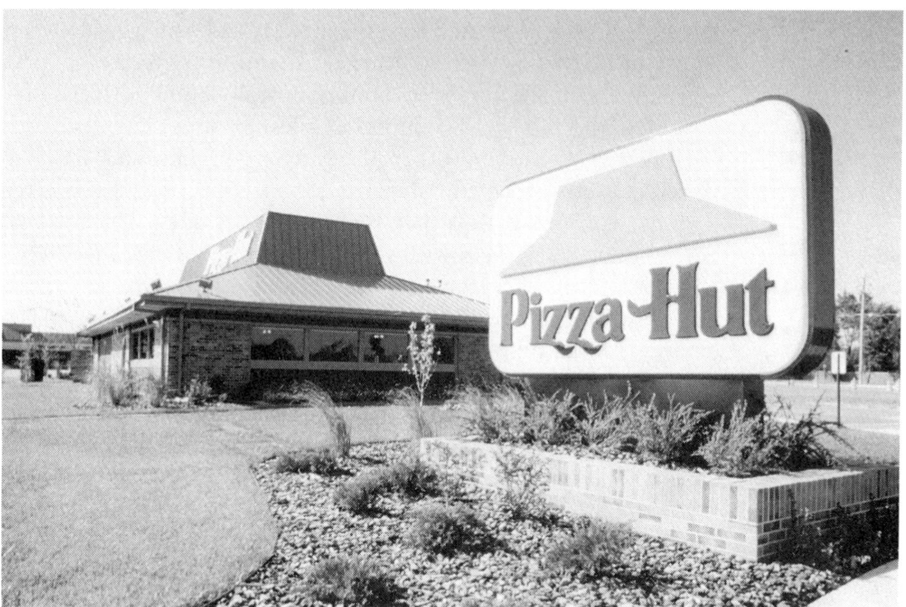

Brands offer a means of identifying an operation to the guest. Here a pizza restaurant's image is enhanced with the Pizza Hut brand. (Photo courtesy Pizza Hut)

in part, from advertising, ultimately, it is the consumer's experience with the product that determines the brand's success. While branding serves substantially the same purpose in hospitality as in other kinds of marketing, the role and importance of branding is undergoing significant changes and achieving a new prominence in hospitality.

Branding[15] uses words, symbols, or designs, or some combination of these, to identify an operation in the consumer's mind. Brands have played a significant role in the hospitality industry since shortly after the turn of the century, when hotel operators like Statler and Ritz began to associate a number of hotels in different cities with their brand names. In food service, Howard Johnsons and Stouffers are two of the earliest brand names. Since the 1950s, branded chains have played a growing role in both lodging and food service. Today, the use of brand names is in a period of exploding growth again. We will discuss some of the recent developments in the use of branding in the hospitality industry in a moment, but, first, we should consider the major functions of branding.

Brands offer operators a way of identifying their operation to guests. If the operation achieves superior performance, that identity helps to "enhance the image" and "raise the profile" of the operation.[16] The brand image helps to protect the operation from competition, particularly if it is supported by a strong marketing communications program. Food service brands, such as McDonald's, KFC, and Pizza Hut, are among the best known brand names not only in North America but in the world.

Brands can be used to segment markets. We have already alluded to Marriott's use of branding. With its Fairfield brand, it is targeting a price-sensitive segment. With Courtyard, it reaches a more upscale segment that is prepared to pay for limited services beyond a superior guest room. Marriott Hotels serve travelers in downtown areas and other places where higher rates are charged and fuller hotel services are expected. Marriott targets the long-stay market with its Residence Inns. Thus, its brands span most segments of the lodging market.

Brands also help with the introduction of new products. When Holiday Inns decided to enter the limited-service lodging market, the name Holiday Inn Express for its "new" product (often an older property that had been converted) drew on the reputation built up over many years in the Holiday Inns name.

Brand equity is the value that gradually builds up in a brand. One useful way of thinking of brand equity is as a reward that accrues over time for satisfying customers. We should note, though, that brand equity can be built, in part, by superior advertising and other marketing communications, although not in the absence of good operating performance. One measure of brand equity is the premium over the book value of its physical assets a brand such as Holiday Inns will bring when it is sold. Another measure is the recognition the brand has from consumers and the market power that confers on the operation. Brand equity, as we just noted, was part of the advantage that Holiday Inns had when it launched Holiday Inn Express. Figure 8.2 summarizes the advantages of branding we have discussed. Field Practice Note 8.1 illustrates the value that brand names can achieve.

Brand loyalty is a desired goal of branding. On a basic level, branding achieves consumer recognition. Prior to achieving brand recognition, the consumer would not know such an operation existed. Building on recognition, with successful operations and continued promotion, a brand can achieve consumer preference. Preference suggests that the consumer, given a choice, will choose the preferred brand over one that is not as familiar. Probably, however, guests will not go very far out of their way if an acceptable alterative or a less expensive one is available more conveniently. The highest level of brand loyalty is consumer demand where consumers will insist on a particular brand and will make a significant effort to follow that purchase decision and even pay a premium price.[17]

Brand loyalty relates, too, to the type of purchase the consumer makes. A brand with which consumers are familiar has an advantage in *convenience-oriented*

Identity
Enhanced Image
Protection from Competition
Facilitates Market Segmentation
Eases Introduction of New Products

Over Time, Builds Brand Equity and Brand Loyalty

Figure 8.2 Advantages of Branding

decisions—the purchase of a snack or a quick lunch in a food court, for instance. A customer on a date, however, might well be *a shopper,* one who would make some investigation to find a preferred location. An operation which had achieved consumer preference would be at an advantage in this decision. For a very special occasion, however, the consumer's buying decision is likely to seek a *specialty* operation and, in this case, there might well be a clear insistence for a *particular* restaurant.[18] It would be rare for a QSR to achieve *consumer demand* (outside of younger customers). A more viable goal for a new operation would be recognition and for a more established operation, consumer preference. Upscale operations, on the other hand, strive for consumer demand in their clientele.

Branding and Product Lines

Product lines are groups of related products offered by a company. In a full-service restaurant, it is possible to speak of the product as a whole: The experience of dining and the menu offerings can be considered together. In QSRs, however, it is useful to think of the menu as a *product line.* While not all food products on a QSR menu are given the distinction of their own brand name, the practice of item subbranding is becoming increasingly common. Indeed, table service restaurants are also identifying house specialties and according them the treatment of a separate subbrand.

Umbrella Brands and Subbranding.[19] Most QSRs have developed brand names for their feature products—names which have become household terms such as Big Mac and Whopper. As competition heats up, companies even go beyond their own proprietary brand names to incorporate other company's branded items on their menus to achieve what Blumenthal calls "category credibility":

> What credibility truly does a product called "Burger King Ice Cream" have? Häagen-Dazs sub-branded on the menu board, says it all—and clearly establishes category credibility. Burger King, therefore, is the "umbrella brand" that carries sub-brands (which may include such sub-brands as its own signature product, "The Whopper").[20]

Ingredient Branding. The announcement of the use of other company's branded products as ingredients is becoming increasingly common and gives us some insight into the power of branding to establish an image of quality and distinctness:

> Manufacturer's brands are starting to appear on menus. Hyatt Hotels room service menu depicts brands and logos such as Hillshire Farm, Oscar Meyer and Louis Real . . . . Olive Garden announces it serves Ocean Spray and Welchs juices. Bennigans' menu features Grey Poupon, IBC Root Beer, Coco Lopez, Sargenot, Heinz, A1 Sauce and so forth.[21]

Cobranding. This practice (also called colocation and discussed further in a later chapter) involves locating two noncompeting brands in one operation. Wendy's,

Field Practice Note 8.1

What's in a Name? Brand Equity

Consumer recognition confers value on established brands, as HFS, Inc., has amply demonstrated. *The Wall Street Journal* put it this way:

> In a celebrity conscious world, brand names, even aging ones, still have cachet and one can do very well exploiting consumers' fondness for the familiar.[1]

HFS began its meteoric rise to the largest hotel franchising group in 1990 when its president, Henry Silverman, acquired the franchising rights to Ramada and Howard Johnson. In 1992, HFS purchased a then bankrupt Day's Inns. In the same year, the company went public, with its stock trading on the New York Stock Exchange. Since that time, as the accompanying figure makes clear, HFS has acquired a number of additional hotel brands and has developed one new brand, Wingate Inns. In 1994, the company began acquiring franchising companies in other business lines. It presently owns three real estate franchise companies and, as this note is written, is in the final stages of acquiring Avis, the car rental company.

HFS defines its customers as its franchisees and acts as their brand manager, handling marketing, reservation services, and quality maintenance.

Silverman sees synergy between his mix of brands. As the world's largest hotel franchisor, HFS can achieve substantial purchasing economies to its franchisees. According to the *Wall Street Journal,* one of the reasons Silverman was interested in Avis was because of its reservations network. Already cross-marketing arrangements between lodging brands and real estate brands see Century 21 realtors with discount cards for HFS hotels while Ramada guest folios tout the advantages of using Century 21.

With a stable of "household names," HFS is reportedly exploring ways to continue its acquisition of franchising companies.

[1]Wall Street Journal, June 4, 1996, pp. A1 and A8.

for instance, and Tim Horton's (a Canadian donut chain) shared premises, particularly on expressways in Canada, for many years before Wendy's finally bought the Tim Horton chain, with the purpose of expanding into more "colocations." In **cobranding,** the two brands are often in quite different fields of retailing. For instance, it is becoming increasingly common for gasoline and food service companies to share a site. Sometimes these two, food service and gasoline, combine with a third retail operation, a convenience store.

In lodging, operators are increasingly willing to locate national brand name restaurants on their premises. Holiday Inns, for instance, is working with a broad range of restaurant companies, including family restaurants such as Denny's,

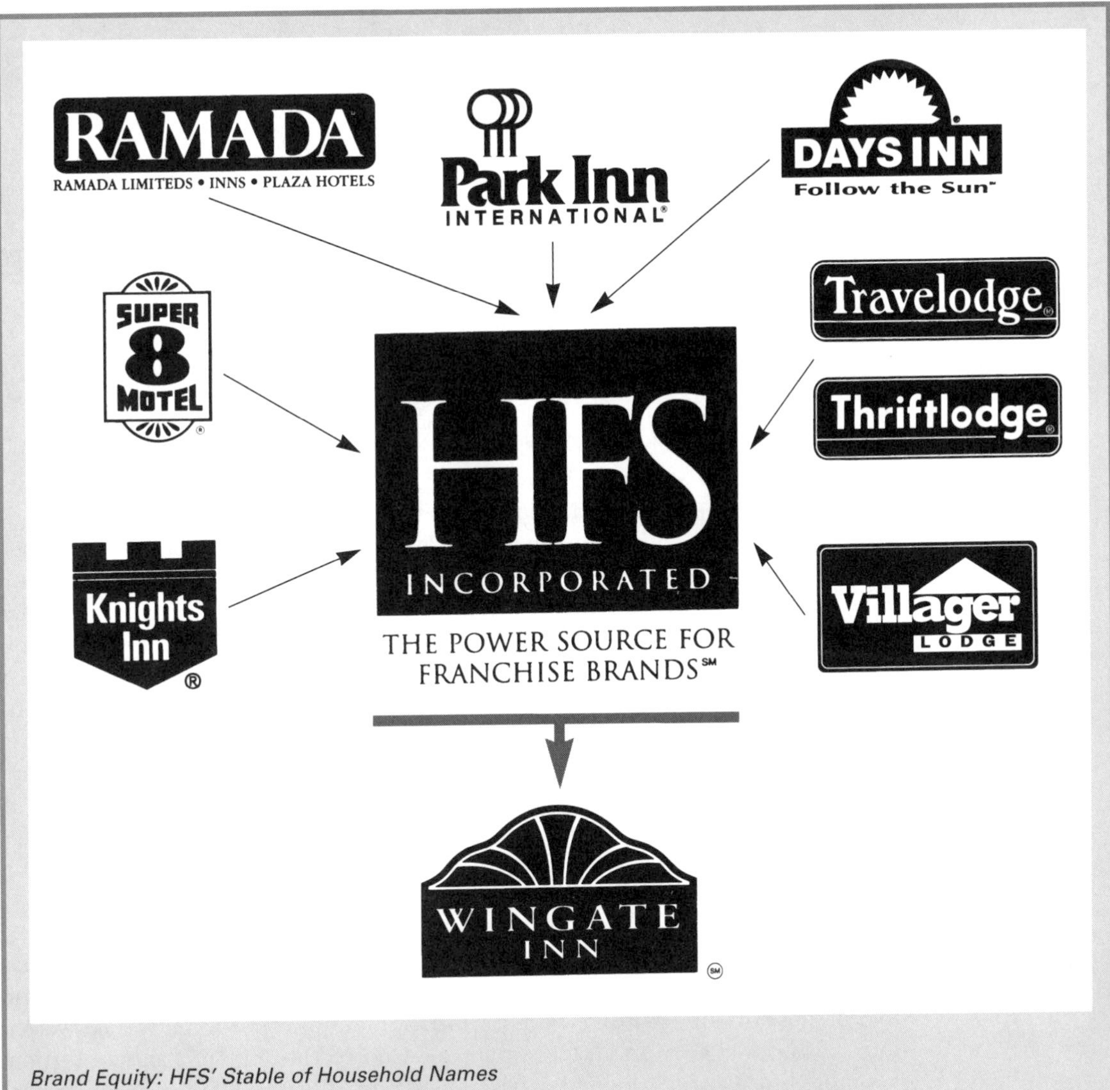

Brand Equity: HFS' Stable of Household Names

Holiday Inn uses branding to segment markets. This Holiday Inn Sunspree Resort targets vacationers. (Photo Courtesy Holiday Inn Worldwide)

Perkins, Country Kitchen, as well as casual dining chains like Bennigans, Steak and Ale, and Montana Steak Co.[22]

Carlson Companies has developed travel company brands that are deliberately planned to fit well with each other—and with the products of other companies. Country Kitchen, for instance, is a family restaurant that can serve as a coffee shop in a Radisson Hotel or as a freestanding restaurant on the same site with Radisson's Country Inns—or the limited-service products of other lodging companies. Carlson, in fact, is opening a triple-branded hotel–restaurant complex where the lodging component is a Country Suites by Carlson. The hotel will be served by two of Carlson's noncompeting restaurant concepts, Italiani's and Country Kitchen.[23] Field Practice Note 8.2 profiles the new triple-branded operation.

The purpose of cobranding (colocating) is to derive synergy from the presence of the two or more concepts. Each draws some clientele of its own and each can serve the needs of the guests patronizing the other operation.

Multiple Branding. In the overbuilt hotel industry, operators have found that a larger hotel can achieve higher occupancies in some markets by dividing itself into two brands. In Fort Worth, Texas, for instance, a 300-room hotel was converted into a 201-room Clarion Hotel (an upscale Choice Hotel brand) and a 99-room Comfort Inn (Choice's limited-service brand). In Houston, a portion of a former Holiday Inn was converted to a full-service Days Inn, while its six-story tower became an 89-room Hampton Inn.[24]

Field Practice Note 8.2 Cobranding Prototype: Lodging and Food Service

Carlson Hospitality Worldwide has unveiled a new hospitality complex near its international headquarters in Plymouth, Minnesota, which features three complementary branded operations. The new unit is a prototype intended to showcase three Carlson Hospitality concepts to attract potential investors from around the world. The three units are a Country Inn and Suites, a Country Kitchen restaurant, and Italianni's, an Italian restaurant concept which Carlson is now expanding rapidly. The restaurants are noncompetitive with one another and, in fact, offer significant synergies with the inn.

Country Inns and Suites is an upper economy chain presently operating in North America but with commitments to open in Latin America, Malaysia, India, and Europe. The Plymouth operation is a three-story structure with 67 guest rooms, including 30 suites. This smaller-than-average property offers an informal setting and one well suited to smaller cities. Country Inns and Suites target both business and leisure travelers and are often located near business parks and local attractions. Over 75 Country Inns and Suites are presently in operation, achieving occupancies in excess of 75 percent, according to the company.

Country Kitchen, a full-service family restaurant, presently operates over 250 units in the United States, Canada, Puerto Rico, and Indonesia. The chain's menu offers nearly 100 popularly priced selections and features full breakfast, lunch, and dinner menus. Menu offerings include items such as chicken, meatloaf, pasta, quesadillas, beef and chicken stir-fries, and specialty desserts, as well as beer and wine. Country Kitchen, when located with a Country Inn and Suites, offers room service to hotel guests.

Italianni's, a concept developed on the basis of two years of market research by another Carlson company, T.G.I. Friday's, is a 230-seat Italian dinner house which features "shared dining"—that is, platters which are passed at the table by the guests. Average checks are $10 at lunch and $14 at dinner. The operation is open for lunch and dinner. Italianni's offers such Italian specialties as cannelloni, grilled chicken fettuccine, shrimp linguini, rigatoni, lasagna, and pizza, as well as a full range of alcoholic beverages. Clearly targeting a traveling family market, Italianni's offers kids the opportunity to craft their own pizza, helping themselves to pizza sauce, cheese, and toppings before handing it to the chef to be baked.

Carlson is not new to cobranding. The company's Radisson Hotels are a good fit with its T.G.I. Friday's restaurants and Country Kitchen can serve as a coffee shop operation in a Radisson Hotel. Carlson Hospitality's other brands include Front Row Sports Grill restaurants and Radisson Seven Seas Cruises. Other affiliated Carlson companies are the Carlson Travel Group and the Carlson Marketing Group.

Source: Carlson Hospitality Worldwide.

Family Brands and Line Extensions. **Family brands,** in manufactured goods, are brands that are used on several products by one company. Sony, for instance, sells many different electronic products under its Sony brand. A **line extension** relates to developing a related product for a somewhat different market. Generally, line extensions try to go up market or down market. In hospitality, line extensions and family branding are often related to one another.

Holiday Inns, for instance, operates the several related lodging products, most of which feature the "family" name, Holiday Inn. Holiday Inns is using these extensions of its product line to reach different market segments. The Sunspree Inns target vacationers, while the Holiday Inn Select targets executives and other business travelers with amenities such as voice mail, data ports, coffee makers, irons and ironing boards, hair dryers, and special work areas in the room.[25] Holiday Inn Express is a limited-service product targeting rate-sensitive travelers. Holiday Inns and Suites are properties that will have suites as 10 percent of their room inventory.[26]

These are either horizontal or downward line extensions from the original Holiday Inns brand. The difficulty of moving *up market* with a line extension is suggested by Holiday Inns' experience with Crowne Plaza. Crowne Plaza finally removed the "Holiday Inn" from its name. According to one authority:

> Efforts to position the Crowne Plaza brand as upscale have been hampered because "having Holiday Inn on it pulled it down." The independent identity could boost Crowne Plaza's market share, allowing for a rate increase.[27]

Another company, Ramada, uses the Ramada family brand as its original brand, Ramada Inns, as well as on its line extensions, Ramada Plaza Hotels and Ramada Limited. As we noted earlier, Marriott associates its lodging brands by adding the Marriott name to Fairfield Inns, Courtyard by Marriott, and Residence Inns. Similarly, Carlson Companies adds "by Carlson" to all individual brands. The advantages of family branding are that each product can benefit from the promotion mounted by all the others and, to a lesser degree, by the company's overall successful operations.

Individual Brands. One of the most successful companies in food service, PepsiCo, chooses to operate its concepts under unique brands, principally KFC, Pizza Hut, and Taco Bell. Note that each of these products is quite different from the other. KFC and Taco Bell are the leaders in their respective—and quite different—QSR segments, while Pizza Hut is principally a limited-menu table service chain. Another concept operating under PepsiCo ownership, Hot'n Now, is a double drive-thru. The lack of a strong relationship—from the consumer's point of view—between these concepts is probably one reason for the separate brand strategy. Another is to encourage competition within the company between subsidiaries.[28]

While many lodging companies have opted for multiple segmented brands, one of the largest and most successful hotel groups, Best Western, uses its single brand to cover a wide variety of properties and service levels. After Holiday Inns,

Best Western is the most well-recognized lodging brand in North America and achieves an annual renewal rate from its member properties in excess of 99 percent. The Best Western view on multiple brands, as expressed by one of its executives, is that

> there is far too much brand clutter in the market place. If you gave a test to most people in the industry, they couldn't tell you what each of the brands and sub-brands offers and how they are distinguished from each other. I truly believe the traveling public is even more confused.[29]

Since both segmenting and use of a single brand seems to be quite successful, trying to answer the question of "Who is right?" is probably a waste of time. Rather, we can conclude that a number of different strategies may be successful, depending on the circumstances and how the strategies are executed.

Brand Bundling. The first brand bundlers were shopping centers in their food courts. While PepsiCo maintains the distinct identity of its food service brands, it has begun to associate them with one another in freestanding buildings. As indicated in our earlier discussion of cobranding, other companies that do not have the same ownership have begun to "bundle" brands that are noncompetitive, sharing a freestanding building.

Brands in Institutional Food Service

Branding has gone from being an oddity to being commonplace in institutional food service, where food courts often replace more traditional cafeteria lines and scramble systems. Aramark has probably gone further with the development of its *proprietary brands* than any other contract company. A proprietary brand has the major advantage of requiring neither franchise royalty payment nor national advertising assessment. Another strategy for holding down payments to franchisors is to invite local operators or new concepts to "try out" at one of Aramark's accounts. In a food court setting, where volume is largely provided from the surrounding environment, lesser-known brands have a better chance of thriving than in freestanding locations. In a food court in Houston, Aramark used four of its own brands, four units operated by a local operating group, and Earl Campbell's Sausage House, the first unit opened by a former football player. (Nevertheless, Aramark did also make room for another four *national* brands.[30])

Branding has become so popular on college campuses that the National Association of College and University Food Service (NACUFS) has developed a series of house brands. These concepts come complete with logos, menus, and promotional materials, as well as information manuals and equipment.[31] Branding is common not only on college campuses but increasingly in high schools. In Richmond, Virginia, the school system operates as a franchisee of Chic-fil-a and Taco Bell.[32]

Health care is certainly no exception to the trend toward branding. The University of Kansas Medical Center is using manufacturers' brands—Weight

Contract food service companies have created their own brands, such as the "Deli Corner," one of ARASERVE's company brands.

Watchers and Healthy Choice—as entrees on its cafeteria line. These branded products sell better than the hospital's own "healthy" entrees! Like many other hospitals, this medical center offers other franchised products. Pizza Hut pizza is delivered to the hospital and a local franchisee also operates a Taco Bell cart in the vending area.[33]

The Power of Branding

The hospitality industry is a highly fragmented, competitive industry. While independents are still important, chains with deep pockets for heavy advertising expenditures play a major role in almost all sectors of the industry. In this competitive free-for-all, branding offers a means of establishing a differentiated identity and a basis for attempting to rally consumer loyalty. The exploding and varied uses of branding tactics summarized in Table 8.4 suggests that hospitality marketers find branding a favored weapon in their struggle for market power. (See Field Practice Note 8.3.)

Brands are a major power in every part of the economy, but, perhaps, one reason they are especially powerful in hospitality is the *intangible* nature of the hospitality product. The brand—whether McDonald's or the Ritz—helps to identify

Table 8.4 Branding Tactics in Use in the Hospitality Industry

Umbrellas and subbrands	Use of individual item brand names by restaurant on menu items
Cobranding	Operating two noncompetitive brands on the same premises
Ingredient branding	Use of manufacturer's brand name for ingredients on restaurant menus
Multiple branding (lodging)	Operating a hotel property under two brand names
Family branding	Pairing the "family name" with different chain brands
Individual branding	Maintaining completely unique identities for a company's brand
Brand bundling	Locating several brands in a freestanding unit or a food court

the operation and make concrete the idea of the particular hospitality offering. It helps operators to stand out from competing products.

PRODUCT LIFE CYCLE

Over the life of a product, the consumer's view of that product may and usually does change. What was once cutting edge becomes something everybody is doing and then, conceivably, something nobody wants to be caught dead doing. Things go into and out of fashion. The idea of a life cycle for products captures this notion of fashion. The **product life cycle** concept, in fact, had its origins in fashion goods.

The style cycle is illustrated in Figure 8.3. In the early days of a new style, only a few fearless innovators are likely to try it. As the product begins to take hold in the growth stage, it spreads to a wider fashion-conscious group, the early

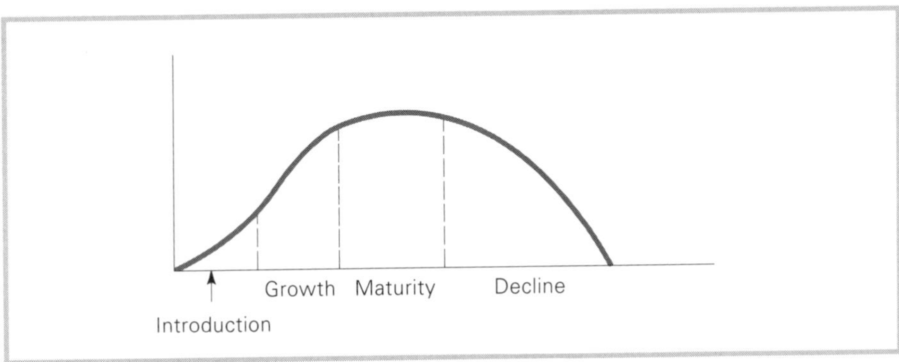

Figure 8.3 The Style Cycle

Field Practice Note 8.3

Birth of a New Brand

The first new construction-only hotel brand in over 10 years, Wingate Inns, got its start as a result of the interest expressed by franchisees of HFS, Inc., in a "new build," midpriced, limited service brand. Rising occupancies and average rates in the hotel business, nationally, accelerated the development of this new brand, and the first three new Wingate Inns opened less than 18 months after HFS's announcement of the new brand.

Market research, which consisted principally of focus groups and individual interviews, was aimed at three target audiences: frequent business travelers who had experience in competitive properties (principally Courtyard by Marriott and Hampton Inns), francisees of other HFS brands, and developers. The result was a hotel that was designed to please those who would use the hotel and those who would need to finance and build them.

Business travelers, HFS learned, spend 2–5 hours a day working in their hotel room. Initially, five room designs were considered, but traveler focus groups rejected some as too office-like and others as not suitable for work. The final balance separates working and leisure areas with an arch. For work, a large, well-lighted desk and a swivel executive chair are provided. Each room has a two-line desk phone with dataport, speaker, conference, and voice mail capabilities, as well as a cordless phone, permitting the guest to transmit data from his or her computer while talking on the phone. Each hotel has a board room and two small meeting rooms, and provides 24-hour access to a business center. Free local calls and no surcharges on long-distance calls eliminate a frequent business traveler's complaint.

Business travelers want comfort, and the Inns need to attract leisure travelers as well. Accordingly, guest room amenities include a recliner chair—or one with an ottoman—as well as a 25-inch television with remote control, an alarm clock radio, and a coffeemaker. Guest rooms are 12 feet by 28 feet, approximately 17 percent larger than average. Each hotel offers complimentary breakfast but no other food service, exercise facilities, and a hot tub. Traveling families are not charged for their children.

Wingate prides itself on its technology. The hotel's computer has four terminals: one for the reservations office, two on the front desk, and one that permits automated guest check-in without assistance. At either self check-in or front desk, the swipe of a credit card will retrieve the reservation, verify

adopters. At the peak of sales, the product has entered the mass market and is said to be mature. During the introduction stage, profits are limited or there may be losses because high promotional costs associated with the start-up are necessary. Profit growth is strong during the growth stage but levels off and begins to decline during the maturity stage.

It may seem surprising that profits begin to decline when sales are at their

credit, assign the room, and produce an electronic guest room key—all in roughly 15 seconds. The speed of transaction and availability of self-service strike at another common business traveler complaint, long lines at check-out and check-in.

Developers and potential franchisees, finally, are pleased with the simplicity of design, which features a rectangular building of three or four stories, heightening the efficiency of land use. Straight building lines help control construction costs.

HFS provides a $250,000 development grant and is committed to spending another $100,000 on marketing in each new Inn's market area. A total of $27 million is committed for marketing in the brand's first five years.

Source: "The Making of a Midmarket Hotel Company," *Lodging Hospitality,* September 1995; Kathleen Cassidy, "Inside Wingate," *Lodging,* November 1995; Barbara A. Worcester, "Wingate: A Tech-Based Brand," *Hotel and Motel Management,* February 19, 1996; I would also like to acknowledge the help of Ms. Janet Jarosz of Wingate in the development of this Note.

peak—until we recall that this is a *product* life cycle, not a company brand name history. *Industry* sales peak and profits decline because many firms have entered the competition in the product area by this stage. With more firms in the market, competition drives price levels down, reducing profit margins severely. Figure 8.4 implies that, once the sales peak is reached, the product is on its way to the bargain basement and extinction.

What was once cutting edge becomes more commonplace and, in time, passes out of style. One example of this in food service is the product Blackened Redfish. The fish is rubbed with spices and then seared very rapidly over a hot fire. The result is a product that is cooked on the inside but that has a spicy, crisp, blackened crust on the outside. When blackened redfish was introduced to a wider market outside Louisiana's Cajun community by Paul Prudhomme, it was quickly added to the menus of leading upscale restaurants as something new. In time, however, mass-market dinner house chains picked up blackened redfish, too. As a result, it became too common for most cutting-edge restaurants that seek to set style. While still offered at some operations, it is no longer as widely popular, nor is it seen as trendsetting. It has, in fact, largely gone out of style.

The restaurant business is subject to cycles in consumer preference, in large part, because "most restaurant chains are built around the exploitation of a simple product or concept."[34] While restaurants experience cycles in consumer acceptance, the experience of McDonald's, Burger King, and Pizza Hut, to name a few long-lasting concepts—is that most successful concepts do not die out but, rather, regenerate themselves as shown in Figure 8.4. When customer counts start to fall, companies review their concept and spice it up with a thorough remodeling or the introduction of new products—or both.

Problems with the Theory of Product Life Cycles

Critics suggest that, for *many* products there is no clear life cycle pattern. Moreover, the life cycle model is not a reliable predictor, even for those products

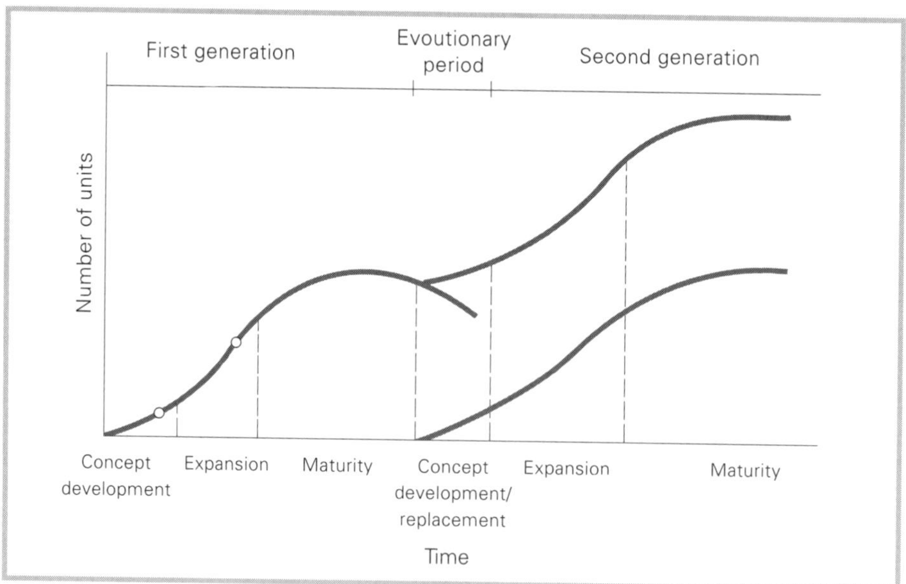

Figure 8.4 Restaurant Concept Life Cycle

Source: Adapted from Technomic Consultants.

subject to fashion's dictates. It is often difficult to judge, with any accuracy, which stage of the life cycle a product is in. "The four major phases," moreover, shown in Figure 8.4, "don't divide themselves in clean cut compartments."[35]

Life Cycle in Lodging? Hotels are assets with a long economic life, commonly 30 or 40 years or more. With the enormous amount of capital required to build them, it is difficult for a style life cycle to affect the overall property. Nevertheless, fashions in decor do affect hotel *restaurants,* in much the same way they do any other restaurant. Moreover, public spaces (lobbies, banquet rooms, and the like) are also subject to aging in appearance. As a result, hotels periodically require major refurbishing.

Another problem the life cycle theory poses is the danger that it will be used as an excuse, that it will become a self-fulfilling prophecy. Perhaps the greatest value in the notion of the life cycle is that it warns us of the dangers of an aging product and of the importance of dealing with maturity.

Responses to Maturity

The characteristics of a mature market are that it is one populated by established companies that are expert operators and marketers with substantial financial resources. Fast food is a good example of a mature industry, one in which corporate giants face off against each other in a mass market.

The responses which maturity dictates to marketers in a mature market are repositioning against other segments, altering some or all of the marketing mix, or a combination of both.

Repositioning. Repositioning refers to finding new markets or market segments. An example we might use is a restaurant whose appeal is to singles and couples aged 25 to 34 without children—such as a roadhouse operation. That age segment of the market is numerically in decline and will be until sometime after the year 2000. This is a time in life, too, when people marry and begin to have children and the roadhouse format might not be judged to be particularly child-friendly.

A repositioning, for such a firm, could involve seeking to broaden its appeal to its present age segment (25- to 34-year-olds) to include families *with* children. As a second step, it could seek ways to appeal to a slightly older group of patrons, say those aged 35 to 40, as a means of hanging onto its present patrons as they age. The repositioned operation would have broadened its target population significantly—but, to do this, changes in menu, operating style, services, and, perhaps, even decor would probably be required. For instance, children's menus would have to be added and menu items for its older, more weight-conscious patrons would need to be expanded, as well. The addition of a play area (perhaps with babysitting supervision) would also help broaden its appeal. Servers would need to be trained in how to wait on families with small children. Redecoration of the dining area might feature a somewhat more restrained tone—without,

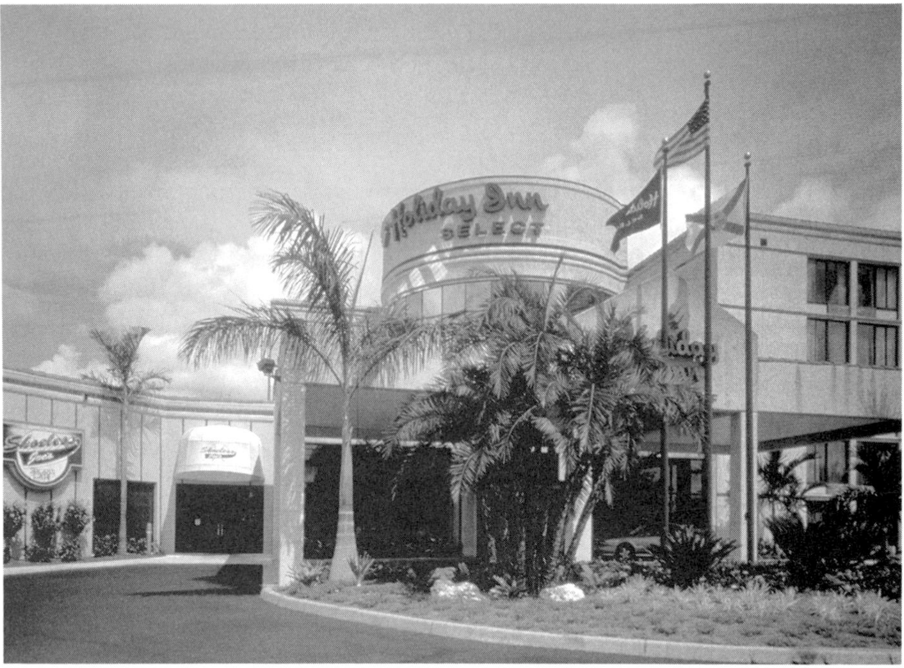

Holiday Inn has used its Express, Sunspree, and Select subbrands to improve its positioning with specific target markets. Holiday Inn Select, such as this one, targets business travelers. (Photo courtesy Holiday Inn Worldwide)

however, losing the "fun" atmosphere which is part of the appeal to its existing clientele.

Another aspect of repositioning is that, as a company changes its target market, it takes on new competitors, the operations that are already serving the alternative target market. Thus, the repositioning analysis needs to take into account not only the needs and preferences of the added market segment but the appeals of the competition to those segments. The new offering must include *competitive points of difference* which will give the operation an advantage, not just a "copy cat" pattern that repeats what others are doing in the market. Thus, a careful consumer and competitor analysis is an essential part of repositioning.

Changing the Marketing Mix. Another approach to maturity involves changing one or more elements in the marketing mix. In the face of growing competition, a company might increase promotional discounting or even lower some of its prices on a longer-term basis. The most common response to Taco Bell's low-price appeal has been the development of value meals which bundle products in a way that raises the check average but reduces the cost to the consumer of the individual items offered in the value meal.

Operations also increase their promotional budgets as a market becomes more crowded. The advertising budgets of QSRs, for instance, have increased steadily for years. The most common response to a tired concept, however, is the development of a new product.

NEW PRODUCTS

The consumer's needs and preferences are constantly changing. What is today's hot product becomes commonplace and then old hat. Some products (e.g., hamburgers and fried chicken) are staples that have a continuing strong appeal. Nevertheless, even established operations such as McDonald's continue to present new combinations of old products, as well as genuinely new products such as McNuggets, to liven up their image.

New Product Functions

New products are added to build and hold the operation's customer base, as shown in the top part of Figure 8.5. Perhaps the most successful use of new products to expand a market is McDonald's introduction of the fast-food breakfast, which opened its stores to a whole new segment. McDonald's sells 25 percent of all breakfasts eaten away from home according to *Time*,[36] suggesting that McDonald's has been well able to hold onto the customer base its status as an innovator first gained it, in spite of increasingly fierce competition. McDonald's has also been very successful in extending its market into snack day parts, particularly with chicken McNuggets.

Ponderosa is another firm that pioneered in the breakfast market, the first steakhouse chain to enter that market. The payoff was an initial substantial increase in customer traffic and average weekly sales. Not only did Ponderosa join a new day part, but many breakfast customers who were first-time Ponderosa customers returned for other meals as a result of their breakfast patronage.

New products are also used to increase sales to existing customers. A particularly effective method of achieving this goal is through the addition of specialty

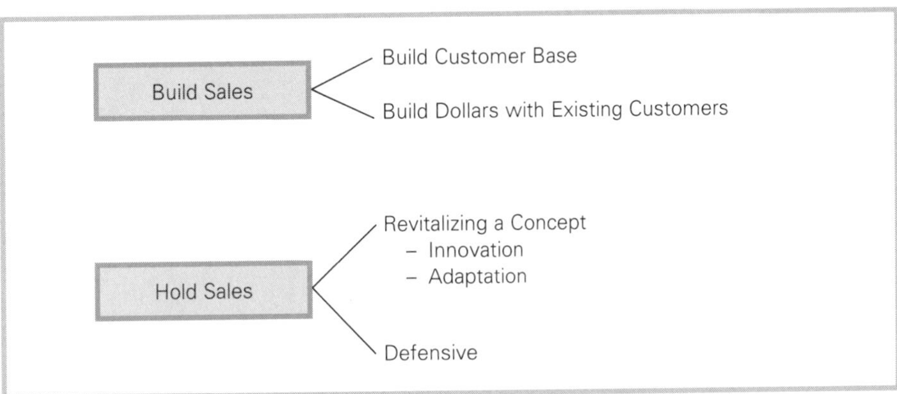

Figure 8.5 New Product Functions

appetizers and other first courses, as well as through the introduction of a taste-tempting dessert menu.

Some new products are added, particularly in limited-menu operations, to permit offering a full meal. A full-meal offering raises check averages and strengthens the QSR's competitive position against family restaurants.

New products have also been used to hold sales (Figure 8.5) by revitalizing an aging concept. Salad bars offer an excellent example of a product that livened up existing operations such as Wendy's and Ponderosa.

Another use of new products is defensive. When a company finds itself losing market share because it does not have a product that has become popular, it is likely to add that product defensively—as KFC did with chicken nuggets in the face of McDonald's success with McNuggets. Figure 8.6 summarizes the functions of new products.

Defining New Products

A new product, according to Technomic Consultants, is any item not present on an operation's menu.[37] That is, even if the product is available elsewhere, if it is new to the operation, then Technomic defines it as a new product. We can distinguish three categories of new product:

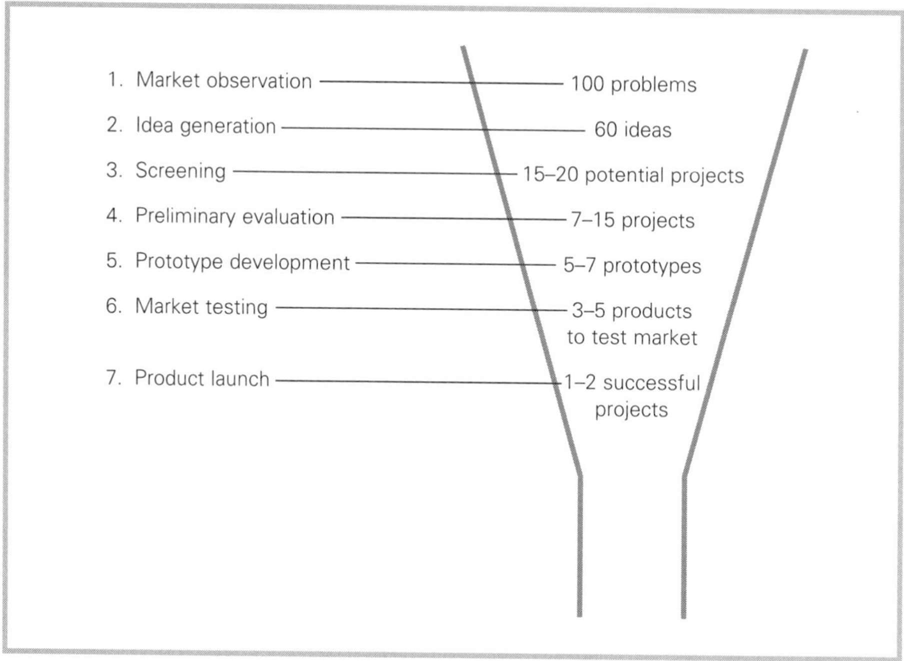

Figure 8.6 The New Product Process: A Funnel Approach

Source: Adapted from Ronald N. Paul, "New Product Development Overview," *Proceedings, Chain Operators Exchange, 1982* (Chicago: International Foodservice Manufacturers Association, 1982).

1. *Imitation.* When several operators added chicken nuggets, they were imitating McDonald's success with the product.

2. *Adaptation.* The bacon cheeseburger—a modification of an existing product by adding one or more new ingredients—is a good example of adaptation. Another example is pizza by the slice. Godfathers, for instance, originally served only whole pizzas, but it introduced pizza by the slice in an effort to convert pizza into a fast food [38] particularly at the luncheon meal.

3. *Innovation.* Wendy's baked potato should be classified as an innovation because it was unique in its execution—a first for fast food. The *first* fast-food nugget product, McNuggets, represents another example of true innovation.

New Product Development

Technomic Consultants' experience with **new product development** in chain restaurants suggests the funnel approach outlined in Figure 8.6. Consumers are surveyed to identify "problems" they experience with the hospitality environment. Some of these "problems" appear to embody ideas, that is, possible solutions to consumer complaints. The researcher narrows his or her focus as a smaller number of these "problems" are identified as potential projects, and a few of these are tried in a test store. A still smaller number make it into formal test marketing, and perhaps one or two of these are successful.[39]

While many new products are tried, few become successful. For instance, the Lite Mac was rolled out with much fanfare but subsequently failed completely except as a public relations exercise. One of McDonald's most successful new products, the McDLT, was, in time, withdrawn but is periodically revived. An important consideration in thinking about new products is that, whether they are, in themselves, successful or not, they add life and change to the operation and add interest for the customer.

Once a product has been identified as meeting a customer need, the process has only begun. Technomic Consultants[40] identifies several factors to monitor in determining the fit with the operation:

1. Existing equipment
2. Company image
3. Long-term objective
4. Volume requirements
5. Profitability contribution
6. Investment required
7. Existing customers

During the product introduction, the product's attractiveness is assessed in terms of customer acceptability and likely gross profit margin/food cost percentage. The supply of the ingredient or ingredients must be assessed, too. When Burger King first added bacon to make a bacon cheeseburger, for instance, the impact on national demand for bacon was so pronounced that pork belly futures rose appreciably on commodity markets.

A final factor in assessing a potential new menu item's attractiveness is its uniqueness. Although a new product may be added defensively in reaction to a competitor's success, it is preferable to have a product that makes a new statement in the marketplace, rather than one that just says "me too."

Concept Innovation

Of course, the most fundamental kind of innovation is at the level of concept. The power of a new total concept is suggested by competitive reaction to it. In the 1950s, a few successes in Polynesian atmosphere restaurants, such as Trader Vic's, set off a wave of imitations that eventually produced variants in most major cities. The success of McDonald's and KFC inspired waves of similar restaurants. Kemmons Wilson and Holiday Inns' successful development of the motor inn, as opposed to the motel *or* hotel of the time, must be credited with setting off a wave of emulation that eventually revolutionized lodging. In recent years, however, some of the most basic concept innovations have been new service forms.

Proliferating Service Forms. The fastest-growing segment of food service is off-premise. Take-out food service operations have the largest share of off-premise sales, followed by drive-thrus and delivery. Another service form that has added significantly to food service sales is late-hour operations via drive-thru or take-out window. (This avoids the security problems of late-hour operations.)

New Product Hazard: Cannibalization

One potential problem with a new product is that it will steal sales from existing products. What is desirable is that the new product will attract new customers. New products are sometimes added as a defensive measure to *keep customers,* in a highly competitive market, by offering them something new and different. However, the ideal new product will result in attracting new customers, not just spreading the existing customers over a larger menu.

New Product Development Procedure

Food Service. The actual procedure for developing a new food product from the idea stage begins with recipe formulation and spells out plating and product presentation details. Operational specifications then indicate equipment needs, production flows, and inventory and labor requirements. At this point, too, suppliers are identified. A menu price is set, product name established, and in-store promotional materials are prepared. The product is now ready for testing in a unit operation.

As a result of test operations, operational procedures and staffing needs are evaluated. If a product passes this stage, it is ready for preliminary market testing in several stores and then for full market testing.[41] Should the product pass this last stage, it is ready for rollout.

Lodging. Marriott has followed a similar general pattern in developing its new hotel products such as Courtyard by Marriott and Fairfield Inns. Product development began with consumer research. Prototypes were designed and tested in Atlanta. Rapid expansion into the national market began once the success of the test was established.

Independent Operations

As we have seen, the introduction of a new product in a chain is a very complex activity. This is true because the product must be evaluated in several markets, fit with many existing units' physical plants, and match the image of the chain. In an independent operation, the process is much less formalized because the owner's eye and experience are available to make informed judgments of the product's success. Although there may be less formal analysis, the same basic factors identified in the chain's evaluation will come into play.

SUMMARY

Service is an *experience* for the guest. For the operation, however, it is a planned event that can be likened to a performance. The service product is made up of the core benefit the guest seeks, facilitating services that are essential to providing the benefit, and supporting services that are necessary to the *marketing* of the service offering.

Because services are intangible, marketers provide cues to help consumers conceptualize a service offering. Among the most important of these is the physical plant and the atmospherics it establishes. The total service offering is referred to as the *concept.* In food service, this includes the menu, the kind of food used and the way it is prepared, the service, price, and atmosphere. Hotel concepts can be broken into two groups, full service and limited service, and these can be further divided.

Branding is used to help identify products and its role in lodging and food service is growing. Figure 8.2 summarizes the advantages of branding. The joining together of brands is increasingly common and includes subbranding, ingredient branding, cobranding, family branding, and brand bundling. Branding is also playing a growing role in institutional food service.

The product life cycle is a useful way of summarizing the impact of the aging of a product. When a product becomes old (i.e., mature), various means are used to rejuvenate the concept: It is repositioned, or the marketing mix is changed. New products play an important role in rejuvenating a concept and in building or holding sales. Many ideas are required to achieve just one successful new product.

◆ Key Words and Concepts

Marketing mix
Product as intangible experience
Intangibility of service
Service offering
  Core benefit
  Facilitating services
  Supporting services
Atmospherics
Supporting cues
Concepts as products
  As experience
  As operating system
Branding
Brand equity
Brand loyalty
Umbrella brands
Subbranding
Ingredient branding
Cobranding
Family brands
Line extension
Product life cycle
Product maturity
Repositioning
New products
New product development
Cannibalization

◆ Discussion Questions

1. The intangibility of service is one of its major distinguishing characteristics. What problems does it present for marketers? How are these problems solved?
2. What are the major elements of the service offering? What role does each play?
3. What is meant by "manipulating the environment"? What are some specific manipulations? What are their effects?

4. What are the elements of the restaurant concept as it is offered to the guest?
5. What is branding? What are its advantages?
6. How do umbrella brands and subbrands relate to one another? What is the purpose of a subbrand? What is an ingredient brand's purpose?
7. What do you see as the pros and cons of segmented branding in lodging?
8. What is the difference between the style cycle and the restaurant product life cycle? How do restaurants deal with maturity?
9. How are new products used in food service marketing?

Chapter 9

When you have finished reading this chapter, you should be able to

1. Define distribution in a hospitality context
2. List the major channel members serving hospitality firms
3. Discuss the role of reservation systems in lodging distribution
4. Describe the conflicts in the channels of distribution
5. List the services provided by franchisors
6. Assess the importance of selling to channel members
7. Evaluate franchising's role in hospitality marketing
8. Define intensive distribution in food service
9. Discuss the needs of hosts and venues

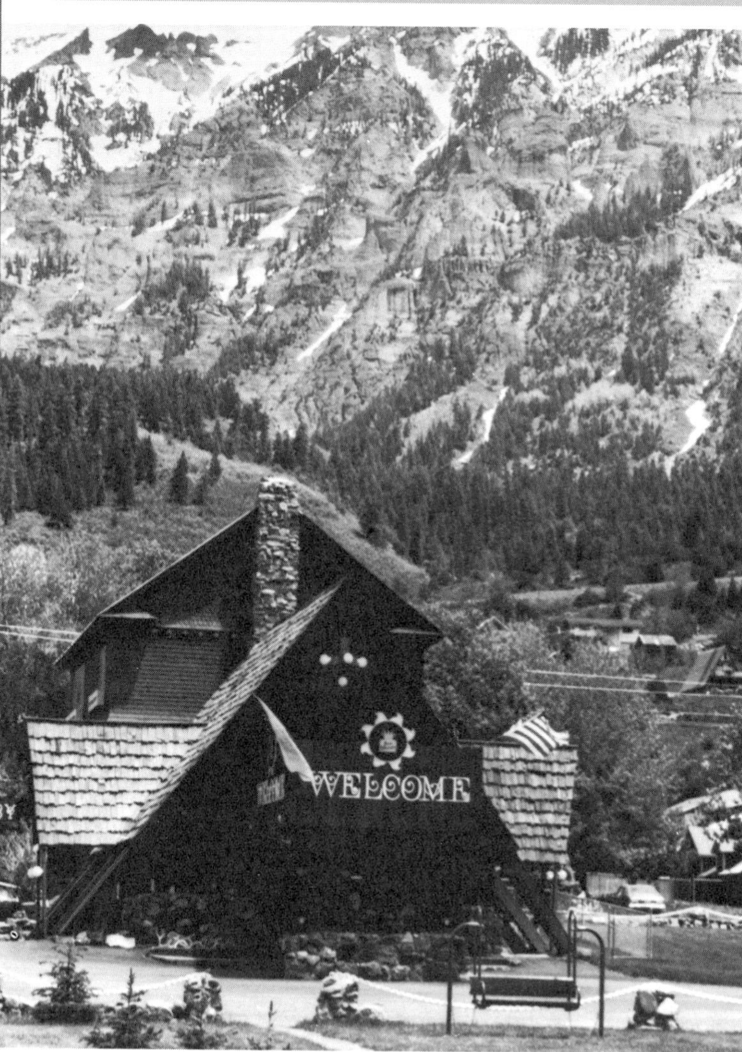

(Photo courtesy of Best Western, International, Inc.)

Place in Hospitality Marketing:

Distribution

PLACE AND PLACES

The marketing mix element place, in hospitality, covers a number of related topics. The next chapter covers location and site decisions. Place is also commonly taken to include the *distribution* of the product, that is, making the product conveniently available in many *places.* As you might expect, a concern with *places* means multiple locations, that is, chains. Most of this chapter focuses, then, on the distribution problems of chains, but our discussion of being *represented* in a market does apply to independent, as well as chain, hotels. In the first part of this chapter, we will consider the concept of distribution in a general way. In later sections, we will discuss channels of distribution in lodging and food service. In a final section, we will briefly consider the place-related topic of logistics.

The Concept of Distribution

If you are downtown in any large city and you are hungry, it does not do you a lot of good to know there is a very fine restaurant in the suburbs—unless you have transportation and lots of time. The same is true in lodging. If your favorite hotel chain has a room available somewhere across the continent from where you are, that information is not very helpful.

For a business, being *in place,* in the many places where the consumer is, is critical to hospitality organizations that want to serve guests in regional or national markets. For restaurants, this means having an operation in as many markets as possible. For hotels, having an operation in a market *is* advantageous, but, where there is a significant market they do not have a property in, it is important for them to be represented there by one or more of the agencies that can help sell business originating in that market. Distribution refers to the strategy of *places,* of being present or represented in key markets.

The word "distribution" comes from the days when marketing was concerned principally with physical goods. To oversimplify a bit, distribution originally was concerned with how to get goods from maker to user—ultimately, how to distribute products in physical space. The *ways* in which hospitality firms go about achieving distribution for their services, that is, being represented in all appropriate places, is the subject of this chapter.

Manufactured-goods marketers have developed three broad categories of distribution strategies. **Intensive distribution** is appropriate for convenience goods. Toothpaste is sold at all drugstores but also in most grocery stores, in local convenience stores, and in lots of other places, as well. The toothpaste company needs to have its product in all those places because customers are unlikely to go out of their way to purchase that product. Intensive distribution is required to catch convenience-oriented consumers when they are ready to make a purchase. The distribution strategy of quick-service restaurant chains is analogous, in food service, to this intensive distribution strategy.

At the other extreme is **exclusive distribution** where there is only one seller in a market. We might think of a great, one-of-a-kind resort, such as the Greenbriar or a very fine restaurant as being similar to this exclusivity. In between these extremes is **selective distribution** which achieves fairly wide market representation.

The Constraint of Market Saturation. If that tube of toothpaste is not sold today, it remains in inventory until it is sold. In services, you will recall, there is no inventory. A service operation puts in place a *capacity.* If that capacity is not used at an economically acceptable rate, the operation will have to go out of business. Unlike the situation with toothpaste, where intensity of distribution literally means having the product in every place where that kind of product is sold, there are limits to how many operations a market can support. Thus, intensity of distribution has a different meaning in hospitality than it does in manufacturing. Where convenience-oriented intensive distribution is the rule, as in QSRs, a big city *can* absorb a large number of operations—but not as many locations as are feasible for a good that can be inventoried.

Selective distribution is a description that fits family restaurants and casual restaurants. A large shopping area might have 5 or 10 or more competing QSRs, but probably only one or two family restaurants and perhaps another more upscale casual restaurant.

This simplified model of levels of intensity of distribution is necessary to understand the dramatic changes that are taking place in hospitality distribution today. In quite different ways, lodging and food service are experiencing increasing intensity of distribution. In lodging, this is coming about through expansion

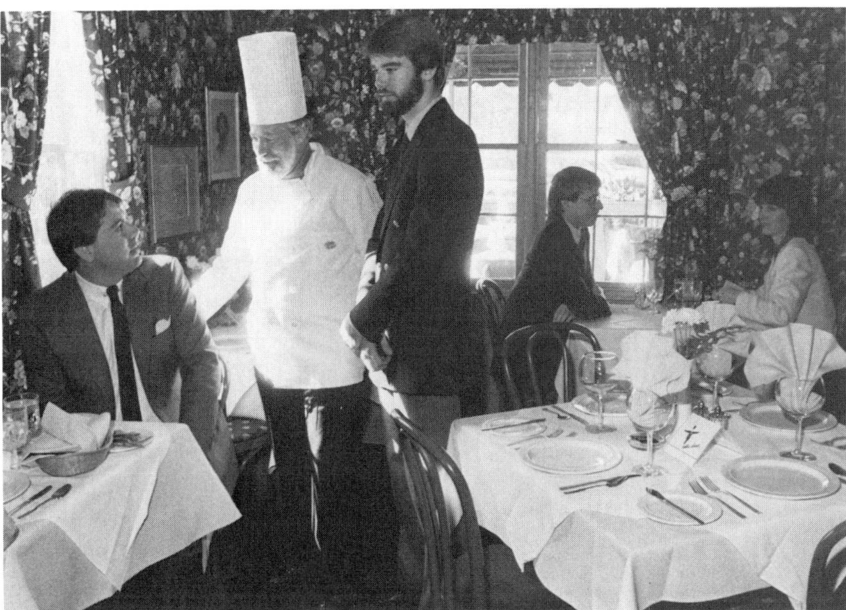

A fine dining restaurant—one of a kind in its community—offers an example of exclusive distribution. (Photo courtesy of Meri Houtchens Kitchens/Picture Cube)

in the *representation* of hotels through a variety of reservation and sales services, while, in food service, the expansion is the result of an expansion in the number of units. Increasingly, however, this is being accomplished with a different kind of downsized, specialized unit.

Channels of Distribution

Channels of distribution are the commercial structure of intermediaries between the provider of a good or service and the ultimate consumer. Some of these channel members in manufactured goods are the more service-intensive *merchant firms,* such as wholesalers and distributors, who take title to the goods, maintain inventories, operate warehouses for that purpose, and provide delivery services. They also have their own field sales organization. Firms such as these supply the hospitality industry with most of the goods used in their operation such as food products, beverages, cleaning supplies, guest supplies, and the like.

Another type of merchant firm is the retailer, who sells to the ultimate consumer, providing final processing and service. Merchant firms set final prices and receive their compensation in the form of the margin between cost of goods sold and operating costs. In taking title to the goods, merchant firms assume the risk of resale and their compensation is the profit on that sale. The overwhelming majority of hospitality units are retailers and thus are members of the channels of distribution.

Franchising offers a company an opportunity to penetrate many markets quickly, with franchisees providing much of the capital. (Photo courtesy of Taco Bell)

Others, channel members, such as brokers and manufacturer's representatives, are *agents*, who do not take title to the goods, generally provide fewer services than merchant firms, and frequently do not control the selling price for products they handle. Their compensation is usually in the form of a commission. Brokers play key roles in the distribution of food products and are also active in providing furniture and equipment to the hospitality industry, as are manufacturer's representatives.

There are major differences between this structure and the one that the hospitality industry uses to serve its customers, but there are also some similarities. Hotel *chains* are, in some ways, a channel of distribution for the owners of individual properties as are **franchise systems.** In lodging, the *travel agent* acts as a *representative* for many hotels and that is increasingly true for other travel reservation services, as well. Airlines, through their reservation services, are becoming a significant factor in hotel sales. The role of representatives is growing and likely to continue to do so.

Restaurants are a combination of manufacturer and service organization, who deal almost exclusively with the ultimate consumer. This is another way of saying that the restaurant business is a retail industry. A very large part of the restaurant industry, however, are also members of franchise systems which are a specialized channel of distribution.

Franchise Systems. Franchising companies provide a number of services to franchisees, principal among which are marketing services and, in the hotel business, reservation services. Franchising has been a major force in both lodging and food service for nearly 50 years.

If a company with a successful concept does *not* expand, others will copy its idea and it will lose the advantage its original uniqueness confers. To protect against this danger, a successful concept needs to achieve distribution, in all appropriate markets, as rapidly as possible. To expand, however, a company must invest capital in physical plant and must develop a large organization not only to manage multiple operations but to direct that management from the area and district levels. Franchising offers a company with a successful operating format an opportunity to achieve widespread distribution, quickly. The *franchisee* provides most of the capital for expansion and the job of managing a large, widespread organization is made simpler by the motivation of the franchised owner.

Other specialized channel members serve principally hotels. These firms, which include, in addition to hotel chains, reservation services, hotel representatives, and incentive houses, will be discussed in the next section.

Hospitality Sectors Differ. While the basic conceptual framework for thinking about distribution applies to both hotels and restaurants, we can best discuss distribution in the major sectors of the hospitality industry separately because the way hotels achieve distribution is different in a number of ways from restaurants' approaches.

LODGING DISTRIBUTION SYSTEMS

Two major forces shape distribution in lodging. The first, franchising, has been a potent force since the early 1950s. While it remains a powerful force, franchising in lodging has changed and is likely to continue to change in the direction of being a supplier of specialized services. The second force is a technology-driven revolution in reservation systems. Computerized communications are revolutionizing the way hotel rooms are sold and heightening the role of intermediaries in the marketing of hotels.

In this section, we will first consider the importance of distribution systems in lodging. Then, as background for an understanding of the changing role of franchising and intermediaries in lodging, we will look at the state of reservation systems today and their likely future. With this essential background, we can turn to consideration of the various channel members.

The Need for Distribution in Lodging

There are two ways we can look at distribution in lodging. The first is as the **physical presence** of properties in markets, while the second is as **representation** in markets. Actually, both are essential to the distribution policy of any hotel chain and the latter is useful to most independents.

Having a hotel in every major market is a desirable goal, first of all, because that is what is required to serve the guest. A hotel has to be *in place* to make it as easy as possible for the guest to choose it. Serving a guest gains revenue for the hotel, but it also gains *access* to the guest which is important for future sales chain-wide. The hotel will happily facilitate the guest in making reservations for her or his next night's stay. Once a guest is in the system, it is easier to retain her or his business for the rest of the trip. An additional advantage of having a property in a locale is that the local people become familiar with the brand and, as a familiar brand, they are more likely to choose it on their travels.

Representation refers to having some agency in every market to represent the lodging system. There are several levels of representation. At the lowest level, if you are reading this in a room with a telephone in it, then there is a "representative" of many hotel chains right there with you—in the form of 800 number reservation services. On the other hand, you might choose to call one of the many travel agencies that are undoubtedly available to you for advice on where to stay.

Travel agents represent all hotels—but, generally, not any one hotel in particular—so they are not an especially powerful tool for a *particular* hotel unless efforts are made to *sell* the travel agent.

If you were with a firm that originated a lot of travel or were responsible for a major convention, it would make sense that representatives of hotel chains would call on you to solicit your business. This might be done, as we shall see, by the sales office of a chain or franchise group or by a salesperson from a hotel representative firm. In these ways, many hotel groups are represented in markets where they do not have a property.

Lodging is highly competitive and so it is important not only to have a known brand name—or a strong local reputation in an independent property—but to have some way of being represented in appropriate markets. One means of such representation is through a reservation service.

Reservation Systems in Lodging

Figure 9.1 gives an overview of the global distribution system (GDS) serving the lodging industry. To understand this system, it will be worth our while to discuss the role of each of the players in the system, who are identified in the left-hand column of the figure.

Referring to the top line of the figure, three sources of reservations are identified. *Individual travelers* may make a reservation through a travel agent or directly through one of the chain hotel central reservation services (CRS). *Business offices* can also make reservations in either of these ways. *Travel agents* can place reservations for their clients directly through the hotel CRS. Another significant set of actors in the GDS are the *airline central reservation services* (second row from the top). They are becoming a major factor in hotel reservations and present an *alternative* to the channels just discussed.

Virtually all travel agencies are on line to one of the airline CRS. That means roughly 45,000 travel agency offices are potential agents for hotel properties and

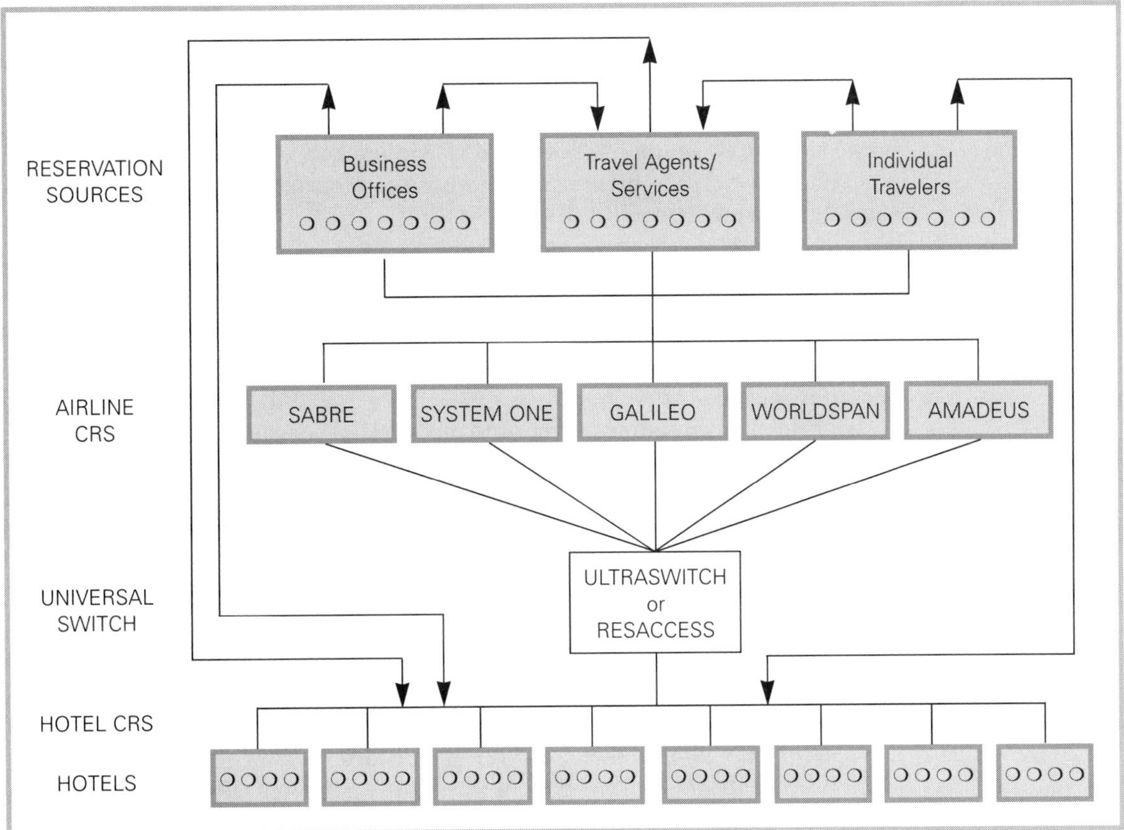

Figure 9.1 The Emerging Central Reservation Network

Source: Chervenak, Keane and Co., New York.

can make reservations *directly by computer* in a way which is faster, more efficient, and less costly for them than is using the *hotel* chain CRS 800 number. As a result of the greater efficiency of the airline CRS for travel agents, this alternative is gradually replacing the agents' direct use of the hotel CRS. In fact, 1993 was the first year that hotel CRS received more reservations via the airline CRS than by 800 number.[1] To the 45,000 travel agent offices, we can add all the airline reservationists, as well as those of car rental companies, because those companies now offer travelers reservations not only for the travel company they work for but for other travel products. For instance, an airline reservationist can make arrangements not only for an airline ticket but hotel reservations, as well as a car rental.

In order for the airline CRS to communicate with the hotel CRS, a third set of GDS actors in Figure 9.1 is required: the *universal switch*. When an airline reservationist (or travel agent or car rental company) receives a request for a hotel reservation, that reservation is dispatched through the airline CRS and passed to the hotel CRS through one of the "switches" which provide "bidirectional interface between any major *airline* CRS and any *hotel* central reservation operation."[2]

The result of the development of the GDS is a vast increase in the distribution system available to hotels. However, it comes at a price. First of all, there are fees for the airline CRS and for the switch for handling the reservation. Perhaps, in the long run, however, the present fees are not the biggest problem. As one knowledgeable industry source put it:

> Stripped of the public relations platitudes, the long term goal of the airline CRS megasystems is to dominate the travel and hospitality industry's global distribution networks.[3]

If, indeed, the airline CRS gain this dominance, future costs for reservations might be even higher than they are today.

The global distribution system presents special problems for *independent properties.* "Airline/travel agent systems haven't yet found a cost-justifiable way to keep individual hotels in their data base. Only hotel organizations with hotel CRS are included."[4] This puts pressure on independent properties to find a way to link to the GDS. The options that are available are all expensive. They can join a franchise group, affiliate with a hotel representative firm, contract with a firm which will provide the GDS connection for a fee, or join a hotel association which has a CRS that is linked to the global system. Several state hotel associations have set up such a service and more are considering it. The average reservation cost, however, exclusive of any travel agent's fee, was $18 in 1995. The size of the fee presents an especially difficult problem to a midpriced property, where room rates are likely to be in the range of $40 to $60. Indeed, the cost of reservation services may be a part of the explanation for the massive movement of midrange and economy properties to join a franchise group.

Most of the intermediaries we have discussed are not only disinterested in any particular property but probably do not even know that a particular property exists. Accordingly, selling to the channel members, which we will discuss later, is a topic that has become very important to the lodging industry.

Lodging Channels of Distribution

The most important channels of distribution in lodging are hotel chains and franchise systems. Travel agents are also playing an increasingly significant role in lodging. Other channel members include hotel sales representatives and incentive houses. Each will be discussed in the following sections.

Lodging Chains

A chain of hotels *looks* very much like one company. Every property sports the same sign out front and all properties achieve a particular standard of services and facilities. This appearance, however, conceals a reality of highly diverse ownership patterns.

Some hotels with the Hilton or Marriott name are owned and operated by that company, but most are owned by an investor group and managed under *management contracts.* While these chains perform many other services, one of their major roles is to provide advertising and sales representation, as well as a reservation network, for their properties in multiple markets. From the perspective of both the customer and the owner of the property, they are a specialized channel of distribution. Many chains not only own and operate for others but franchise, as well. We will, accordingly, concentrate our discussion here on franchise systems.

Franchise Systems in Lodging

The largest single brand in lodging in number of rooms is Holiday Inns, with over 365,000 rooms. The largest single brand in number of properties is Best Western, with over 3,400 hotels and motels. The largest *group* of franchises is Hospitality Franchise Systems (HFS), which operates six brands covering 4,400 properties and 435,000 rooms. Choice Hotels, which also operates six brands, is the second largest group of franchises, with about 3,500 properties and 300,000 rooms.[5] These and other franchise (or membership) systems[6] provide four basic services to their affiliated hotels.

A National Brand and Marketing Program. It is axiomatic that the lodging customer is away from home and so a place to stay with a brand the traveler can trust has an advantage. To support the brand and promote its membership's properties, franchise chains pool advertising assessments to mount national and regional advertising and promotional campaigns. The system also distributes directories which let travelers know where the system has properties, at what rates, and with what facilities.

Sales representation in key cities is an important part of the national marketing program. Specialized sales offices pursue group business, while regional offices call on local originators of travel to sell their brand. In many ways, then, the franchise system is a specialized kind of agent for its individual properties, and nowhere is this channel member aspect more clear than in the chain's reservation service.

Reservation Systems. Each lodging system maintains a reservation system which usually relies on a centralized computer reservation system and 800 number phone centers. As we noted earlier, the GDS and airline CRS are playing a growing role in lodging reservations. On the other hand, the more reservations a lodging group can take directly from the guest, the lower its reservation costs will be because it will not have to pay fees to outsiders.

While larger chains operate their own reservation systems, smaller organizations contract with other companies which specialize in telemarketing for their reservation service. These contracting companies provide the reservations entirely in the lodging system's name and the guests are not even aware they are dealing with another organization.

A franchise system appears to be just one company, but franchise chains are really an alliance of many independent owners with the franchising company. (Photo courtesy of Holiday Inn Worldwide)

Quality Assurance. With 3,000 to 5,000 individual hotels and motels in the largest lodging systems, the possibility of problems at a few of those properties is very real. Given the importance of providing the guest a positive experience to secure repeat business, maintaining quality in the system is important to all properties. Lodging systems have minimum physical standards which are upheld at the time of entry of a property into the system. Efforts to maintain continuing operating standards rely on inspection systems, but, as a practical matter, punishing a property that does not comply is difficult because of the legal implications of the threat to cancel the franchise which is, effectively, the only sanction available. Increasingly, franchise companies rely on shorter franchise contracts[7] (five years or less; one year at Best Western) and simply decline to renew operations that do not live up to standards. Some lodging systems have also begun to rate their own properties and publish superior ratings in their own directories,[8] as a way of reinforcing good performance.

Buying Cooperatives. Many lodging groups maintain buying co-ops for products used in their properties, as well as for local and regional advertising. This benefit is not an aspect of guest room distribution as such, but it does have an important marketing impact. To the degree that these co-ops achieve operating savings, they help properties keep rates at competitive levels.

Training Programs. The better lodging systems provide a training program for key property level executives, as well as videos and training manuals for hourly employees. Like the co-ops mentioned previously, the training programs have an impact on cost and they also help to standardize the quality of service.

Changes in Franchising

In the early days of lodging franchising, the franchisee "did whatever the franchisor wanted." It was "basically a kind of autocratic environment."[9] There was a significant degree of loyalty between franchisee and franchisor. In the mid-1980s, however, franchisees gained the right to hold the franchises of more than one franchisor's brand. At about the same time, franchisors began to engage in "conversion franchising," in which a property would change from one franchise to another. During a period of severe overcapacity and several years of operating losses for most in the industry which lasted into the early 1990s, many hotels changed brands and competition emerged among franchisors for properties to convert. As a result, franchisors have become more like suppliers of services than the quasi-bosses, they once were and franchisees have become more like customers than subordinates.[10]

One major factor driving franchisees to consider changing franchises has been cost. After payroll costs, franchise fees are typically the second largest expenditure for a franchised hotel.[11] As Table 9.1 demonstrates, there is a very considerable spread between the least and most expensive franchisors.

Conflict in the Channels of Distribution

Impact. Impact can be defined as "the effect on a particular hotel of a franchisor converting or developing a property that maintains the same brand affiliation in the franchisee's market area."[12] Impact can result in one or more of the following unfavorable effects: lost market penetration, a diluted average rate, increased marketing expenditures, lost food and beverage revenues, and a fall in the value of the hotel in resale.[13]

An owner of one property, for instance, found that "the franchise company granted new franchises [in his market] every time the hotel achieved an occupancy over 75 percent."[14] The franchisor's reservation system's volume was gradually spread over more and more properties until, at the end of a three-year period, the original franchisee's fees had amounted to 52 percent of the room revenue generated by the franchisor's reservation system!

The problem of impact is being lessened as more lodging systems, under pressure from franchisees and state and federal regulation adopt positive measures to deal with it. Some lodging systems have developed written impact statements providing for payment where impact can be proved. Some chains have adopted exclusive territories. One chain defines exclusive territory as a 3-mile radius in a downtown metropolitan area or a radius of 20 miles in a suburban area.[15]

The "problem" of impact, however, is built into the franchise relationship. The decision to expand favors all the franchisees—except those nearby:

Table 9.1 Highest and Lowest Franchise Fees as a Percentage of Room Sales*

Budget		Mid Rate		First Class	
Brand	% of Room Sales	Brand	% of Room Sales	Brand	% of Room Sales
Five Highest Brands, by Rate Group					
Holiday Inn Express	9.34	Days Inn	8.99	Marriott	9.91
Comfort Inn	8.98	Country Lodging	8.84	Radisson	8.95
Howard Johnson Inns	8.85	Ramada	8.68	Sheraton Suites	8.91
Hampton Inn	8.61	Howard Johnson	8.68	Crowne Plaza	8.90
Travelodge	8.56	Holiday Inn	8.57	Western	8.80
Five Lowest Brands, by Rate Group					
Budget Host	0.75	Best Western	1.94	Preferred Hotels	1.49
Microtel	2.71	Park Inn	6.04	Clarion	5.83
Best Inns	4.12	Comfort Suites	7.12	Doubletree Suites	6.53
Passport Inns	4.79	Quality Suites	7.12	Doubletree	6.53
Scottish Inns	4.79	Quality Inns	7.13	Guest Quarters	6.53

Source: Hospitality Valuation Services/*Lodging*, July 1995.
*Percentages are based on calculations by Hospitality Valuation Services over a 10-year period.

> All the hotels in the chain benefit from more representation and more funding for advertising. However, the individual franchisee pays for these benefits if his hotel loses business to a new member of a chain.[16] The franchisor says it is vital for the brand to expand for recognition and referral. "True but not in my back yard" responds the franchisee. . . . There will always be two sides to the impact issue.[17]

Assessing Franchising as a Lodging Channel of Distribution. Realistically, lodging franchise brands are unlikely to ever regain the unique market power they had in the early days of lodging franchising. The dominance of the market that Holiday Inns once had is not in sight for any of the present firms. This is true simply because there are so many of them; that is, competition among franchisors is so intense. It seems likely, however, that those franchises which are most successful in the long run will owe much of their success to wide distribution of their product, combined with effective representation in many markets by other channel members.

To assess franchising from the point of view of individual properties, we might note that less than 5 percent of hotels converted to another brand in 1994 and the total number of conversions has been in the range of 1,000 to 1,200 properties

Howard Johnson is just one of many brands operated by HFS, a company that identifies its mission as service to its franchisee customers. (Photo courtesy of HFS Inc.)

since 1990.[18] Much of the conversion seems to have been driven by the desperation of owners during a period of overcapacity in the industry, combined with a recession in the general economy.

Conversions from chain to independent have been falling since a recession-driven peak in 1992. During the same period, independent-to-chain conversions have increased. The behavior of the customer, in this case the franchisee, strongly suggests that a very large proportion of properties are at least satisfied enough with their affiliation to maintain it and that many properties without an affiliation are finding it to their advantage to join a brand. Small chains and independents provided the largest proportion of conversions in 1994, while midscale and economy properties saw the largest number of brand changes. It is not surprising that smaller, less prestigious properties have found it advantageous to seek to bolster their image through an affiliation with a brand.[18]

From the perspective of the franchisor, it seems clear that franchising is a powerful form of distribution for the franchisor's brand. Steven Rushmore has pointed out that the fees of the lowest-cost franchisors (and membership organizations) in Table 9.1 probably represent the minimum cost of providing franchise services. While some of the differences between low- and high-cost franchisors may result from higher advertising budgets, these differences also suggest that hotel franchising is currently quite profitable for many franchisors.

Impact, in this very competitive market, is not likely to go away as a problem for either franchisee or franchisor, but there is every indication that it is on its way to a reasonable resolution. The high cost of some franchises remains a problem with many franchisees, but new, lower-cost franchise (and membership) groups are entering the market and something very similar to price competition appears to be emerging among franchisors as discounting comes to franchising and franchise rate negotiation becomes more common.[19] In fact, *Lodging* characterizes competition among franchisors as cutthroat.[20]

We should note that a franchise is not necessary for every property. Where a hotel's guests are business travelers or tourists and come from a variety of places, a franchise will probably be a good investment. On the other hand, if a hotel's business is obtained largely through local contacts and reputation, it can probably succeed without the expense of a franchise. Similarly, hotels that depend on group business may find that their own sales force is strong enough to secure meeting, conference, and convention business.[21] Another case in which a franchise may not be required is when "the destination becomes the primary drawing card," such as is the case with some resort locations.

The Travel Agent

There are both wholesale and retail channels for travel products—including hotel stays. *Travel wholesalers,* such as American Express, buy blocks of hotel rooms and other travel products, such as airline tickets, at discounts and resell them to retail travel agents. In this, they resemble the *merchant* wholesalers we discussed earlier in the chapter because they actually commit to rent the rooms in advance and earn their profit as the margin on their resale.

Retail travel agencies, employing some 300,000 agents, sell travel products to end users. Travel agents book over 95 percent of cruises, 90 percent of airline tickets, 50 percent of car rentals, but, as of 1994, only 25 percent of hotel rooms.[22] At one extreme of the agencies' clientele is the individual tourist or business traveler. At the other end of the spectrum, travel agencies often act as a "travel office" for companies and make all their travel arrangements. Some of the products sold by agents are the packaged tours referred to previously, but the greatest part of most agencies' business is the sale, on commission, of individual travel products such as airline tickets and hotel stays. The airlines have capped the commissions they will pay to travel agents at $50 per ticket. In some cases, this has resulted in travel agencies, for the first time, levying a fee on the traveler. It has also improved somewhat the position of hotels with travel agents because agents can still earn a full commission on the sale of a hotel room.

While the typical travel agency is a small firm, there are some very large travel firms, and the growth of the global distribution system and the capping of airline commissions have put increasing pressure on the smaller firms.

Other Travel Companies. We have already noted that reservationists for airline companies and auto rental companies can reserve rooms for guests. The travel company making this reservation receives a fee for this service.

Other Specialized Channel Members

Representation in particular markets is provided by **hotel sales representative companies.** "Hotel reps," as these firms are called, have their own sales force and often their own reservation centers. Smaller hotel reps operate in only one or a few markets, but larger firms operate on a worldwide basis.

According to *Hotels,* the 25 largest of these firms represented 2.5 million hotel rooms and over 19,000 properties worldwide. The largest, Utell International, represents "6,800 hotels from the Algiers Hilton to the Elephant Hills Hotel in Victoria Falls, Zimbabwe." Its clients include small independents, as well as international chains. Utell segments the products it represents into three groups: deluxe city center hotels, resorts, and a special division for Caribbean resorts. Another hotel rep firm, Lexington Services Corporation, takes a somewhat different approach, representing such well-known hotels as "the Broadmoor in Colorado Springs and the Knickerbocker in Chicago. They do not need a famous flag to represent them or a fancy booklet; rather they want an on-line system to help world wide travelers reach them."[23]

Incentive houses supply a variety of rewards for employees of companies who win awards in sales contests and similar competitions. These rewards include all-expense hotel stays and other travel products. Thus, they are a channel between the hotel and the company offering the award and, ultimately, the guest who wins the award.

Assessing the Use of Travel Intermediaries. The advantage for a hotel of working with travel agencies is widened representation. Travel agents send hotels business they could not otherwise get. The disadvantage, of course, is travel agency commissions. Some hotels reason that their business comes to them because of their unique advantages—location near an attraction or on a major travel artery. Since the hotel would be full anyway, they reason, why pay commission? While this logic used to fit large parts of the lodging industry, most operators now recognize the value of the additional business travel agencies bring—and hotel occupancies are generally not at a level where there is no room for "additional business."

SELLING WITHIN CHANNELS

As we noted earlier, travel agencies present a problem in that they have no special ties to any particular property. This problem, however, can be offset by setting policies that make it attractive for travel agencies to do business with a particular property or chain. Experience of successful operators indicates that a hotel chain's commitment to use travel agents must start at the top and must be communicated to all hotel staff levels. Hilton Hotels maintains a number exclusively for travel firms staffed by agents especially trained to work with travel agents, provide specialized meeting or management facilities and a help desk to provide answers to agents' other questions. Commission payment has been centralized to ensure prompt payment and Hilton has established a Travel Agent Advisory Board made up of travel agency and Hilton executives. Hyatt trains staff to refrain from criticizing travel agents in the presence of a client. [24] One effective program for selling within channels is Radisson's "Look to Book," which is described in Case History 9.1.

An important accommodation to travel agencies is a reservation system that provides full access to all of the information on a hotel that is available to the hotel company's own reservationists. Called a *seamless connection,* this kind of access provides the travel agent full rate information and an accurate picture of room availability. Since the information can be called up on the agent's terminal and used in making reservations, it speeds the agent's work. While putting all the rate-discounting information in the hands of travel agents might be expected to endanger the hotels' rate structure, Radisson and Hyatt have both reported that the actual impact on average rate has been nil.[25]

Selling to travel agents is certainly not limited to the chain level. One of the most effective means, especially for resort properties, is the "fam (familiarization) trip" which provides free or reduced-price accommodations for employees of travel agencies who do business with the hotel. Fam trips normally include a required tour of the property, during which a manager or salesperson shows off the special features of the hotel.

Hotel chain and franchise organizations have sales staff who specialize in calling on travel agents, as do hotel sales rep firms. The focus of this sales effort is concentrated on geographic markets which generate a lot of business for a chain or particular hotel. Some hotels and chains offer specialized training programs for travel agencies in how to sell hotel rooms. A travel industry consultant points out that "many travel agents lose hotel business simply because they fail to ask for it."[26]

The Future of Reservations

With the continuing rapid development of individual access to the Internet, there is a distinct possibility that the volume of reservations coming directly to hotels from individuals will rise dramatically in the near future. As a measure of the already enormous volume of traffic on the Internet, E-mail messages were estimated at one billion in 1995 and are expected to rise to one trillion by the year 2000.[27] The Internet offers access to more than 30,000 customers, and Carnegie Mellon reports there were 12,000 travel systems on the Net in 1995. Hotels, destinations, and other travel service products can establish a "web site" which displays pictures, rates, packages, and a description of their facilities.

Developments, to date, foreshadow an explosion of activity for lodging on the Internet, both in terms of making information available to travelers and providing reservation services directly to individuals. While these applications are still in their early stages, the Internet has the potential to revolutionize distribution systems over the next 20 years. In fact, given the pace of change we are currently experiencing in technology, the revolution could happen in much less than a generation.

DISTRIBUTION IN FOOD SERVICE

Food service and lodging have key characteristics in common. **Franchising** plays a key role in both businesses. Distribution—in the form of a retail presence in markets—is also important to both businesses. The revolutionary development in food

Case History 9.1 Selling Through Channels: "Look to Book"

Travel agents book about 13 airline reservations for every hotel reservation. A few of the airline tickets do not represent overnight business but most do—so the ratio suggests that travel agents are not booking as many hotel rooms as they could. Carlson Hospitality executives reasoned that encouraging travel agency employees to book more hotel rooms was good business for the travel agency (more commisions and better service to clients)—and, if they booked those rooms at a Carlson-affiliated hotel (Radisson Hotels, Country Inns and Suites), then it could be very good business for Carlson and its franchisees.

"Look to Book," a patented frequency program, was created to give agents an incentive to ask for the hotel booking and to reward travel agents who book hotel rooms (and other Carlson travel products such as cruise bookings or car rentals) with Carlson companies. The "Look to Book" program allows individual travel agents to automatically and electronically accumulate award points at the rate of 10 points for every U.S. dollar booked. Agents are eligible to enroll and earn points in the program by simply booking a room-night at Radisson through global distribution system. By completing approximately *20 Radisson bookings per week for a year, an agent could earn a seven-day cruise in the Caribbean aboard the ultra deluxe SSC Radisson Diamond!* Other prizes include: stays at Radisson or Country Inns and Suites hotels, airline tickets, car rentals, a cordless telephone or fax/phone combination, designer luggage, compact disc players, color television sets, jewelry, exercise equipment, and so forth. Also, as a part of improving service to travel agencies, Radisson enhanced its reservations technology to ensure confirmations in seven seconds or less. The improved reservation system also ties negotiated rates together through a system called Best Available Rate Search (BARS) to ensure the lowest negotiated rate on behalf of an agent's corporate travel program client. "Seamless service" allows agents to view total hotel inventory and to book accommodations from directly inside Radisson's reservation system.

More than 130,000 travel agents in 74 countries—more than 30 percent of the world's automated travel agents—have enrolled in "Look to Book" and new enrollments continue at approximately 5,000 per month.

Radisson attributes a 35 percent increase in revenues through the GDS to "Look to Book." Approximately $4 million in merchandise and travel awards have been earned by travel agents since the program's inception.

Sources: Lodging, November 1994, pp. 64—70; Radisson Hotels International.

service distribution is the increasing emphasis on multiplying **points of delivery (PODs)** in a development that has been called **intercept marketing.**[28] One *contrast* between the two is that there is nothing in food service analogous to the reservation systems so important to lodging. Another is the absence of any other significant market intermediaries.

Intercept marketing basically means bringing the food to where the customer is. This Kentucky Fried Chicken mobile unit is in a grocery store. (Photo courtesy of KFC Corp.)

Franchising in Food Service

Earlier in this chapter, we discussed the fact that franchising is an important organizational tool for a company that seeks to expand quickly and preempt the market. The factors (other than reservation systems) that are important in lodging are also important in food service franchising. Since their impact is somewhat different and there are some additional considerations, we will briefly discuss the services food service franchising organizations provide their franchisees.

A National Brand and Marketing System. Ronald McDonald is said to be second only to Santa Claus in recognition. Since McDonald's has been one of the largest advertisers in the world, spending over 2 billion dollars[29] on marketing, Ronald's recognition factor is no accident. Advertising is so important to a restaurant chain's success that one of the fastest growing chains in the United States, Boston Market, has organized its franchising and growth strategies around a common measure of advertising's geographical penetration, the ADI (area of dominant influence, see Chapter 3).[30]

Quality Assurance. One of the most important continuing services of a franchise system is field support, which includes inspection and guest opinion monitoring systems. In addition, franchisors provide for the development of improved operat-

Ronald McDonald and his friends are well-known figures, a testament to McDonald's advertising. (Photo courtesy of McDonald's)

ing tools and techniques such as management information systems. Another critical franchise service is the development of new products.

New Products. As restaurant concepts mature, the public tires of them. To keep customers from going to the competition, new products are a prime means of keeping a concept lively (see Chapter 8). The franchisor has the responsibility for developing new products from ideas into operational concepts and then to market-tested products. One of the richest resources in the new product development process is the franchisee. The Egg McMuffin, for instance, was first developed by a McDonald's franchisee.

New product development is not limited to new menu items. It also includes new and adapted *restaurant concepts*. PepsiCo's KFC and Taco Bell, for instance, have developed a conversion program which retrofits existing KFC stores into KFC/Taco Bell outlets.[31] Arby's has developed a new brand, Roast Town, which will be operated as a dual brand with Arby's. Test units with the new dual branding have seen 50 percent sales increases. Roast Town is Arby's entry into the home meal replacement market developed so successfully by Boston Market. Arby's is also testing two additional dinner-oriented concepts and is considering partnerships with breakfast, dessert, and snack brands.[32]

Buying Co-ops. Many franchise organizations work with franchisees to operate a buying co-op. The franchisor has a critical quality control role in approving suppliers of food products. In some cases, however, the franchisor also sells products to franchisees. At Domino's, for instance, 90 percent of the food products used by franchisees are sold to them by a subsidiary of the franchisor. This has led to some conflict which we will discuss later.

Training Programs. As in lodging, franchisors develop training programs and audiovisual support for these programs. This can be a cost-effective means of ensuring standardization and an important contribution to improving the quality of service and reducing training costs.

Assessing Franchising as a Mode of Expansion

Franchising is a tool for rapid expansion, but it also threatens control of operations by the franchisor as franchisees seek greater freedom and higher profits. The issues of growth and control deserve further discussion.

Growth. In the early days of a new concept or on entering a new territory, when franchisors need rapid growth, franchisors adopt practices oriented to meet that need for growth. Some franchisors expand by using a "master franchise," which grants the right to develop units in a fairly wide territory. The master franchisee usually contracts to develop a certain number of units over a specified time period. In some cases, the master franchisor has the right to subfranchise to others as a part of the expansion plan. The franchisor gives up a significant degree of control in ceding a large territory to a master franchisee.

Boston Market, one of the fastest growing companies in food service, uses a kind of master franchise, an "area developer, to achieve rapid market penetration—as well as advertising and operational efficiencies."[33] This company chooses people with a proven record of business success and regards area developers as partners who are granted the right to "open 10 to 100 stores . . . which is a multi million dollar business."[34] On the other hand, it does not abandon control since the franchise agreement gives it the right to buy back the franchise territory.[35]

Control. Franchising gives significant control over operations to the franchisee. While the franchise contract specifies many controls of the franchisor over the franchisee, courts tend to favor the franchisee as "the little guy" and so legal enforcement of these contracts is often difficult. Franchising also gives the franchisee the profit from the operation (after paying franchise fees). Companies that are well established in the market often limit the number of franchises a franchisee may receive, which, effectively, limits the franchisee's territorial control.

The dilution of profit from franchising is, in some cases, dealt with by an aggressive buyback program. PepsiCo, for instance, bought back many franchised units. This worked very well during a period of rapid growth in the market and improvement in operations, but the emphasis on increasing owned operations has been called into question in the face of profit setbacks:

> McDonalds scored nearly three times more in operating profit, from about $2 billion less in revenues. And McDonalds did so while owning only 20 percent of its chain . . . . In contrast, Pepsico owned 54 percent of its domestic Pizza Hut, Taco Bell and KFC Units.[36]

Conflict in Food Service Franchising

Food service franchisees are more closely tied to their franchisors than are lodging companies because of special-purpose buildings and highly specialized operating skills which might not translate readily to another concept. While there has been conversion activity from time to time, much of it has come about as a result of the purchase of entire chains to secure additional locations for the purchaser. Another occasion for conversion has arisen when a chain has been forced to go out of business due to financial difficulties and has been purchased by another company.

While the competition among franchisors for franchisees that arose from conversion franchising in lodging has not developed in food service, there is no lack of conflict in food service franchising systems. The conflict has taken the form, however, of lawsuits and lobbying of legislative and regulatory bodies. *Fortune* characterized the state of franchising in the United States as "deeply troubled," noting that most markets are crowded.

Since 1990, the number of complaints filed with the Federal Trade Commission against franchisors by their franchisees has been growing at a rate of over 50 percent, "numbering in the hundreds." Franchising advocates argue that the rate of business failure, which they estimate at about 5 percent, is lower for franchisees than for independent businesses. Others argue that these claims are based on data taken from the 1980s. More current studies by economists at Wayne State University and UCLA suggest that current failure rates for franchisees have risen so that they are about equal to those of independent businesses, in the range of 25 to 35 percent.[37] Four sources of conflict—inaccurate financial information, encroachment, conflict of interest on the part of a franchisor–supplier, and problems with franchise renewal—are discussed in the following sections.

Inaccurate Financial Information. Although regulated by both federal and state agencies, franchisor financial information is claimed by some franchisees to be unduly rosy. For instance, 26 franchisees of Cajun Joe complained in an arbitration proceeding that sales were overestimated and costs "grossly underestimated" so that profit projections were overstated.[38]

Encroachment. **Enroachment** is the term used in food service to describe the problem we have already discussed under the heading of *impact* for lodging franchisees. In 1993, a group of KFC franchisees successfully lobbied for a bill in the Iowa legislature which prohibits a franchisor from locating a new franchise within three miles of an existing franchise.[39] The result, reportedly, is that major franchisors slowed or halted the granting of franchises in that state.

Some franchise expansion is taking place in the form of downsized units. Franchisors argue that, even if these locations are near existing franchisees, they constitute an entirely different market of store or shopping mall patrons who would not go outside to eat a quick lunch, anyway. Franchisees argue that (1) the smaller unit downgrades the image of the franchise and (2) people who have already eaten at a sub shop or hamburger chain or some other restrictive concept are less likely to patronize the franchisee later that day or in the near future.[40]

One franchisee of McDonald's who had five new stores built close by, with a resulting drop of 35 percent in sales, summed up his view of encroachment:

> Remember the franchisor is in the business of maximizing his revenues, even if that means saturating your market with competing stores.[41]

Conflict of Interest. The franchisor's ability to *require* product purchases from its own distribution center is severely limited by antitrust laws. Nevertheless, there is a gray area in practice which relates to supplies provided for the purpose of maintaining quality. Eleven Domino's franchisees have filed a lawsuit under the antitrust laws, alleging that they are overcharged for raw dough and that the franchisor, who must approve all suppliers, is acting in a manner which discourages alternate suppliers from entering the market. A similar suit was filed in 1993 by a group of Little Caesar's franchisees.[42]

Franchise Renewal. Most cancelations of franchises are for unpaid costs and relatively few disputes arise, considering the huge number of franchises there are in operation. Nevertheless, as franchisors try to tighten operations in the face of growing competition, franchisees become concerned. Field Practice Note 9.1 explores a potential dispute in the making as this text is written.

Food Service Franchising Assessed

Franchising remains a powerful force for the distribution of a chain's brand and for rapid expansion of a concept. The problems we are now seeing in food service franchising (franchisees claiming that the franchise deal did not work out as advertised; or that their franchised territory has been encroached on with new franchises; or that the franchisor is abusing its power to approve suppliers) suggest that there are common pitfalls to this form of business organization.

To these difficulties should be added the fact that the franchisee is completely in the hands of the franchisor for vital business services, such as advertising, and product development. Franchisors are often strategic business units of larger companies and, as such, can be sold. When this happens, there is often a change in relations within that franchise community, as well as a good deal of change in business direction—and even sometimes a period of confusion and management turnover. Thus, while franchising *can* achieve the franchisor's ends of rapid growth, a potential franchisee should look very carefully at the deal offered—nor-

Field Practice Note 9.1

Franchising 2000 and Franchise Renewal

"Franchising 2000," McDonald's new business plan, includes provision to grade franchisees on seven specific criteria: customer satisfaction, market share, operational standards, employee development, financial viability, capital involvement, and the operator's daily involvement in operations and with other McDonald's operators. Franchisees earning a grade of A or B will be rewarded with opportunities to renew their franchises and expand to other units. Franchisees receiving lower grades must take remedial measures if they want their franchise renewed.

In response to this initiative, 200 franchisees have formed an independent association, called Consortium Members, Inc. A former McDonald's franchisee, Richard Adams, expressed the members concerns:

> How McDonald's regional staff grades the stores has to be consistent. We're going to monitor that and the timing of the various phases of implementation [of Franchising 2000]. We're going to try to make sure its done fairly.

The franchisee's stake in renewal is suggested by a profile of the consortium's members:

> The typical member has been in the McDonald's system for a decade or more, owns 2.3 stores, has a spouse and/or child active in the business and wants to continue as a McDonald's operator. The members typically depend on the equity in their restaurants for their retirement, and stock in the corporation represents a major part of their [financial] holdings.

Membership in the consortium is anonymous, suggesting that McDonald's franchisees may not feel absolutely comfortable with airing their grievances, actual or potential, in public.

Source: *Nation's Restaurant News,* April 1, 1996, pp. 1 and 96.

mally a contract that is highly favorable to the franchisor—to be sure that it meets his or her goals.

INTENSIVE DISTRIBUTION: INTERCEPT MARKETING

There has always been an advantage for a chain to having numerous restaurants. More units can reach more customers and achieve a higher level of market share. Over the past few years, QSRs have learned that they can operate in what are called *nontraditional locations,* such as hospitals, schools, colleges, expressways, and virtually any other place, as well as in freestanding restaurants. Learning from this

Carlson Companies' Country Kitchen Restaurants can be franchised as freestanding restaurants, as this one is. The company also franchises restaurants in Country Inns and Suites and in Radisson Hotels, two other franchise brands offered by Carlson Hospitality Worldwide. (Photo courtesy of Carlson Country Hospitality)

experience, restaurant companies have begun to think in terms not just of restaurants but of points of distribution (PODs).

Points of distribution (PODs) are scaled-down versions of a concept. They often rely on menus that are more limited than in a full concept, as well as miniaturization, modularity (production and service modules which can be assembled in different ways), and, sometimes, mobility. The presence of a known brand, careful choice of target market, and a high-traffic site are key points in achieving a successful POD operation.[43] Several different kinds of PODs are in use. Some of the most common are as follows:

Towers or modular upright merchandisers. These may be self-serve or a visible full-serve display. Usually floor standing and taller than eye level, it can be a warmer, a refrigerator, or a merchandiser for shelf-stable products.

Carts or modular cart systems. Ideal for intercepting customers and due to their mobility capable of serving as a satellite unit, carts are more often service units than they are "prep" units.

Kiosks. The kiosk is a self-contained minirestaurant. With the possible exception of needing outside storage space, the kiosk is a "standalone" intercept marketing vehicle. The typical kiosk requires approximately 120 square feet.

Custom facades. The facade is a frontispiece of trade dress and upgrades existing food service space into a branded food concept relatively simply, easily, and cost effectively.[44]

This scaled-down Taco Bell unit provides a low-investment route to intensive distribution and extends food service to locations that could not otherwise support it. (Photo courtesy of Taco Bell)

Two concepts are important to understanding the development of intercept marketing. They are *hosts* and *venues.*

Hosts and Venues

Hosts. According to Blumenthal, "A host is a business location or locations where high traffic is likely to offer potential high-volume sales of food or food service products." Examples are discount stores, grocery stores, malls, colleges and universities, airports, manufacturing plants, and theme parks. The key to the concept is that hosts provide the food service vendor with access to the host's traffic. Hosts seek food service PODs to enhance their environment, satisfy consumers, gain revenue, and, in commercial establishments such as stores, to drive incremental traffic.[45]

Venues. The place provided by a host for the operation of a P.O.D. or other scaled-down food service operation is called a "venue." In a way, a venue is analogous to a location for a freestanding restaurant. A venue, however, not only includes the place but also defines the customer. A venue on a college campus means that students will provide the bulk of the guests, whereas one in a mall means that shoppers will be the main customers, and in a manufacturing plant, we would expect workers to be the predominant traffic in the area.[46]

Food service companies seek venues because of a scarcity of traditional sites and because those traditonal sites that are available are very expensive. Chains' traditional operations face severe competition, but a venue offers exclusive or nearly exclusive access to a significant traffic flow.

Who Operates PODs?

Some operators of PODs are quick-service restaurant companies such as Taco Bell or Burger King. They often serve products which have been partially prepared in one of the their regular units. Others, however, are miniaturized versions of more service-intensive specialty restaurants such as Olive Garden, Pizza Hut, and Au Bon Pain. Contract food companies are major operators of PODs. Some contract companies operate under franchised brand names, while others use their own brand names or their own brands in combination with franchised national brands in a food court.

OTHER INTERCOMPANY MARKETING AGREEMENTS: ALLIANCES

Cooperation between companies can take many forms. Referred to as alliances, strategic partnerships, or joint ventures, these cooperative arrangements sometimes involve franchising. For instance, Radisson Hotels formed a strategic partnership in Europe with SAS Hotels. SAS Hotels undertook a joint marketing program with Radisson Hotels and changed its name to Radisson SAS Hotels. One of the stipulations of the agreement was that SAS hotel properties would take on the Radisson franchise. On the other hand, some alliances simply provide foor cross-marketing. Field Practice Note 9.2 considers several examples. Other alliances between hospitality companies and their suppliers are described in Case History 3.1 and Field Practice Note 14.1

LOGISTICS

Logistics pertains to moving goods for the purpose of supplying operations. Since the advent of QSR chains, concerns with logistics have become more significant in food service. With the coming of PODs and the increasing use of commissaries, this topic is likely to become even more important. Logistics is, in many ways, an operations function but, in developing place strategies, marketers must also take into account the problems of the physical distribution of the product.

Many chains prefer not to operate their own distribution system and find working with locally or regionally approved suppliers more efficient. Economies of purchasing may be achieved through *national contracts* that secure a lower-than-normal price for all chain and franchised units. Suppliers still provide distribution services through normal channels.

The working arrangements that emerge as most common are one of three. If the chain uses distributors, then all of the services—stocking and maintaining

Logistics companies such as Martin Brower provide physical distribution to many food service chains. (Photo courtesy of McDonald's)

appropriate inventory levels such as ordering, financing, warehousing, and delivery—are provided by wholesalers who pass these costs along in their markup. Chain units and franchisees are generally limited to buying from *approved suppliers*. The problems the chain solves with this option are those of quality and cost control. Use of approved suppliers is achieved through initial approval of the supplier and by inspection of products in transit and receiving controls at the unit. In the case of a large supplier, the chain may maintain an inspection team on the premises of a manufacturer or wholesaler. Inspectors make unannounced visits to wholesalers' premises or may meet suppliers' trucks at their destination and inspect contents against standards for both quality and quantity.

A second alternative is for the chain to maintain *distribution centers* that accept orders from units much in the same way that wholesalers do. Some chains go even further and maintain *commissaries* that manufacture food products for resale in the chain's units. The higher the *degree of integration* (i.e., the more of its channels it owns), the greater the level of control afforded the chain. In fact, some units operate commissaries principally to maintain quality control, rather than to effect savings, though economies of distribution are always a consideration.

A third option, third-party logistics, involves outsourcing the logistics function to a specialized company which takes over the entire logistical process. This is the arrangement that McDonald's has had with Martin Brower for some years. The logistics firm undertakes all the functions needed by the customer firm,

Field Practice Note 9.2

Corporate Alliances

Corporate alliances are formed to strengthen the partners' brands and to improve their efficiency in marketing and operations. Alliances permit "the partners to retain their independence—and in most cases, their financial control—while they raise revenues or cut costs"[1] Partnerships improve sales, because they help upgrade services while each partner reaches new customers. Cost savings come from "sharing segments of the business system" and from eliminating activities at one company or both through outsourcing.

Corporate alliances in the hospitality industry involve cross-marketing arrangements between two or more hospitality companies or between a hospitality company and one of its suppliers. In some cases, the alliance is a way to explore a possible merger but, in most cases, each firm intends to remain independent.

Pizza Hut has alliances—with Hilton Hotels, Marriott International, Choice Hotels, and HFS—to provide pizza delivery to hotel guests. Participating hotels display a table tent in guest rooms advertising the service. This provides a service that hotel guests want while helping Pizza Hut increase its sales. Pizza Hut pays a commission to the individual hotel for each order delivered and a smaller commission to the hotel franchinsing company. As in any good partnership, everybody benefits.

Carlson Hospitality International has developed a cross-marketing arrangement between Carlson Travel and the European firm, Wagonlit. Carlson Travel has excellent coverage of North America, while Wagonlit's strength is in Europe. The result of the alliance is that each firm has increased its global presence. The two partners intend to merge, and the alliance in Europe is known as Carlson Wagonlit.

HFS has developed a "Preferred Vendor Program" that offers certain vendors access to HFS' franchisees and their customers in return for discounts to the franchisees, advertising support for HFS brands, and payment of commissions to HFS. One agreement is between Visa and HFS. When HFS takes a reservation on its 800 number, the HFS reservationists will ask, "Would you like to guarantee that reservation with your Visa card?" Thus prompted, most guests do choose to use their Visa card, which has a lower discount fee than many other credit cards. HFS franchisees benefit immediately from moving guests to a lower cost card and Visa also supports HFS brands' marketing programs.

including warehousing, transport, product tracking, breaking bulk, small deliveries, custome brokerage, insurance, and related functions.

SUMMARY

Distribution involves making the product conveniently available to the customer, either by physical presence in a market or by representation. Convenience products (like QSRs) use intensive distribution to reach consumers wherever they are.

Another HFS alliance is with C.U.C. International, a discount travel firm. When making a reservation, HFS reservationists ask guests if they are interested in a discount travel club. If the guest is interested, he or she is referred automatically over the phone to C.U.C. HFS brands benefit because, for instance, a Day's Inn guest will be enrolled in a "Days Inn Travel Club," which C.U.C. operates, helping to build brand loyalty. (Days also operates its own travel club.)

HFS reservationists offer other services to callers. They will offer to reserve a car with Alamo Car Rentals if the traveler is going to be in a city in which Alamo has an agency. HFS and its franchisees have become the largest outside providers of sales to Alamo, and, in return, Alamo has joint advertising programs with HFS brands and provides them with marketing funds. Other alliances between hospitality companies and their suppliers are described in Case History 3.1 and Field Practice Note 14.1.

Experience with a wide variety of alliances at McKinsey and Company, an international consulting firm, suggests these points of caution when firms are considering alliances.[2]

1. Customer demographics and usage patterns should ensure a good fit between the partnering firms, and their brand images should be compatible.
2. Expectations and operating guidelines should be agreed to in advance, and benefits and risks between the partners should be balanced.
3. "Bundling" of products in a joint offer should give guests some real advantage and not just offer a package that guests would prefer to put together themselves.
4. Alliances can be costly in terms of executive time and can lead to disagreements, so conflict resolution mechanisms should be built into the agreement.
5. Each party should be assured of its ability to control its service offering and protext its brand image.

Source: I would like to thank several people for their help in assembling the information for this Note: At HFS, Janice Jarosz and Daniel Tarantin; at Pizza Hut, Chris Romoser; and at Radisson, Tom Polski.

[1]David Earnest and Thomas D. French, "Corporate Alliances: After the Honeymoon." *Wall Street Journal,* May 13, 1996, p. A20.

[2]Ibid.

Channels of distribution in lodging include chain and franchise organizations, as well as travel agents, airline and car rental ticket agents, hotel sales representative companies, and incentive houses. In lodging, the growth of the global distribution system (GDS) has intensified the role of intermediaries such as travel agents and other travel companies. Franchise organizations continue to be important but have much less power over their franchisees because of growing competition among lodging franchisors for franchisees. Food service is essentially a retail business and franchise companies are the only significant distribution channel active in the industry.

There is conflict in the hospitality channels of distribution centering around issues of impact (hotels) and encroachment (food service), accuracy of franchisor financial information, conflicts of interest, and problems with franchise renewal.

The growing use of mobile and downsized points of distribution (PODs) supports a move toward intercept marketing in food service, that is, providing guests with food service wherever they are.

◆ *Key Words and Concepts*

Intensive distribution
Exclusive distribution
Selective distribution
Market saturation
Channels of distribution
Franchise systems
Physical presence
Representation
Reservation systems
Lodging channels of distribution
  Chains
  Franchise systems
  Travel agents
  Hotel sales representative companies
  Incentive houses
Selling within channels
Distribution in food service
  Franchising
Points of delivery (PODs)
Intercept marketing
Conflict of interest
Franchise renewal
Conflict in food service franchising
Impact-Encroachment
Hosts
Venues
Alliances
Logistics

◆ Discussion Questions

1. What are the differences in the way distribution is achieved between lodging and food service?
2. What are the degrees of intensity of distribution? How are they matched to products offered and consumer buying motives?
3. Who are the typical channel members in the distribution of manufactured goods? What differences are there among them?
4. Who are the principal channel members in hospitality distribution?
5. How are reservation systems changing distribution in lodging?
6. Under what circumstances is it possible for a hotel to operate successfully without a franchise? When is a franchise necessary?
7. What is meant by "conflict" within franchising? How is this conflict different between hotels and food service?
8. What is meant by "intercept marketing"? How is it changing food service marketing?

Chapter 10

When you have finished reading this chapter, you should be able to

1. Describe the major strategic issues related to location
2. List the factors that will be considered in avaluating a location
3. Discuss site evaluation factors
4. Explain the difference between food service and hotel location studies
5. Identify the important factors in a hotel feasibility study

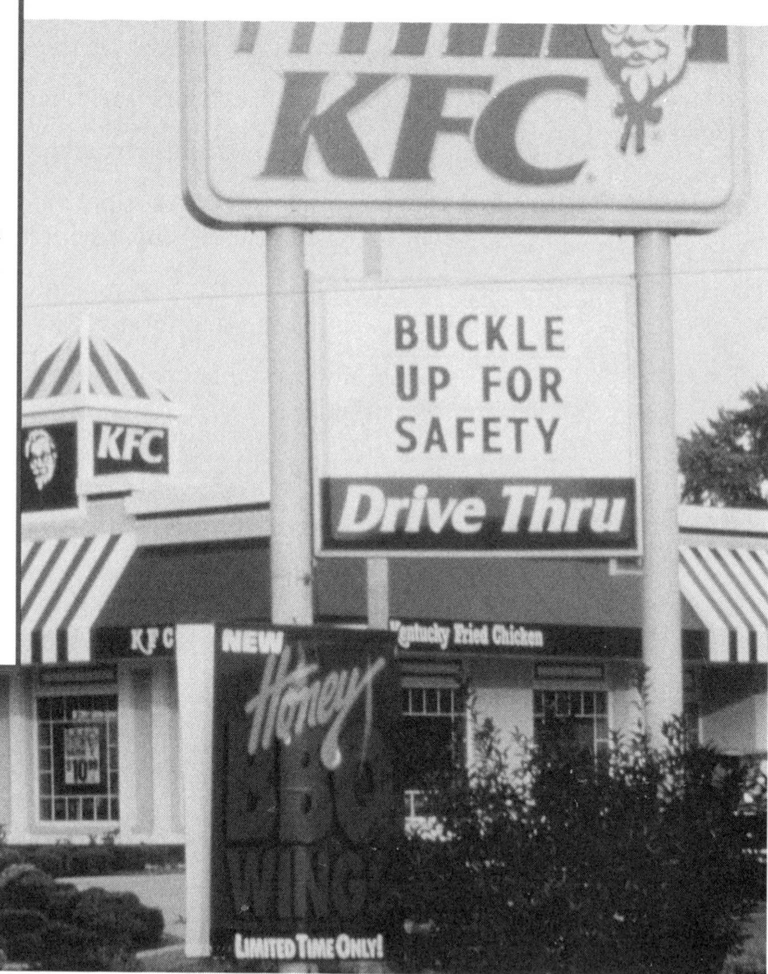

(Photo courtesy of KFC)

Place in Hospitality:

Location

One major difference between hospitality marketing and conventional marketing is dramatically illustrated in the contrasting ways they handle the concept of place. Conventional marketing is concerned with "placing products," that is, with getting products from the manufacturer to the final seller, the retailer, and to the ultimate consumer. Location, if it is mentioned at all in most marketing textbooks, receives a page or two of discussion and much of that is concerned with the location of *factories and warehouses,* rather than the location at which the consumer is served. In contrast, we will devote this chapter to location and site selection, a subject of major importance in hospitality marketing.

LOCATION

It is the oldest chestnut in our field; yet it is so true that it bears repeating. Ellsworth Statler, founder of the Statler Hotel chain and one of the pioneers of marketing in our industry, once said, "There are three factors necessary for the success of a hotel. They are location, location, and location." In our discussion, we need to look at both the strategic and the tactical issues related to location because Mr. Statler was right: Location *is* a crucial issue in hospitality.

LOCATION STRATEGY

At the most basic level, companies must decide in which area they will locate their units as they expand. In the early days of motel chains, for instance, Quality Courts operated east of the Mississippi, Best Western west of the Mississippi. Holiday Inns began as a regional chain in the southeastern United States and gradually expanded into adjoining areas. LaQuinta Motor Inns has followed a similar strategy. Concentrating in a region and expanding the company's territory gradually into adjoining areas permit a company to draw market advantage from the reputation and customer base of established units. When companies move into a new territory they are not known in, they often experience tough sledding until they are established. This was the case, for instance, with a company as well established as Holiday Inns when it first entered the West Coast market in the United States.

Clustering

One strategic approach to the problem of location is clustering. **Clustering** refers to locating several units in the same geographic area. In describing its business plan, for instance, Boston Market indicated:

> There are 211 ADIs [areas of dominant influence—see Chapter 3] across the country. However, about two thirds of the U.S. population is concentrated in 60 key ADIs. We have prioritized our development efforts to make these 60 ADIs our primary targets for rapid development.
>
> Our experience indicates that rapid, concentrated penetration of select ADIs is a superior strategy to more diffuse, generalized development across a large number of markets . . . . Concentrating our stores by ADI helps us establish critical mass by quickly obtaining the best location and building consumer awareness and loyalty . . . . Concentrated market development leads to operating efficiencies in many areas, including management, training, marketing and administration. It also allows us to use television advertising sooner than would be the case with a more scattered expansion strategy.[1]

Clustering, then, offers economies of scale within the cluster. However, loading a number of new stores into a territory involves the risk of *cannibalization,* that is, one of a company's stores stealing its business from another of its stores. In fact, Boston Market's sales volume in new stores was initially inadequate. Boston Market indicated "that its (clustering) strategy requires *at least* 18 months to absorb the effects of cannibalization."[2]

Although clustering can be overdone, the reverse is also true. Wendy's expansion into Canada some years ago illustrates some of the problems. Early success in the Toronto market encouraged Wendy's to move into other geographic markets in Canada, some over 1,000 miles away. In several markets, Wendy's did not have a large enough store base to generate the sales needed to support expensive television advertising or to mount a significant campaign in other media. Operations management was hard put, too, to supervise such a large territory and the quality of the operations suffered. Although these problems were subsequently solved by a very energetic turnaround management team, the company experienced several bad years.[3]

Field Practice Note 10.1 shows the relative desirability, based on supply and demand, of nine major areas of the United States with respect to "restaurant opportunities" as determined by one group of market researchers.

Location Type: Freestanding or Part of a Larger Unit

Another strategic location issue is location type. Some companies seek only freestanding locations, whereas others specialize in locations in malls, office buildings, and other areas where traffic is provided by other tenants. Increasingly, however, companies are choosing to move into malls and other complex units, even though their principal location strategy may favor freestanding units.

The move into malls results from several factors.[4] The number of available freestanding locations is limited and many of the best are already taken. Limited availability of freestanding sites means not only difficulty in obtaining a site but also a substantially higher cost for those freestanding sites that remain. Mall locations, though expensive, are not as overpriced relative to the volume they can deliver.

Market research indicates, moreover, that the mall visitor market is a particular kind of target market. The principal restaurant patronage motive is the convenience of food service located in the mall. In effect, the mall's traffic provides a customer base and access to a target market that can only be reached by being in the mall. No market is captive. Malls of any size have several kinds of food service, so that competition is present. Nevertheless, a mall location provides privileged access to the mall's customers. Although competition *is* present, there will usually be only one operation for each concept and this exclusivity is not available in other locations. Indeed, in today's mature food service market, the freestanding unit commonly must fight it out with several neighboring competitors that offer a similar concept.

The mall location presents a somewhat different marketing situation than freestanding units. The unit's physical arrangements are less flexible and the occupancy cost (i.e., rent) per square foot is usually higher. Accordingly, companies have developed downsized units that can recapture high rents through high sales volume—in successful malls. A key point in a mall location is that sales volume is basically a function of the success of the mall and that a successful food service operation in an unsuccessful mall is quite unusual.

The presentation of the unit is different, too. The unique physical facility and the visibility found in a freestanding unit are not available in a mall. Instead, presentation issues involve the amount and kind of signage permitted and the number of feet of counter space available.

Promotion costs for a small chain operating exclusively in malls are likely to be somewhat less because they rely on the traffic provided by the mall. Companies that have a significant number of freestanding units, however, probably have to maintain their promotional activity to support their freestanding units. Malls do

Field Practice Note 10.1

The Best Locations in America to Open a Restaurant

Restaurant and Institutions Magazine and Equifax National Decision Systems have developed a model which identifies where demand for restaurants is relatively high and the supply of restaurants is relatively low. *Supply variables* which the model takes into account are the number of eating and drinking places, total eating and drinking place sales, and sales per location. *Demand variables* are number of households, median income per household, annual per household expenditure on eating and drinking away from home, and share of household income spent on eating and drinking away from home. The location results are compared to other locations in the same census region in order to establish a relative position.

Source: *Restaurants and Institutions,* May 15, 1995, p. 58.

Restaurant Opportunities by Region

				Eating and Drinking Locations				
Region	Restaurant Opportunity Index	1994 est. Households	1994 est. Median Income	Locations	1994 Total Sales (000)	Per HH[a] Expenditure	Demand per Location	Income[b] Share
1. East South Central	135	3,371,776	$29,261	15,259	$6,043,477	$1,770	$409,257	5.98%
2. West South Central	118	7,861,405	28,044	42,036	14,244,739	1,757	340,923	6.31
3. South Atlantic	116	14,176,613	31,350	70,082	26,442,389	1,795	371,923	5.68
4. Mountain	110	3,944,446	32,946	19,507	7,224,667	1,802	358,913	5.55
5. West North Central	105	4,349,091	32,052	22,127	8,052,827	1,793	337,101	5.64
6. East North Central	101	12,783,539	34,586	69,428	23,895,114	1,815	340,235	5.37
7. Pacific	97	13,676,869	35,614	80,650	26,247,401	1,862	343,727	5.14
8. Middle Atlantic	93	10,019,741	34,051	58,103	18,801,832	1,823	316,101	5.34
9. New England	87	4,321,121	37,299	24,882	8,447,613	1,883	322,201	4.88
UNITED STATES TOTALS	100	97,472,896	34,617	526,842	179,648,530	1,843	340,991	5.32

[a]HH = households.
[b]Household expenditure as percentage of median income.

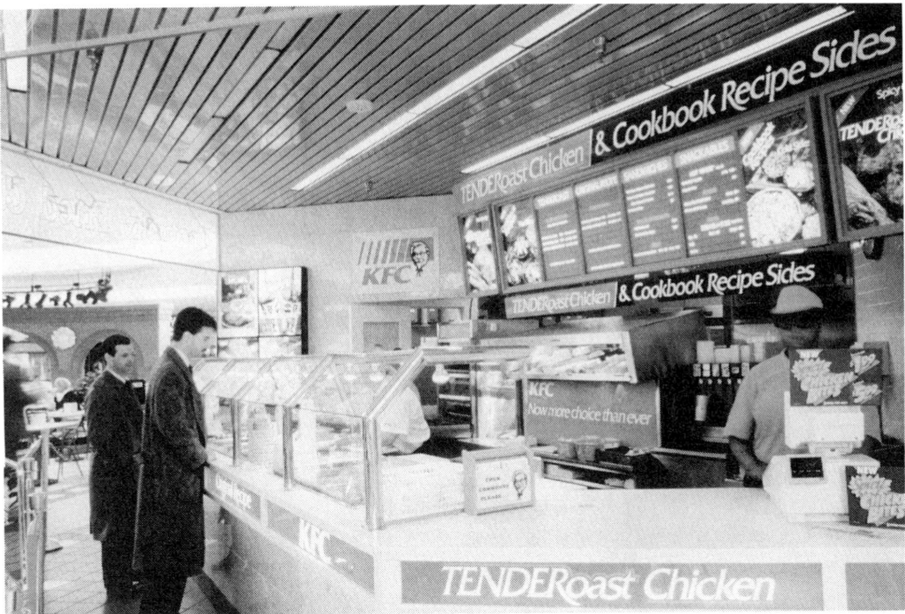

A freestanding unit presents a different marketing problem than an in-mall location, where the traffic is provided by mall patrons. (Photos courtesy of KFC)

offer advantages to new or relatively unknown concepts just because traffic is provided. On the other hand, a strategy of using only mall locations will, in time, limit the growth of a chain simply because the number of successful malls is limited. Moreover, large chains that operate several different kinds of locations do have to accept that not all of their mall units' volume is *additional* sales. There is some cannibalization because, for instance, a person eating fried chicken in a mall for lunch is less likely to be a dinner customer for fried chicken that evening.

Colocation

Colocation, as the name implies, involves putting two or more concepts in one location, generally two noncompetitive concepts. Arby's has developed Roast Town, a concept intended to compete in the home meal replacement market, a different market segment than the one Arby's has traditionally served.[5] The Roast Town concept will colocate with existing Arby's QSRs.

McDonald's and Amoco have announced a chain of cobranded stations after a year long test of the concept and McDonald's has announced a similar alliance with Chevron's Food Mart, a convenience store. Alliances between food service chains and oil companies are particularly attractive since service stations often control prime real estate.[6]

Where colocation is with another retailer, the restaurant benfits from the traffic that firm generates and, in turn, provides a service to the retail customers which

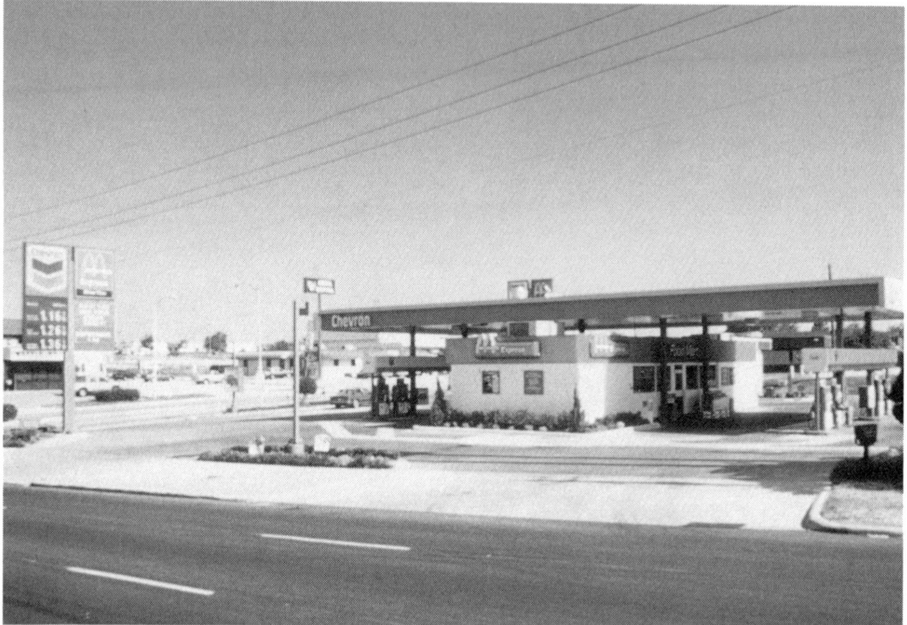

When two powerful noncompetitive brands occupy a site together, the result is improved sales, as each brand benefits from the draw on the customer base of the other brand. (Photo courtesy of McDonald's Corp.)

enhances the location. Where colocation is with another food service firm, both firms share the cost of the land, some building costs, and gain from exposure to the customers of the partner. Morning donut customers, in effect, become afternoon ice cream customers.

Funnel or Magnet?

Most chain operations and many independent operations seek high-traffic locations. We can liken these locations to a funnel under a waterfall: if you keep both hands firmly on the funnel, the water will flow through it. In funnel locations, such as those occupied by major QSR operators like McDonald's or KFC, there are so many prospective customers in the area that stores are almost certain to do a high volume of sales. Funnel locations, however, do have the disadvantage of being located on very expensive real estate which means high rent or fixed capital costs.

The analogy to the magnet in locations is the very distinctive operation located out in the country, away from everything, or in a small town, away from major population centers. In such a location, there will be little or no drop-in business; people have to drive a considerable distance to get there. The country location, however, offers advantages in creating a unique ambience: scenery, quiet, open space, and the like. Moreover, the real estate cost is likely to be much less than in high-traffic urban locations and this helps hold down fixed costs. In order for such a location to succeed, however, the *operation* must be the magnet, offering a distinctive experience in menu, quality of food, and excellence of service that will draw customers a significant distance.

In paying for a high-traffic location, operators expect that location will help *push* volume through their operation. A magnet location requires an operation that will *pull* customers to it.

TACTICAL ISSUES

Once the broad outline of a location strategy is established, specialized effort is needed to analyze particular location decisions. We will distinguish between a *location decision* and a *site decision*. As an example, in a location decision, a company might decide to expand into a general part of a city, such as the neighborhood of a new mall or office park, or on a particular side of town. Once a decision is taken to locate in an area, a site decision that involves a particular piece of land is required. For every retail location decision, an average of four sites are evaluated, according to John S. Thompson, a location and site selection consultant.[7]

Evaluating a Restaurant Location

A restaurant location is best evaluated in terms of the potential access it affords the operator to customers.[8] A trading area can be defined for an existing operation or estimated for a new one. The "quality" of the population is assessed, as is the location's access to that population through the roadway system for transportation. The likely direction of major traffic flow is also significant. Finally, competition in the area must be studied. We will review each of these factors briefly.

Trading Area. A trading area encompasses the region from which 70 to 75 percent of a unit's business is drawn. In an existing unit, the trading area is estimated from studies of the unit's patronage. In a new unit, the trading area would need to be estimated. This estimate would be made on the basis of sales volume at other retail establishments in the region, the performance of other units in similar locations (if the proposed operation is part of a chain, these data are much easier to come by), and very often from responses to questionnaires or interviews with prospective customers.

Population and Its Characteristics. When a trading area has been defined, its characteristics are studied in depth. A key factor is population, in particular, its density, demographics, and psychographics. A densely populated area is generally preferred simply because the more people there are, the more mouths there are to feed.

Although for fast-food and other popularly priced operations population density is the key, the demographics of that population are also important. For instance, the presence of families with children would be a highly favorable factor for some operations but less important for others. For an independent seeking to serve the upscale carriage trade, population density would be less significant than the income statistics for the area. As this last case makes clear, the operator is not interested in everybody in the trading area but rather the market segment or segments targeted.

A feasibility study needs to take into account the current market situation, but it also needs to look ahead. A location analysis should project population growth for the area and also estimate the size of the total population and the market segment or segments for five years into the future.

Finally, the population's psychographics or lifestyle is of interest. An operation that offers family dining with country style barbeque might be interested in one psychographic segment in an area, whereas a Red Lobster might target a somewhat different group. We need not be surprised, however, if these two operations are found side by side: The trading area they draw from probably contains an adequate number of both market segments to meet the needs of such operation.

Relation to Roadway System and Traffic. The key to the location is the access it offers the unit to target populations. Whereas population in the immediate area is important to many operations, access to people via the roadway or other transportation is often even more important. Driving time from centers of population is a commonly used measure of the convenience of the location. Driving time will be affected by the quality of the road system leading to the site and any physical barriers between the site and the population center.

The impact of any physical or social barriers on traffic should also be assessed. **Physical barriers** include factors such as unbridged rivers and large bodies of water, as well as mountains and freeways that do not have convenient crossings. **Social barriers** include industrial areas, slums, and—curiously—extremely affluent areas,[9] as well as areas with congested traffic.

Distance. As we just noted, distance from population is a good *proxy* (i.e., indirect measure) for convenience. We should keep in mind, however, that *acceptable distance* is defined differently for different operations. Most convenience stores, for instance, serve a trading area within a radius of 1/4 mile to 1 mile, but a fast-food unit area may draw residents from a radius of 1 mile to 1 1/2 miles. On the other hand, fine dining establishments often pull customers from much greater distances.

Table 10.1 describes good, fair, and bad driving conditions for nearby and more distant locations. Field Practice Note 10.2 highlights the advantage of measuring a market in terms of driving time instead of just distance.

Local Traffic. A fast-food operation, in particular, but other mass-market operations as well, will be interested in the volume of traffic in the area. In downtown and other highly congested areas, pedestrian, rather than vehicular, traffic can be the significant measure. In general, the more traffic and the greater the traffic flow, the better the location for popular-priced restaurants. For upscale restaurants,

Table 10.1 Factors Affecting Driving Time

DISTANCE 0 TO 5 MILES

Ideal Driving Conditions

Quick and easy access to a freeway direct to the site. On-ramp (from zip code center to freeway) and off-ramp (from freeway to site) combined distance must be less than 1 mile.

Semilimited access such as a network of not more than two *major* arterials. Up to 1/2 mile on residential roads.

If the zip code population center is within 1 mile of the site, good residential roads.

Adequate Driving Conditions

Semilimited access such as a network of not more than three *major* arterials. Up to 1/2 mile on residential roads.

If the population center is within 2 miles of the site, good residential roads.

Poor Driving Conditions

Blocked or otherwise poor network.

All other conditions.

DISTANCE 0 TO 5 MILES

Very Good Driving Conditions

Quick, easy access to a freeway direct to the site. On-ramp and off-ramp combined distance must be less than 1 1/2 miles.

Semilimited access such as no more than two *major* arterials direct to the site.

Poor Driving Conditions

All other conditions.

Source: Adapted from John S. Thompson, *Site Selection* (New York: Lebhar-Friedman, 1982).

however, the *quality* of traffic is also of interest. Truck traffic can yield fast-food business but is unlikely to be a source of white-tablecloth business.

Other Sources of Business. In many locations, nonresidential sources of business are the most significant. For instance, offices or plants, as well as theaters, schools, colleges, and medical facilities, have large numbers of employees who are potential customers and also draw a significant volume of visitors. In the central business district (CBD) and in shopping centers, retail stores are the major source of traffic.

Field Practice Note 10.2

Distance or Driving Time

The area enclosed in the circle in the accompanying figure is a market area defined by a 3-mile radius from a hypothetical QSR location in Chicago, Illinois. The drawback to this market definition is highlighted by contrasting it with the shaded portion of the map which marks a trading area that is within a 5-minute drive of the location. Note that some of that 5-minute drive area is actually *more* than 3 miles from the location.

Using a *distance*-based market definition results in the inclusion of a substantial population that can not actually reach the restaurant in a short enough period to make them probable customers, while excluding some who are within reasonable drive time. In fact, not every household within the circle has equally convenient access to the restaurant. The reason for the difference is undoubtedly accounted for by barriers to transportation and other peculiarities of the local roadway system. A location decision based on distance would be distorted by an inaccurate customer profile and a seriously overstated population as shown in the bottom part of the figure.

Distance has been used in the past largely because the only way to determine drive time was to get behind the wheel and experiment. That was time consuming, especially if measurements were needed from a large number of points. What has changed all this is the availability of computerized drive times as a part of the census. Called TIGER (Topologically Integrated Geographically Encoding and Referencing) files, TIGER is essentially a collection of electronic road maps. When incorporated into a computer mapping system, TIGER can be manipulated, as was done in the accompanying figure, to produce drive times.

With expensive real estate, companies need to be sure the market they are paying for is one that can effectively reach them. For this purpose, drive times are the best information.

Source: Scott Purlee, "Driving Influences," *Restaurants and Institutions,* April 15, 1995, p. 30. Map and data courtesy of Scott Purlee, Analytical Directions, Inc.

The Gravity of Large Centers and Traffic Flow. Perhaps the leading academic theory of location analysis is the gravity model set forth by David L. Huff. This model estimates the probability of consumers patronizing a retail area.[10] The factors the model weighs in this estimate are the size of the shopping area, travel time for the consumer to reach the center, and the impact of the amount of travel time on patronage at the particular kind of shopping center.[11] (e.g., a large regional mall versus a small strip mall). In general, the larger the center, the larger the variety of goods offered, and the shorter the distance from the consumer's home, the greater the likelihood of patronage.[12] Retail sales volume in the center, then, is positively related to the pull (likened to gravity) of the shopping area—reflected both in size and variety of goods—and proximity to customers. Thompson speaks of an

Cumberland Avenue and Irving Park, Chicago, IL

Variables	3 Mile Radius (Circled Area)	5 Minute Drive (Shaded Area)
Households (1994)	71,198	58,090
Population	178,862	145,536
Population square mile	5,962	6,930
Total employees (day time population)	86,877	64,673
Median Household Income	$39,140	$38,589
Total spending on food away from home		
Fast Food (000 omitted)	68,130	54,819
Service Restaurant (000 omitted)	79,497	63,965

The river and freeway in the center of this picture and the mountains in the background all constitute physical barriers that shape traffic patterns in Phoenix, Arizona.

"inbound bias," indicating that shoppers gravitate toward centers of retail activities.[13] Being located between a center of population and a shopping center that exercises a gravitylike pull, then can give significant advantages to a location, assuming a favorable site.

Competition. The presence of competition in a neighborhood is often a favorable indicator. Fast-food rows and restaurant rows are testimony to the fact that a good central location can support several restaurants and that the presence of a number of restaurants in an area will increase the draw of food service traffic to the area, much as the gravity of large retail shopping centers do in Huff's model.

The first step in assessing competition is to plot the competition on a map of the area and to note location in terms of street and cross-street, size of unit (number of seats; square feet), and the type of outlet and its estimated sales. The competitive analysis should discriminate between direct and indirect competition. For instance, a market study for a fast-food chicken restaurant analyzed competing locations in two direct categories: fast-food chicken and other fast food. In addition, it identified, in a third category, all other restaurants such as coffee shops and family restaurants.

Although the presence of competition can be a favorable indicator, it is clearly possible for a location to be overstored. One means of assessing this possibility is

In many downtown locations, foot traffic rather than vehicle traffic is a prime consideration.

to estimate the sales volume of the competing operations in the area. If the competitors are able operators but not doing an acceptable level of volume, this should signal a caution to the location analyst. On the other hand, a concentration of outmoded or indifferently operated competitors may signal an opportunity. In effect, if they can survive while doing an indifferent job, that is evidence of strong demand on which a currently fashionable, well-run operation should be able to capitalize.

Site Evaluation

Our division between location and site analysis is a useful way to approach the material we have covered. At this point, however, we should note that it is in some ways artificial. Although general location analysis can proceed first, followed by site analysis, in many cases there are not two separate processes but one interactive process. If there is no site, then reviewing the location is a waste of time. If there are sites, it immediately raises the question of whether this is a good location. In practice, landowners and their agents are continually approaching restaurant chains with proposed sites, so that a site proposal could even initiate the analytical process. The reader, therefore, should keep in mind that the factors cited earlier regarding location are often reviewed more or less simultaneously with those we are about, to look at. They are all fundamental to analysis of the site, too. It is true, however, that the detailed review of a site is likely to be the last step finished before a site is acquired.

As a starting point in site analysis, the traffic patterns (considered in general earlier during our analysis of the location) need to be reviewed again. This time the traffic patterns need to be related to a specific piece of property. Factors to be considered are traffic volume count, ease of traffic flow, and (as appropriate) quality of traffic. As Figure 10.1 shows, the exposure to traffic is maximized by a corner location. For this reason, a corner location is almost always preferable when available.

The access from the roadway to the site is evaluated on the basis of ease of ingress and egress. Where left-turn lanes, left-turn pockets, or traffic control lights or stop signs are present, these are favorable factors because they facilitate access for left-turning traffic. If traffic is highly congested at the site or if access is restricted to right-hand turns, these can be seriously unfavorable factors.

Adequate size of the site, itself, to provide room for both the building and the necessary parking, is crucial. The cost of the site will also be a significant factor. Demand for prime real estate is strong and, with many good locations taken, real estate prices continue to escalate. Restaurant building costs have risen, too. Accordingly, fixed-asset requirements, including land and other capital costs, need to be reviewed in the light of the property's forecasted volume in order to be sure

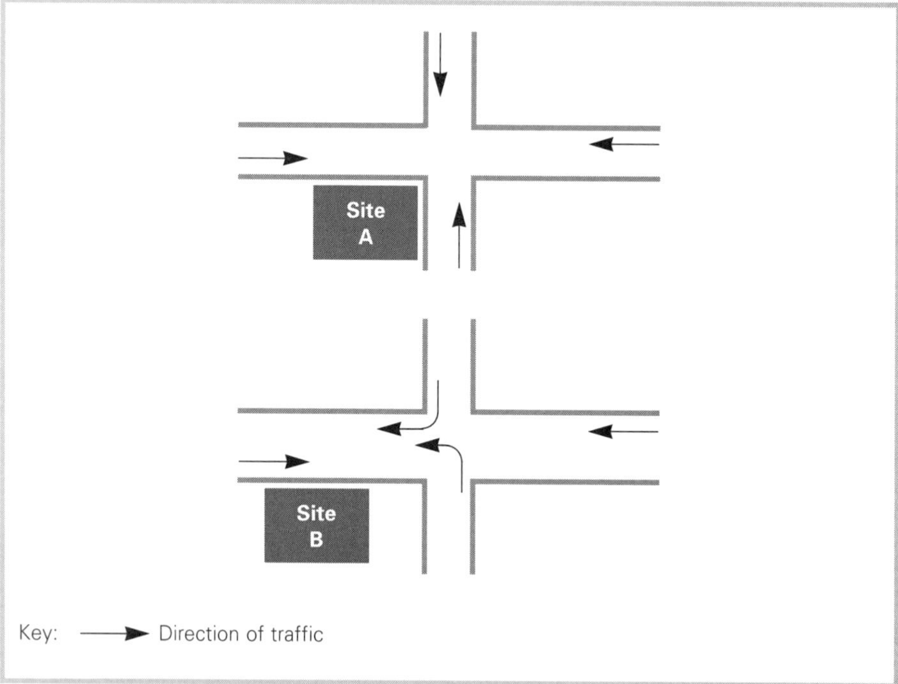

Figure 10.1 Corner Locations Are More Readily Visible and Accessible to All Traffic

Source: Adapted from John S. Thompson, Site Selection (New York: Lebhar-Friedman, 1982), p. 62.

that the planned operation will generate the necessary level of sales and profits to justify them.

The visibility of the site to traffic is important and the *relative* visibility is significant, too. Here, we refer to the possibility that the site might technically be visible yet lost in the clutter of other building and activity in the area. Under these circumstances, any special provisions or problems related to making the property stand out from its neighbors with signs, special treatment of the exterior, or other efforts to heighten the visibility of the propsed operation would be of particular interest.

Land use in the surrounding area should be examined. Activities in the area can serve as a magnet for traffic, as in the case of a theater, or can be a distinct disadvantage, as in the case of a factory or other activity that pollutes the immediate environment with odors, excessive noise, or just an ugly appearance. A final factor is site terrain and whether it presents problems for the building and parking required.

Given the complexity of the location and site analysis, it is not surprising that most restaurant chains have real estate departments that specialize in the analysis and acquisition of land for the company's use.

HOTEL LOCATION: THE FEASIBILITY STUDY

The hotel location and site analysis has many similarities with the restaurant location and site decision just described. There are, however, some fundamental differences. First, the feasibility study—as the documents developed to support a hotel construction decision are named—is more concerned with the overall financing picture for a proposed property than is typically the case in food service. Because a hotel decision is so capital intensive, the feasibility study must consider not only total project cost but "the financial structure of the deal and the tax implications of the resulting profit and loss in the context of the owner's total portfolio."[14] A hotel feasibility study, then, emphasizes financing considerations to a greater degree than is the case for restaurant decisions.

Second, a hotel developer looks at a larger service area than does the typical restaurant. Most hotel location studies will evaluate the entire community as a market. In larger cities, specific area will be evaluated, but that area will generally be much larger than the typical restaurant's trading area.

A third difference is that although market analysis is restricited to the area in which the project site is located, guests are expected to come from areas far removed from that site.[15] In the case of resort hotels, conference centers, and convention hotels, a study of demand in distant cities may be undertaken, but, with most properties, the demand from travelers in other cities is inferred from a study of "local demand generators and attractions."[16] and a study of "rooms actually occupied in local hotels and motels".[17]

The contents of a hotel feasibility study include a site review and area evaluation, a market demand analysis, a review of economic and demographic indicators, a competitive analysis, facilities and concept recommendations, a forecast of income and expense, an estimate of total project cost, an economic value estimate, and a return-on-investment analysis.[18] These factors are discussed next.

Project Site and Area Evaluation

The size and topography of the site must be assessed to be sure it is suitable to the proposed project. Similarly, the location of the site relative to key highways and interstates should be considered, as should the site's ease of access for motor vehicle traffic.

Demand Analysis

Demand is analyzed by major segment, including at least three: commercial, meeting, and vacationer. Demand is estimated by two methods. Using what is called the "build-up approach," demand is estimated "through a series of interviews with people connected with travel generators." These interviews determine the amount of demand each source attracts on a weekly or monthly basis, along with other important visitor characteristics such as length of stay, number in party, and spending habits. The alternative to build up "recognizes that an area's transient demand can be estimated by totalling the rooms actually occupied in local hotels and motels."[19] That is, actual demand and its trend are estimated. These two estimates can then be used as a check on one another.

Market Characteristics

Trends in demographic and economic indicators are reviewed as a basis for supporting the demand projection. For instance, in one model study, the history of the following indicators was used to project commercial visitation to the area: retail sales, employment, occupied office space, thruway traffic, and airport passenger and cargo traffic. Similar bases were used to project meeting and convention volume, while vacationer visitation was based on highway traffic, past tourist visit statistics and visits to nearby attractions.[20]

Analysis of the Competition

The analysis of the competition is always set in the context of the demand in a particular market. Well-qualified competitors, for instance, are not as much of an immediate threat in a market that is severely underbuilt as in one that has excess capacity. A competitive survey needs to evaluate the strengths and weaknesses of existing competition; this may be used to argue for the particular kind of facilities to build in a specific locale.

It is necessary to assess not only direct but also indirect competitors. For instance, in a resort community, condominium rentals are a potential factor. It is important, too, to assess future competition. Many properties that are announced are, for one reason or another, never built. Those that have been granted building permits and obtained financing, however, are very likely to be built. Those that are under construction are almost certain to be finished.

Other Study Contents

Based on analysis of demand and competition, a recommendation as to facilities is made and, on the basis of that recommendation, the cost of the facility can be estimated. Income is estimated based on demand projection and competitive analysis and the cost of operation is also estimated based on facilities and assessed occupancy levels. Profit is forecast by comparing income and expense. Since the final estimates typically are concerned with a minimum 30-year life, the entire project involves judgments that go beyond the typical marketing study.

Informed Judgment

It is important to underline the degree to which a hotel feasibility study relies on estimates, judgment of interviewers as to meaning of statements, and judgment of the feasibility study authors as to the extent and interpretation of trends. The location decision patterns in the hotel industry are somewhat less precise and formalized than is the case with food service chains.

The feasibility study is commonly used internally to confirm management's original decision on a proposed location, but another and probably more significant use of the feasibility study is to secure debt financing for the proposed property. Because the hotel company will spend tens of thousands of dollars on the feasibility study and as it is intended for use by them to secure financing, there is often an unspoken pressure on the feasibility analyst to come up with a positive answer. The study's use as a confirmation of the earlier, informed judgment by senior management under these circumstances is open to question.

Site selection is sometimes relegated to a secondary role. As one chain executive told the author, "We are more flexible than a no-name because of our marketing strength and brand recognition. We are interested in convenience to areas of commercial and recreational activity, but we can afford to take a location three or four blocks from the very center because our customers will come that far-at least in a central business district location."[21] That same executive, however, noted that site location relative to traffic and activity areas was considerably more important outside the central business district.

Marriott's Courtyard properties offer another example of the use of less than prime sites because of the strength of the brand. Company officials have indicated that some Courtyard locations are actually hard to get to the first time but that guest demand for the Courtyard property is strong enough that guests will make the effort to find the property. We should note, however, that, in these locations, the property is serving guests who have business in the immediate area and, hence, want to stay nearby. Such a location strategy would almost certainly not be appropriate if the property was counting on a significant amount of off-the-road tourist traffic.

SUMMARY

Location strategy involves the selecting of the general region in which a company will operate; how it will expand that area; and what type of location it will use (freestanding, for instance, in-mall, or colocation). The tactics of locating a particular operation involve both location and site selection. *Location* refers to a general area within a city, while the *site* is a specific piece of property. Location analysis requires the definition of a trading area and then a study of the area's population, roadway and transportation system, and the area competition. Traffic patterns and the volume of traffic are important points to consider.

Site evaluation, which is often conducted simultaneously with location analysis, considers the same factors but with respect to a specific piece of property. In addition, site evaluation considers ease of entrance and exit from the site, the site's visibility, nearby land use, the size of the site, and its cost.

Hotel location analysis is usually documented in a feasibility study following a rationale that is similar to that for restaurants. Hotel location decisions, however, emphasize financing aspects of the proposition and generally look at a larger service area, often a city as a whole. A peculiarity of hotel decisions is that most of their business comes from other areas, and so regional and national travel patterns must be considered.

◆ Key Words and Concepts

Location strategy
Clustering
Location type
Colocation
Funnel or magnet
Trading area
Population characteristics
Roadway system
Physical barriers
Social barriers
Gravity model
Competition and location
Site evaluation
Site visibility
Feasibility study
Demand analysis
Market characteristics
Analysis of the competition
Feasibility studies and informed judgment

◆ Discussion Questions

1. What are the major strategic issues related to location?
2. What are the advantages and disadvantages of clustering?
3. What are the principlal issues in evaluating a location? How do these issues differ from those used in site evaluation? How are they similar?
4. To what degree is informed judgment a part of a hotel feasibility decision? What impact does this have in making the hotel location analysis different from the process for food service?
5. How important is site in a hotel decision in a downtown market? In a suburban market? How do you account for any differences?

Chapter 11

When you have finished reading this chapter, you should be able to

1. List common pricing objectives
2. Explain what determines price
3. Describe the rationale for food service pricing methods
4. Discuss hotel pricing practices
5. Define yield management and its pitfalls

Holiday Inn®
ENJOY OUR
LUNCHEON BUFFET
$3.95
SUN. THRU FRI.

(Photo courtesy of Holiday Inns)

The Price of Hospitality

A pioneer in food service marketing, George Rice, describes the role of price in marketing:

> The basic purpose of price is to capture the value of the product in the consumer's mind.[1]

Rice does us a favor by directing our attention to *value* and associating it with price. *Price* is of interest to *sellers* because it is the means by which they recapture cost and make a profit. *Customers,* however, are really more interested in what they get for price, that is, in value. For this reason, some marketers speak of **price/value** rather than simply price.

In hospitality, value for the consumer can be defined as:

$$\frac{\text{Product} + \text{Service} + \text{Location} + \text{Ambience} + \text{Image}}{\text{Price}} = \text{Value}^{2}$$

We can illustrate the meaning of this equation briefly in terms of *enhancements of value* with examples:

Product enhancements such as guest room amenities, or just the artistic arrangement of the garnish on the plate

+

Service enhancement—perhaps related to an unusually well-trained staff or a particularly accommodating central reservation service

+

Extra location appeal such as those with unusual convenience or the social prestige of having the "right address"

+

An ambience designed to be current that captures the aspirations—for speed, modernity, luxury, or some other value—of the target market.

+

An image supported by advertising and promotion

= enhanced value

Enhancements of this kind—or a combination of several—should improve the consumer's perception of the operation. These improvements support and can be reflected in the *price* charged for the value provided.

In this chapter, we will consider price first by examining price objectives and then the determinants of price. Next, we will turn to pricing methods in the industry, first in food service and then in lodging.

PRICING OBJECTIVES

In multiunit organizations, there are usually well-thought-out company policies that support specific **pricing objectives.** In businesses that are smaller and run more informally, these may not be explicitly stated or even consciously thought out, but close examination will reveal an unstated set of goals that consistently lie behind pricing decisions. Some pricing goals emphasize sales, whereas others focus more on profits. This is a matter of emphasis; profit requires sales—and sales imply a profit. Both sales and profit goals, then, are invariably involved, to some degree, in all pricing decisions. We will also examine personal goals and situations where profit is a secondary consideration, at most.

Sales-Oriented Pricing Goals

Taco Bell's value pricing strategy began as an experiment by franchisees in a depressed market. Another Taco Bell franchisee experimented with value pricing to improve Sunday sales. These experiments were so successful in 1986 and 1987 that by 1988 "the value concept was adopted and spread across the country."[3] These price *reductions* were intended to drive sales and they did. Sales from 1987 to 1990 rose 60 percent.

A less dramatic, but more common pricing practice is to meet the price level in the market. In fact, this is a pattern found not only in hospitality but in many other service industries.[4] The **sales-oriented goal** here is to protect market share. The logic of protecting share is that the level of price is set by the competition and the costs of the operation are set by the going rate for labor, food products, and supplies. Since the operation is (or should be) managed as efficiently as possible in order to minimize the usage levels of food, labor, and other resources, there is a very limited range of discretion for pricing. Since the market sets final price, profit margins reflect efficiency of operation, rather than (monopolistic) market power.

What management *can* control, to a significant degree, is sales levels. It tries to do this by meeting competitive prices and by developing more effective strategies based on the nonprice elements of the market mix. The principal means of pursuing such a strategy are service enhancements, new products, and increased advertising. The upgrading of the ambience of fast-food restaurants by market leaders some years ago, which was quickly followed by other operators, is an example of nonprice competition, as is the growth in promotional spending by hospitality chains. All of these are attempts to differentiate the product and increase sales without engaging in competition on price. The rationale, in effect, is that if you lose share, it is difficult to regain your market position. Whatever profit margin is currently manageable through maximum efficiency in operations will be applied to the operation over time, so that maintaining sales volume really determines the dollar amount of profit. Although a certain premium can be extracted for new and unique products, the general rule is that *pricing must meet the competition* except where strong differentiation exists.

Profit-Oriented Pricing Objectives

Sales oriented goals can also be **profit-oriented goals.** The Taco Bell value pricing initiative increased volume relative to fixed costs sufficiently to raise profits by over 75 percent from 1987 to 1990.[5] A part of this increase in profit came from increased volume and some of it came from restructuring the company by reducing middle management. In fact, reducing operating costs in order to become more price competitive is a tactic being used by many firms in and outside of the hospitality industry today.[6]

Lodging companies commonly use a target rate of return on investment (ROI) to evaluate an operation. Price levels are expected to support an operation that generates enough revenue to cover the company's operating format (i.e., luxury, midrange, or budget, for instance) and meet the company's profit target. Properties that cannot perform at this level are disposed of.

Following this reasoning, when a property's occupancy level falls, room rates are often actually raised to maintain target profit levels. Some observers argue that raising prices in the face of falling demand is illogical. The fundamental logic, however, is that a hotel is a financial asset that should perform at a certain ROI level. When it can no longer do so, the building, or at least the land, can be converted to other uses. In the meantime, price is used to ensure that profit targets are met. This tactic, however, is not available to operators in markets where there is an oversupply of rooms. Excess capacity tends to drive down prices regardless of profit levels.

Restaurant corporations, too, view restaurant concept and individual operations as financial assets. Food service conglomerates acquire fledgling firms with the intent of expanding the concept to a larger territory. If that concept does not measure up, the restaurant will be sold or converted to another concept. For

Taco Bell's value-pricing initiative cut prices but increased profit as sales bounded ahead. (Photo courtesy of Taco Bell)

instance, after five years of trying to develop a successful Chinese dinner house concept, Darden Corporation closed all of its China Coast restaurants. About half the units will be converted to Red Lobster or Olive Garden[7] and the rest, presumably, will be sold or otherwise disposed of. While these decisions involved an assessment of the viability of the entire concept, it seems likely that the *price level* those concepts supported was not adequate to yield a level of sales to meet ROI targets.

We should note that although most restaurant companies use profit and ROI goals in evaluating new locations, they would rarely try to maintain volume in a soft market by raising prices as hotels sometimes do. Theirs is a price-sensitive product and higher prices would spell lower sales. Hotel guests (at least during the business week) have urgent reasons for their travel and are usually traveling on expense accounts; hence, they are generally less price sensitive.

Personal Pricing Goals

Many independent, family-operated units are viewed by their owners as a source of "a living," which they may define as enough to survive on, enough to live comfortably on, or enough to accumulate an estate to leave their children. Whatever the goal, it is a highly personal one and particular to these people.

In operations such as these, the owner's lifestyle decision is basic to goal setting. Typically, the goal will be expressed in terms of a satisfactory return on sales because more elaborate and sophisticated return on investment calculations are beside the point—at least from the subjective view of the owner. Pricing decisions are likely, in these circumstances, to be aimed at maintaining the status quo, that is, supporting the operation at its current size and with its current clientele. Prices, then, tend to be set by the level of the competition's prices and "what we've always done."

Pricing in the Nonprofit Operation

In a way, nonprofit operations have the most rigidly driven profit-based pricing goals of any. To see this clearly, we need a special definition of "profit" to include "negative profit," that is, a subsidy. If a school lunch program's operation has a city appropriation of a certain size from the school board, say $150,000, then the operation must *lose no more* than $150,000. The budgeted loss is best thought of as a negative profit. Thus, price levels that will yield that "profit" must be rigidly adhered to.

Some nonprofit organizations, on the other hand, base their price to consumers on *ability to pay.* This is true, for instance, of congregate meals for the elderly in the United States. Those who cannot pay anything, receive their meal free; others pay what they can up to some level that is called the price. The number of meals an operation such as this can serve is determined by revenues from sales, per capita subsidies of one kind or another from the federal government, and donations and grants from local government and charitable organizations.

School lunch prices to the consumer reflect subsidies from several levels of government. (Photo courtesy of ARASERVE)

Another, quite different kind of operation, the private club, subsidizes operations with membership dues. The *real* price in subsidized operations lies in the subsidy goal the operation sets with local funding sources—or, in a club, with the members.

THE DETERMINANTS OF PRICE

The classic **determinants of price** are demand, supply, and competition.

Demand

Demand is, first of all, a function of people—that is, of the population and the kind of people who make it up. A young population demands one kind of product, older people another. Income level and other factors considered in Chapter 3 as the basis for segmentation should help you to think about qualitative changes in demand. To take one example, the growth in the aging population that will begin around 2010 as baby boomers begin to turn 65 will probably result in fundamental changes in the nature of demand.

While price is a *result,* in part, of **demand,** we should note that demand is determined, in part, by price. When hotel rooms cost the same on weekends as they did during the busy weekdays, hotels had very low weekend occupancies. When weekend prices were cut dramatically, occupancy in many urban center hotels increased just as dramatically; that is, demand increased.

Price Sensitivity. Demand for some products is more sensitive to price. Weekend room demand is a good example of such a product which is said to be *price elastic.* Weekday demand for rooms in a business center, as we have said, is relatively insensitive to price (price inelastic), at least in the short run. A person who needs to do business away from home *must* have shelter and probably requires certain amenities and so will pay what he or she has to for accommodation. (If guests perceive themselves to have been gouged on price, however, they may stay home next time and do business by phone.)

Relevant Range. Price sensitivity is not a fixed matter. In the booming 1980s, people seemed relatively indifferent to fine-dining prices, but then, as a recession developed, many fine-dining restaurants found it necessary to rewrite their menus, introducing lower-priced dishes and eliminating costly ones. Economic conditions and the climate of opinion had changed. There is some range of prices within which people will accept price changes. Move outside that range and the chances are that your product will be perceived as over- or underpriced. As the experience of fine-dining restaurants in the late 1980s and early 1990s indicates, changing conditions may change the **relevant range** of price sensitivity, as well.

Supply

In this section, we will consider the cost of goods, labor, and capital needed to operate a hospitality establishment. In any short-run time period, it is possible to estimate **supply** and, hence, food costs with reasonable accuracy. As with any good, scarcity relative to demand will bid up the price: A bad freeze in Florida that destroys the orange crop can mean higher orange juice prices for the coming year, for instance.

Over the longer run, however, there is less certainty. Malthusians in each generation, such as Thomas Malthus who originally stated the proposition, assert that the population is growing faster than the food supply. To date, they have been wrong; food gluts and government control of prices and problems with distribution have been the major food problems, but, in 1996, the possibility of grain and other food shortages loomed once again. In the longer run, of course, Malthus may be proved right with dire consequences for much more than the hospitality industry.

Labor is another basic input to hospitality. Since many jobs in our businesses do not pay well, they are taken by younger people who are getting their first job or working while in school. The decline in the youth work force that began in the late 1970s has created a significant shortage of workers in some markets. While that trend turned around in the early 1990s, there is still a shortage of young workers in many local markets and this bids up the price of labor.

Part of that labor shortage, however, is a function of hospitality pay rates. When price in any market is low, less will be offered and this is true for hospitality labor, as well. At the low wage rates that have always prevailed in most of our hourly jobs, there is a limited supply of workers who can be recruited. As a result of the relative shortage of labor, there is a premium on increasing productivity. Any labor supply shortage raises labor costs and forces hospitality to bid up its price to consumers.

The third element of supply is capital. Lodging is particularly capital intensive and hence hotel construction—the source of increases in supply of rooms—is sensitive to interest rates and capital availability. Food service is less capital intensive than lodging but still requires significant investment in plant and equipment. Both lodging and food service go in and out of fashion with lenders and investors. When in fashion, capital is available on easier terms (i.e., lower interest rates). When out of fashion, expansion is more difficult and expensive.

Competition

Competition in virtually all areas of the hospitality industry is intense. The intensity of competition means that it takes a very strong competitive point of difference to gain any premium in price over the competition. Competition results in more innovation for the consumer—but also means any innovation that is effective will probably be copied by competitors if it can be.

Competition within the industry is fierce, but competition with other industries for the consumer's time, attention, and spending is stiff, too. There are many substitutes for hospitality products. Frequent communication by phone, fax, and E-mail may replace some business trips (and accompanying room-nights). In food service, the toughest competitors are the grocery store, which offers a wide range of convenience products, and the home.

Quick Service Restaurants responded aggressively to Taco Bell's value pricing with value meals of their own. (Photo courtesy of McDonald's)

Interindustry Competition. When it comes to discretionary spending, a meal out can be forgone to purchase a compact disc. A weekend vacation might be skipped to purchase a new piece of computer hardware, a camera, or a new stereo. The level of price matters not just relative to other hospitality firms but also relative to other discretionary uses of the consumer's dollar. To put it another way, price *is* related to cost (supply) but also to demand, that is, what consumers see as a good value. This, in turn, relates to competition not only within the industry but also to what substitutes are available and what other goods and services cost.

The interaction of demand, supply, and competition are the broad forces within which pricing objectives must be set. They also set the boundaries for pricing practices in food service and in lodging.

PRICING METHODS IN FOOD SERVICE

In this section, we will consider cost-based pricing and gross margin contribution pricing and the analytical tools they use. We will also consider break-even analysis briefly here and in more detail in the appendix to this chapter. Finally, we will assess demand-based pricing and discuss contract bidding.

Cost-Based Pricing Methods

Eric B. Orkin describes the **cost-based pricing** method as it is widely used in food service:

> Typically, an operator will establish a target food-cost percentage that is his operating goal. The target percentage is derived most commonly from current industry "wisdom" and occasionally from analysis and projections. The percentage is then converted to a "menu pricing multiplier" by taking the reciprocal of the percentage. Thus, if the target food cost is 40 percent the multiplier is 2.5 (that is, \$1/.40 = 2.5). The ingredients for each menu item are costed and the total is multiplied by the multiplier to yield a "ballpark" price.[8]

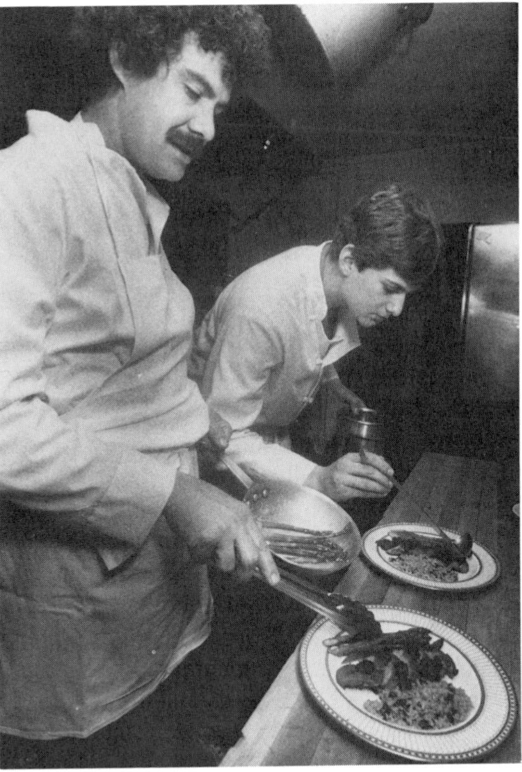

Labor cost is related to the size and quality of a crew needed to service a particular concept. (Photo courtesy of Don Chidester/Image Works)

The ballpark figure, we should note, is just a starting point which should be adjusted up or down to match competitive price levels. If a restaurant cannot produce a product at a competitive price level that yields an adequate margin over cost, it might decide to drop the product from its menu. When the product is popular and cannot be dropped, menu placement and other merchandising strategies may be used to move as many guests' choices to other products as possible. (See "Menu Merchandising," Chapter 14.)

Cost-based restaurant pricing is simple and straightforward. However, its critics argue for approaches that take into fuller account dollar gross margins (as opposed to percentage margins) on different items and the impact of selling price on gross margin. The term "gross margin" refers to the amount remaining from the selling price after the cost of goods sold (i.e., food cost) has been deducted. In a restaurant,

Selling Price – Food Cost = Gross Margin

We should recognize *why* simple cost-based pricing is so common. In a highly competitive market (as we noted earlier), where costs and selling prices are determined largely by the market, operators reason that price is largely a competitive issue. Where the consumer is shown to be price sensitive, operators are likely to meet the competition on price but concentrate on other elements of the marketing mix except during periods of low volume when competitive activity makes price discounting a competitive necessity.

Is Labor a Variable Cost? Some argue that time-and-motion studies should be used to develop a standard labor cost for each product on the menu. There is a real question, however, as to whether labor is a *true* variable. By way of clarification, *variable costs* are those that vary directly with sales, while *fixed costs* do not vary with sales. If you sell one more steak, will labor cost rise by some constant number of dollars or cents?

Another way of looking at labor cost is to see it as related to the crew size needed to service a particular food service concept within some range of volume. In effect, for menu pricing purposes, this means labor cost is a *mixed cost,* that is, a cost with both a fixed and a variable component. Up to a certain level of sales volume, labor cost is fixed by the minimum crew size. Beyond that level, however, labor cost is variable—that is, it will increase with incremental sales.

If labor *and* food costs are to be used as the cost base in establishing a ballpark figure, then a multiplier can be calculated in much the same way as described earlier. For instance, if prime cost (i.e., food and labor) is budgeted at 60 percent, then a multiplier of 1.67($1/.60) should be used against food and labor. It is important to emphasize again that the "ballpark" figure is a starting point, however it is computed, which is adjusted to competitive price levels.

Gross Margin Contribution Pricing

Gross margin contribution may be defined as the margin contributed to all other costs and profit after variable costs have been covered. **Contribution pricing** focuses on *dollar contribution* level, rather than just food cost percentage. In the discussion that follows, we treat food cost as the variable cost. A menu, for instance, might list steaks and pasta, with pasta having a low food cost in spite of a fairly low menu price on that item. Steaks might require a fairly high price but still have a higher food cost. For simplicity, we can reduce the menu to the two items shown in Table 11.1. It is clear from the table that we would rather sell the steaks with the "bad" food cost percentage than the spaghetti in spite of its "good" food cost percentage, because spaghetti does not yield the dollar contribution. You can not bank percentages, only dollars.

Another good example of a menu-pricing decision based on contribution reasoning is the cut-rate banquet price that was discussed in Chapter 1. It was a highly competitive price—a dollar over cost—offered in order to attract very large pieces of business. The profit per meal was modest because a steak dinner was priced at only a small margin over food cost. However, the resulting sale of thousands of bowling banquets made a very large total contribution.

Full Costing. Ultimately, the price per unit must recapture the unit variable cost and the fixed cost that must be allocated to every unit sold. Some pricing decisions may use contribution analyses to justify a price below full cost. These can be acceptable in special situations, such as slow-volume day parts or off seasons, when

Table 11.1 Simplified Contribution Pricing Example

Menu Item	Food Cost	Menu Price	Food Cost Percentage	Contribution Margin
Spaghetti	$1.125	$4.50	25%	$3.375
Strip steak	$6.000	$15.00	40%	$9.000

any margin above variable cost will be a contribution to fixed overhead and profit and help maintain the cash flow that is necessary to meet payroll and other regular cash outlays. Ultimately, however, these sales are subsidized by other, higher-margin sales. Clearly, sales revenue overall, must recapture full cost, including a reasonable allowance for profit, if a firm is to stay *in* business. Still, in some special cases, it is better to have some contribution than no sales at all.

Break-Even Analysis. Another cost-oriented tool used in pricing is the break-even point (BEP). The BEP is reached at the point where total dollar contribution from sales, after variable cost, just equals total fixed cost. **Break-even analysis** is helpful in analyzing a decision to add a service or facility and to analyze the price and contribution levels required of the new service or facility. Break-even *pricing* is sometimes appropriate in nonprofit operations. Finally, the *form* of break-even analysis can be used to examine the feasibility of reaching a *target return*. In such a case, a target level of desired profit is considered a "cost" and the sales required to achieve that level of profit computed. The process of break-even computation and the uses of break-even analysis are discussed in more detail in the appendix to this chapter.

Sales Mix. Most menus include several items. The price of one item has a significance of its own but needs to be seen in relation to other prices. The performance of the whole menu is what determines final profit. A high food cost percentage (perhaps dictated by low competitive price levels) on one item may be balanced by a low food cost percentage on another. Through menu placement, menu language, and other merchandising techniques, moreover, lost-cost, high-contribution items may be featured to push sales. Low-contribution items—which need to be on the menu because of a need for coherence in product offering or to meet competitive pressure—can be "buried," as we noted earlier, in order to minimize their sales. (See Chapter 14.)

Because the many items on the menu need to be considered, any break-even computation must be based on an assumed **sales mix,** as well as on the cost and contribution of individual items.

Cost-Based Pricing Assessed

Cost-based pricing is the most common practice among most service industry firms, including food service.[9] Cost-based pricing, however, runs the danger of

One common way of maintaining list prices but responding to local competitive conditions is couponing. (Photo courtesy of Pizza Hut)

ignoring the consumer. It assumes the market or competitive level of prices accurately reflects what people are willing to pay. In effect, we are letting our suppliers and competitors tell us what our prices should be.

It is easier to make that sound silly than it is to get around the fact that, for many hospitality industry products and services, the going rate *is* determined by competitive forces, rather than clever managers. Where the product is undifferentiated, as with hamburgers and economy rooms, competitive price levels are probably good proxies (i.e., indirect measures) for the level of prices the market will tolerate. Where there is uniqueness or a high degree of service intensity, however, more latitude in pricing based on consumer demand is available.

Demand-Based Pricing

In some situations where a product has unique advantages, "what the traffic will bear" determines price. Well-located resorts can often follow this practice during the high season. There are only so many room-days available in January in five-star resorts in Arizona—and lots of people who want to fill them. Under these circumstances, prices during the high season are generally based on the most that the traffic will bear.

When a new hotel comes into a market (assuming that market is not overbuilt), it can set a price based on the maximum customers will pay and limit discounting severely. This is sometimes called **skimming**—as in skimming the cream off the market while the property is new. An opposite tactic with a new product is **penetration pricing.** Where competition is expected to develop quickly, as it generally does in food service, an attractive price may be offered to seize as large a share of the market as possible quickly. The hope is that the seller can hold onto the customers when competition develops.

Chain food service operations can, through test marketing, get a clearer picture of what price will maximize revenues. Many independent operations, however, assume they cannot afford to experiment with several prices and so competitive or traditional price levels are often accepted as the best proxy for demand.[10] On the other hand, independent operators (and chains for that matter) that offer table service have available, according to food service operator and consultant Bill Main,[11] a well-qualified source of information for pricing and that is their service staff. Main notes that, in most operations, pricing is done by the chef or food production manager. These people, however, tend to be *cost focused.* Servers, on the other hand, are customer focused; they are the people who are closest to the customers and interact with them for a living. Accordingly, when Main is ready to introduce a new item on his menu, he asks his service staff's views on what people would be willing to pay for the item. This becomes an important input to the final price-setting process which is a collaboration between the chef (or kitchen manager), front-of-the-house managers, owners (or general managers), *and* servers. This process, Main has found in his own restaurants and those of his consulting clients, will result in a price that represents value to the guest. Main continually reassesses menu prices, using his servers as a vital source of intelligence on consumer reaction to prices.

Selecting the Final Price

Pricing in food service usually begins by determining cost in order to set the minimum price. Adjustments are then made to reflect the operator's best judgment as to the price customers are willing to pay. In the final analysis, it is an entire menu that is being priced and some items—to meet competition—may be below the target cost percentage, whereas others, the lower food cost items, will make up for that. Now, the **final price** must be set.

Price Points. Quick-service restaurant prices tend to end in 9 or 5. Some view adjusting the last digit for psychological factors as irrational. However, attempts to "prove" that such factors do not affect consumers have had, at best, mixed results and the intuition of operators is that adjusting that last digit in popular-priced restaurants affects the way consumers perceive prices. *The first figure* is apparently more significant to customers than other digits. For instance, "consumers perceive a greater distance between 69 cents and 71 cents than between 69 cents and 67 cents. As a result, restaurateurs are more reluctant to move a price from 69 cents to 71 cents than from 62 cents to 67 cents. *The length of the price* or the number of digits in its field is also a sensitive point with consumers. Thus, the distance between $9.99 and $10.25 is *perceived* as much greater than the distance between, say, $9.75 and $9.99."[12]

Main's experience in *table service restaurants* suggests that price perception below and above $5 differs. Under $5, he asserts, pricing should be in increments of 25 cents and 50 cents. In effect, if a product can be sold for $3.15, the consumer is unlikely to notice the difference if it is sold for $3.25. Over $5, the increments consumers notice are $.50 and $.95. Thus, an item offered for $8.75 could be offered for $8.95 without any impact on consumer value perception.

Price Range

Most operators have a range of prices they regard as fitting their target market. A coffee shop chain, for instance, may eliminate entrees that are priced below $3.50 and above $9.95. Fast-food sandwiches rarely go above $2.50 for a single main item or above the $3 to $4 range for "extra value meals." One reason for fast food's limited success in the dinner market to date may be the consumer's unwillingness to "believe" in the value of the typical higher-priced dinner item in that setting.

One coffee shop chain found the price of shrimp, a popular item, escalating in a way that would require the chain to price it above its regular **price range.** Management felt that the effect of violating its upper limit would be to make the whole restaurant appear more expensive to the consumer and so, reluctantly, removed one of its best sellers from its menu, replacing it with another seafood product that fit the limits.

Lower limits are important, too. For instance, the cost of a bottle of wine might justify a price of $12, but that low a price—in a fine-dining restaurant—could cheapen the appearance of the entire wine list. And so, like the item that was too expensive, that particular wine might have to be eliminated from the wine menu if a higher price did not seem reasonable in the light of guest value perception.

Finally, range needs to be considered not only in terms of the absolute levels of the top and bottom but also of the distance between them. Menus with too large a spread between individual prices may encourage the customer to choose the lower price, perhaps by bringing a concern about prices in general to the forefront of the consumer's mind.

Price Changes

From time to time, it becomes necessary to increase prices in the face of food cost variations and the consistent long-term trend toward higher wages. Practice in the field is to avoid large adjustments or too frequent adjustments. Some restaurant chains try to hold the frequency of **price changes** to once a quarter. A number of operators change their entire menu periodically, adding items which fit in the appropriate price range and dropping items which have become too expensive.

Red Lobster, for instance, has begun to feature chicken and beef items on its menu in reaction to high seafood costs. It is also adding shrimp fajitas to the menu,[13] doubtless because shrimp, in combination with tortillas and other ingredients, has a lower food cost than a shrimp platter. There are many good reasons for the growing popularity of pasta, but, certainly, one reason for that trend is that pasta with chicken is likely to be much less expensive than a main dish made up solely of chicken. The favorable effect on gross margin of a price rise is achieved by substituting lower-cost items in this way but without making the change apparent to the customer in a price change.

Following Price Changes. The question of whether to match price changes of competitors *automatically* can be answered only in a qualified way. The basic determinants are the competitive situation and the customer's price sensitivity. Even in a tightly competitive market, there are alternatives to price reductions that should be reviewed such as the menu changes we have just discussed. To take just one possibility, what would happen if the revenue likely to be lost were spent on increased advertising and promotion?

The final determination, however, is the customer's. If price is a major consideration, as it very often is in fast food, for instance, it is hard to hold out against a competitive price reduction. Where more upscale operations achieve a high degree of differentiation, on the other hand, it may be easier to hold the line on prices in the face of some competitors' reductions.

Contract Bidding

Organizational customers often invite sealed bids in competition for a large sale such as an association holding a convention or a large institution requiring a food service company to operate its food service over a period of a year or more. Price is often only one dimension—the contract may go to the operator who has the best reputation—and perhaps the best relations with key members of the organization's buying center. The price bid, however, will certainly be an important factor in awarding the contract.

The bid is likely to be a complex document. For instance, an institutional contract may offer different terms depending on whether the bidder is prepared to make a capital investment in the food service facilities of the client. Complete knowledge of the contractor's own costs and organizational capabilities, as well as the priorities of the institution's buying center, is essential. In many cases, as noted previously, contracts are awarded not to the lowest bidder but to the one who is judged to be best qualified to meet the client's needs. The final contract stipulating price levels or pricing methods, as well as payments to the client, will often be subject to further negotiation once the bid is accepted in principle.

HOTEL PRICING

Setting room rates involves judgments about a more capital-intensive business than food service and one with a much higher fixed-cost structure. Room rate judgments, moreover, are typically set in the context of a property life of 30 years or more. Accordingly, one might expect pricing methods to be different from those used in food service, and, in many ways, they are. There is, however, an underlying similarity because the fundamental problems are the same: recovering cost, assessing consumer demand, and earning a target profit.

The Cost Basis for Hotel Rates

For many years, the rule of thumb in estimating hotel prices has been that the room rate must equal one dollar per thousand dollars of investment in the hotel. Like most rules of thumb, this one is more suggestive than precise. As price levels have changed dramatically over recent years, it is amazing that it can preserve any relevance. No one would, however, use it to *set* rates.

The **Hubbart formula**—developed in the 1950s by a committee of the American Hotel and Motel Association chaired by Roy Hubbart—bases rates on the operating and capital costs to be covered, including a target profit. Revenue required to meet the target is divided by the estimated number of room-nights sold per year. The Hubbart formula, then, is based on a break-even model with a "fair return" defined as a part of the costs.[14]

Projected rates for a new property must be reviewed as part of the feasibility study to see, at the very least, if they will cover costs with an adequate margin of safety. Otherwise, under ordinary circumstances, debt financing is not likely to be forthcoming. Existing properties can adjust rates more realistically to other revenue possibilities in the hotel, principally the opportunity for good profit performance in food and beverage and—to a lesser extent and only in some properties—to revenue derived from commercial rentals. There is no question, however, that the room rate is the principal factor, along with occupancy levels, for determining revenue and profitability.

Demand and Competition. When the market for rooms in a town begins to expand, new hotels will typically come in at significantly higher rates. This is true, not only because the investment cost of new construction is higher than the capital cost of existing properties, but also because many guests will pay more for new facilities. As new facilities enter the market, occupancies in older properties drop as a result of business lost to the new properties, but rates often rise to offset their fall, moving up under the umbrella of the top rates charged by the new properties.

Lodging Supply Segmentation. Lodging supply is divided into the five segments shown in Table 11.2.[15] Most guests enter the market with the price ranges of their favored segment in mind.[16] Competition between properties is most intense within categories, but there is competition between segments, particularly between adjacent segments (i.e., between luxury and upscale, upscale and midpriced, etc.). The designation "all-suite" has a deluxe sound to it, but, in practice, there are all-suites at virtually every price level. The services provided are similarly varied.

Room Rate Range Tactics

Properties in the limited-service and economy segments generally have only one or two room types and charge the same basic rate for each type, with additional charges for each additional person in the room. There are sometimes exceptions to this "one size fits all" approach for suites or large family rooms.

Luxury, upscale, and, to a lesser degree, midpriced properties generally have a number of room types which range in price. The practice of having a minimum of three rates, preferably five, gives front-office staff and reservationists an opportunity to "sell up." The object is to have several levels of rooms and rates, each differentiated from the other by physical features—size, location and view, higher floors, and so forth. Front-office staff and reservationists are trained to sell the higher-priced rooms first but move to a lower category rather than lose the guest. The result, if properly executed, is a satisfied guest *and* a high average rate.

Discounting. Very few rooms are sold at "rack rate," the hotel's equivalent of list price. The reasons for **discounting** rooms seem to cover almost every contingency—except for the traveler who does not know enough to ask for a special deal.

Table 11.2 Lodging Supply Segments

Segment	1995 Average Rate	Typical Brands
Luxury	$113.69	Four Seasons, Ritz Carlton
Upscale	76.82	Hilton, Marriott
Midpriced	57.84	Holiday Inn, Best Western
Limited service	44.16	Hampton Inn, Comfort Inn
Budget	34.45	Motel Six

[a]Rates shown are for January 1995. Smith Travel Research, *Lodging Outlook*, March 1995.

Premium prices can be charged for rooms with particular features such as an attractive view. (Photo courtesy of Ritz-Carlton, Laguna Niguel)

The author noted a listing of 17 special rates prominently taped to the side of a front-desk machine at a Florida inn at which he was staying. The four-letter abbreviations followed by a fuller identification are reproduced in Table 11.3 and suggest the range of discounts offered. The eighth item is particularly revealing.

Every hotel market is in a local market[17] and "must respond to business conditions in [its] local market." Special discount rates are generally a function of demand in a particular geographic market. Most of the special rates in the Florida hotel in Table 11.3 were almost certainly applied at that property during periods of slack demand. Still, the practice of discounting is widespread and, as Figure 11.1 indicates, increases as the price level rises. Both the size of the dollar discount and the percentage of discount to rack rate increase with average rate increases.

What Drives Lodging Discounting? The obvious driving force for widespread price discounting in lodging in recent years is overcapacity and heightened competition. More recently, supply and demand have been in better balance. A second factor, discussed at length in Chapter 7, is that, as with most services, there is no inventory. A hotel's unused capacity has no value the next day, and so there is pressure to sell *now.* There is still another factor, however, we should consider and that is the cost structure of a hotel. The cost of renting one more room is low—a few guest supplies, some linen, and a small amount of housekeeping payroll, perhaps something between \$5 and \$10. If the rate on the room is \$60 and the variable cost is \$7.50, the contribution margin is \$52.50 based on rack rate. This leaves

Table 11.3 Some Lodging Discount Categories

Abbreviation	Full Designation
AAAA	Senior citizen/AAA/any 50 percent discount card, etc.
COMP	Any Comp per (management person's name)
CORP	Corporate rate
CRUS	Cruise packages, including food, drinks, room, etc.
EMPL	Employee discount
EXIT	Exit Information Guide Coupon
FFAM	Flintstone family fun rates
SELL	Discount to sell to keep guests from walking out
SEPT	September Club Member
SPEC	Special company rates
SSSS	Company Saver Rates
STAY	Any discounted rate due to extended stay of 7+
NEGT	Negotiated rates with Drive, Viking Princess, etc.
RACK	Normal rack rate
ROCK	Company Rock Bottom Prices
GOVT	Government/military rate
SMER	SMERF groups, i.e., Athletic, Wedding, Reunions, Dive

Source: Noted at a hotel front desk.

considerable room for discounting. Beyond that, however, is the fact that the hotel has a high-fixed-cost structure. Finance and related charges alone account for roughly 25 percent of sales. These charges, the minimum crew size wages, contracted repairs and maintenance, and marketing, for instance, are all fixed costs that must be paid. Accordingly, there is a real *need* for that contribution margin. In a high-fixed-cost industry with a product which has a high contribution margin and *cannot be inventoried,* discounting is a likely practice during any slow period. What makes discounting convenient—really, automated in many properties—is yield management.

YIELD MANAGEMENT

Yield management is a technique that was first used by airlines to match ticket prices to the level of demand for a particular flight. The system has been adapted for hotel reservations (and other businesses serving travelers, such as car rental companies and theme parks) to adjust rates for a given time period to demand for

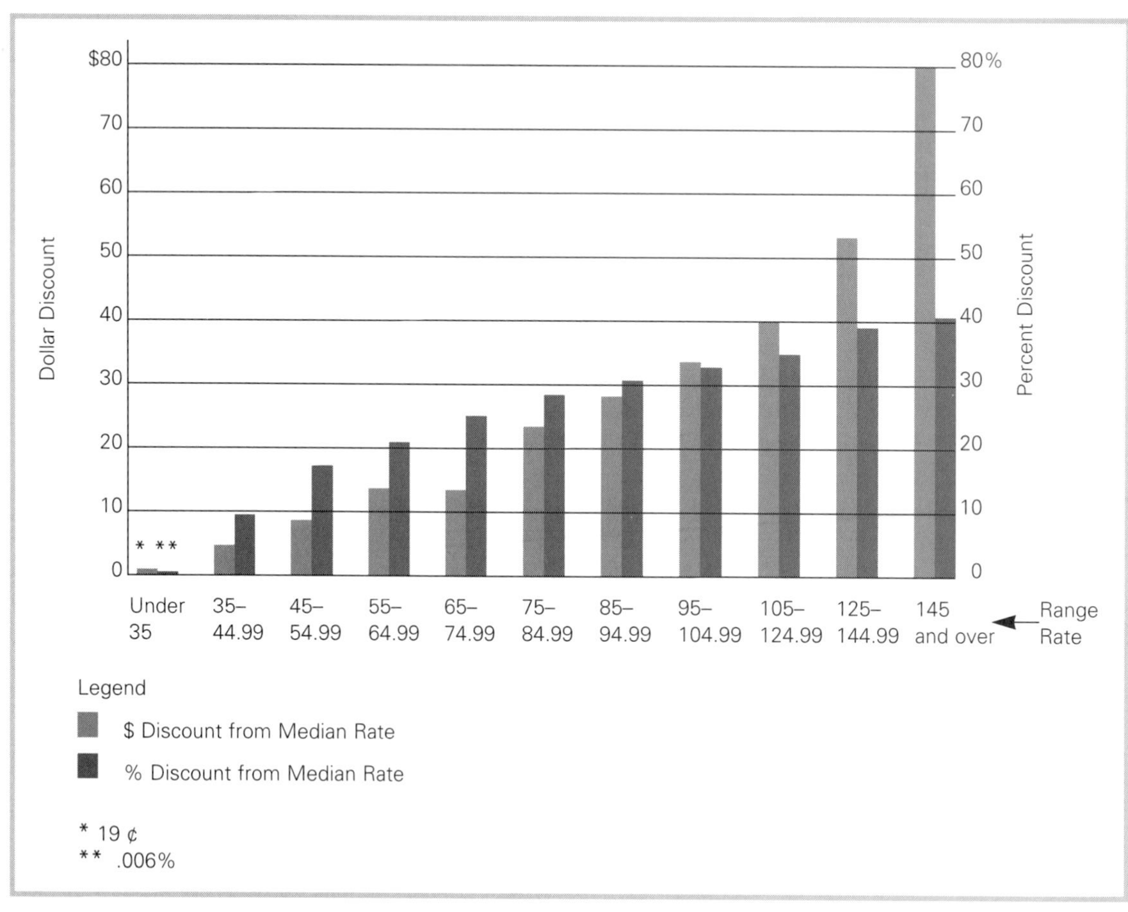

Figure 11.1 Discounting by Rate Group

Source: Data, Smith Travel Research, *Lodging Outlook,* April 1994.

accommodations in that time period. In very high demand periods, few, if any, discounts are given. In low periods, on the other hand, special rate categories are opened to attract price-sensitive market segments, such as clergy, teachers, government employees, and service men and women. Yield management, then, is a system intended to maximize revenue—and, in the short run, it undoubtedly achieves this end. While yield management is here to stay, we will have occasion later in this section to wonder what its long-term impact is on the hotel business's rate structure and image with the guest.

Management might wish for a world in which every room was rented every day at the posted rack rate. In practice, the industry occupancy has ranged between 60 and 65 percent during the first half of the 1990s.[18] In a five-year period in one chain, rooms rented at *full rate* declined from 55 to 15 percent.[19] In lodging, there is, as we just noted, no way to inventory unused capacity. Today's unrented room has no value tomorrow and so there is pressure to rent the room at a discount. The question arises, however, as to when to discount and what the appropriate discount is. Yield management has been designed to rent as many rooms as possible while generating the maximum rate possible at a given level of demand. The object, then, "is to use your capacity in the best (most profitable) way possible."[20] Yield management, as we noted, was developed in the airline business where it has come to be accepted. Its reception in the hotel business has often been less friendly.

A yield management system does not require a computer, but most systems have now been reduced to a computer program. A growing number of hotel system CRS incorporate yield management in their operation. The construction of a yield management system begins with a review of demand for a property, usually over a period of years. This review identifies periods when the property is likely to be full; when it will have a fairly good occupancy, filling some nights and not others; and when its slack seasons are. This review will also identify days of the week that are always slow and other regularities in demand variation.

To oversimplify somewhat, the next step is to use this historical pattern to forecast demand for the future, updating it with any special events, usually for at least one year out. For periods when demand is expected to be light, reservation agents are given maximum discretion with rates, while, for busy periods, special rates are available only to special categories of guests such as regular corporate clients. The forecast is updated, usually weekly, and daily for the next 30 days.

The way yield management looks to the guest when it is put into practice is important. The guest should not get the impression of a "rip-off" and so there should be some real value considerations the guest can understand involved in yield management price decisions. Cornell researcher Sheryl Kines says that acceptable practice requires:

1. Information on the different pricing options be made available to guests.
2. Substantial discounts be given in return for restrictions on cancelation of prepaid reservations.
3. Reasonable restrictions be accepted as a trade-off for a discount.
4. Where different prices are charged, there should either be restrictions—such as a cancelation restriction—or the product offered should be different.[21]

Marriott's practice of "rational pricing" is widely cited in the travel trade as an approach to discounting that is fair, understandable to the consumer, and profitable to the company. Marriott offers advance purchases with nonrefundable rates. These rates offer excellent discounts, but, in return, the consumer assumes some risk. The president of one hotel contrasted this with the yield management "systems used by most hotels" which he saw as "day to day systems which are geared to raise rates when a hotel reaches a certain occupancy."[22]

Pitfalls in Implementing Yield Management

Proper training and motivation of reservations staff and anyone else who deals with guests and their reservations is critical. *Two* kinds of training are needed, for tact and for competence. When special rates have been advertised during an off period, for instance, once reservations reach a certain level, that reduced price will no longer be offered. If the reservationist is properly trained, he or she will say, tactfully, "I'm sorry, all of those rooms are sold out" and try to book the guest at a higher rate or offer alternative dates or accommodations elsewhere within the system. Poor training can yield a more annoying, "Sorry. We're going to fill that night so I can't give you that rate." Disgruntled or indifferent employees are given enormous leverage for harm to the system's reputation in a situation like this.

Competence is no small issue, either. Rate structures have become extremely complex and—regrettably—it happens sometimes that the guest understands the rate structure better than the reservationist and either has to explain it to that person or, worse, argue with him or her. This leads to a loss of respect for the hotel or chain and a cynicism about hotel rates.

Finally, Kines suggests that one of the dangers of yield management is a possible "focus on short term profits." If rates are maximized for a night for a hotel full of guests, most of whom are resolved never to stay there again because they feel they have been overcharged, then the cost of the benefits of yield management will have come at too high a price.

PACKAGE PRICES

Both lodging and food service operators see it as advantageous to sell a package of goods and services rather than individual items, and that perception is matched by quite different benefits to the consumer.

The greatest use of **package pricing** in lodging is in resort pricing, which has always had a strong packaging element in the American plan (all meals included in the price) and modified American plan (breakfast and lunch included). Weekend hotel rates—aimed at guests wanting a short vacation—commonly include some meals and often a free cocktail. The *all-inclusive resort* price usually covers all the costs of a vacation, including transportation, ground transfers, food, and lodging. Alcoholic beverages are included, too, at some resorts. The package enables the guest to know the total cost of an outing or vacation. Usually, the package sells for less than the total of the items purchased separately and so offers a discount that is also attractive.

The packaging makes for a more predictable level of sales for the operation and secures a greater total volume of sales. It also bolsters the sales of the weaker of the packaged services.[23] Although the package reduces the percentage margin of profit somewhat, it provides incremental sales and improved total profits.

In quick-service restaurants, a major thrust of value pricing has been the bundling of several products to offer the consumer a bargain such as a "value meal", while giving the operation enough incremental sales volume to offset the

Package prices are a common feature in resort properties. In this case, special off-season rates also represent an attempt to manage demand.

reduction in margin percentage represented by the discounting of items in the package.

SUMMARY

Price represents value to the customer and a means to recapture costs and earn a profit to operators. Sales-oriented pricing goals seek to maintain or increase market share. Most commonly, service prices meet competitive levels. Increasing market share can result not just in maintaining profit but increasing it when volume increases are large enough. Profit-oriented pricing goals treat the operation as a financial asset and seek to support a planned return on investment. In smaller, owner-operated organizations, personal pricing goals seek to support more personal lifestyle goals.

Price and demand interact, each affecting the level of the other. As price increases, demand generally declines, but this relationship depends on the price sensitivity of the customer. Price sensitivity exists in some *relevant range* and is not the same at all price levels. Price is also affected by supply, being higher for scarce goods. A third price determinant is competition. Competition within hospitality is intense, and, as well, hospitality goods and services face competition from other goods and services.

Cost-based pricing is most common in the hospitality industry, but cost must be combined with competitive levels in setting price. Break-even analysis is helpful in making price decisions. Demand-based pricing is most common in situations where the product is unique. In setting the final price, consumer perceptions are critical to determining exact price points.

Hotel pricing has a cost-based element (recovery of capital and operating costs) but responds to levels of demand and competition, as well. *Yield management* is a technique which seeks to match room rates with the level of demand at a particular point in time. Implementing yield management successfully requires sensitivity to guest perceptions and careful training of employees. To be seen as fair by guest, rate concessions should be made only where there are restrictions on that rate or the product offered is different

◆ Key Words and Concepts

Price/value
Pricing objectives
  Sales-oriented goals
  Profit-oriented goals
  Personal pricing goals
Determinants of price
Demand
  Price sensitivity
  Relevant range
Supply
Competition
Pricing methods
  Cost-based pricing
  Gross margin contribution pricing
Break-even analysis
Sales mix
Demand-based pricing
  Skimming
  Penetration pricing
Final price

Price range
Price changes
Hubbart formula
Room rate range tactics
Discounting
Yield management
Package pricing

◆ *Discussion Questions*

1. What is the significance of the term "price/value"?
2. Did Taco Bell's use of value pricing pursue sales oriented or profit-oriented goals? Why?
3. Give an example of a price-sensitive market segment. What makes them price conscious? Give an example of a market segment that is not price sensitive. What explains their point of view?
4. What kinds of competition face hospitality? Be specific and give examples.
5. What are the strengths and weaknesses of cost-based pricing and gross margin contribution pricing? Which do you prefer? Why?
6. Discuss what is meant by demand-based pricing. What information is readily available on guest price perception?
7. How prevalent is discounting in lodging?
8. What is yield management? What benefits does it offer? What problems does it present?

Appendix
Break-Even Analysis

This appendix shows the form of break-even calculations and illustrates some of its uses, particularly as they bear on pricing. A break-even point (BEP) can be computed in terms of the number of units required to be sold to break even or in terms of the dollar level of sales required. In general, the BEP is reached at the point where total contributions (Contrib) from sales (S), after deducting variable costs (VC), just equal total fixed costs (TFC). Recall, first, that

$$\text{Contrib} = S - VC$$

We can now define the break-even calculation in units and in dollars.

IN UNITS

The break-even point is equal to total fixed costs divided by the contribution per unit in dollars or

$$\text{BEP} = \frac{\text{TFC}}{\$\ \text{Contrib}}$$

For instance, in a new banquet operation, total fixed costs will be $50,000 per year for permanent staff, depreciation, and miscellaneous overhead. Assume an average banquet check of $20, a food cost of 25 percent, and other variable costs, including variable labor, are 15 percent for a total of 40 percent. First, compute the contribution:

$$\text{Contrib} = S - VC$$

$$= \$20 - .40\ (\$20) \text{ or } \$20 - \$8$$
$$= \$12$$

Next compute the break-even point in number of meals:

$$\text{BEP} = \frac{\text{TFC}}{\text{Contrib}}$$

$$= \frac{\$50{,}000}{\$12} = 4{,}166.6 \text{ banquet covers}$$

In other words, just over 4,165 banquet meals need to be sold to cover total fixed costs, that is, to break even.

IN DOLLARS

The break-even point is found by dividing the total fixed costs by the contribution rate (Contrib %)

$$\text{Contrib \%} = 1 - \text{VC\%}$$

Using the same example,

$$\text{Contrib \%} = 1 - .40 = .60$$

$$\text{BEP} = \frac{\text{TFC}}{\text{Contrib \%}}$$

$$= \frac{\$50{,}000}{.60} = \$83{,}3333.33$$

Break-even *pricing* is sometimes appropriate in nonprofit operations. In most food service, however, break-even analysis is used as a cost-based support to marketing decision making. We have assumed a price and checked to see at what level of sales volume that price would cover cost. This is useful information because we can assess the projected sales volume figure against what we think is realistic.

Let us consider one further example to show how break-even analysis supports marketing judgments. Assume a motel is considering adding cocktail service in its restaurant in the evening. Total fixed costs (TFC) are estimated at $500 *per week;* the average selling price of a drink is tentatively set at $4.00 and the variable costs (VC) are 30 percent or $1.20 per drink. The resulting contribution rate is 70 percent or $2.80 per drink.

IN UNITS

$$\text{BEP} = \frac{\text{TFC}}{\$\ \text{Contrib}}$$

$$= \frac{\$500}{\$2.80} = 178.6 \text{ drinks}$$

Assuming guests will have 1.2 drinks, on average, then 148 guests (178.6 ÷ 1.2) must be served per week, or just over 20 guests a night. Management can assess the probability of attaining that sales volume at that price.

IN DOLLARS

$$\text{BEP} = \frac{\text{TFC}}{\text{Contrib rate}}$$

$$= \frac{\$500}{.70} = \$714.28 \text{ or, at \$4.00 per drink, (178.6 drinks)}$$

In this case, the desirability of the new product addition (a cocktail lounge) is dependent on the price of drinks and the number of sales likely at that price.

Another way break-even analysis can be used is to determine the point at which a *target return* (TR) will be reached. In the banquet operation used earlier, assume management judges that a target return (TR) must be $25,000 above fixed costs. Using the same form of analysis and defining "break even" ("BEP") to include the target return—*in units:*

$$\text{“BEP”} = \frac{\text{TFC + TR}}{\text{\$ Contrib}}$$

$$= \frac{\$50{,}000 + \$25{,}000}{\$12} = \frac{\$75{,}000}{\$12} = 6{,}250 \text{ meals}$$

A similar calculation for the motel's cocktail hour assessment in which a weekly profit of $500 is judged an acceptable return can be made—in dollars.

$$\text{“BEP} = \frac{\text{TFC + TR}}{\text{Contrib \%}}$$

$$= \frac{\$500 + \$500}{.70} = \frac{\$1{,}000}{70\%} = \$1{,}428.57$$

In each case, management can now assess the likelihood of achieving the required sales target at the assumed price.

The break-even calculation can also be shown graphically. The banquet department's decision is depicted in Figure A.1.

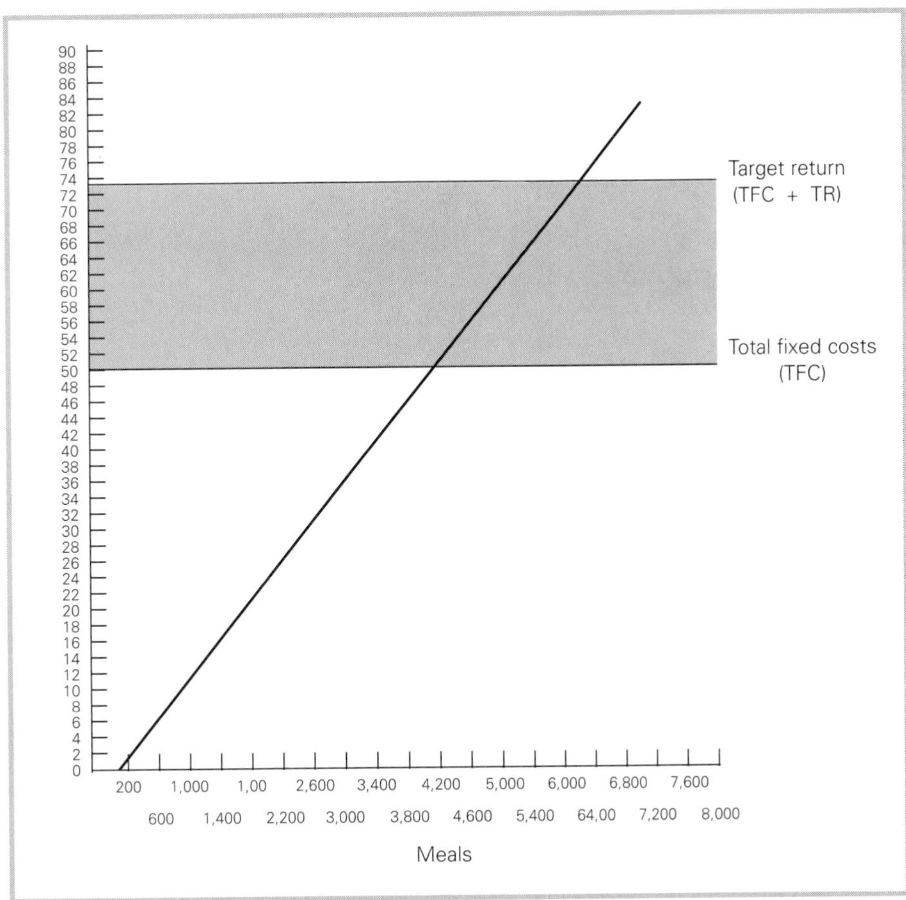

Figure A.1 Break-Even Point and Target Return for Proposed New Banquet Operation

Chapter 12

When you have finished reading this chapter, you should be able to

1. Describe the major components of marketing communication
2. Discuss the objectives of promotion
3. List the five considerations in advertising planning
4. Identify four advertising audience segments
5. Define "cut through the clutter"
6. Identify the major media used in advertising

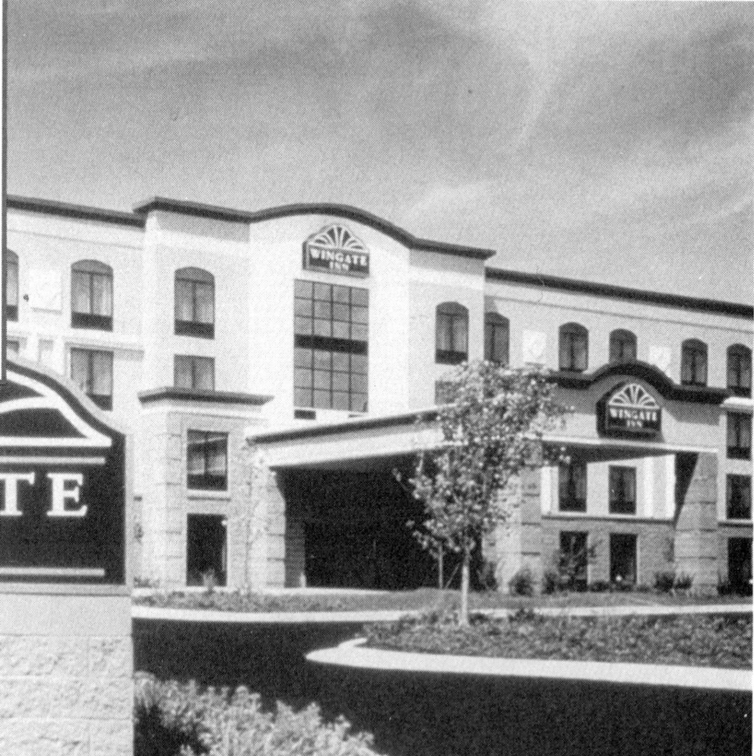

(Photo courtesy of Wingate Hotels)

Marketing Communication:

Advertising

You have just opened your own restaurant and you realize you need to let people know you want their business. Your first job is to *inform* potential customers that your restaurant is open and offers certain benefits. Second, you need to *persuade* potential guests that your offer is a good one. After you have been open for a while, you will find—in the face of all your competitors' marketing communication programs—that you need to *remind* guests of your restaurant and its offering. In other words, you need to *promote* your restaurant.

Because marketing communication or promotion includes activities such as advertising and selling, it is the element of the marketing mix many people think of first when marketing comes to mind. Indeed, some people confuse promotional activity with marketing. They think selling is all there is to marketing. We have postponed our discussion of marketing communication to the end of the marketing mix to emphasize the dependence of marketing communication on the *product and service* offered, the *place* in which it is offered, and the *price* at which the offer is made. This said, however, we need to emphasize that this is a case of last but not least. Indeed, promotion is so important that we devote two chapters to it. In this chapter, we will look at advertising and, in the next chapter, we will look at sales promotion, public relations, and personal selling. Before we turn to our discussion of advertising, however, it is appropriate to introduce the major forms of marketing communication.

PERSUASIVE COMMUNICATION

The terms "promotion" and "communication" are sometimes used interchangeably in marketing, but promotion is a *particular kind* of communication, persuasive communication. A good commercial motivates the consumer—to prefer the advertiser's product, perhaps to go out and buy now. The methods used to address *mass audiences* are advertising, sales promotion, and public relations. Personal selling involves representation on a person-to-person basis. We begin with brief definitions of each.

Advertising employs various impersonal mass media on a paid basis to communicate with people. Mass-media advertisements include not only newspaper advertising and radio and television commercials but also signboards and other media such as direct mail, which can be used to address large numbers of people without any personal contact.

Sales promotion, discussed in the next chapter, is used to stimulate immediate purchase. It includes all promotional activities other than personal selling, advertising, and publicity that attempt to persuade the consumer to purchase. In food service, the most common forms of sales promotion are "deals" such as coupons, premium merchandise, and games. Hotels use family packages, seasonal promotions and special events, and frequency programs. Sales promotion strives to enhance value and is generally aimed at achieving a specific purchase goal.

Personal selling, also discussed in Chapter 13, generally refers to sales calls made by a company representative on prospective or existing customers. These calls can be face to face, but the use of the telephone in personal selling is of increasing importance in hospitality companies. We should note, too, that personal selling also includes "selling up," the work an effective waiter or waitress or desk clerk performs in persuading guests to increase their level of expenditure.

Public relations is a marketing tool that seeks unpaid media coverage of a company's products, services, and activities. Public relations will be discussed in greater depth in Chapter 13.

THE OBJECTIVES OF MARKETING COMMUNICATION

Stimulating Demand

The basic objective of marketing communication is to persuade the consumer to buy, that is, to stimulate demand. We can distinguish, however, between stimulating primary demand and stimulating selective demand.

Primary Demand. **Primary demand** refers to generic demand for the product itself. Demand for food and shelter are good examples of primary demand. For these basic hospitality products, however, primary demand already exists. Still, organizations, such as state travel promotion agencies, have as their basic job promoting primary demand for travel.

Some Of Our
Towns Are Full Of People
You Can't See.
Walk the wooden sidewalks of a Colorado ghost town or the sacred rooms of our Indian ruins, and you'll discover something you may have left behind. Your imagination. Suddenly the town fills with cowboys whooping it up on a Saturday night. Or, at Mesa Verde, the chants of the Anasazi echo off canyon walls.
That's the incredible thing about Colorado. The variety of things you'll see. Even if you're the only one who can see them. Spark your imagination with a free Colorado Vacation Guide. Write or call toll-free and ask for extension 1007.
COLORADO
1-800-433-2656
Colorado Tourism Board, Box 38700
Dept. 1007, Denver, Colorado 80238
Name
Address
City
State
Zip

State tourism boards and other travel promotion agencies have charge of stimulating primary demand for travel, as well as selective demand for their particular state or region. (Photo courtesy of Colorado Tourism Board)

Individual firms, moreover, may need to promote primary demand when they have a new product. Such was the case with hospitality condominium companies selling time-shares (ownership of the right to use a condo for a specified period of time) when they first came on the market. They needed to explain to consumers what the time-share concept was and how swapping networks (arrangements to trade a time-share in one place for use of a facility in another place) gave them a flexible vacation medium.

Market leaders, who have the lion's share of a market, sometimes advertise to stimulate primary demand. "When you own the pie," as the saying goes, "you want it to grow." McDonald's lifestyle advertising, for instance, depicts QSR dining occasions—father and son, mother and daughter—as socially approved ways for families to get together.

Selective Demand. When the battle is for the consumer's patronage in an established market, the emphasis is on differentiation of the offering from that of the competition, that is, on stimulating demand selectively—"our" brand rather than "theirs." Within the domain of stimulating **selective demand,** however, there are several possible objectives, not all of which can be achieved by marketing communication alone.

Hierarchy of Objectives

Table 12.1 shows several possible levels of consumer involvement with a company's offering. Getting to the next level is a marketing plus, a progressive set of

Table 12.1 Hierarchy of Objectives in Marketing Communication: The AIDA Model

	Stage	Consumer Reaction
A	Awareness	I see there's a new . . .
I	Interest	I wonder if . . .
D	Desire	I'll give them a try on . . .
A	Action	Well, here I am.

marketing achievements. All marketing, of course, is aimed, ultimately, at securing purchase and a loyal customer base.

Promotional Objectives. A new operation, or the first unit of a chain in a new territory, has as its primary goal to gain consumer *awareness* that the operation is there. At a grand opening, the unit may seek to gain the community's *interest* and the early burst of promotional activity about the unit's offer of product and ser-

Use of Ronald McDonald and other familiar "cartoon characters" in McDonald's advertising—just because of their familiarity—*help keep viewers or readers aware of McDonald's even if they don't attend to the spoken or written context of the ad. (Photo courtesy of McDonald's)*

vice should help achieve this goal and move the customer on to the next stage, *desire*, which should lead to *action*, that is, to *trial*. Table 12.1 provides an acronym, **AIDA,** to help you remember these important stages.

Although promotion continues to be important in keeping the company name and offer before its target markets, once trial occurs, the quality of the operation will be crucial in the guest's decision to return. "Reminder" advertising is appropriate; indeed, in most markets it is essential. However, no advertising can fill seats or rooms for long in an operation that does not deliver what the guest wants. Case History 12.1 suggests that advertising can actually have an adverse effect on sales when the operation is not delivering what the guest wants.

Promotion plays a key role in fulfilling all marketing objectives up to the point where trial is secured. We should note that all elements in the marketing mix have a place in this process. A convenient and viable location helps in securing awareness; a pleasing ambience and convenience can be important factors in securing repeat patronage. Once consumers are aware of an operation, a competitive price can also be a supporting factor in developing interest, evaluation of the offer, and trial. Indeed, special price offers can even be used to secure awareness.

When trial is secured, however, the *quality of the product* becomes crucial. Promotion's role remains important thereafter as a reminder as suggested in Figure 12.1. In Figure 12.1, marketing communication has a primary role up to the point of trial (the dotted line in the figure). From that point, promotion has a secondary, reminder role. Once the consumer's trial of an operation begins, operations people play the primary role in pleasing the guest and moving her or him on to becoming a repeat customer. For hospitality operations, that top step is the true goal: adoption and repeat business.

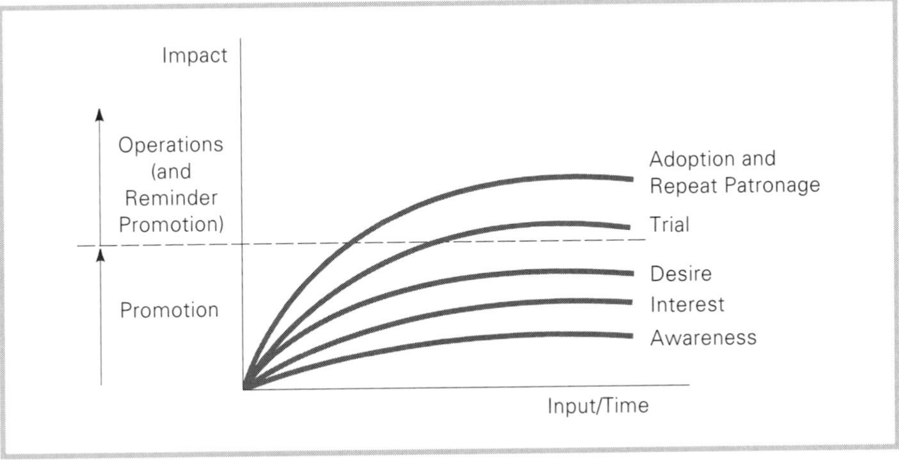

Figure 12.1 Operations Takes the Lead After Trial but Promotion Retains a Secondary, Reminder Role

Case History 12.1 When Advertising Is the Wrong Solution

When Dick Benefield first joined Arthur Treachers as executive vice president of a Treachers' franchise, the concept was a very successful one. The *product* was excellent and advertising support was strong. Benefield's operations were among the most successful in the entire Treachers franchise community. Then, for a variety of reasons, the franchisor's business experienced difficulties. The franchise was sold to another company and franchisees complained that the shift from an Icelandic cod product that was breaded in the unit just before preparation to one using Canadian cod which was "predusted," that is, breaded before freezing, resulted in loss of quality. Predusting covered any blemishes, so checking for quality at the time of receiving and cooking was no longer possible. In addition, the cooking process was altered by the use of predusted fish. The predusted product took longer to cook. As a result, more of the moisture in the fish was cooked out into the batter coating with the result that the product was gooier.

Before the difficulties for Benefield's units began, advertising expenditures were less than 4 percent of sales. Later, in an attempt to achieve a turnaround in one market, advertising expenditures were raised to 10 percent of expected sales for a six-month period. During that period, however, sales declined 25 percent and so advertising and promotion expenses ended up near 15 percent. In fact, during this period, this market had about 30 percent *new* customers. As one of Benefield's colleagues put it, "If our sales were down 25 percent and we had a 30 percent increase in new customers, we were losing 50 percent of our regular customers."

Source: Adapted from Thomas F. Powers, "MIE Hospitality" (Guelph, Ontario: University of Guelph, Advanced Management Program for the Hospitality Industry, 1983).

ADVERTISING IN THE HOSPITALITY INDUSTRY

Advertising in hospitality, believe it or not, was once somewhat out of favor. With their earlier product-oriented mode of management, most restaurants limited advertising to a promotional push when a new unit opened. Hotels generally limited advertising to informational purposes: signboards along highways and dignified ads in the hotel trade press to secure referrals from colleagues in other cities. Those days are gone, probably forever. With the increased importance of advertising and the growth in advertising budgets, clear formulation of the objectives of a company's program becomes essential.

Measurable Objectives

For a plan to get the most for its advertising dollar, it must have objectives that are specific, measurable, and attainable. Here are five which are good examples of appropriate objectives:

1. Increase consumer awareness levels.
2. Improve consumer perceptions of the company.
3. Support the successful introduction of a new product or service.
4. Increase sales at a particular meal occasion.
5. Support a short-term promotional program.[1]

The growth in marketing sophistication and advertising budgets is a response to the increasing levels of competition across all segments of the industry. Richard Good traces the growth in food service advertising to a shift to "a mature marketplace" in which fighting for market share has replaced the earlier relatively easy expansion. This is a marketplace where development of new concepts and new products is a major competitive strategy that requires advertising and promotional support.[2]

Because restaurant advertising expenditures are escalating rapidly—McDonald's marketing expenditures are about $2 billion for 1996[3]—advertisers have a special problem of their own making: consumers so bombarded with commercial messages as to make them indifferent. Thus, advertising has a special and growing need to "cut through the clutter" of the saturated media with advertising that can gain and hold the prospect's attention. Lodging advertisers have the same problem and, as the battle of the franchise chains in lodging continues to heat up, they are supporting growing advertising budgets.

Image Versus Promotional Advertising

Two basic and somewhat different goals of advertising are building or sustaining an image and creating an immediate sale, often by supporting other promotional activities such as a coupon campaign or other special offer. Advertisers that have limited budgets must often make a difficult choice between the two extremes of image and immediate sales. Some see advertising to secure consumer action as undermining image. "Every advertisement is a part of a long-term investment in the personality of the brand. Deals will get you somewhere but they cost you too much by cheapening the brand image."[4] However, the case for promotional advertising is compelling, too. As one marketing executive put it, her company emphasized advertising at the regional and local levels tied to the special selling situations in these markets. "Image is wonderful," she said, "but if you want to move traffic, you promote."[5]

There is no clear-cut answer as to whether advertising to support image or to support sales promotion is "the best." In practice, operators do some of both; they try to design sales promotions so that they support their image. Where budgets

The objective of this product-oriented ad is to use a special price to move volume now. *Notice, though, that the ad* can *be seen as emphasizing Pizza Hut's long-term policy of always offering specials that are good buys, that is, of supporting the image of Pizza Hut as offering affordable dining. (Photo courtesy of Pizza Hut)*

are generous and competitive position is strong, there will probably be more image advertising. McDonald's, for instance, is a leading image developer in hospitality. On the other hand, the need for short-run sales results drives some chains to a much higher proportion of sales promotion support. McDonald's, by the way, is among the most efficient of practitioners of sales promotion. Its "Monopoly" game promotion is a good example of a promotion that drives traffic and yet builds image. McDonald's—a place "sponsored" by a clown and featuring playgrounds, "cookie people," and an (apparently) walking Big Mac—has a "fun" image. The Monopoly game is a logical extension of that fun theme, offering the chance to play America's most popular board game for instant wins with 100 million prizes and the fantasy of the top million-dollar prize. During the 1995 holiday season, McDonald's issued over a half billion game pieces.[6]

ADVERTISING PLANNING

Five **key considerations in advertising planning are:** target audience, message, media, timing, and budget. Table 12.2 lists these considerations and links them to key points, discussed below, with respect to each.

Table 12.2 Advertising Planning

Considerations	Key Points
Target	Emergents—loyals—switchers Multiple decision makers Diverse population
Message	Unique selling proposition (USP) Cut through the clutter
Media	Broadcast, print, roadside, direct mail
Timing	Continuity—flighting
Budget	Object oriented

Target

As with any marketing activity, advertising planning begins with research on the customer. Specific considerations include customers' product/service preferences and their viewing, listening, or reading habits. A necessary precondition for advertising planning is a good comprehension of the operation's consumer profile. Demographics are important, but an understanding of *lifestyle* is perhaps more fundamental. A household made up of two 35-year-olds with a combined income of $100,000 could, after all, be two lawyers or two plumbers.

Four Audience Segments. Four **key audience segments** need to be considered in designing advertising. Each of these requires a somewhat different approach.[7] A first group are *nonusers* who are aware of the product but have rejected it—as, for instance, some older customers have done in regard to fast food because of health concerns. Nonusers of the type described "are relatively unimportant." People your product does not have a good fit with are just not a very promising segment. There is, however, another kind of nonuser who *is* important, the *emergents*—young people and recently arrived immigrants. These newcomers to the marketplace are a growth segment of the market in that they have not yet formed buying habits. Advertising to them should follow the form of ads for new products, seeking to create awareness and build brand image.

Two more established groups are the *loyals* and the *switchers.* The goal with loyals is to reinforce brand loyalty and discourage switching. Advertising offers justification for people's behavior in remaining loyal, in effect, reassuring them that they are making the right choice. Loyal customers are important. According to an American Management Association study, "65 percent of the average company's business comes from current satisfied customers."[8]

Loyal users of competitive brands, however, present a more difficult picture. It may be hard even to get their attention and harder still to get them to try an alternate product. "Indeed, one measure of loyalty is the size of the price discount required to get customers to change brands."[9]

Switchers are fickle. Price promotions can attract their patronage, but they are likely to switch to something else if the discount is no longer available. Being a familiar brand with a good image is helpful when top-of-mind awareness is a major factor in the purchase as it is for many QSR customers. Even then, however, the effect of advertising on switchers is shortlived.[10] The four audience segments are presented in summary form in Table 12.3.

A study of hotel advertising supports the notion of the importance of advertising to loyal customers. For business travelers, a critical step in the lodging patronage decision is for the hotel to become a part of the "evoked set." The evoked set, you may recall, is the list of possibilities that come into the customer's mind when a buying decision arises. The indications are that advertising *alone* may not be able to "promote chain-name awareness."[11] This brings up, the possible need to offer a special inducement to try an operation. A "get acquainted" introductory offer, perhaps one that includes a one-time discount, is one possibility. The discount associated with the trial offer can be thought of as the cost of getting into the individual's evoked set, since experience with a property is crucial to that objective.

Targeting Multiple Decision Makers. Not all advertising is directed at the ultimate consumer. Meeting planners are decision makers who place business for others who *are* travelers. They include corporate travel offices, and social, group, and association organizers. These organizational segments, which were discussed in Chapter 3, are the most common targets for personal selling.

Targeting a Diverse Population. Some large segments in North America are based on ethnic heritage and many of these are growing. For instance, African American, Hispanic, and Asian persons made up 22.3 percent of the U.S. popula-

Table 12.3 Four Target Audiences

Audience	Possible Appeals	Comment
Nonusers		Not really potential customers
Emergents	Similar to selling a new product; create awareness and image	Have not yet formed their buying habits
Loyals	Confirmation of loyalty as the "right choice"	65 percent of most firms customers are repeat users
Switchers	Name awareness, price, deals	Hard to retain as customers

Source: Data deribed from David W. Stewart, "Advertising in a Slow-Growth Economy," *American Demographics,* September 1994, pp. 40–46.

tion in 1990 but will be 28.4 percent by the year 2005.[12] Advertising to ethnic market segments often requires a different approach than is appropriate for the general market. One such case was the Sizzler steak house chain:

> In the general market Sizzler is seen as a blue collar destination where friends get together for a good time. For Hispanics, however, Sizzler is seen as being more elegant. To dine out at a Sizzler is more of an occasion, a special event for families. To create a new market position for the chain Al Pinto stresses the quality of Sizzler's food in the Spanish language commercials and reinforces the affordable price.[13]

Ethnic-oriented advertising agencies, such as *Al Pinto Publicidad* which created Sizzler's Spanish language program, specialize in serving companies that want to reach these markets.

Message: Unique Selling Proposition

A **unique selling proposition (USP)** states the theme for a campaign and often becomes its slogan. An effective USP summarizes the reason to buy. It needs to demonstrate that the offer is desirable. Moreover, it can not be a "me too" offer; the appeal's *uniqueness* must be clear to achieve differentiation. The USP should make a promise that is believable and that can be fulfilled. The strongest appeals are product *benefits* which are the personal appeal to the buyer. They tell what use the product is to the customer. *Product attributes* are characteristics or features of the product that generate these benefits. If attributes are cited, the related benefit should be clear.

Bob Evans Farms has developed a branded lunch program "Lunch Savors." The "Lunch Savors" program USP is summed up in the tag line, "Where else can you find lunch this good for a price this small?" The commercial lets customers know that Evans offers "10 great lunches for $3.99 or less." The *satisfaction* of a good meal and the *saving* of a low-priced lunch are key appeals captured in the tag line.[14] A similar message—good food and a bargain—is conveyed by a Hardee's tag line: "Big Taste—Little Money."

In a Kenny Rogers Roasters television ad, a woman in a business suit is returning home with her young son in a baseball uniform—and they are carrying a large shopping bag from Kenny Rogers Roasters. The mother serves the prepared meal—rotisserie-roasted chicken and all the "fixins"—to a group of family members. Rogers, a country and western star for whom the chain is named, can be heard singing, "This Place Called Home" in the background. As the ad ends, a voice over gives the tag line, "Remember what a home cooked meal can bring to the table. Kenny Rogers Roasters. There's goodness here."

When McDonald's says, "You deserve a break today," the message conveyed is a complex one that includes the idea that a McDonald's meal or snack will be a pleasant experience, that is, a deserved reward in the midst of a harried life. Moreover, it implies the notion of solving time pressure problems. The break saves time. Visually, a McDonald's ad suggests a particular experience that goes well beyond food: social acceptability, family solidarity, fun times, and so forth.

Just as tag lines in a television commercial sum up the message in words, the visual content is often used as a summary visual device: smiling faces, happy people, good times. Pictures play a similar role in print ads, particularly for hotels. "The pictures in a hotel advertisement effectively make a promise to the customer—a promise that certain benefits will be delivered at the hotel."[15]

Cut Through the Clutter. As we have already noted, the consumer is bombarded with messages. The problem of gaining and keeping the attention, let alone the credibility, of the viewer is a major one that is summed up in the phrase **"cut through the clutter."** This is a key goal of designing an ad that gets the operation's message across.

One of the ways of doing this is with a print ad's headline. The headline provides a hook to attract the reader's attention. Some are simple, "50 Percent Off!" while others strive to be catchy: "The Only Resort to Resort To" (Long Bay Beach Resort, Tortola, British Virgin Islands).

Humor will attract attention but humor is difficult to do successfully. At Long John Silver's, consumer focus groups told executives that they found the company's ads somewhat stodgy and boring and that "they liked humor in ads and ads that were different from the norm." Long John Silver's built a campaign around

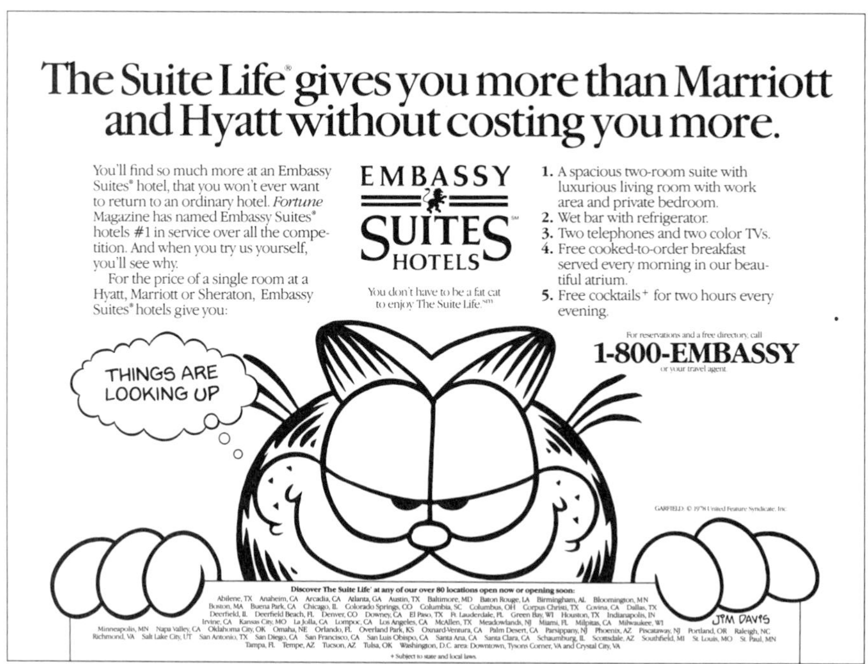

Comparative advertising is impolite and combative. For just that reason, it cuts through the clutter. Everybody, it seems, likes to watch a fight. (Photo courtesy of Embassy Suites Hotels)

a "spokesperson," "Mr. Norman Bigfish, Chairman" (part puppet and part human in costume). Mr. Bigfish was a large blue fish seated, in one ad, behind an imposing desk in an office. The company's marketing executive vice president explained the company's reasoning: "When you have a tiny budget [in this case, $50,000,000] compared to the big guys, the ultimate risk is that you won't be noticed. We've got to be a little different." The theme line for the campaign was "Where great fish is a big deal."[16] Unfortunately, after a few months, Long John Silver's had to discontinue the Bigfish campaign which apparently did not catch viewers' attention.[17]

Sonic, a regional chain with headquarters in Oklahoma, was more successful in promoting its competitive points of difference with a humorous commercial called "Warming Bin 101," poking fun at the burger operations that use prepared menu offerings rather than made-to-order products.[18]

Another technique to get attention is the highly aggressive comparative advertising campaigns that have become a centerpiece of marketing for runners-up among the hamburger chains: the much discussed burger wars. However, this technique is certainly not limited to burger chains. El Pollo Asado, a *broiled* chicken chain, following a similar tack, took on the fried chicken leaders of its segment with a series of television commercials that featured a counterperson asking, "Y'all want greasy or extra greasy?" and handing out red and white striped baskets of chicken. The red and white buckets were eventually replaced with plain white ones after Kentucky Fried Chicken went to court to claim infringement of its service mark.[19]

Spokespersons are often used to cut through the clutter by personifying the company and its appeal. With Mr. Bigfish, that did not work out too well, but Big Boy—a mythical figure atop Big Boy restaurant signs—has become a landmark in many cities. Probably the most successful spokesperson is Ronald McDonald, who is said to have a name recognition factor second only to Santa Claus. The visual image associated with the company and its message, through, constant repetition makes for efficient communication. The sign of the stylized clown for most people in North America will instantly be associated with McDonald's restaurants. McDonald's animated products are also well known.

Real people are used, too, and often with great success. Dave Thomas, president of Wendy's, has been very successful as an easygoing, humorous spokesperson for that company. Bill Marriott has served as an effective spokesperson for Marriott Hotels. Subway uses actors to portray cab drivers Bucky and Vinny as they drive through different cities discussing the merits of Subway, of course.[20] Even spokespersons, however, can wear out. KFC's long-time symbol, the Colonel, *Nations Restaurant News* reports, was shelved and replaced with a campaign "that promotes families."[21] It is possible, however, that we have not heard the last of the Colonel because he is a favorite with many KFC franchisees.

Promises, Promises. One danger in clever and ambitious copywriting is that of overpromising. The expectations aroused in the consumer by the advertising

Some operations use the device of a "mythical person" to symbolize their company. Just glimpse at the figure in the lower right of this ad, and you will know instantly who is offering the generous breakfast pictured.

message will haunt the operator that cannot fulfill them. Holiday Inns built a major advertising program around the tag line, "No surprises":

> One advertising expert explained that this campaign sensitized the customers to any failure of service and boosted complaints significantly. With its huge network of franchisees, Holiday could not really guarantee that all guests would have perfect accommodations.[22]

Advertising Media

The principal **advertising media** used in the hospitality industry are electronic (television and radio) and print (newspapers and magazines). Outdoor advertising is important, too, as is direct mail. The telephone and telemarketing are increasing in significance, especially for hotels.

There are two common benchmarks in assessing advertising media, **cost per thousand** (**CPM,** where M stands for thousand) and **gross rating points (GRPs).**

To compute the cost per thousand (CPM), the cost of the ad is divided by the rated audience in thousands. If an ad—to use a simple illustration—costs $10,000 and reaches 500,000, the CPM would be $10,000 ÷ 500 or $20. This should be regarded as a very rough benchmark because it ignores the issue of waste circulation (people who, though they use the medium, do not really see or attend to the ad as well as people who do see it but who are not really potential customers). On the other hand, it also undercounts in print media because it registers circulation only and ignores the impact of multiple exposures, that is, where a magazine or newspaper is read by more than one person. Finally, the cost-per-thousand measure ignores the question of the **impact** of the particular medium on the target audience. Escalating costs in traditional media have driven advertisers to consider nontraditional media, some of which are described later in Field Practice Note 12.1 (see page 347).

In addition to cost, media have three key characteristics: reach, frequency, and impact. *Reach* refers to the number of households exposed to a particular ad during a particular time period. *Frequency* refers to the number of times within that time period that a household is exposed to that message. Based on estimates of the number of persons viewing or reading a medium within the average household, reach and frequency can also be expressed in terms of the *number of persons* reached and the *number of times* the persons are exposed to the message. Reach and frequency can be specified numerically and used to compute *gross rating points* (GRPs). Gross rating points are computed by multiplying reach by frequency.

If an ad reaches 70 percent of the homes in a market with an average four-time frequency, that schedule has a GRP of 280. Note that the word "gross" in GRP is used because there is duplication in coverage. A very high GRP does *not* mean nearly everybody in the audience has been reached. Many people may have missed the ad, whereas others may have seen it several times.

Gross rating points are a measure of the *weight* of the advertising delivered by a particular schedule. If another schedule delivered 350 GRPs, it would have more weight than the 280 GRPs computed previously, but *the GRP figure does not tell us what combination of reach and frequency is used.* The media planner also faces decisions regarding reach and frequency as separate considerations. The decision to be made is whether extensive coverage of a large audience (high reach) or intensive coverage (frequency) of a more limited target should be emphasized. Too frequent an exposure results in boredom; overemphasizing reach at the expense of frequency may mean an ad makes no impression at all because it is seen so infrequently. In general, some repetition is helpful; too much results in boredom, in tuning out.

Impact involves a more subjective judgment of the quality of the exposure. An ad attempting to reach women executives would likely be more effective in the magazine *Ms* than one in *Playboy* because the credibility of the magazine would be higher and the reader's respect for it likely greater for the target audience.

We can turn now to a brief overview of the principal media which are shown in Table 12.4. Field Practice Note 12.1 discusses some alternative media used in food service.

Broadcast Media

Television. Television often results in lowest-cost-per-thousand reached, but it has a very high *total* cost. For this reason, large chains are the major users of television advertising. They have advertising budgets large enough to afford television's efficiency. So significant is television to restaurant chains that television ADI (areas of dominant influence) boundaries are a significant factor in restuarant expansion planning, as we noted earlier in the case of Boston Market. In fact, an

Table 12.4 Types of Media

Broadcast media	
Television	Excellent reach, high total cost Combines sight, motion, and sound
Radio	Highly targetable Less costly than television Good reach of travelers
Cable television	Highly targetable Good reach of hotel guests Fragmented market
Print media	
Newspapers	Some targeting possible Printed word is credible to many
Magazines	Targetable, prestige, high-quality reproduction
Newspaper inserts	Flexible, low-cost print medium Good campaign distribution vehicle
Roadside media	Directional, very brief message
Direct mail	Excellent targeting, high CPM Good coupon distribution vehicle

advertising threshold can be computed indicating the number of units in a market needed to justify television advertising. If television advertising is necessary to the success of the particular concept, then the **market entry threshold** calculations shown in Table 12.5 will indicate whether it is feasible to enter that market or not.

The power of television comes from its ability to combine sight, motion, and sound—and to tell a story. Often, commercials simply inform, but many tell a story to dramatize a point and persuade the listener.

Despite its strengths, television advertising comes in for frequent criticism. The escalating cost, particularly of network television, has meant that budgets may no longer provide for sufficient frequency. With the growing use of shorter commercials, television suffers from escalating clutter as the number of commercial messages rises. Although television offers the greatest reach (number of people exposed), a logical by-product of extensive reach is poor selectivity. The chances are very good that television reaches many who are not in the target segment. The ability of the listener to mute commercials and channel surf during commercials has also had an impact on television's effectiveness. For all the reservations we may have about television, however, it is clearly the most powerful medium for mass marketers who can afford it.

Radio. Radio is less expensive in terms of absolute costs and so can be used by a wider range of operations. Radio is also more targeted because the various

Table 12.5 Calculation of Market Entry Threshold

Assumptions

Typical unit sales volume	$1,000,000
Percent of sales to local advertising	4%
Local advertising budget available per unit per year	$ 40,000

Experience in this company is that 250 GRPs every other week are required to get its message across.

Cost in this market for 250 GRP schedule is $10,000 per week.

An every other week 250 GRP schedule will cost $260,000

$260,000 ÷ $40,000 = 6.5 restaurant units

From these calculations, the company should not enter this market unless it thinks the market can support seven restaurants or that some alternative advertising schedule can be made to work.

station types (i.e., progressive, contemporary, middle of the road, news/information/sports, talk, easy listening, classical, country and western, and ethnic) each offer a highly differentiated listnership. Radio is often used in conjunction with television to provide frequency in an overall campaign.

Radio can also be used to reach people in their cars and, thus, is a good medium for travelers, particularly during drive time (roughly, 6:00 to 10:00 A.M. and 3:00 to 7:00 P.M.). A disadvantage of radio is the limited attention of the listeners, most of whom are doing something else such as housework, driving, or studying while listening.

Other Electronic Media. Cable television and other video options, such as videocassettes, share regular television's audience. Cable, like radio, is a highly targetable medium because the individual cable channels have a distinctive body of viewers. Cable television is available in virtually every hotel room in North America and is, therefore, a powerful, if highly fragmented, medium for reaching travelers.

Print Media

Newspapers. Newspapers are generally published daily and so provide great flexibility since the message can easily be adjusted daily, if necessary. Newspaper advertising provides the credibility of the written word, perhaps because newspapers are read for current information. Newspapers provide a broad-based readership that helps build awareness of an establishment among key publics. They offer possibilities for targeting where ad placement is specified by section (e.g., sports, financial, women's, society, travel, etc.). Newspapers are often used to distribute coupons to a wide audience. They are generally effective in supporting promotions, but some argue they are not as effective for image-building goals.[23]

Magazines. This medium offers demographic selectivity and many national magazines publish regional editions which offer geographic targeting. Specialized magazines—sports, hobby, special interests—offer other targeting opportunities, too. Local and regional magazines also offer some obvious geographic planning advantages. Many magazines have a higher prestige than other media and the high-quality reproduction that is generally available improves the impact of the message. Superior reproduction of photos is especially important to travel and resort advertising. Since magazines are often read by more than one person, they have a "pass along" readership factor built into their circulation numbers.

Newspaper Inserts. There are two kinds of specially printed sections for insertion into newspapers. The kind most frequently used by hospitality operations are co-op inserts for which several advertisers share the cost. The insert is usually printed in color and offers greater flexibility, as well as lower cost, than newspaper advertising. Coupons distributed by insert have a higher redemption rate than those in a newspaper advertisement. Co-op inserts contain only advertising for noncompetitive products and services. So-called solo inserts are generally one or two pages and cost three to five times as much as co-op inserts. Thus, solo inserts are usually limited to chains and the advertising co-ops of franchise organizations. They do make an effective medium, however, for special events such as grand openings.

Roadside Media

Billboards and other signs are especially useful for giving directions. They are also used to reach general audiences, but only when the message can be simply stated. The upper limit of message length is roughly seven or eight words. Circulation figures are available; they are based on the number of cars that pass a display each hour.

Direct Mail

Many independent operators favor direct mail. These operators find they cannot take advantage of large-circulation media such as television, radio, and newspapers in spite of their favorable CPM because of their high total cost. Moreover, they prefer the greater targeting and personalization possibilities of direct mail.[24] Specialized mailing lists are available from list suppliers. The best list, however, may well be the one compiled from an operation's own customers. When an in-house list based on customer addresses is used, it is important to realize that a direct-mail campaign is only as good as the mailing list used. By requesting undelivered mail be returned to you by the post office (for a nominal charge), you can "clean" your own list by examining the returned mail.

Some operations use a customer list to mail a newsletter that features items about staff and guests, as well as information about special holiday meals, wine tastings, and other promotional events. Some hotels use a similar newsletter approach to advise frequent guests of busy dates when reservations may be hard

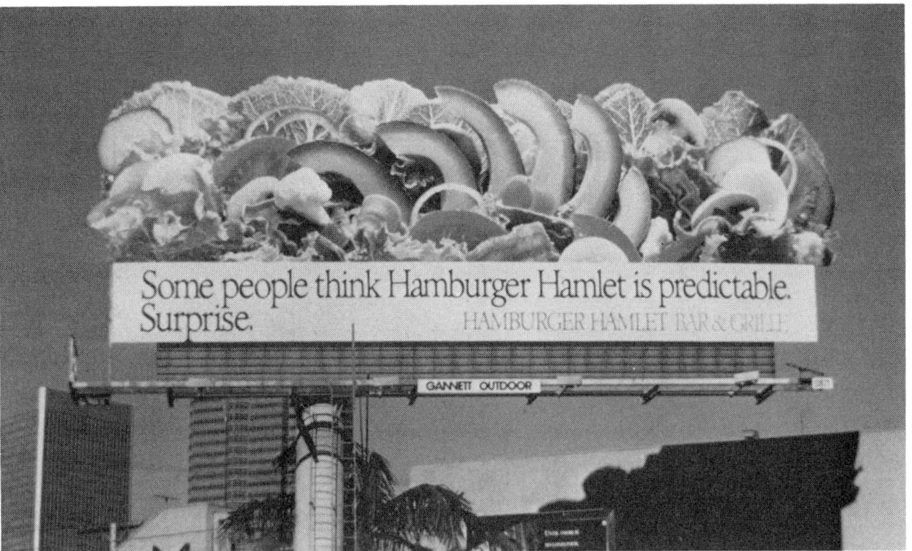

The short time a traveler is exposed to a billboard limits the message length, putting a premium on creativity. (Photo courtesy of Outdoor Advertising Institute)

to get. Frequent-guest programs that award points for each dollar spent in a restaurant or premiums for each visit to a hotel also give operators an excellent mailing list.

Direct mail is often used for coupon distribution. In a "feathered" mailing, only a certain percentage of the list is sent out each week. This helps avoid the crush that can result from sending out several thousand coupons all at once.

One drawback to direct mail is its high CPM. Another is its image as junk mail. This last difficulty can be overcome to some degree, however, by personalization or by conferring an "insider's" feel in a newsletter. Including a coupon in a direct-mail piece can also convert junk mail to something of potential value to the prospect.

Due Bills. **Due bills,** or trade-outs, are a means of trading merchandise or services for advertising. Although the practice is used in other industries, it has special attraction for hospitality. In any but the most luxurious hotels, for instance, the incremental cost to the hotel of renting a room is about $5.00 to $10.00. The cost of setting up and cleaning up a meeting room is very little, and the incremental cost of doing so may be zero if the staff used is on duty anyway. When the rooms that are traded would otherwise be vacant, they have no little or cost to the hotel.

On the other hand, to a radio station that wants to stage a weekend sales meeting, the vacant space does have value. If the radio station can trade radio time for rooms, it gets a good buy—a no-cash transaction—and the hotel gets advertising for a very small outlay.

This page is one of a three-page booklet that Pizza Hut used, offering a total of 18 coupons. (Photo courtesy of Pizza Hut)

Even with food service, food cost is the only necessary element of cost in a trade-out. Note, however, that if the trade—for rooms or food—permits use to take place at any time, then trade-out guests may displace regular guests, in which case the true cost is measured by lost revenue. Accordingly, trade-outs make the most sense when they apply to slow periods.

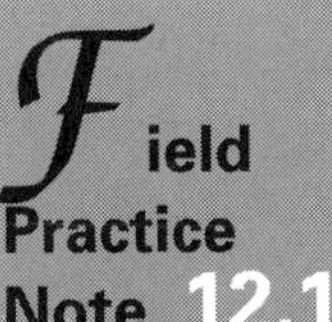

Alternative Advertising Media

"The increasingly high cost of traditional media forces you to look at alternative outlets and resources," according to a marketing director for McDonald's 140 units in Atlanta, Georgia. "You may not have broad reach but you do get frequency." Pizza Hut and McDonald's are engaged actively on the Internet and some QSR chains are sponsoring racing cars. Other nontraditional media are being developed with mass-transit operators, sporting goods, sporting events, and even automatic teller machines. According to *Nation's Restaurant News:*

> Poly-wrapped busses, which utilize every square inch of vehicle surface, including the roof, to create a visually arresting effect, are a medium deployed in some markets by Taco Bell and Ohio based Donato's; New York City's "branded car" plan, which saturates interior ad surfaces of individual subway cars with one advertiser's message, is popular with Blimpie International; Burger King has its name attached to a regulation sized series of collector baseballs; a host of quick service operators, including Little Caesars, Burger King, and KFC are couponing themselves on the tops of ATM receipts.

Source: Theresa Howard, "Operators Take Note of Alternative Advertising Venues," *Nation's Restaurant News,* April 1, 1996.

Trade-outs can often be arranged with local media by the unit manager. These arrangements, properly handled, can have a beneficial public relations impact, in addition to the monetary benefit of the trade, because of the personal contact with local media personnel. Brokers are also available to make such arrangements on a national or regional basis.

Timing

The timing of the campaign often relates to the timing of the customer's purchase. A direct-mail program aimed at selling office Christmas parties would be illtimed in July but probably also in December. If the decision is normally made in November, late October or early November would fit well with the time the customer needs the information. Radio ads aimed at gaining Mother's Day patronage should start roughly one month before the event.

There are two possibilities to consider in scheduling advertising, **continuity** and flighting. Some advertisers aim for continuity by scheduling ads evenly throughout a campaign. An alternative to continuity is **flighting.**

A "flight" of advertising refers to the periodic use of advertising in a medium during a campaign—an "on" period. The flight is then followed by a period of silence in that medium—an "off" period. Flighting is used in some cases because of budget limitations. The advertiser referred to in an earlier example judged that 250 GRPs were required in a market to achieve an impact. If the cost of 250 GRPs per month is $10,000 and the advertiser's budget will only allow $7,500 a month, it might be possible to have three one-week flights followed by an off period and then repeat that pattern the next month. When flighting is used with television advertising, some advertisers seek to maintain continuity in another, less expensive medium such as radio.

A perennial timing issue is whether advertising should concentrate on periods of low volume to build them up or should be used to build strong periods to make them even better. At a recent marketing conference, a group of restaurant advertising executives discussed this issue and concluded that advertising in purchased media should be concentrated on strong periods until the unit is operating at capacity during those periods. They also noted that in-store advertising (see Chapter 14) should be used to promote the off period to the guests who were in the unit during the high-volume period, perhaps offering them a deal to come back in the low-volume time. The moderator summed up the discussion in this way:

> Suppose that you do most of your business on Friday, Saturday and Sunday. If you are not operating at maximum capacity on those days, the logical thing is to work to make the weekends better since that is the propensity of your customer's buying behavior. You go fishing when the fish are biting.[25]

Panelists agreed that, in the situation described previously, they would spend 90 percent of their advertising dollars on the strong weekend business.

Budget

One common way to set the advertising budget is as a percentage of sales that is judged affordable or which is comparable to what others in the industry are spending. The main advantage of this method is that they simplify decision making. Some might even argue that they are simple minded. Adjusting advertising to match sales in a poor year, for instance, can result in decreasing advertising at a time when falling sales suggest *more* advertising is called for. Spending at the industry average lets your competitors set your advertising budget for you.

A preferred method is to set advertising objectives and then spell out the steps necessary to accomplish that goal—or goals. For instance, a company might seek to raise consumer awareness for an operation in appropriate markets, to secure a heightened level of name recognition, or to increase the level of trial. The steps judged necessary to achieve any or all of these goals can then be laid out and costed. If the cost of attaining the objectives exceeds the budget, more realistic objectives can be set, perhaps moving toward the desired goal over a longer period of time. The advantage of this approach is that results of the advertising program can be measured against the goals set for it.

THE ADVERTISING AGENCY

Advertising agencies come in all sizes, ranging from a one-person shop to international agencies with billings in the billions of dollars. Full-service agencies offer *creative, media-buying,* and *market research* services. In addition, a full-service agency will provide *campaign planning.* In many cases, these agencies will be involved not only in the advertising but in the design of sales promotion programs and, indeed, in all elements of the company's marketing program.

There are also a wide variety of specialized agencies such as creative boutiques, independent media-buying services, and market research firms.

The disadvantage of using a group of specialized agencies is that the client (i.e. the company's management) is called on to coordinate the work of a group of highly specialized experts and, often, management lacks the expertise to undertake this coordination. The result can be expensive and frustrating.

While large companies use major agencies, a town of almost any size invariably has a small independent agency that will be very interested in assisting the independent restaurateur or providing local advertising services to a franchised hotel or restaurant. Although a small agency obviously does not have the depth of a larger firm, it does have people experienced in the creative work of developing an ad campaign, including, especially, layout and art work. It also should have expertise in media-buying processes in the local community. Moreover, a relatively small account will usually be able to get the attention of the small agency's top people.

Some firms develop their own in-house ad agencies to maintain tighter control over advertising and to save the commission or fees that an outside agency would levy. One problem with this approach is that these companies lack an *outside independent* judgment of the company's marketing program, which is one of the vital advantages a strong agency offers its clients.

SUMMARY

Advertising is one of the major forms of marketing communication. The others are sales promotion, personal selling, and publicity. The objective of advertising is usually selective demand for a particular company, but market leaders and firms introducing unknown products may seek to stimulate primary demand. Advertising aims first to move consumers to awareness and then to interest and desire and, ultimately, to action (AIDA). Advertising has a key role up to the point of consumer trial. From that point, pleasing the guest through good operations becomes key, but advertising retains an important reminder advertising role. Some advertising is designed to burnish image, while other efforts are aimed at immediate purchase.

There are five considerations that underlie advertising planning: target, message, media, timing, and budget:

Target. The audience for advertising can be divided into the segments of nonusers, emergents, loyals, and switchers. Organizational targets offer multiple purchase opportunities. Advertising aimed at consumers must take into account diversity in the marketplace.

Message. The unique selling proposition (USP) is often summed up in a tag line. While product attributes are important, the consumer benefit is crucial. A message must be designed to "cut through the clutter" of other advertisements.

Media. The chapter summarizes the strengths and weaknesses of the principal media: broadcast (television and radio), print (newspapers, magazines, and inserts), roadside, and direct mail. Due bills are a form of swapping hospitality services for advertising.

Timing. Advertising must be timed to reach the customer at the point when he or she is most likely to be influenced to purchase. Continuity in advertising is desirable but may be too expensive, in which case, flights of intermittent advertising may be used. As long as a unit is operating below capacity during its peak period, advertising effort should be concentrated on the peak time, rather than on slower periods when the consumer's propensity to buy is lower.

Budget. The budget should be planned with specific goals in mind, rather than simply mimic the industry's pattern of marketing expenditures.

Advertising agencies may be divided into full-service firms and firms that specialize in one or a few of an agency's functions. One of the key advantages of a strong agency is that it brings an expert outside independent judgment to a firm's marketing decisions.

◆ Key Words and Concepts

Primary demand
Selective demand
AIDA
Measurable objectives
Image versus promotional advertising
Key considerations in advertising planning
Key audience segments
Multiple decision makers
Unique selling proposition (USP)
Cut through the clutter
Advertising media
Cost per thousand (CPM)
Gross rating points (GRP)
Impact
Market entry threshold
Due bills
Continuity
Flighting

◆ Discussion Questions

1. What is meant by "hierarchy of objectives"? How does it relate to marketing communication? How does it relate to operations?

2. Give examples of measurable advertising objectives. How would you obtain the measure appropriate to each objective?
3. What are the pros and cons of image and promotional advertising? What deciding factors would determine which you might use?
4. What are the main considerations in advertising planning? What key points relate to each?
5. How can an effective USP "cut through the clutter"? Give examples of campaigns you believe have been effective in achieving this goal.
6. Discuss the uses and weaknesses of the measures CPM and GRP. What is meant by "impact" in advertising?
7. What are the strengths and weaknesses of television as an advertising medium?

Chapter 13

When you have finished reading this chapter, you should be able to

1. Describe the three main types of dealing
2. Discuss the role of special events in promotion
3. Explain how news is defined by the media
4. List the steps in effective crisis management
5. Assess the cost effectiveness of public relations
6. Describe the sales process

(Photo courtesy of Merrill Lynch & Company, Inc.)

Marketing Communication:

Sales Promotion, Public Relations, and Personal Selling

In this chapter, we continue our discussion of the important topic of marketing communication. Sales promotion and public relations are impersonal media which aim at large numbers of consumers. In this, they are like advertising and are often used in conjunction with it. Personal selling, on the other hand, is directed at individual decision makers.

SALES PROMOTION

Sales promotion is a "marketing communication activity which offers an incentive to immediate action."[1] It is a way of building immediate sales within a given time period. Whereas advertising is used to influence consumer *attitudes* over a period of time, the primary purpose of promotions is to stimulate immediate purchases.

A good sales promotion, ideally, should not just stimulate sales but also support the company's image. Table 13.1 offers 10 purposes a sales promotion might serve.

The most common form of sales promotion in food service is dealing. Deals involve the use of coupons, premium merchandise, and games. **Discounts** are another common form of promotion. In upscale operations, **special events** are used to achieve much the same purpose, that of enhancing perceived value for the purchaser.

Most sales promotion activities are keyed to the environment of the moment. Couponing, which works on the price side of price/value, is especially popular

Table 13.1 Ten Reasons to Use Promotions

1. To encourage *trial* of your restaurants among noncustomers and former customers.
2. To stimulate repeat business from present customers; to build customer loyalty through promotional rewards.
3. To increase your business during specific day parts or days of the week.
4. To increase party size.
5. To increase check averages.
6. To introduce new food items or services such as breakfast bars or carryout.
7. To help offset competitive advantages or actitivities; to take the focus off competition and put it on you.
8. To capitalize on holidays, seasons, or special events.
9. To create an *event* and add excitement to your restaurant several times a year because your *customers enjoy* promotions and like the extra activity associated with them. In other words, simply for the *entertainment* value.
10. To stimulate *employee* enthusiasm and involvement. When customer promotions are properly mechandised to employees, they almost always have this important side effect.

Source: Adapted from Robert H. Marriott, Jr., "Promotions—A Key Piece in Your Marketing Puzzle," *Proceedings, Chain Operators Exchange, 1987* (Chicago: International Foodservice Manufacturers Association, 1987).

during recessions when consumers either have less money in their pockets—or are afraid they soon may have. In more prosperous times, on the other hand, the emphasis shifts to events that enhance value such as games and premium merchandise.

Promotions, like any element of the marketing mix, need to be targeted to—that is designed to reach—a relevant consumer segment such as families, senior citizens, teens, children, or singles. Sales promotions are not a spur of the moment activity and, especially in multiunit companies, they require considerable advance planning. For instance, Marriott suggests that key management people should be consulted six months in advance of a promotion and unit managers should have a written guide for a promotion at least 30 days before the event begins so that necessary staff training can be accomplished.

Marriott suggests several ways to evaluate the cost effectiveness of a sales promotion:

- The 4-to-1 formula: If a promotion costs $1,000, it should recover the cost and generate incremental sales of $4,000 or $5,000 in all.
- A premium promotion (discussed further later) may be judged successful if all the premium merchandise is used up.
- Coupon redemptions should be at a rate at least sufficient to pay for the media purchased (direct mail, newspaper, point of purchase inserts, etc.) in incremental sales and profit.

Customary practice in the industry for measuring the impact of a promotion is to compare the operating results in the four-week period immediately preceding the promotion with the four-week period during the promotion and the four-week period after it. These comparisons sometimes need to be adjusted. If unusual events (e.g., a major football bowl game or a blizzard) occur during any of these periods, some adjustment must be made in evaluating the results. According to Marriott:

> Most operators are in agreement that major promotions should be introduced no more than three to four times a year although simple discounts can be offered as often as monthly . . . . Customer and employee interest can be maintained from four to six weeks, although a few have been successful as long as eight weeks. A minimum of four to six weeks should be allowed between major promotions.[2]

Several **concerns** are commonly expressed **about promotions:** the loyalty (or lack of loyalty) of deal-prone customers; the potential, real or *perceived,* for erosion of product quality and service; discounting to present customers with no resulting real increase in sales; and the potentially negative impression created among consumers that may erode years of chain positioning efforts. The conclusion, however, of CREST research is that the evidence suggests these concerns are "unsupported and appear to lack relevance."[3] In fact, CREST concluded that, although dealing can have widely varying effects, generally all of them are good. Deals appear to have the effect of increasing brand loyalty and they generate more excitement than do new product introductions.[4]

Dealing: Three Main Types

The three most common forms of promotion are coupons, offers of premium merchandise, and games.

Couponing. Coupons effectively reduce prices to consumers (if they use the coupons before their expiry date). They are an inducement to buy *now* (i.e., within the promotional period). Coupons are most commonly distributed by newspaper or direct mail and are used most during slack economic periods and during off seasons. The larger the discount offered, generally the higher the redemption rate.

Couponing is most commonly used in fast food, but hotels sometimes use coupons, usually distributed by mail or in magazine ads, to promote weekend or off-season business in a targeted audience or as a means to introduce the hotel to new customers.

Couponing in off seasons, particularly in fast food, often results in drastically reduced margins. A BOGO (buy one get one free), for instance, effectively means that if an operation has a food cost of 30 percent at full price, it will have a 60 percent food cost on a meal when a BOGO coupon is redeemed. On the other hand, because food cost on soft drinks is low (commonly less than 10 percent on post-mix dispensed products) and most customers have a soft drink (that is not discounted) with their meal, the combined food cost percentage may work out to be more in the order of 50 percent. As one operator put it, "It's better than having the store stand empty. It covers the payroll and leaves something for profit."[5] In

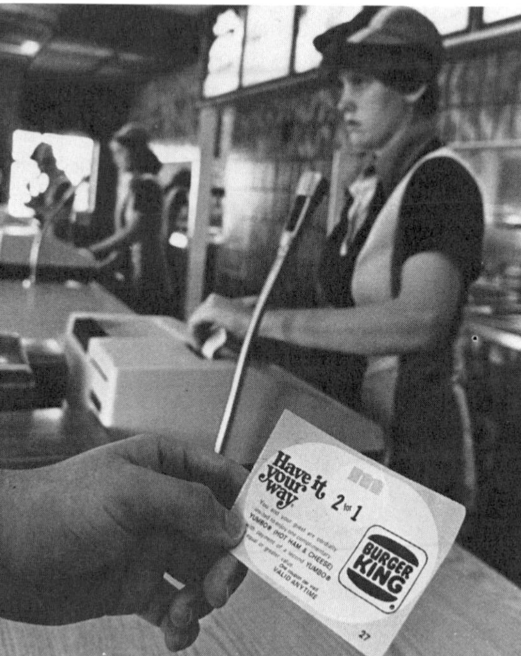

Couponing can be used to introduce a new item or to build volume in slow periods. BOGOs (buy one, get one free), however, are very expensive to the operator and, if used too frequently, can accustom the guest to "waiting until the special is offered." (Photo courtesy of Burger King)

fact, the effect of heavy discounting in an off season does seem to be to bring people out into the snow of January and February and into the slush of March and early April, thus increasing industry sales in a time when people might otherwise prefer to eat at home. Moreover, Marriott indicates, "[a]bout half the people who use coupons are new triers" (i.e., someone who has not purchased in the last few months).[6]

Bounce Backs **Bounce-back** coupons are given customers at the time of purchase in hopes that they will return to redeem them. Bounce backs have a significantly lower cost because there is no cost of distribution, a particularly important consideration for a small chain. One operator noted that coupons distributed by newspaper for his company had a media cost associated with them that was about 20 times that of bounce backs.[7] The redemption rate of that firm for bounce backs was 7 to 10 times greater than for newspaper coupons.

Marriott lists the following common and effective uses for bounce backs:

- Increase visit frequency.
- Bring customers back during different or additional day parts or days of the week.
- Stimulate trial of new food items.
- Induce first-time customers to return.[8]

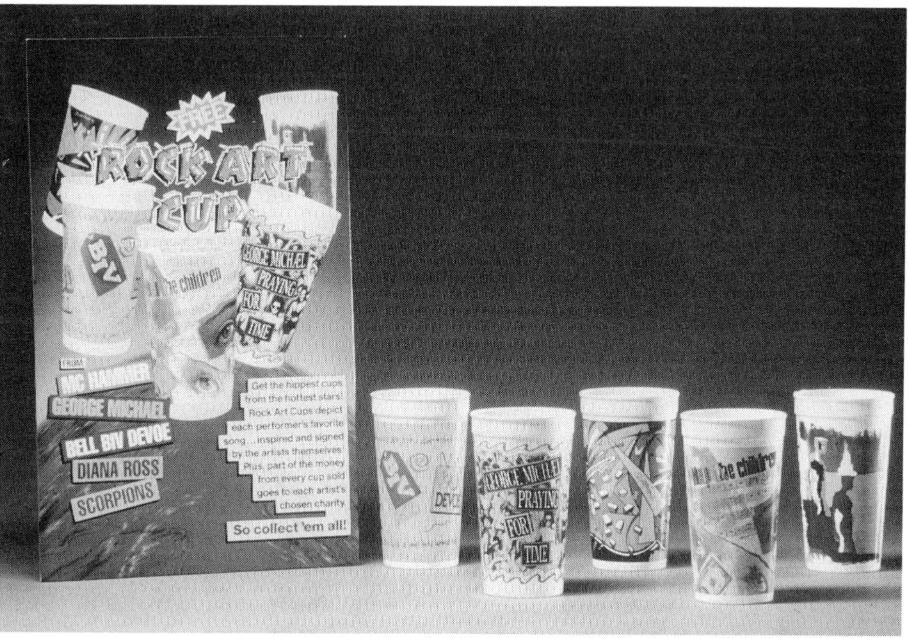

This series of five cups featuring famous rock artists encourages repeat patronage. As the point-of-purchase poster says, "Collect 'em all." (Photo courtesy of Taco Bell)

Premiums. Premium merchandise is usually sold at cost with any purchase of a food or beverage item. Toys and special drinking glasses are common premiums. These are often offered in sets of 3 to 6 with the goal of getting consumers to collect the entire set, thus encouraging repeat patronage. The "bargain" on the promotional merchandise is an extra feature associated with a visit to the store. As such, it is seen as adding or enhancing value. Premiums are sometimes referred to as self-liquidating promotions because the cost of the merchandise is usually covered by the amount paid by the customer.

Games and Sweepstakes. Sweepstakes are often built around a ticket given out with each purchase. In one kind of game, the symbols, words, or numbers from two or more tickets must be matched. This form of promotion requires frequent visits by the customer to increase the probability of winning and so promotes repeat business. For a game to have significant impact, however, top prizes have to be really large to compete for attention with lotteries and other events.[9]

How do games add value? They add a note of excitement to a visit to a restaurant. Winners of a free soft drink or serving of french fries or other food item are just common enough to make the game interesting, particularly for younger customers. The top prize offers at least the satisfaction of a fantasy about a trip to the Caribbean or a new car to every customer.

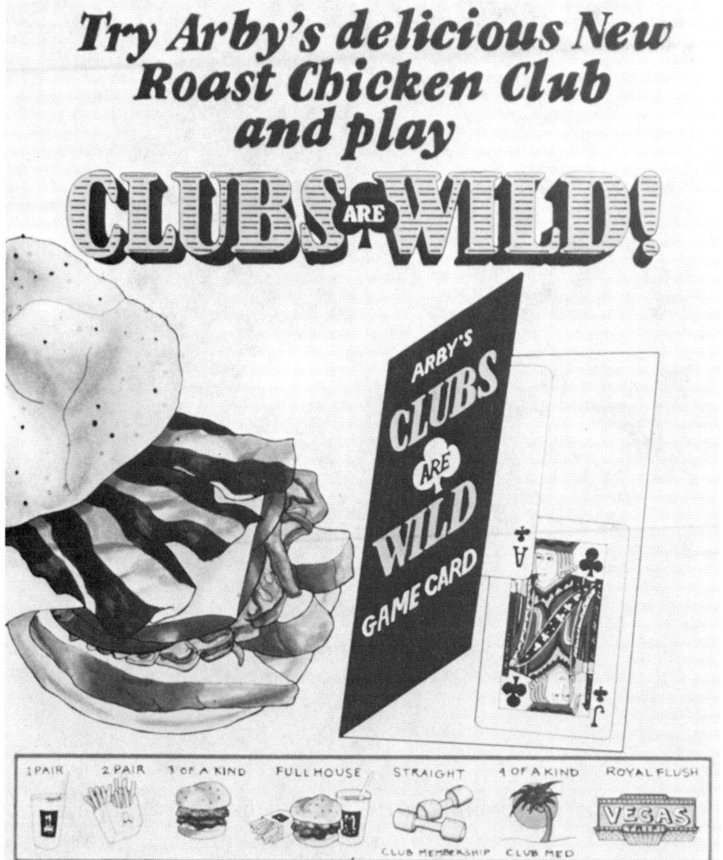

Games and sweepstakes offer the guest some excitement, the fantasy of a really big win, and lots of low-cost prizes to keep things interesting. In this way, they enhance value. (Photo courtesy of Arby's, Inc.)

Other Forms of Sales Promotion

Discounts: "Sales." Perhaps the most common form of sales promotion is the sale. Whether supported by other advertising or just by in-store signage or a "special" clip on in a menu, discounts, like coupons, work on the price side of value to enhance the price/value relationship. They are most often used during off-peak sales periods. The "early-bird" special attracts people to eat the evening meal early when the dining room is not crowded. Sales on slow days sometimes bring an offer of a special price for a second dinner.

Another use of discounting is to introduce a new product. Sometimes, there are "limited-time only" offers, while, in other cases, a free or reduced price is offered on another item, such as a soft drink, when the new item is ordered.

The danger of discounting is that it can cheapen the product's image and, if repeated too often, can accustom customers to the availability of a discount. In one QSR operation featuring fish, for instance, where discounts were available every week on certain days for a protracted period, the units found they were doing almost all their business on the discount days and practically standing empty on nondiscount days.[10] Indeed, when a discount on fish products was extended to Friday, one unit had to hire off-duty police to keep order in the line of cars which extended well down the block and around the corner. A moment's reflection suggests that such a prominent display over a price reduction, when repeated week after week, could result in cheapening the operation's reputation for quality and service. In some situations, however, discounting becomes a competitive necessity or (as with couponing in the off season) a means of stimulating incremental business during slow periods.

Special Events

Successful special events offer at least two advantages as promotions. They create volume in a designated period. Moreover, they frequently generate favorable publicity and word of mouth.

Table service restaurants, during their slow months, use ethnic or special regional cuisines to attract guests to celebrations such as a St. Patrick's Day dinner, Valentine's Day Special, Mardi Gras Week, and the like.

Partnerships. A number of independent restaurants and chains have found that their suppliers are happy to have a chance to work with them on a promotion. For suppliers, a successful partnership means enhanced sales of their product and a closer relationship with their operator–customer. A wine tasting provides a useful example. The wine supplier provides the restaurant with wines for tasting (free or at a reduced price), as well as promotional materials such as booklets, regional wine maps and posters. Sometimes, the purveyor provides a member of its staff or an outside expert as a lecturer at the tasting. The restaurant offers its regular customers an interesting "free" event or perhaps levies a price which still makes the tasting a bargain for the guest. The result is very likely a full house for dinner that evening. Moreover, the wine tasting can provide an excellent kick off for a new wine list and a campaign promoting the sale of wine with dinner.

Hotel restaurants can use all the promotions that a freestanding restaurant can, but dealing is not as common. Hotels can also offer special weekend packages that include tours of local cultural centers—art galleries and museums for instance—or packages built around sports or cultural events with tickets or other entrance fees built into the package price. The result can be both favorable publicity and increased room and food sales on otherwise dull weekends.

PUBLIC RELATIONS

Public relations refers to the relationship that a firm has with its special **publics,** as well as the general public. Any firm has *directly related publics:* consumers, employees, suppliers, intermediaries (e.g., travel agents), and stockholders. Each of these has a somewhat different point of view and interest in the company. Other *special publics* can be identified: people working in the firm's political and regulatory environment, community opinion leaders (e.g., clergy, teachers, or key people in civic and business organizations), and, not least, the firm's own employees. Finally, there is the general public, a collectivity that includes everybody in a community—or, for a chain, in a region or the nation. The management of the process of positioning the firm as a business citizen and communicating that position to appropriate publics constitutes public relations. Public relations transcends marketing and embraces the strategy of the firm.

A key starting point in public relations is simply to always have the public's interest in mind in establishing operating policies and procedures. That is, a firm must intend to be a good citizen and to behave responsibly and honestly. To do right, however, is not enough: The firm must take steps to see to it that its publics are informed about its action.

What Is News?

One of the major advantages of public relations as a medium of communication is its credibility. The news is written by a disinterested third party. An ad or commercial obviously presents the advertiser's point of view. A news article (even if it is an edited version of a firm's press release) is seen by the reader as objective and factual. Moreover, the same amount of advertising space would surely be costly. Clearly, then, it is in an operation's interest to present information in that form—as news—whenever possible.

Interesting the media in your story, however, is far from easy. Many hospitality operators fail to understand the editorial problem of the media and present their story solely in terms of their own interests. They do not know what is **newsworthy.** What is needed is to look at the story from the point of view of the general reader or viewer of the particular medium being targeted. A plush new banquet room is news to the operator, but a release about its features and cost probably looks like disguised (and free) advertising to the media. On the other hand, if the room is named for a prominent early settler or a famous figure from the area and dedication ceremonies are held with appropriate dignitaries in attendance, that may be legitimate news.

Tools of Public Relations

Events and happenings—sometimes manufactured for that purpose—are the grist of the PR mill. These might include speeches, public service activities, and awards and news conferences. Grand openings and dedications of new or renewed facilities often have a news angle—or can be given one. The promotional special events found in our earlier discussion on sales promotion are a good source of news stories. A part of the planning of any such event should include the development of a press kit—press releases, fact sheets, and photos. Where the event is a culinary one, it is worthwhile to include recipes and, as appropriate, a biography of the chef. Inclusion of photos can result in a substantial increase in the amount of space devoted to the story if the photos are used. Photos will also improve potential impact on readers.

Favorable publicity is available as a result of special achievements of staff (sometimes just their hobbies are of interest) and any recognition accorded members of the organization. These may include those related to civic responsibilities, as well as activities and offices in trade associations. Visits of celebrities to properties are often interesting, and the cost of having a photographer on hand will usually be amply repaid by more prominent coverage. If the celebrity is of sufficient interest and the media are notified in time, television stations may send camera crews. Whatever is done, however, must be within the bounds of what is acceptable to the celebrity guest.

Corporate charities are often developed, in all candor, with a view to doing well by doing good. That is, they accomplish charitable goals, but they also yield favorable publicity. Companies often sponsor an activity permanently to increase their public relations impact and to secure a linkage in people's minds between the company and the institution. McDonald House, residences for families of children who are seriously ill, is probably the best known in our industry, but smaller organizations can make a significant impact in their market area. Tim Horton's, a chain of donut shops, maintains summer camps for handicapped children. A major portion of the camps' budget is covered by contributions from the company and its franchisee organization, but it also collects contributions from customers in coin boxes displayed in all stores. An important aspect of both the McDonald House and the Tim Horton's camps is that they involve a significant public, the franchisee, in the campaign, furthering their commitment to the franchising organization.

News is generally conveyed to the media in a press release. Chains and large operations may have a PR person on staff. Smaller operations rely on a talented manager, part-time PR counsel, or assistance from their advertising agency.

Hazards of Publicity. A word of caution, however, is in order before we conclude this section on getting out the good news. The very strengths of public relations—that the message comes by means of a disinterested third party—contains a very real hazard. With advertising, the advertiser controls, absolutely, the content. Publicity, on the other hand, is controlled by the editorial staff of the media. In some cases, the message comes out garbled, simply a case of confused facts. Worse is the situation where an editorial writer chooses to make fun of the release's contents or, worse still, sees a silly side to the story. The result can be negative PR. Care should be exercised, therefore, in preparing releases, and the risks inherent in any release should be evaluated before the decision to send out the release is made. Field Practice Note 13.1 illustrates the potential risks—and rewards—in a public relations event.

Field Practice Note 13.1

Public Relations Can Cut Both Ways

The story in the *Wall Street Journal* began, "Taco Bell has rung a sour note with the city of Philadelphia." It seems that Taco Bell announced on April 1 that it had purchased the Liberty Bell, one of America's great patriotic symbols and was renaming it "the Taco Liberty Bell." According to a company news release, "People have been adopting highways for years. Now we're going one step further by purchasing one of the country's great historic treasures." The release indicated the purchase was a part of a corporate effort to trim the national debt. The news release supported full-page advertisements in major national and regional newspapers at a cost of $300,000. The day was April 5.

Then, at noon, the company issued another news release calling the whole thing "The Best Joke of the Day." April Fools'! In the immediate aftermath of the event, there was some question as to who had been the fool. The *Wall Street Journal* said "some observers considered the whole thing a "high profile publicity gaffe." *Nation's Restaurant News* reported that the National Park Service director blasted the announcement "as false and cheesy. The Liberty Bell belongs to all Americans; it is not now nor will it ever be for sale under any circumstances."

The event quickly took on partisan overtones in an election year. The Secretary of the Interior saw dark motives: "It's no wonder there was such an immediate and forceful public reaction. People know the new Republican Congress has an agenda to auction it off, shut down and give away our national heritage to the special corporate interests who financed their campaigns. This ad must have seemed like the GOP's latest sellout." Apparently, a lot off people in Philadelphia in particular were not amused. Independence National Historic Park and the city's chamber of commerce had their phone lines jammed with irate callers.

Taco Bell, on the other hand, seeking to reverse sales declines, claimed the resulting PR was worth $22 million and saw the event as a great launch for a $200 million advertising blitz with the slogan "Nothing Ordinary About It." Taco Bell did make a $50,000 contribution to help in the presenvation of the Liberty Bell.

Rick Warner, editor of *Nation's Restaurant News,* assessed the event positively. "In spite of the ire of a few customers and expenditures of $350,000, the plank gave the chain millions in free publicity. The attention grabbing ploy served not only to tout the new advertising campaign but also to reinforce Taco Bell's image as a hip, rebellious restaurant chain that is anything but staid."

Sources: *Wall Street Journal,* April 2, 1996, p. B3., *Nation's Restaurant News,* April 15, 1996, pp. 1, 4, and 25.

Crisis Management[11]

Unfortunately, the news is sometimes bad. Accidents, fires, food-poisoning incidents, and similar untoward events do occur. Most managers would prefer to hush these events up, but, if the news does get out, experience suggests that getting the facts straight and then telling the truth about them is the best policy. It is also

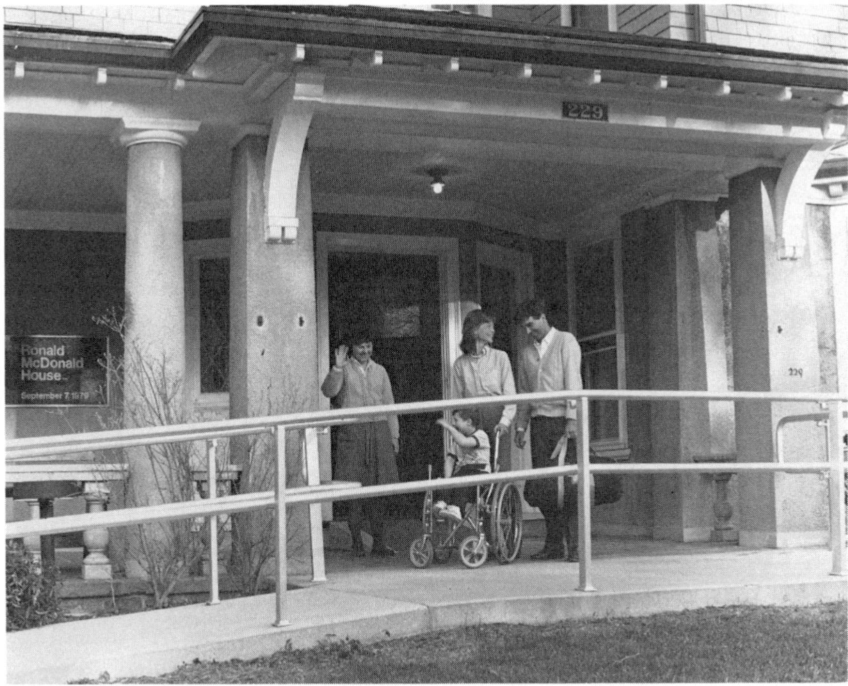

Programs such as Ronald McDonald House build goodwill in the community and help involve franchises in a companywide program, helping to buttress franchisee loyalty. (Photo courtesy of McDonald's)

advisable to develop procedures in advance of need to deal with emergencies. Unfavorable publicity can often be avoided by careful planning.

The first steps in **crisis management** must be taken *before* the crisis. First of all, as noted at the outset of this section, a company's policies and procedures should be constructed with great care to be in the public interest. This is good sense and the conscientious thing to do, but it also minimizes the possibility that any crisis will be traced to the company's negligence.

A second step in advance of the crisis is to have contingency plans in place which have identified the company's key crisis points and anticipated how these might be handled. These plans need to be flexible, however, because the nature of a crisis is that it—and the information demand it creates—is inherently uncontrollable. In most cases, there should be a designated spokesperson for the organization. This person should be a decision maker who will be accessible and who has the facts. Where some facts are in doubt, the spokesperson should offer to get the information and make it available.

Within the company, the communication process should have a structured pattern that is easy to follow when people are rattled. The two most difficult dangers of a crisis are *panic* and a *sense of urgency.* Panic often leads to extreme reactions and the sense of urgency encourages people to rush—and, thus, sometimes be intemperate. Knowing who the spokesperson is releases employees from unnecessary pressure and keeps the communication in the hands of a person who has the necessary information and background to deal with the press. There should be clear channels of communication *within* the company to get the word on the crisis to the company's own people. This is appropriate for reasons of morale but also because employees, both on and off the job, are in contact with the public and should know the facts. A waitress or waiter cannot meet a guest's query with a "no comment."

The Cost Effectiveness of Public Relations. With the escalating cost of paid media, public relations efforts have become more and more desirable. On the other hand, public relations is not free. There is a cost to preparing releases, photos, press kits, and so forth. That cost is generally minor, however, when set alongside the cost of purchasing similar space or time for ads. Moreover, although a specific selling message such as that found in advertising cannot be incorporated, the impact of publicity is often greater (at least at the awareness and interest levels) than a similar amount of space or time devoted to advertising because news coverage has a higher credibility than an ad does.

PERSONAL SELLING

Selling is something every reader of this text will need to do. All who live and work in a modern organization have to sell their ideas and also have to sell themselves

All of a property's staff need to be ready to be part of the sales team. (Photo courtesy of Don and Pat Valenti/Taurus Photos)

to their colleagues. Moreover, selling to the customer (i.e., working directly as a sales representative) is often a job with which people get involved in the years immediately after their formal education is finished. Moreover, as people work their way up in organizations, they reach a stage, even in operations, where they need to represent their organization to people outside it—really another form of selling. Whether directly or indirectly, selling is something you will surely do. This section, then, speaks quite personally to you.

Personal selling is a very expensive medium for getting an operation's message across. The high cost is accounted for by the overhead required to support a salesperson: transportation, entertainment, office space, phone bills, and so on. Perhaps even more significant, the sales process, properly executed, involves an expensive salesperson who, realistically, is able to spend relatively little of his or her time in face-to-face selling contacts with prospects. Most of a salesperson's time is expended in getting ready and following up.

Personal selling should only be used where the size of the sale justifies the expense. For instance, in the hotel business, sales representatives are used to sell rooms business to groups and to solicit referrals of visitors from companies that have a significant volume of visitors. They are also used to sell meetings and banquets and other group function business. In Chapter 9, we referred to "selling within channels" and personal selling is also an important tool, particularly for hotel chains, in selling to travel agents and other channel members. Personal selling is the major medium used by contract food service companies to obtain new accounts. In our discussion of the selling process, we will use the hotel business as our principal example.

While we are mainly concerned, here, with the work of the sales staff, the total sales effort includes the whole staff, especially those "marketing ambassadors" who interact with guests—such as servers and desk clerks. A 180-room inn with a 75 percent occupancy averaging 1.2 persons per occupied room caters to between 30,000 and 60,000 people in a year. There is no way a sales representative can deal with that number of people—yet all guests are subject to selling while in a hotel. The desk clerk tries to sell to gain a high average rate; if he or she is not a good salesperson, then a low average rate results. A waitress or waiter raises the check average by selling not just meals, but drinks and desserts and so forth. Alternatively, if not trained to sell, the server takes the order and slings the hash. Moreover, the *quality of service interactions* is what sells repeat customers.

Selling is part of everyone's job, but not everyone is charged with the responsibility of dealing with prospective guests outside the hotel. Whole books have been written on selling, and the student who is interested in a career in hotel sales—or in a sales staff job with a contract catering company—will require specialized training as part of his or her preparation for full-time work in sales.[12]

THE SALES PROCESS

Selling begins well before the call and, properly speaking, never ends because keeping the customer is an important part of the sales rep's job. The major divisions of the selling activity are prospecting, planning the sale, making the approach, making the presentation, closing the sale, and following up your sale and your customer. We will consider each.

A first step in **prospecting** involves developing sales leads from whom prospects are identified. Prospects are people who need to use your property and can afford your rate structures. The heart of prospecting, then, involves reviewing sales leads and identifying prospects from among them.

Sales Leads

The search for sales **leads** can begin no further away than the nearest Yellow Pages. Scanning that classified directory to see the businesses that are not already being served by your property and that might require rooms or meeting accommodations is not a highly sophisticated activity—but it can yield plenty of leads. There are also other directories of trade associations and membership lists for local organizations that may suggest particular people within organizations. Scanning the directory of meetings for the day at competitive hotels is both customary and quite productive. Your friends in the community and your present customers are also a good source of leads. At the lead-gathering stage we might say "the more the merrier," but, in the next stage, the emphasis is on quality as we move from leads to prospects.

Qualifying Prospects

A **qualified prospect** is a person who has a need for, or an interest in, using your property and who controls a large enough piece of business to justify the expense of a sales call. Qualified leads would include people who *book* a significant number of guest rooms or meeting rooms and people who make decisions about these bookings. Thus, qualified prospects can include secretaries, as well as travel office managers, sales or training managers, and other management people. To be productive, salespeople should spend most of their time talking to people who are responsible for placing or referring business. Secretaries are often key gatekeepers (see Chapter 2) in an organization. Some helpful hints on getting along with secretaries are summarized in Table 13.2.

Cold Calls. Not all sales calls, however, are made on qualified prospects. One way of generating leads and qualifying them is to call on new prospects about whom you know very little. These calls may be made as what we might call targets of opportunity when other business brings you into the area with a few minutes to spare. Alternatively, **cold calls** may be made as a part of a coordinated effort called a sales blitz.

A sales blitz is a concentrated series of sales calls, usually cold calls. The blitz consists of an organized, concerted attack on some particular market or markets by a number of people. In many cases, the target may be a geographic area (downtown north of First Street), but it might also be organizational (all institutions of

Table 13.2 Pointers for Selling Yourself to Secretaries

1. Give the secretary your business card.
2. Consider giving the secretary a brochure with your card. It may, at the least, help her or him to remember you next time.
3. Speak clearly and audibly; help the secretary get the correct pronunciation of your name.
4. Don't give the appearance of being grouchy or unhappy if you have to wait. Accept any waiting patiently and cheerfully.
5. Be friendly but not fresh. The waiting room is not a cocktail lounge.
6. Don't be overly friendly as a means of getting in to see the boss. It is too obvious and may backfire.
7. Don't try to pry confidential information out of the secretary.
8. If you have a gripe about the company, find out who the correct person is to take it up with and discuss it with them. Don't gripe to the secretary!
9. Don't treat the secretary like a piece of furniture. When she comes into the room where you are waiting, smile, speak to her, or otherwise acknowledge her as a person.
10. Remember, you are the guest—act like one.
11. If you are in doubt about how to act, the best course is to underplay your role.

Source: Adapted from Frederick A. Russell, Frank H. Beach, and Richard H. Buskirk, *Selling: Principles and Practices,* 11th ed. (New York: McGraw-Hill, 1982), p. 199.

higher education in the city). Sales blitzes are sometimes conducted with the help of hotel and restaurant school students, although, more commonly, the blitz uses sales staff from several of a chain's properties. Sometimes operating staff may join in the blitz, too.

Cold calls are basically an information-seeking activity. They may sometimes result in actual sales, but, most often, they yield leads and qualified prospects.

Planning the Sales Call

A sales call requires careful planning. A planned sales call, in contrast to a cold call, should be made on a particular prospect. The more you know about that prospect, the better you will be able to develop a strategy for selling him or her. Two general kinds of information are helpful: company information and personal background on the individual prospect.

It is important to know as much about the prospect personally as you can. For instance, the area the prospect lives in may tell you something about his or her social position and aspirations. Club or civic affiliations, hobbies, and interests sometimes offer opportunities for small talk during the interview preliminaries. A note of caution is in order, however. This is a business call, not a social visit and considerable care needs to be taken not to intrude on the privacy of the prospect.

A good deal of information may be available from the prospect if you develop the art of listening. Certainly, the specific information about a function being planned may only be available from her or him.

The key in planning a sales call is to have particular objectives in mind: You need to know what you want to sell and what approach you intend to make to the prospect, that is, what interests or needs you think will gain the strongest response. You should know what information you still need, what points you propose to make, and, roughly, in what logical order.

For hotel sales, a canned pitch (a memorized sales presentation) is not likely to be effective, but a logically thought-out sales presentation that is organized to include the necessary information and appropriate appeals will almost always make a better impression than an unplanned chat. The people you are calling on are usually busy and accustomed to giving and receiving information in an organized way.

The Approach

The first few moments with the prospect are crucial. First impressions, moreover, are lasting. It is worth your while, therefore, to develop an **approach** that will (1) gain the prospect's *attention,* (2) gain his or her *interest,* and (3) provide a smooth *transition* into your sales presentation. Students of the art of selling have identified several more or less standardized approaches that are of varying effectiveness. Several of these will be discussed later.

First, though, we need to note that *getting in the door* is not always easy. To avoid wasting time cooling your heels, it is often best to arrange an appointment. This may be done by phone. If the person you are trying to contact, however, is hard to reach by phone, a letter stating the purpose of your visit and requesting an appointment may be the best course.

Once through the door, the task is to gain favorable attention and begin the sales presentation. We can turn now to consider several strategies for the approach.

The Introduction Approach. "Hello, I'm Jane (or John) Smith from XYZ Hotel." Certainly, this is the most common approach, but, very often, only the prospect's good manners prevent him or her from saying, "So what?" Although an introduction may be appropriate at the start of the conversation just for the sake of politeness, it is a good idea to know what you are going to say right after that in order to gain interest and attention.

The Consumer Benefit Approach. If you are seeking referrals of individual visitors from a secretary, you may find an effective approach is to begin by telling her not about your hotel but about your secretary's club—or whatever method you have of recognizing people who refer guests. It is important to avoid sounding like you intend to bribe this prospect, but a friendly, "I'd like to invite you to join our secretary's club," followed by an explanation of how the club functions, will usually not offend.

Bringing a prospect to the property gives the salesperson a chance to show off the product. The act of hospitality offers a friendly context for the sales interaction. (Photo courtesy of The Ritz-Carlton, Laguna Niguel)

For the person who is responsible for booking meetings and seminars, the consumer benefit approach may come as a question: "How would you like to have a meeting where *all* the coffee breaks and meals are served *on time*?" Whatever distinctive *difference* your property offers can serve as the basis of such an opener. If your property is ready to offer price concessions, the appeal may involve a flat statement, "We can save you 10 to 20 percent (or whatever is an appropriate percentage) on your next meeting—and our food and service are tops, too."

The Invitation. Probably the best setting for a sales call is your property itself. Where the amount of business warrants your expenditure of time and money, an invitation to join you in the property for a meal can be most effective. An invitation to dinner may be warranted, but breakfast or lunch are more common business meals.

When your guest is in the hotel, a tour of the property is in order. Certainly, the prospect should be shown those areas that concern the sale—the guest rooms and the banquet facilities, for instance. People are also interested in the back of the house and passing through those areas gives you a chance to cater to that interest and show "how things really work." You can also introduce the prospect to some of the key players in the property such as the chef and executive housekeeper. These people can do a lot to help you make the sale. Incidentally, it brings the sales office closer to the operations people when they are given the feeling of helping to land a sale.

Some notice that this tour is in the offing is essential so that people can reserve some time to meet your guest and also so those responsible can spruce up the cleanliness of their area. An unannounced tour into a dirty-looking kitchen could cost you a sale.

The Presentation

Having made a good first impression by your appearance and gained attention and interest from the prospect by your opening, you are ready to persuade the prospect to buy. Your first step is to establish a definite need: "I understand you are about to make arrangements for your March sales meeting." Having recognized the need, you must show that you and your organization represent the solution to the prospect's problem. This requires that you also establish the credibility of your **presentation.** Finally, your presentation should be pointed toward gaining action *now.*

Establishing credibility involves two dimensions: the credibility of your property and organization and your own personal believability. It is nice to think that everyone knows how good your property's service is and you may hesitate to brag about it. In fact, however, this may really be a central point for someone who has never been a customer.

Building Confidence. There is no perfect script that will secure a sale every time. There are, however, some general guidelines and techniques that are time tested:

Make Conservative Claims Do not claim more than you can produce. If you are conservative early in the conversation, you are more likely to be believed later.

Be Positive in Your Outlook Above all, do not knock your own organization, your boss, or your associates. In general, stay with positive statements. Sometimes negative things have to be said but, in general, accentuate the positive.

Describe the Experience of Your Firm A "story" will often catch the listener's interest, so do not hesitate to briefly tell about successful functions at your property or how you won the repeat patronage of a particularly loyal guest.

Testimonials Build Confidence Provided they are not overemphasized, testimonials from your customers may help convince a prospect of your organization's excellence. One way to do that is the implied testimonial. Invite the prospect to pick up the phone and call one or two of your regular guests (always after you have secured permission and never so often as to be a pest). Many people will not take you up on this suggestion, but it impresses them with your confidence in your property's ability to perform. Some sales reps like to carry copies of letters thanking the hotel for particularly successful events.

Invite a Tour or Visit Where the size of the sale warrants it, the best sales tool you have is the property itself. Encourage the prospect to come by so she or he can see what you have to offer.

A Friendly Interchange Although the sales call is not a time to act the part of the prospect's old pal, especially on the first meeting, it is supposed to be a friendly talk. The chances are you will be pleasantly welcomed because hotel sales reps are usually received almost on a social level.[13]

You should be willing to listen during the conversation as well as talk. If you do all the talking, not only do you appear to be pressuring the prospect but you cannot hear what he or she has to say.

Ask Questions If you find the prospect does not have much to say, you may want to ask questions to be sure your audience is with you. The tone, as well as the content of the prospect's reply, may signal belief or doubt and can then give you a strong clue as to how you are doing. Some salespeople actually feel they are best able to control the direction of the conversation by relying on questions. Questions give the prospect a chance to talk, the sales rep gets a lot of feedback, and the questions can be used to steer the conversation from topic to topic.

Listen Active listening involves making eye contact. Let your facial expression show your interest with a smile or a frown, as appropriate, to show you are involved. Lean forward, nod your head or shake it, and, generally, let your demeanor say you are fully engaged in this conversation.

Do not Argue If you win an argument and lose a sale, you are *not* ahead. Where disagreement does seem unavoidable, it is probably best to indicate interest in hearing another point of view on that subject.

Handling Competition

You cannot ignore the competition, but one of the oldest maxims of selling is, "Don't knock the competition." Running the competition down makes you sound petty and your motives are, to say the least, suspect. The best approach is probably, in essence, "It's a fine organization but we can probably fit your needs better because . . . ."

It is generally best not to raise the subject of the competition, but the chances are the prospect will. For this reason, it is important to know your competition: their strengths and weaknesses relative to those of your organization. You should be able to anticipate the points a prospect will raise and, in preparing for the call, you should try to have answers ready.

In some cases, you may want to consider listing the advantages of each property or organization on a piece of paper. In this process, you may have to concede some points of difference to the competition, but, clearly, you want to be confident that, on an overall comparison, you will come out ahead.

Handling Complaints and Objections

People will have heard good and bad news about your operation. C. DeWitt Coffman, a man with many years of hotel sales experience, advised: When confronted with a complaint, "Never try to justify the mistake. Never challenge or question the complaint. Remember, there is no way a salesperson can win an argument." The response Coffman suggested: "I'm sorry" or "We're sorry." And, then, he urged the sales rep to thank the prospect: "I appreciate your letting me know about this situation" and indicate your desire to have another chance.[14]

In a way, objections to your selling proposition and complaints about the operation should be welcomed because they tell you about the prospect's points of resistance and show you where you need to concentrate your effort.

The Close

Nobody bats a thousand and no salesperson makes every sale he or she tries for. Still, the **close** is the moment all of your efforts have been pointed toward. This is the time at which you get undeniable evidence of success or failure. The fact is that many salespeople shy away from asking for the order. Perhaps it is the starkness of the yes or no answer or maybe it is just that people have been brought up to feel it is impolite to ask directly for something. Some salespeople feel their presentation has been so effective that people will just be ready to buy and they need not directly ask for the order. However, if a sale, not generalized goodwill, is the object of the call, it is necessary to *ask for the order.*

Assumptive Close. One way to close is simply to assume you have made the sale and act on that conclusion. Questions such as these fit this kind of close: "How soon do you think we can have your rooming list?" "Do you want to write up the menu now or would you like some time to consult with your people?" One of the best is to ask to use the phone "so I can block the space for you."

Standing Room Only. If you are not certain the sale is yours but feel now is the time to close, you may want to indicate that the time of year is a fairly busy one and suggest a reservation to protect the client. If prospects think there soon may be no room at the inn, they may be more ready to let you help them. It is important, though, not to use this close in a way that untruthfully exaggerates demand, because, eventually, you will be found out and, then, there goes your client's trust and your reputation for truthfulness.

The Trial Order. If you feel the prospect is really not ready to buy, consider asking for this order (or even an order for another, smaller event) as a trial: "We'd like a chance to prove ourselves to you."

If you cannot get a firm order, get a tentative commitment, and indicate that you will call back for a confirmation at a point named by the prospect. The point is, if at all possible, obtain some form of positive commitment from the interview. Movement from lead to prospect and movement from prospect to an active

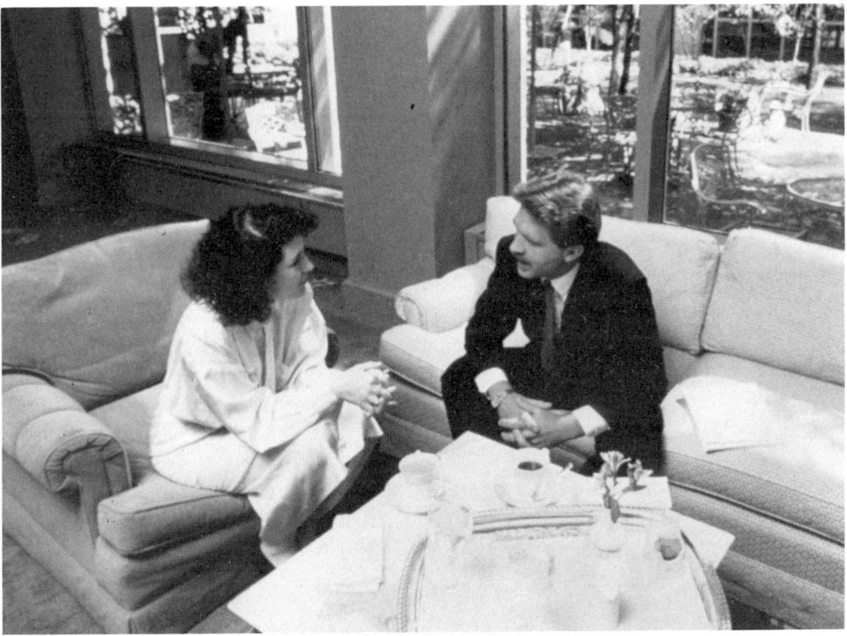

If a sale is the object of the call, the salesperson must ask for the order. *(Photo courtesy of Leif Skoogfors/Woodfin Camp)*

account if not a sale *this* time are both positive developments that can lead to the sale next time.

Calling Back. There are at least two reasons to call back: because you did not get the order the first time and to service the account if you did.

Getting the Order. There is an old saying that "the third time is a charm"; another saying is that it is "the third call that sells." In fact, there probably is no magic to the number 3, but the idea that repeat sales calls are usually necessary to land an account is generally correct.

Servicing the Account. Once a sale is made, it is important to follow through on service. This means that, if you booked the business, you should be in the property when the function takes place to check with your customer. If there is a problem, you are in a better position to pass the concern on to the *right person* in your organization than is the guest who cannot very well know your operating crew as well as you do. The danger, of course, in this part of servicing the sale, is that you come to be seen as meddling on operations' turf. This means that tact is called for.

After the function is over, there is a need for a further call-back for several reasons. First, a few days after the function, your contact may have had reactions from others in his or her organization. If they are unfavorable, it is important for you to make whatever amends that may seem appropriate. If they are favorable, that is an ideal lead-in for you to sell the next piece of business.

Another reason for a follow-up call relates to the competition. If you are reading the function boards in their lobby, as you should be, you can be reasonably assured that they will return the compliment. Just as a function in a competing property is a trigger for you to go after an account, you can expect that a meeting or banquet in your hotel will stimulate competitive calls on your account. The logic of *keeping* your account argues for aggressive follow-up on your part after the sale.

Sometimes a call-back on an account simply serves the function of keeping the lines of communication open, maintaining your contacts, and staying current on what is happening in that organization. Calls of this kind can be brief and often fitted between more carefully scheduled calls on other accounts in the area.

Staying with It

Sales work can be discouraging. There are a lot of turndowns and even more calls from which there are no traceable results. The best analogy is to baseball: Nobody bats 1.000, and people who bat .300 are real heroes. Field Practice Note 13.2 gives an overview of the selling process.

SUMMARY

Sales promotion, which is often supported by promotional advertising, offers an incentive to immediate purchase. Deals, the most common form of sales promotion in popular-priced hospitality operations, include coupons offering reduced prices, premium merchandise, and games. Deals enhance consumers' price/value perceptions by offering a bargain or adding to the excitement of the operation. In upscale operations, special events play a similar role.

Every business has publics to which it must relate and public relations (PR) is an important part of a company's marketing communication program. For a release to be acceptable, however, it must be newsworthy. Many kinds of events lend themselves as sources of publicity. With rising media costs, PR is becoming increasingly cost effective. A program of crisis management begins before the crisis with the establishment of policies that are in the public interest. It is important to know what steps are to be taken by whom in a crisis.

Selling is something everybody needs to do in their work and in their lives. Studying the selling process, then, is useful to you even if you do not intend to pursue a career in sales. Everyone in your organization needs to be on the sales team. If you do become a salesperson, selling is a very costly promotional medium. Therefore, you need to make effective use of your valuable time. Selling is used only where large dollar sales are at stake, such as in contract food service, in selling to travel intermediaries and other channel members, and in the hotel business. In hotels, good accounts are those that have multiple room bookings or meeting and banquet needs you can meet. The sales process is summarized in Field Practice Note 13.2.

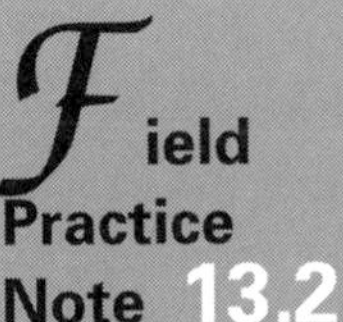

An Overview of the Selling Process

Field Practice Note 13.2

Precall Stage

Prospect for sales leads by researching directories, as well as by contacting personal acquaintances and your present customers.

Qualify prospects by determing whether each lead has a large enough need for your services to justify a call.

Planning the call requires:

- Information on the *account,* that is the company or organization
- Information on the *prospect,* that is, the individual, both of a business (position, title) and a personal nature (interests, background)
- Organization of the presentation in terms of the necessary information and the appeals that will be important to the prospect

The Call

Making the approach involves getting in the door. This means gatekeepers like secretaries and receptionists are important. It also requires that once you are there you get the prospect's *interest* and *attention* and make a *smooth transition* into your presentation. Approaches may involve and *introduction* (which alone is usually not enough), identification of a *consumer benefit,* and an *invitation* to visit the property.

The presentation, in terms of the facts you state and your personal demeanor, must establish your credibility and that of your company. Some keys to gaining the prospect's confidence:

- Make conservative claims
- Be positive in manner and outlook
- Describe your firm's success and experience
- Use your sales brochure, particularly in conjunction with meeting and banquet prospects
- Use testimonials to further establish your property's credibility
- Invite the prospect to visit the property
- Be a friendly visitor
- Ask questions, especially if you are not sure what the prospect's reaction is
- Listen attentively to what the prospect says
- Never argue
- Handle discussion of the competition, questions, and complaints or objections to your presentation in a positive manner.

The close is the moment when you get the sale—or don't. One way or another, you have to *ask for the order.* Some common approaches to the close are:

- *The assumptive close—*
  "When can we have your rooming list?"
- *Standing room only—*
  "Let me check to be sure we have enough space to handle your group."
- *The trial order—*
  "We'd like a chance to prove ourselves to you."

Remember, any form of future commitment is a positive outcome of a sales call.

Postcall

Calling back is essential.

- to follow up on earlier effort and obtain an order
- to service established accounts

◆ Key Words and Concepts

- Sales promotion
  - Dealing
  - Discounts
  - Special events
  - Partnerships
- Concerns about promotions
- Bounce backs
- Public relations
- Publics
- Newsworthy
- Hazards of publicity
- Crisis management
- Personal selling
- Prospecting
  - Leads
  - Qualified prospects
- Cold calls
- The selling process
  - Approach
  - Presentation
  - Close

◆ Discussion Questions

1. What is the major purpose of sales promotion?
2. What are the major forms of sales promotion in food service? In lodging?
3. How frequently can promotions be mounted? What is a desirable duration for promotion?
4. What are the advantages and disadvantages of public relations?

5. What are the major steps in crisis management? Have you ever been involved in a crisis in an operation you worked in? If so, how do you assess the way it was handled?
6. Under what circumstances is personal selling used? Where is it not indicated?
7. What are the main steps in the sales process? How do you assess the importance of each?

Chapter 14

When you have finished reading this chapter, you should be able to

1. Explain the basis for local marketing
2. Discuss why local area marketing is growing
3. Describe chains' problems with local marketing
4. Define merchandising and explain its importance
5. Describe the role of personal selling in local marketing
6. Explain the property level marketing mix for hotels
7. Discuss the elements of propety level marketing communications

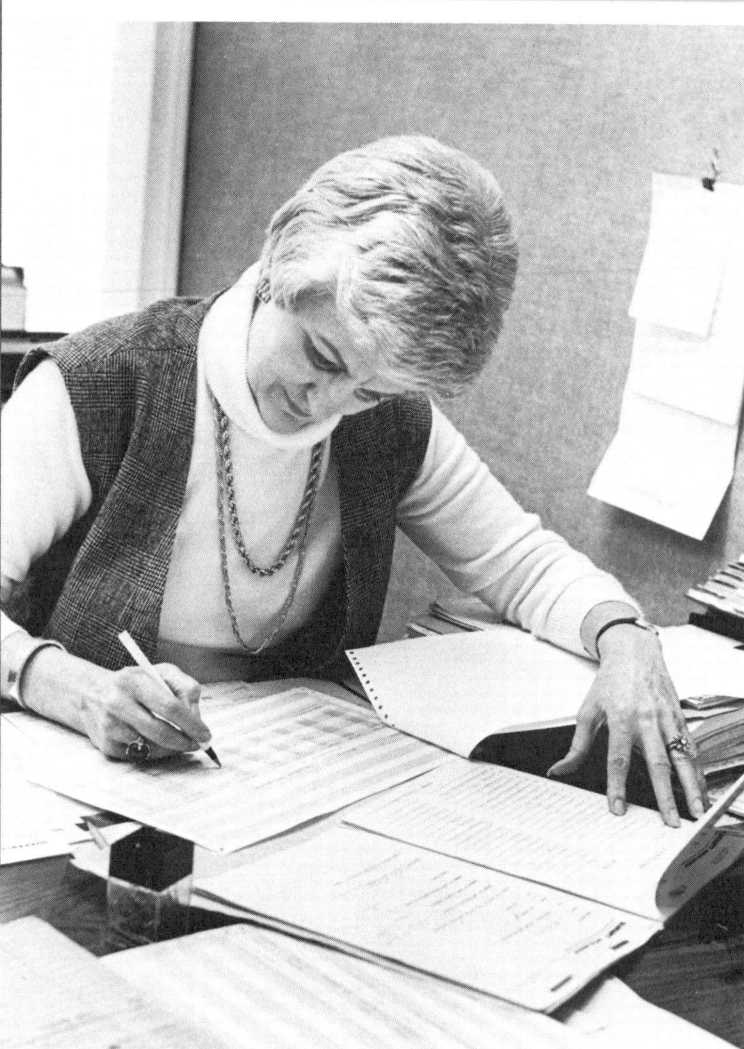

(Photo courtesy Allan Carey/The Image Works)

Marketing at the Unit Level

Marketing at any level of a company draws on the same basic body of knowledge, but the *perspective* at the unit level is different.[1] Not surprisingly, marketing in the unit is characterized by a "hands-on" approach. In the restaurant or hotel operation, marketing is something which managers often *do* themselves, rather than a process orchestrated for many players.

As more segments of the hospitality industry reach a mature stage of development, where competition only goes from fierce to fiercer, hospitality managers are seeking whatever advantage in the marketplace they can find. One chain's strategic marketing effort is met by the strategic marketing effort of its competitors. New products are matched by other new products and special pricing brings competitive price reactions. Promotion must compete not just with all other hospitality promotion but with all the other advertising. Consumers are bombarded wherever they turn! Marketing at the local level is, however, by its nature, much more targeted; it is closer to the consumer and offers opportunities for personal touches which are just not possible in regional or national programs. It is also an activity in which an individual manager can make a real difference in an operation's success—and, incidentaly, in the manager's own success.

The subject of unit marketing is likely to be of special interest to students in hotel and restaurant management programs because the most likely place in which you will be practicing your management and marketing skills following graduation—and for some years thereafter—is at the unit level. Moreover, while marketing at the chain level is the principal concern of specialized staff people, unit level marketing is, more often than not, work that is done by the unit manager—if it is to be done at all. While medium and larger-sized hotels may have sales representatives, many smaller full-service hotels and limited-service properties do not have a specialized sales staff. Very few restaurants have sales representatives. As a result, unit level marketing and sales fall to the manager and to other operations people. An understanding of the broad perspective of a companywide marketing program *is* vital—but competence in local marketing could prove to be a practical skill that will be useful in the near term future.

Marketing in a multiunit company is a top-down process. The company's image and market position are determined at the headquarters level and units operate under the umbrella of the chain's concept. The marketing challenge at the local level is different. The companywide marketing job is to establish and enhance the identity of the company in the marketplace on a very broad scale.

In contrast, at the unit level, the concern is to burnish a *local* identity as an integral part of the community. The **community** may mean a town, but it can also be a mall or a region of just a few blocks in a large city. In fact, unit level marketing, particularly in food service, is sometimes called **neighborhood marketing.**[2] By whatever name, the unit marketing task is to translate, for the local market, a national image into a vital local one. By becoming an important local institution with a network of contacts and activities, operators seek to make an international brand like Holiday Inns or McDonald's become, to local people, "our Holiday Inn" or the hometown's very own McDonald's. Local area marketing is no substitute, in a multiunit company, for a national or regional strategy. In fact, the more the local effort can dovetail with the wider effort, the better. The goal of coordinating local with companywide marketing is to achieve the best of both worlds: a strong national image *and* a strong local identity.

In this chapter, we will be concerned with units of regional and national chains because they have a need to give themselves a local identity that complements their chain image. This does not mean, however, that independent operations do not need to be concerned with localized marketing. Quite the contrary, for the independent, *all* marketing is unit level marketing. We will not be discussing the independent specifically here, but virtually everything in this chapter applies to independent operators. In fact, successful independents are usually the best local marketers in any area.

Though all hotels can apply restaurant local marketing techniques to their food service operations, the role of local marketing and the manner in which it is carried out in connection with rooms business is different, in a number of ways, from that applied to restaurants. For that reason, separate sections of this chapter will be devoted to unit level marketing in food service and in lodging. Before we come to those sections, however, we should focus our attention on some elements which apply across the hospitality industry.

THE BASIS FOR LOCAL MARKETING

As with any marketing task, local market analysis begins with the **customer** and must include the **competition.** The nature of the *hospitality product* has a major impact on localized marketing and—to meet the needs of the operation's particular market—the *company's offering must be adapted* to that market's special needs and conditions.[3] Finally, **database marketing** improves an organization's ability to target customers. These five topics affect all hospitality organizations' unit level marketing. Accordingly, it is important for us to consider each of them briefly before we turn to an examination of local marketing in restaurants and property level marketing in hotels.

The Customer

Analysis of the customer involves a study of local customers' characteristics such as the demographics of the market area and of the unit's present customer base. Figure 14.1 shows a portion of a population analysis for one market area used by a consulting company specializing in local marketing. Data for such a profile can be drawn from local census reports or purchased from contract suppliers.

Local marketers need to understand the customers' behavior—as, for instance, what brings guests into the area and what they are doing while they are there. Included in this analysis would be a review of the major traffic generators (e.g., shopping centers, schools and colleges, and entertainment centers such as amusement parks, theaters, and sports centers). It would also be important to identify the major centers of economic activity, including factories, office buildings, and retail centers.

While this information would be a useful part of a market overview for a hotel, the hotel would be interested particularly in those segments which generated a significant volume of out-of-town business. Customer segments of interest to the hotel's sales team would include: corporate business travelers, potential conference and meeting customers, tour groups, athletic teams, and local government. For hotels with a restaurant, of course, local food service customers would be of interest, as well, not only for the sales they generate but as a source of referral for rooms business.[4]

As a part of understanding the customer, we need to understand the local economic environment. For instance, two similar restaurants, one in a booming suburban market and another in a depressed town or region, would face quite different marketing challenges. The suburban unit might be successful with value-added offers such as service enhancements, premium merchandise offers, or new products. The unit facing an adverse economic climate might find that promotions built around special pricing—couponing, value meals, and the like—were the only successful approach to its customers.

The kind of economic activity that characterizes the local market is also significant. A hotel, for instance, operating in a manufacturing center such as

A.S.A.P. **Abbreviated Store Area Profile**

DENNY'S ABBREVIATED STORE AREA PROFILE
200 Morton Blvd.
Hazzard, KY 41701

POPULATION REPORT

	TOTAL U.S.	LEXINGTON, KY A.D.I.	NEIGHBORHOOD (3-Mile Radius)
POPULATION (#)	244,956.000	928,152	9,246
Projected Growth 90–95(%)	4%	3%	-3%
Historical Growth 80's(%)	11%	7%	0%
Historical Growth 70's(%)	10%	21%	25%
HOUSEHOLDS (# HH's)	91,037,200	353,440	3,342
Average HH size (1980 People/HH)	2.69 people	2.79 people	3.07 people
Projected Growth 90–95(%)	6%	8%	3%
Historical Growth 80's(%)	20%	18%	12%
Historical Growth 70's(%)	35%	37%	39%
URBAN /RURAL MIX (%)			
HOUSING	74%/26%	45%/55%	30%/70%
1980 Median Home Value (Owner-Occupied)	$49,687	$37,447	$24,300
% Owners/% Renters	715	75%	71%
% Single Units	5%	8%	14%
% Multiple Units	24%	47%	5%
% Built pre-1970	74%	47%	31%
% Built pre-1950	37%	14%	56%
% Built 1950–'69	37%	14%	56%
AVERAGE HH INCOME($)	$33,242	$27,429	$22,758
RACIAL MIX			
% Black	12%	6%	3%
% White	83%	93%	96%
% Other	5%	1%	1%
AVERAGE AGE	35 years	35 years	34 years
GENDER (Male/Female)	49%/51%	49%/51%	48%/52%
MARITAL STATUS (Persons aged 15 +)			
% Married	55%	60%	63%
% Single	23%	24%	21%
Other	23%	16%	16%
% HH'S WITH CHILDREN (Aged 0–18)	40%	44%	50%

Figure 14.1 Population Report from a Restaurant Market

Source: Contract Marketing, Mentor, Ohio.

Pittsburgh or Dayton would present a different marketing outlook than would a hotel in a major recreation destination such as Orlando or Las Vegas. Personal selling to key local accounts would play an important part in a manufacturing center, while selling to travel agents, a national reservation system, and brand advertising would play a greater role in a recreational destination market.

Competition

A listing of all competitive establishments in the market area and their locations should be compiled as background information for developing a unit's marketing program, but detailed study can generally be limited to direct competitors. Direct competitors will be similar to "our" operation in terms of facilities, services, and price. If there is any doubt as to whether an operation is a direct competitor, the operation should be included in the analysis. Any plans (or even rumors) for expansion should also be included.

For hotels, competitive analysis should include the size of the hotel (number of rooms), its rack rates, and estimates of its rates for special rate categories (i.e., corporate, groups, tours, etc.). The meeting and banquet facilities offered, including capacities and typical prices, should also be detailed where these are a significant component of the competitor's operations and the hotel's restaurant(s) should also be assessed. An important element of a competitive study is an assessment of the quality of service.

For restaurants, a competitive survey should include an analysis of menu offerings and prices, physical plant and ambience, and quality of food and service. Information on the number of seats, parking lot capacity, hours of operation, and estimates of sales volume by meal period for each day of the week are also vital.

For both restaurants and hotels, a vital piece of information is who the competitor's customers are. A profile of customers should be prepared on the basis of observation and conversations with suppliers and with competitor's management. Another valuable source of information is your own employees who are often acquainted with employees at competitive operations.

The purpose of the study of competitors is not simply to amass information. Rather, it is intended to provide a foundation for evaluating competitors' strengths and weaknesses compared to our own. From this comparison, a differentiation strategy for the *local* market should emerge which covers all elements of the marketing mix.

Operations and Marketing

In Chapter 7, we talked about the "hospitality marketing cycle." In this cycle, conventional marketing communication processes are used to attract customers, but the performance of service people in the organization determines the success in converting interested prospects into customers—and first-time customers into regular guests. The product we offer for sale is really the guest's experience which, in turn, is dependent on the performance of the entire organization. It follows that a successful localized marketing program calls for good operating results for the

The product—that is, the guest's experience—depends on the performance of the entire organization. (Photo courtesy of ARAMARK)

guest—and good working relationships between operations and marketing people at the unit level.

The Offering

The identity of a chain or franchise brand goes a long way toward defining an operation and its offering. Typically, the brand identity will dictate the markets the operation targets, the quality and price levels of the product offering, and, often, even the ambience, size, and other physical characteristics of the operation. There is, nevertheless, considerable opportunity, within these parameters, to individual-

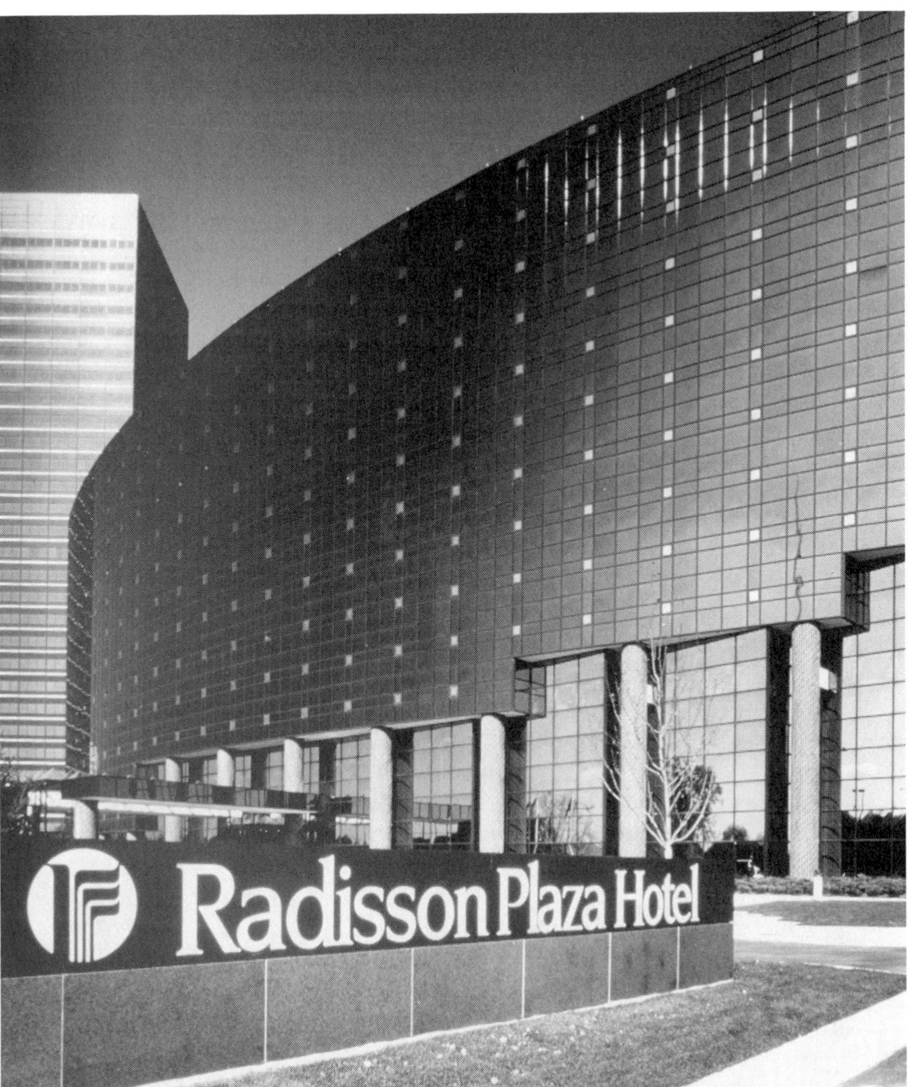

The chain identity of a hotel usually determines target markets, price levels, and often physical characteristics of the property, but properties can still customize themselves to meet local market needs. (Photo courtesy of Radisson Hotels)

ize a product offering to the local market. For instance, a hotel needs to decide whether to seek local business for weekends, as well as *which* group rates to offer and *when*. A high-occupancy hotel might decide to maintain full rates and to limit the availability of rooms at low rates for such markets as government employees, clergy, and high school athletic teams. Where function business is strong, local service clubs might not be an attractive banquet target because of the price concessions such groups expect.

On the other hand, a less fortunate property might seek out those very targets and this, in turn, could affect services offered, as well as prices and promotional strategy. For instance, targeting weekend family rooms business could mean developing a package of services aimed at children—and their parents' peace of mind—with special supervised activities such as pool parties, Saturday videos, cookouts, and the like.

Here is an example of a local market decision for a restaurant unit. Should we seek tour bus business? The sales volume that segment provides can be very attractive—but it can also disrupt service to regular patrons unless special arrangements are made to take care of tour groups. As another example, if a restaurant is located in a high-luncheon-traffic area but has slow evening business, it might seek out special targets for evenings such as local residents, seniors, or group business among its luncheon guests.

If a competitor has a particular advantage in the market, that might lead an operation to tailor its product offering to try to offset that advantage. A new hotel, for instance, faced competition from a well-established older property. The older property had been purchased some years previously at a much lower cost per room than the newer property and, accordingly, could be profitable at a lower average rate. Rather than try to match the older hotel's lower weekend rate packages, the newer hotel offered enhanced services, including all-you-can-eat buffets and entertainment activities that used its superior recreational facilities. The property's advertising—coupled with these product adjustments—helped support a value image for the property in the weekend market in spite of higher room rates.

These examples suggest that "who we are," while defined to some degree by the brand's umbrella identity, can, nevertheless, be customized to a significant degree to meet local market conditions.

Database Marketing

The term "database marketing" (also discussed in Chapter 4) refers to the use of information on an operation's existing customers to improve target marketing efforts *to* those customers—and people like them. Database marketing is not really new to the hotel business. Upscale hotels, for instance, have maintained guest histories for many years. What *is* relatively new, however, is the computer technology which makes guest history and other databases much easier to use and economically feasible for use in virtually any property. Restaurants have recently begun to collect similar information, using data from registrations for promotional programs such as "Birthday Clubs" (offering a free or reduced price meal to guests, usually children, on their birthday) and frequent-guest programs. Building a customer database is an expensive and time-consuming process, but it offers several advantages. It permits the operation to:

1) Communicate with, service and profile existing clients;
2) Segment those clients by type to better understand and serve them;
3) Prospect for new business by targeting those with characteristics similar to existing customers;

4) Respond quickly and appropriately to prospective clients who come to you; and
5) Analyze sales by individual customer and groups over time, and after special promotional efforts.[5]

The database should yield information such as customer name, title, company name, home and work address, and method of payment. In hotels, the database can provide information on the source of reservations, lead time for reservations, prior usage patterns (including frequency of stay), responses to promotions, and special preferences.[6] In restaurants which use a frequent-guest program as a basis of building a database, it is also possible to capture information on frequency of patronage and average check, thus, identifying *which* patrons are most valuable to an operation so they can be *singled out for special recognition.*

Another term for this approach to enhancing a marketing program with information about existing customers is **loyalty marketing.** The information in an operation's database is used to reinforce the loyalty of present customers in three

PRIORITY CLUB WORLDWIDE

PRIORITY CLUB® APPLICATION

❑ Yes, I want to enroll in the Priority Club program, and I agree to all program terms and conditions.†

Preferred Title: ❑ Dr. ❑ Mr. ❑ Mrs. ❑ Ms. ❑ Miss ❑ None Gender: ❑ Male ❑ Female

First Name ______ Middle Initial ______ Last Name ______

Social Security Number __ __ __ - __ __ - __ __ __ __
(to be used as your Priority Club number)

(If you are not a U.S. resident, call 1-800-272-9273 and ask the Priority Club Service Center for a membership number.)

Credit card number to be used to guarantee your Holiday Inn hotel reservation:

❑ MasterCard (MC) ❑ American Express (AX) ❑ Diners Club (DC)
❑ Discover Card (DS) ❑ Visa (VS)
Card# __ __ __ __ __ __ __ __ __ __ __ __ __ __ __ __ Exp. Date __/__ Mo./Yr.

Home Phone (____) ______ Business Phone (____) ______

Preferred Mailing Address: ❑ Home ❑ Business

Street Address ______
(No P.O. Box; U.S. addresses only)

City ______ State ______ ZIP Code/Postal Code ______ Country ______

Choose one of the following two collection options:

A ❑ I want to collect Priority Club points. I understand there is a $10 annual fee to join the Holiday Inn Priority Club Program, and that I will be entitled to membership through December 31, 1996.

❑ I am enclosing a check or money order for my fee payable to Holiday Inn Priority Club.

❑ Please charge my annual membership fee to the credit card indicated previously.

______
Signature (required for credit card payment)

B ❑ I want to collect frequent flyer miles/credits automatically from one of the following frequent flyer programs. I understand the membership fee will be waived, and I agree to use my frequent flyer number upon check-in for mileage credit.* (Please check one.)

❑ Air Canada ❑ Asiana Airlines ❑ Lufthansa ❑ Sabena
❑ American Airlines® ❑ Delta Air Lines ❑ Northwest Airlines ❑ Thai Airways International
❑ Ansett Australia ❑ KLM ❑ Qantas Airways ❑ United Airlines

* Priority Club card will not be issued. Airline responsible for issuing mileage credit will send statement showing mileage received as a result of Priority Club membership. Redemption of airline awards is subject to terms and conditions of airline program. Participating airline alliances may be added or deleted from the Priority Club program at any time without notice.

______ ______
(Name as it appears on your frequent flyer card) (Frequent flyer number)

† For complete program terms and conditions, call 1-800-272-9273.

Complete, then fold, seal, and mail today.

For many hotel companies, the process of accumulating a database begins with a frequent traveler club, such as the one at Holiday Inn. (Photo courtesy of Holiday Inn Worldwide) ways, with rewards, recognition, and by making it painful (or costly) for them to switch. First of all, customers are rewarded for repeated patronage with bonuses in the form of free meals, complimentary rooms, or upgraded services (from a room to a small suite at the same price, for instance). The airline frequent-flyer clubs are probably the best known and most widely established ways of *rewarding* customers and many hotel chains have copied the technique. Casinos have an interesting way of recognizing regular patronage among "slot high rollers." When a member of the casino's slot high roller club begins to use a machine, she or he inserts the membership card in a card reading device on the machine. A microchip in the slot machine keeps track of the volume of play and relays that information to a central database. Players receive premiums in the form of complimentary goods or services based on their volume of play.

Experts judge *recognition* to be one of the strongest ways to motivate repeat patronage.[7] The maitre d' in an upscale hotel, for instance, will look at the registrations for the day to spot patrons who have been there before in order to be ready to greet them by name as they arrive in the dining room. Where a hotel has a guest history system, guest's previous wishes and preferences can be retrieved and "remembered" at the front desk and by the service staff in the hotel's food service outlets. The recognition of an individual addresses the ego needs of that individual at a basic level.

The accumulated rewards in a loyalty program, such as a frequent-diner club, make it *painful to switch* to another operation. If a guest stops patronizing an operation and switches to a competitor, the guest loses the accumulated points—and, thus, has an actual cost of lost benefits. No one would count on this potential loss as the major motivation to continued patronage. It can be counted on, however, to provide the guest with a reason to give an operation another chance when the inevitable happens and somebody makes an error.

As we have already noted, there are significant details in local marketing requirements and practices that differ between the restaurant business and hotels. Accordingly, we can examine the needs and practices of each industry in the next two sections.

LOCAL AREA MARKETING IN FOOD SERVICE

The definition of a local area varies from one restaurant company to another. Some firms uses a 1½-mile radius, while others talk of a 10-minute drive time. On the other hand, for companies operating expressway restaurants, "local" target markets include such segments as trucking companies, tour line operators, and commuters. The customers in these segments do not live near the units in question. What makes theses guests "local" is their transportation patterns, which lead them to travel through the unit's market area on a regular basis. Settling on an appropriate definition of "local" for a particular operation *is* important, but we will be more concerned with what to do about the local market, however defined, than with the specific geographical definitions of local.

Local marketing in food service includes institutional food service, as well as commercial restaurants. The "fourth-floor snack bar" and the "main cafeteria of Johnson Hall" may well present local marketing problems and success in institutional food service requires attention to local marketing issues.

Why Local Marketing in Food Service Is Growing

Perhaps the most important reason for the growing emphasis on local marketing is because that is where the customers are. According to one marketing study,

> 30 per cent of all food service customers base their decision to dine at a particular restaurant on their proximity to the restaurant. *Over 70 per cent of all diners travel less than 15 minutes to get to a restaurant with over 80 per cent of these travelling less than 10 minutes. One in four diners travels less than 5 minutes.*[8]

There are competitive reasons, too, for food service's growing interest in local marketing. They arise from qualitative and quantitative changes in competitive conditions. Food service organizations once expanded opposed only by out-of-date independents. Today, they face well-established regional and national firms, many with deep pockets and large advertising and promotion war chests. The number of restaurant units in most markets, moreover, has increased dramatically in the past 25 years. In fact, growth has been such that many restaurant companies have turned to overseas markets for major expansion opportunities. In the saturated North American market, to adopt a marketing warfare analogy, local area marketing is the equivalent of house-to-house fighting.

Changing economic conditions contribute to the escalation in competition. During the period of food service's earlier expansion, in the 1970s and 1980s, population and work force growth was rapid and so there were more customers each year. Competition took place in an expanding market. Today, however, conditions have changed dramatically. Work force growth has slowed and so there is less growth in the customer base. Customers, moreover, are more conservative because of unemployment concerns and fear of restructuring.

The way the restaurant world looks to consumers has changed, too, after a generation and a half of the ascendancy of chain restaurants and limited-service concepts. In the 1960s, the standardized chain restaurant was *welcomed* as it pushed aside many "Ptomaine Palaces" with their varying standards of cleanliness, sanitation, and quality. Standardization was new and people were glad to see it as a safe haven, especially when traveling. Today, standardization is the rule and the trick is, increasingly, to deliver standardized quality, with national or regional brand recognition *and* a local flavor.

Local marketing is needed to deal with the local competition because economic and social conditions vary so widely from city to city or, indeed, between neighborhoods in any one city. A different response is needed in a posh suburb, in a poor neighborhood with high unemployment, and at an expressway location. In each of these and the many other possibilities, customer needs and wants are different. Different competitors loom, too, in each market, and need distinctive responses. If, for instance, couponing is rife in one market, some reaction is indicated to retain share. Diverse locations, too, have different time-of-day and day-of-week peaks and valleys—and, therefore, lend themselves to different volume-leveling techniques and promotions.

A final reason for using local area marketing relates to firm size and the degree of market penetration a firm has achieved. Independents and small chains cannot compete in the conventional advertising media against larger—and more well financed—national chains. In other cases, even large chains may have one or a few units located in markets where they cannot buy media efficiently; they do not have enough units to absorb the cost of media, particularly television. In these circumstances, local marketing is still a viable opportunity.

CHAIN RESTAURANTS: ISSUES FOR LOCAL MARKETING

Not all multiunit organizations emphasize local marketing. Local store marketing raises issues for chains related to budget priorities, as well as organizational problems. We will consider each briefly.

Budget Priorities

At the headquarters level, the view is often that setting aside a portion of the marketing budget for local marketing is inefficient because national brand marketing benefits *every* unit, while local spending helps only one or a few units.

Organizational Issues

At the headquarters marketing department, moreover, extensive market research can be used to shape all elements of a program, and various scenarios can be simulated, assuming different levels of cost, response rates, and the like. This effort heightens the likelihood of achieving the maximum profitability in any outcome. Market research and planning skills are located at headquarters—while local marketing decisions are generally made by operations people in the field. The dollar amounts of local marketing decisions, moreover, are not large enough to justify extended study or a lot of high-priced talent.

In the field, the unit manager and her or his operations supervisor probably lack the training, background, and skills for formal market research. Moreover, they are pressed for time and so are unlikely to favor time-consuming formalized market studies. As one senior-level marketing manager put it: "It's worth remembering when you ask for a written plan, that the person you want to develop it is probably already working a 70-hour week." Many companies are concerned, too, that time spent on local marketing—since it will be done by the unit manager—is time spent away from unit operations.

Another organizational issue involves supervision. A senior-level marketing manager stated that supervising all the local marketing programs he was technically responsible for was "like managing 50 brands."[9] In local marketing, each problem is different. Time constraints on the headquarters marketing staff pose as much or more of a problem as do time pressures in the field. Accordingly, central-office marketing people tend to avoid involvement in local marketing decisions.

The Field Marketing Manager. One way of addressing the problem of time pressures on headquarters marketing is to establish an intermediate staff position. This person reports to the company's director of marketing but has his or her office in the field at an area or district office. In one national chain, Olive Garden, whose avowed strategy has been to "build a nation-wide chain one neighborhood at a time," the company opted for a field-based staff. Each field marketing person focused on 30 to 40 restaurants.[10]

Whatever the difficulties local marketing presents to chains, it is clear that it is claiming a significant share of marketing budgets in successful companies. At McDonald's, operators pay 2 percent into a local advertising cooperative (as well as another 2 percent into a national advertising fund), and individual stores spend an additional 1 to 2 percent out of their own budget, advertising in their local market. Pizza Hut spends 2.3 percent on advertising in local markets. Hard Rock Cafe spent less than 2 percent in 1995 but, only two years earlier, that company had no local marketing program. Hard Rock's entry into the local promotional battle is accelerating, driven by the increased local advertising of its competitors. Hard Rock had three marketing people on the staff of each store in 1995, a sales manager, a salesperson in charge of the visitor market, and a public relations person.[11]

Organizing Field Marketing

Experience suggests that certain key factors are essential to a successful local marketing program. These include resources, standardization of decisions to increase control and reduce executive time commitment, and provision of expert marketing support to operations people who are making decisions outside the area of their major expertise.

First of all, marketing's major role in *local* marketing is to provide resources. These resources encompass not only a local marketing budget but marketing manuals and resource binders, including camera-ready copy for ads and other suggested campaign material. A very important resource, is standardized financial planning in the form of a break-even formula which quickly indicates to the operator what level of incremental sales is required to pay for the costs of promotion. With that figure, the operator can make a reasonable estimate of whether the proposed local promotion will be profitable or not. At one company, for instance, the rule of thumb is a flow-through of 35 percent of incremental sales to the bottom line. Thus, if the program is to cost $100, the *incremental sales* required to carry it are $100 divided by 35 percent, or $285.

Some chains have developed elaborate break-even work sheets. Experience, however, suggests that unit and district managers find them too time-consuming to use and so local marketing efforts fall off. To avoid this problem, a company's headquarters group can develop standardized deals, which units may offer without the submission of detailed break-even calculations. These promotions are selected for proven results in test markets. All that is required for a manager to implement one of these "approved deals" is an estimate of the incremental volume and approval by the area manager, subject to the local marketing budget. Note that this approach specifically locates the authority and responsibility for this level of marketing in *operations.*

Some companies provide specialized local marketing personnel in the headquarters marketing department who act as expert advisors to area and store managers. They can also respond to specific problem store situations at the behest of the director of operations. While some companies have people on staff full time to work on local marketing, another solution is to hire a specialist marketing firm. A firm such as Contract Marketing (of Mentor, Ohio) will assist headquarters marketing staff in developing chainwide local marketing policies and then work with store managers and area supervisors in implementing the program.

Establishing a Local Area Marketing Program

We can now look at a local marketing program from the perspective of a unit manager. The first step in developing such a program is to define its objectives. Next, the manager must identify the information regarding customer and competition needed to assess the local market. Then, the operation's entire marketing mix needs to be assessed in terms of the local marketing conditions.

Defining Objectives. Local marketing programs should have concrete goals, for instance, to raise traffic or check averages or to offset a particular low-volume day part. Objectives should be stated in specific terms, such as "to increase AM snack sales by 10 percent next month" or "to increase early dinner sales by 50 customers per week over the previous month."

Here are two examples of programs with specific objectives which are based on offering the customers an incentive. For instance, *to build volume* in an off-peak period, one university established a gourmet coffee club. Club members who purchased a personal mug and used it during the period between the breakfast and lunch rush (9:30 to 11:30 A.M.) received a discounted price.[12] The coffee club increased sales substantially and the incremental volume helped carry the operation's costs during that slow day part. Early-bird specials are another widely used variant of the same tactic. They offer reduced prices to increase sales in the slow mid- to late-afternoon period. Early-bird programs achieve their objectives in markets where there is a significant number of seniors or others to whom the special and its timing have an appeal.

Defining the Customer. The process of local market planning begins with the identification of the customer. This requires definition of the restaurant's trading area which can be specified either in miles or in travel time. At one company, marketers and operators follow what they call "The Rule of Ten." The manager is asked to get a map of the local area and—in prime meal time traffic—drive 10 minutes in each direction from the unit, marking the end of each trip on the map. When the points are connected, the operator has defined the probable limits of the unit's local market. Field Practice Note 10.2 discusses a less time-consuming computerized means for measuring travel time.

Once the boundaries have been determined, the manager needs to know who lives and works in the area. Census data will give a great deal of information on the demographics of the census tracts that make up the trading area. Scouting out the area by driving through it will help estimate the size and character of the working (i.e., daytime) population. Driving the area will also locate concentrations of customers—people who live in apartments or work in office or industrial complexes, as well as senior citizen housing centers and schools and colleges. These centers should be marked on the market map, as should major *destinations* in the area such as recreation centers, parks, shopping malls, and churches. Conversations with employees, customers who live in the area, and suppliers can supplement this intelligence gathering. The information on the map should be supplemented with estimates of population, employment, or visitation for each major center identified. Estimates of the relative size of these centers can generally be verified (or adjusted) on the basis of a few phone calls.

Competition. As an initial step, the direct and indirect competition in your trading area should be identified and located on the market map. Classifying competitors as direct or indirect involves a judgment of the marketplace. To give an example, all QSRs can be viewed as directly competitive with each other. Their indirect competitors are family and casual restaurants. On the other hand, in a particular market, because of conditions such as location, some operations in another category might be viewed as direct competitors. For instance, a family restaurant and a QSR located next door to each other *might* see each other as directly competitive.

Once direct competitors are identified, their strengths and weaknesses should be assessed to lay the groundwork for a competitive differentiation strategy *for the local marketplace*. It is also important to keep tabs on what competitors are doing on a continuing basis. One way to gain valuable information while boosting staff morale is to offer to pay the cost of a "shopping visit" to competitive operatrions by staff members, to be followed by a report to management. This has the added advantage of making the staff more aware of competitive pressures.

The Local Area Marketing Mix

Product. As we noted at the outset of this chapter, the core of any local marketing effort must be excellence in operations. Without good food and friendly, prompt service, the guest simply will not return. As one operator put it: "If you are not executing at a great level, you're going to lose business."[13]

Product variation to meet local demand offers, potentially, both risks and rewards. Adding a local item to a chain operation's menu may add local appeal, but may also run the risk of confusing the concept for patrons from outside the area. Still, when identified as a "local favorite," even a company with a tightly focused concept can benefit from some effort to accommodate local interest. An interesting approach to this problem of localizing product is demonstrated by a buffet offered in many KFC units. While only 30 products are offered at any one time, operators may choose from over 300 items which have been approved for the buffet. Thus, locally popular items may be included in what is still a standard product: the buffet.

Price. While setting an exact price chainwide can present antitrust problems, the general price level for the menu is usually established for a chain concept. On the other hand, "specials" and "limited-time offers" may be required locally, to meet the immediate competition or special local conditions.

LOCAL MARKETING COMMUNICATION METHODS AND MEDIA

While product and pricing *are* important local marketing variables, the most prominent place in local marketing is filled by marketing communication. We can classify marketing communication media into five broad categories: merchandising, advertising, sales promotion, personal selling, and community involvement.

Merchandising

Merchandising in the hospitality industry is concerned with efforts at or very near the point of purchase. The classic examples of merchandising in food service are the wine display and the dessert cart, but merchandising extends beyond these obvious examples.

Menu Merchandising. In food service, the most potent marketing tool is the menu. Think of the menu as an advertising medium. The menu is, in effect, a sophisticated product brochure.[14] A leading expert on the use of menus in marketing, Bill Main, estimates that in an average table service restaurant, somebody opens a menu 150,000 times a year. With such a powerful advertising medium available right at the point of purchase, it makes sense to plan the menu to take advantage of what we know about how consumers use menus. In practice, guests do not read menus. Rather, their eye passes quickly over the menu, most commonly in the patterns shown in Figure 14.2. In this hurried scan, the guest takes in just the highlights, about 20 percent of the menu, according to Main. Field Practice Note 14.1 details a number of suggestions for using the menu in merchandising.

Merchandising Zones. Moving beyond the menu, there are many other rich opportunities for merchandising *within* the restaurant. In fact, Tom Feltenstein, chairman of the Neighborhood Marketing Institute, urges that a substantial

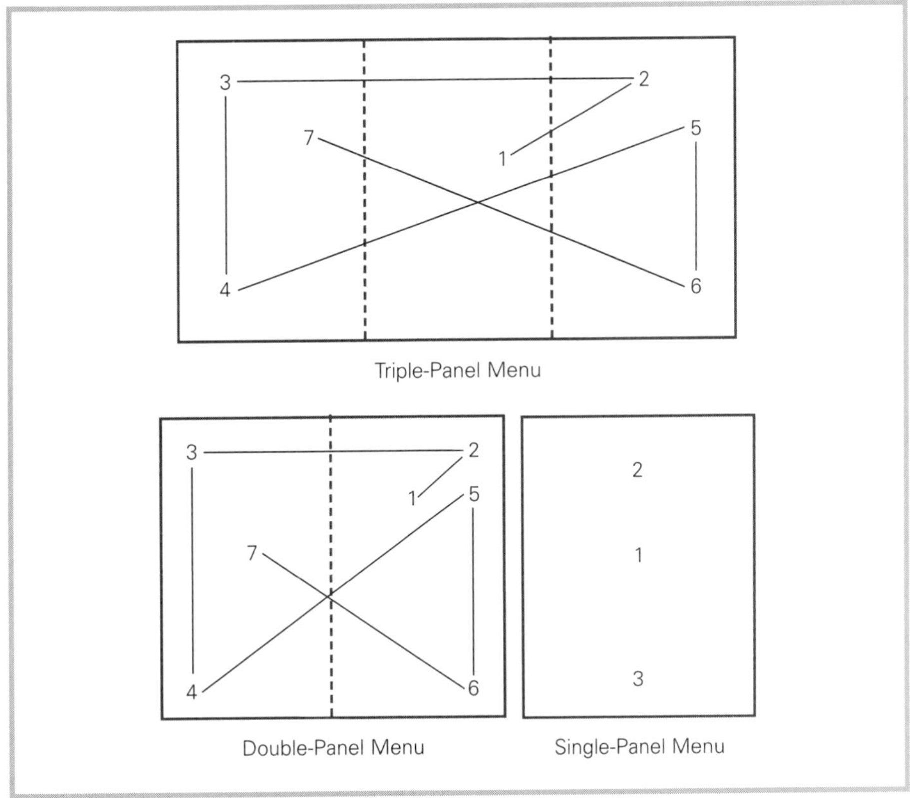

Figure 14.2 The Pattern of a Typical Menu Reader's Eye Movements

Source: Bill Main, "Menu Marketing," 1995 Marketing War College.

portion of the restaurant's marketing budget be spent inside the restaurant. He calls this emphasis on in-store merchandising **four walls marketing.**[15]

Four walls marketing goes after the most susceptible of prospects, those who have already decided to buy. Efforts to enhance the value of the guest's experience are a critical part of marketing which aims to secure repeat patronage. Efforts to "upsell" and to direct the guest's attention to high-margin selections contribute to improved sales volume and profit. Table 14.1 treats the restaurant as a promotional medium. It summarizes some of the major opportunities for selling to the guest directly inside the restaurant. It also suggests media that can be used for that purpose. The various *zones* identified in Table 14.1 are what Feltenstein calls "message centers, places where the guest's eye goes." As shown in the table, these merchandising opportunities include quick service, as well as table service restaurants.

In addition to merchandising directly to the guest, an "employee zone" offers opportunities for activities which address the guest indirectly, through **internal marketing** directed at employees. One of the most powerful of these is a brief *preshift meeting* of guest contact employees at which the day's menu, house spe-

Field Practice Note 14.1

Menu Merchandising

According to a national authority on menu marketing, a menu should be user friendly, in effect, telling a story about interesting menu items. **Descriptive menu copy** should "present a word picture of a menu item which instantly appeals to the full range of the guest's senses of sight, smell and taste." Here is an example of one such menu description:

> CAJUN STYLE FLORIDA RED FISH
> Tender filets of fresh Florida redfish lightly breaded with our own Cajun blend of seasoning, then pan seared to a golden brown.

Guests do not study the menu. In fact, they read only about 20 percent of it. To help hurried guests choose—and to help them choose items with a high profit—menu planners need to make use of techniques which will highlight high-contribution-margin items. For instance, the highest-selling item on the menu will be the *first* menus item listed—and the second highest will be the *last* item listed. This suggests that menu items which have to be on the menu because of guest demand but which carry a low profit margin should be "buried" in the middle of the menu listing.

Other techniques for making menu items stand out are **boxing** or **shading** the listing, the use of signature **icons,** and the identification of new items. The use off these devices will generally result in an increase in sales of the item of 15 to 20 percent. In one case, a small Italian flag was used as a signature icon with an Italian specialty and increased sales of that item 30 percent. Identifying an item as a "Specialty of the House" also produces strong positive results. In one operation, a Mexican sandwich priced at $5.25 was selling 50 orders a day. On the new menu, the price of the item was raised to $5.95 but the item was listed as a "special"—and sales rose to 80 sandwiches a day.

Care should be taken in the way price is listed on a menu. For instance, using large type to indicate price will focus the guest's attention on price as will listing all prices in a neat row, one under another. Instead, prices should be tucked into the copy for each menu item. Since customers judge the experience of a restaurant on the entree prices, every effort should be made to hold down those prices. Then, appetizers, side dishes, and desserts can be priced with a higher contribution margin, achieving the overall profit goal.

Source: This note is based on a presentation by Bill Main, "Menu Marketing," at the 1995 Marketing War College, March 25–28, 1995, Palm Beach.

cialties, service tips, and similar topics are discussed. These meetings present an ideal opportunity to restate the goals and methods of a *suggestive selling* program. Other indirect merchandising opportunities are presented by a suggestion box program, incentives, a communications program in the employee dining room, and other employee communications media such as a newsletter and bulletin boards.

Table 14.1 Four Walls Merchandising Zones and Merchandising Media

All Restaurants		Table Service Restaurants	Quick Service Restaurants
Lobby Zone	*Bathroom Zone*[a]	*Dining Room Zone*	*Front-Counter Zone*
Welcome mat Hanging mobiles Displays Host preselling Brochures Sampling Wall posters	Dessert audio Posters Special event calendar Cleaning schedule	Menu Specials board Matches Posters Displays Wine cart Dessert tray Sampling Gift certificates Bounce-back coupons	Menu board Register toppers Counter cards Wall posters Premiums Condiment stand Bag stuffers Bounce-back coupons
Pay Phone Zone	*Office Zone*	*Bar Zone*	*Drive-Thru Zone*
Signs and posters Memo pads	Hold message Answering machine Phone scripting	Point-of-purchase displays Drama drinks Bar menu Drinks coasters Specials board Activities: ◆ Upselling ◆ Entertainment	Menu boards
Table Top Zone	*Delivery and Carry-Out Zone*	*Car Valet Zone*	
Table tents Place mats Menu clip-ons Wine list Napkins Comment cards	Car signage Bulk order pads Take-out menus Magnets Bounce backs	Thank you card Activities: ◆ First greeting ◆ Vacuum car ◆ Wash windshields	

[a] Forty percent of customers go to the bathroom before ordering dessert.
Source: Adapted from Tom Feltenstein, "The Newest Wave in Neighborhood Marketing," Presentation at the Marketing War College, March 26, 1995.

Moving outside the four walls, Feltenstein identifies a "parking lot zone" in which cleanliness, landscaping, directional signs, and ease of access can enhance the guests' experience, making them welcome on arrival and seeing them off in a pleasant way when they leave.

Finally, the "property line zone"—outside the restaurant but still in the control of the operation—provides many "message centers" for communicating with guests and passersby (in malls, the term would be "lease line zone.") Some of these are the restaurant marquee, a sign on the building, awnings, banners, and posters, and an outdoor menu. An outdoor dining area and a children's playground enhance the guest's experience—and convey an important message to passing traffic about the experience on offer.

Four walls marketing at this unit begins at the front door—with a point-of-purchase poster. (Photo courtesy of Taco Bell)

Merchandising in Institutional Food Service. While a large part of a contract food service company's marketing effort is aimed at clients (i.e., the buying center[16] of an institution such as a hospital, college, or business), virtually all of its marketing effort aimed at the individual user, the guest, is at or near the point of purchase. Referred to as **on-site marketing,** these efforts are, in effect, merchandising.[17]

Contract food service companies object to the term "captive audience," but it is true that they face many of the same customers every day. One way to increase the perception of variety and the desirability of the offering is through the use of popular restaurant brands. Some companies, such as Marriott, make use almost exclusively of national franchise brands in their food service accounts, operating as franchisees. Others such as Aramark have developed their own brands but also use national franchise brands.

The choice of using either an in-house brand or a better known franchise brand poses some hard choices. For instance, taste tests convinced one company that its in-house brand pizza was a better product than that which they could offer under a franchise from a well-known national pizza franchisor. On the other hand, the national brand would outsell the house brand by 4 to 1. The substantial increase in pizza sales, however, resulted in cannibalization of other menu items—and the franchised product carried a significant royalty, on the order of 8 to 10 percent. Clearly, the decision regarding a merchandising technique needs to be made in the light of its impact not just on sales but on profits, as well.

While some account managers are inclined toward merchandising, as elsewhere in food service, many are not. Accordingly, contract companies develop **turnkey merchandising programs** which have all the details worked out for the unit manager for use in a large number of their accounts. One type of promotion used by contract companies is the special event. "Turnkey" special event kits that include recipes, promotional ideas, mats for printing flyers, and other printed media, as well as training manuals and supporting merchandise, are developed and distributed on a monthly basis. In one special event, a "Cowabunga Beach Party," employees wore cutoffs, beach hats, sunglasses, and wild t-shirts. Other themes events have been built around are Mardi Gras, St. Patrick's Day, and parties with a "Fifties" motif. Another merchandising program, which illustrates the importance of integrating merchandising efforts with operational concerns, is discussed in Case History 14.1.

Advertising

Local advertising is used for such purposes as supporting a local promotion, publicizing a local sponsorship, or reaching key local target audiences such as college and university students, seniors, and tourists. Direct mail, usually including coupons, is a common local medium and especially helpful as a response when a new competitor is opening—or an established competitor is launching an aggressive sales drive. Much of a chain restaurant's local advertising may be accomplished through an **advertising co-op** made up of all operators in an area. This advertising is usually an areawide effort which receives considerable assistance and sometimes direction from chain headquarters.

Local "image" advertising that emphasizes the unit's local identity may be useful, subject to budgetary constraints. Some low-cost possibilities include notices on neighborhood/supermarket bulletin boards, bumper stickers and decals, directional and reminder advertising on bus benches, and transit ads (especially when the route leads past the unit).[18]

Sales Promotion

Local sales promotion can help the operation respond to local competitive conditions. When everybody is couponing in a market, a unit in that market probably needs to coupon—whatever the chain's national strategy is. Promotion also offers unique opportunities to burnish a local image by partnering with successful local enterprises.

Joint Promotions. Sometimes called a cross-promotion, this tactic pairs two complementary businesses. For instance, a movie theater and a dinner house restaurant might promote each other by distributing each other's coupons. In return for their effort, each establishment gains access to a somewhat different stream of customers. When a locally well-known partner is chosen, there is the added advantage of being associated with that firm, a kind of indirect endorsement. Careful attention to joint planning in advance of the promotion is

Case History 14.1 Merchandising a Coffee Program in Institutional Food Service: The Java Program

Coffee is a popular item in any food service operation and can be a highly profitable one, as well. A large contract food service company invited its three coffee suppliers to participage in a "shoot-out competition" to develop a program for merchandising coffee as a premium product. The winner of the competition was guaranteed a three-year lock on the food service company's coffee bean business.

The old means of presenting coffee was simply to have a coffee pot available to customers on a burner. This approach, however, had an institutional, unexciting look. The task was to design a presentation that had a retail look but which could also be integrated into operations where space was at a premium.

The keys to operational success in the winning submission, dubbed the Java Program, were these:

1. A small "footprint" (i.e., one which required minimum counter space). Coffee brewers were located in the back of the house so that all front-of-the-house space could be used by the revenue-producing Java thermal containers.
2. Provision of backup product—a second pot in back so there would always be plenty of coffee for the guest.
3. A sightline in the coffee container so operations people could tell how much was left.
4. One of the critical factors in choosing the successful bidder was the supplier's willingness to commit its field staff to giving operational support to the Java Program. This field support has been critical to the success of the Java Program.

A high-quality coffee bean was selected using taste panels and competitive analysis against the two major retailers of prepared coffee. Product quality is maintained by testing with an expert taste panel twice a year.

The product is supported by a generous supply of merchandising materials. A logo was developed for the new coffee program. There is a mobile hung over the display which repeats the design theme and colors and an illuminated sign goes behind the product on the wall. Table tents are also used in dining areas and travel mugs repeating the logo are on sale.

This program builds a premium price—and the merchandizing supports that price. The results are a 7 to 14 percent increase in coffee sales with a product that is highly profitable at 10 to 20 cents less than the retail competion's.

Source: Ian Bell, Vice President of Marketing, and Susan Barclay, Vice President of Marketing, Versa Services, personal interviews, February 1995 and May 1996.

important to assure: that each partner has the potential to gain a significant advantage from the effort; that both parties are fully committed to the project; and that costs and other efforts are shared equitably.[19] ("Partnering" is also discussed in Field Practice Note 9.2.)

Frequent-Diner Clubs. Some restaurants use a promotion based on rewards for repeat patrons such as bonuses of free or discounted meals and other prizes. While **frequent-diner clubs** yield significant repeat business, they do have a significant start-up cost, estimated at $4,000 to $5,000. At Arby's, however, frequency of patronage increased for club members from 1.6 to 2.8 visits per month, while discounts and bonuses lowered check averages by only one cent. Arby's used a "smart card" for its frequency club with membership information embedded in a magnetic strip. One very important aspect of the frequency club is the database it yields. Balancing the costs of the Arby's program, for instance, was the significant improvement in direct-mail results afforded by the compilation of frequency club transaction data. Knowing which items customers ordered permitted tailoring coupons in mailings. Because of this micromarketing, mailing response rates rose from the 5 to 10 percent level to a 38 percent rate.[20]

A much simpler promotion, but one that is highly effective and has some characteristics in common with the frequency club, is the birthday club mentioned earlier. Bringing a young person's family into the restaurant on his or her birthday encourages frequency—and the membership list yields valuable data that can start a restaurant on its way to database marketing.

Personal Selling

Restaurants, of course, cannot afford the cost of personal selling to reach individual guests, but calling on centers where there are large numbers of customers makes good sense. For the vast majority of restaurants, this work will be done by the manager since very few food service operations can justify the cost of a sales representative. Called **prime prospecting** by Contract Marketing, this tactic draws on the marketing intelligence we discussed previously. The essential ingredient is identifying the major institutions which have large numbers of potential customers under their roof. Large plants or office complexes may be willing to distribute "introductory offer" coupons with paychecks, offering an additional fringe benefit to their staff—at no cost to themselves. Nearby churches will have organizations that may be willing to accept and distribute coupons to their members, such as seniors' clubs. Colleges, hospitals, and other large institutions may also be willing to distribute coupons to employees and clientele.

To make the contact necessary to launch such efforts, a personal call by the manager is necessary. Contract Marketing advises that the following steps are appropriate:

1. Identify the key person to be contacted at each Prime Prospect (usually the plant manager or the personnel manager).

2. Send a letter of introduction to the key person, signed by the unit manager, indicating the company's interest in its neighbor and that the manager would like to meet briefly with the contact.
3. When the letter has had time to arrive, the manager calls for an appointment.

Preparation for a sales call is of crucial importance. The manager making the call needs to have a clear objective and even a sort of flexible script ready for the contact[21] (see Chapter 13). For those who are making their first sales call, training and individual coaching are highly desirable.

Community Relations

One of the ways to build a local identity is by having unit personnel involved in local activities. This is particularly true for the unit manager. The manager's membership in a service club, the local chamber of commerce, or convention and visitor's bureau and/or involvement in local charities give the unit visibility. They also give the manager opportunities for networking which can be a significant source of business. While these activities have little or no dollar cost, because of the competitive pressures for excellence in operations and for tight cost control, a manager's time away from the unit *is* a significant cost. The value of being a local notable is hard to measure, but that hardly means it is without real worth in the business of making a firm a good local citizen.

Some activities burnish the organization's image and simultaneously bring an increase in sales volume. Among the most popular and effective are team sponsorships. In some cases, team uniforms are provided by the restaurant (with the restaurant's name included on the uniform), the understanding being that team meals and other functions will be held in the restaurant. One way that the uniforms can be funded is for the restaurant to give a discount for all team meals—and credit the discount to a fund to pay for the uniforms. Another related approach involves community clubs, churches, and other organizations. To support a fund-raising effort, restaurants contribute a set percentage of the sales of any group function to the charitable group's treasury, or pay a set percentage on receipts turned in by an organization's members. Note that these kinds of efforts tie any contribution to specific sales.

One highly effective local promotion is a joint effort with a local radio station, called "a remote." The station broadcasts from the restaurant, often in conjunction with a drive for a local charity. Both radio station and restaurant gain from supporting a local initiative and the broadcast often brings significant traffic to the restaurant, resulting not only in increased sales but new customers. In most cases, however, the "remote" will be tied to the restaurant's advertising and some advertising expenditure is usually a condition for the remote.

Evaluation

The problems of evaluating advertising make a study in itself and so we will confine the discussion here to the customary practice found in companies studied.

NOW PIZZA HUT DELIVERS TO YOU.

©1994 Pizza Hut, Inc. ® and TM designate registered trademark and trademark of Pizza Hut, Inc. Limited delivery area.

This Pizza Hut delivery ad is prepared centrally to achieve the high-quality art that food advertising requires. The blanks are furnished to units so that they can imprint their store location and the exact offer based on local market conditions. (Photo courtesy of Pizza Hut)

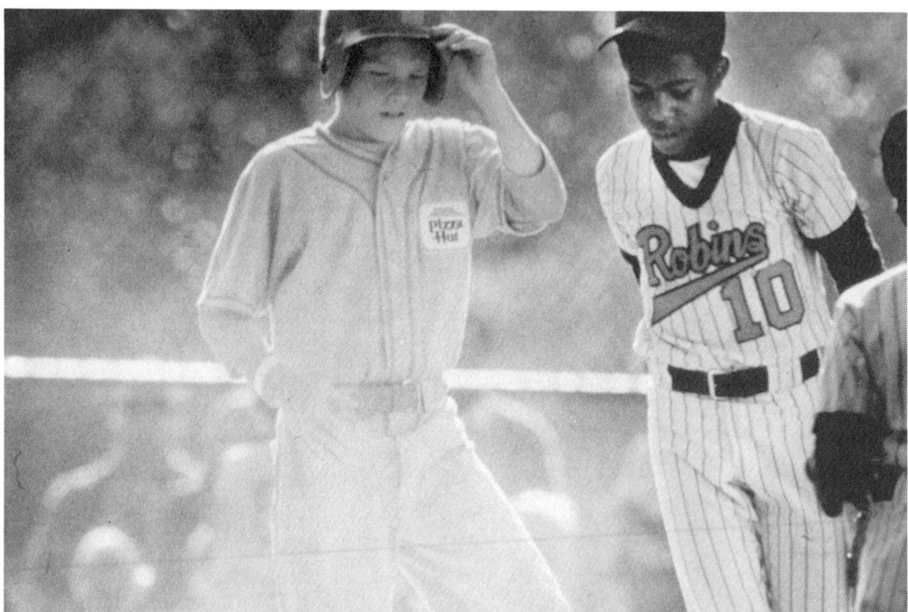

Team sponsorship builds local identity. Team meals can also be a source of revenue. (Photo courtesy of Pizza Hut)

Coupon returns provide an indicator of relative success and a dollar sales value (and discount value) can be attributed to them. Most operations compare sales during the promotion period with earlier periods (same weeks last month, same weeks last year). In addition to dollar returns, however, there is a value that is hard to quantify that relates to new trials, heightened goodwill, and a burnished *local* image.

PROPERTY LEVEL MARKETING IN LODGING

Property-based marketing activities have a long tradition in lodging, but they have, until very recently, been largely confined to personal selling. Today, however, three elements of the mix—product, price, and promotion—are vital elements in a hotel's local marketing program. While place, in the sense of location, is not a variable once the property has been built, it does go a long way to determining who the target market will be. We should also note that the preceding section on food service local marketing *can* be applied to a hotel's restaurant(s). In fact, hotels with restaurants have an ideal tool for gaining local referrals of rooms business. A successful, well-promoted restaurant (and bar) is perhaps the only means to attract local people into a hotel on a regular basis. Once guests are there, it is important to please them with good food and service to make friends with them.[22] What follows, however, deals principally with marketing of rooms and group functions.

Product

For most hotels, the product—as a physical entity—already exists but the product for sale is really the guest's experience. That experience can be designed and redesigned jointly by the efforts of marketing and operations. For instance, packaging the property in conjunction with nearby attractions—theme parks, shopping destinations, theaters, and other cultural institutions—shapes the experience offered leisure travelers. Partnering with these attractions makes sense, too, because joint marketing efforts make marketing dollars go farther.

The way a property is positioned, that is, which customers it targets and which competitors it needs to beat to gain those customers, shapes the product, too. For instance, in Vancouver, Delta Hotels has two hotels within a mile and a half of each other, both of about 400 rooms with significant meeting capacity. One is much nearer the airport and is positioned as an airport convenience buy. The other property offers itself as an urban resort. While there is some competition between them, only one bids on airline crew business and the other is sole bidder on sport fishing business.

Price

Rates are almost entirely a property level decision. Rack rates, although used in only a minority of cases in renting a room, are the point from which setting other rates—corporate rates, weekend rates, tour group rates, and the like—starts. Rack rates are generally set by the property's management team. In some chains, however, rate setting is done with the advice and approval of the company's headquarters. Very few people actually pay rack rates because of the prevalence of discounting but also because of the way hotel rooms are sold today. As the president of one chain put it:

> We don't sell rooms any more by room type. We sell by customer type and so we have rates for national corporate travel, local corporate travel, the tour market, the weekend family market, to name just a few. Our rates today are geared towards the customer's needs and what the customer will pay rather than what was once the old standby, room type.[23]

Special rates are sometimes negotiated at the chain level with very large buyers such as airlines, but most discounted rates vary from property to property and the degree of discount is set by the property's management. Which groups to extend special rates to is a property level decision. The hotel's rate decision is based on "what doors we want to open or close"—that is, which segments to go after and which to discourage—"to achieve the best possible revenue."[24]

The day-to-day **yield management** decisions as to when to "open" and when to "close" special rate categories are also made at the property level based on daily or even more frequent assessments of probable demand for particular periods. While the decision to open or close lies with the properties, some companies, whose headquarters are on line to each property's front desk, can monitor the practice of individual properties in real time. The role of such monitoring, however, is basically advisory in nature. If a hotel front office is in constant need of advice and consistently makes decisions that lead to under- or overbooking, it is likely that some other arrangements, such as additional training, will be undertaken.

Promotion: Marketing Communication

Offering the right product to the right customer and pricing both competitively and profitably *are* critical to a property's success, but the offer must be communicated and this job, more than any other element in the mix, is identified with the hotel sales and marketing function. The broad concerns of marketing involve issues like product and price—which are operational functions in the hotel industry and are the concern of the general manager and his or her management team. The sales function in smaller properties is often an important but additional duty of the manager's. In larger hotels, a staff of one or more salespeople carries out this work. We can identify four principal means of communicating the property's message to its customers and prospects: advertising, personal selling, sales promotion, and public relations.

Property Level Advertising. Database marketing is increasingly being used to transform advertising into "narrowcasting" rather than broadcasting. That is, advertising is being addressed to the hotel's regular customers—and to people like them. Database marketing can be especially powerful in crafting individualized advertising such as direct mail and telemarketing. Advertising an individual property in the mass media, more common among resort hotels and upscale properties, is usually limited to media in major point-of-origin markets and to advertising in the local market supporting special promotional events.

Personal Selling. "The sales function," says one hotel executive, "is 99% focused on the local market. Corporate sales [i.e., the national sales office] is strictly a service function. They are selling national accounts for the [individual] hotels". He describes a property sales program as having an "inside out" focus. By this, he means:

> You start as close to your hotel as you can and keep spreading until you have developed enough relationships and business to give you the results you are looking for. The cost of securing business increases as the propensity to buy decreases. When sales people go to a city 100 miles away, maybe 25 percent of the population have a propensity to buy but when you go as far as 250 miles, perhaps it's gone down to 15 percent and when you go 750 miles, it may be down around 8 percent. In Bangkok the traffic is so bad that three blocks is a great difference. Winter has the same kind of effect in a northern city like Saskatoon.[25]

Personal selling is an expensive medium and must generate significant revenue to offset its cost. Consequently, sales calls target sources of multiple-room nights or meeting and banquet business, rather than individual sales. The target of the sales call is often not the guest but the person making the buying decision. In the corporate market, for instance, three common means of making room bookings all rely on someone other than the guest for the buying decision.[26] In some companies, the manager's secretary in the concerned department makes the reservation. In other companies, an in-house travel department handles the reservation, while still others contract with a travel agency for these services.

In the first case, the hotel's sales representative must establish what the needs, budgets, and preferences of the client company's different departments are. The first few calls on a new account in this category can be thought of as similar to a mapping expedition. Early on, the focus of attention needs to be on finding out where reservations decisions are being made. A common method of motivating the person making the booking is the "secretary's club" which, from time to time, recognizes the help of its members at receptions, dinners, or other functions at the hotel. Some properties offer individual incentives (usually complimentary meals or weekend accommodations) to secretaries based on the number of rooms they book.

In the second case, that of a travel manager, the sales problem is simplified but, in some ways, more difficult. There is only one person to contact and sell but that person may be harder to reach and convince because he or she is the target of every other sales rep. A powerful tool in selling such a person is a visit to the hotel and a well-planned tour of the property that shows off its best features.

In the case of the travel agency, the individual making the booking is likely to have two goals: "To make the very best selection for the client and to protect the business interests of the travel agency . . . . To the travel agency, the prompt payment of commissions and recognition of the agency's role is very important."[27] Some other possible multiple-booking markets are identified in Figure 14.3.

Sales Promotion. Advertising often has long-run goals such as making the property better known and burnishing its image. Sales promotions may enhance a

Local Social Clubs
Fraternal, Religious, and Ethnic Organizations
Government Offices and Military Installations
State and Regional Conventions
Travel Agents
Tour Operators
Motor Coach Companies
Airlines
Hospital and Other Health Care Organizations
Educational Institutions
Professional and Amateur Sports Organizations

Figure 14.3 Local Sources of Multiple Room Bookings

Source: Adapted from Christopher W. L. Hart and David A. Troy, *Strategic Hotel/Motel Marketing* (East Lansing, MI: American Hotel and Motel Association, 1986), p. 152.

property's image, for instance, by partnering with another successful company or an entertainment or cultural institution, but its major purpose is generally to stimulate immediate sales during a specific time period.

Weekend packages are a common promotion aimed at buoying up a soft part of the hotel's sales week. They often involve a partnering arrangement with a local attraction such as an amusement or theme park or sports team, a shopping center, or a theater. Partnering offers a prestigious association and, where cost sharing is part of the arrangement, it also has the advantage of stretching the property's marketing dollar further.

Public Relations. While the "general public" in the local market is one important target, a property has many publics toward which it may want to direct PR efforts. Travel agents may be one such public, while others are local corporate accounts, regular customers in distant cities, and trade and professional association executives. A hotel's own employees are a critical public. General media publicity about the property, as well as targeted media such as an in-house newsletter, can be an important adjunct to an internal marketing program.

A basic tool in public relations is a press kit. A press kit may be prepared for special occasions such as a hotel grand opening or a special promotional event. It is also helpful to have available a press kit describing the property and its features so that a request from the media can be met immediately and comprehensively. A press kit should include a general description of the hotel; a "fact sheet" giving critical data on factors such as size, capacity, history, and so on; pictures of the property's main features; and copies of recent special event releases.

An important aspect of public relations is community involvement. Executives and other employees are encouraged to be active in local organizations to heighten the visibility of the hotel in the community. As appropriate, these activities may be the focus of news releases by the property. Similarly, employee achievements, awards, and sometimes even hobbies provide potential for news stories.

The specialized promotions referred to earlier may also be of enough interest to make news. Where this is the case, a special press kit may be prepared. For instance, if an ethnic theme dinner were the object of promotion, the press kit might include a general release on the event, as well as recipes, the chef's biography and picture, and a photo of the hotel.

SUMMARY

Local area marketing is a special case of the general field of marketing that is action oriented and hands on in its approach. More often than not, local marketing is done by the unit manager. Local marketing is based on the customer, competition, and the company's offering and successful operations is basic to its success. Database marketing can improve local targeting, and loyalty marketing offers regular customers rewards and recognition for repeat patronage and tries to make switching to other operations costly.

Local area marketing in food service is growing in importance for the following reasons: Many patrons come from the nearby areas; competition has become more intense and there is less growth in the market; changing consumer tastes dictate giving a national brand a local identity; different local markets have widely varying conditions; and many restaurants cannot afford to compete in media markets such as television but can afford a local marketing program. Some chain restaurants question local marketing, because it takes resources away from national brand advertising and because local efforts are usually not backed by extensive market research. The role of the headquarters unit in local restaurant marketing is to supply resources, both financial and in terms of expertise, and to develop standardized programs and procedures.

Local marketing uses the product, price, and promotion elements of the marketing mix. Product can be adapted to the local market in food service by developing local specialties and lodging companies use local partnerships and positioning to adapt their product to local conditions. Prices in food service largely follow the pattern of the chain, but specials and "limited-time offers" can meet local competition. In lodging, pricing is a property level function which includes setting rack rates and making yield management decisions about which discounts to offer and when.

Local restaurant advertising often involves advertising co-ops, but some advertising by individual units is also done. Sales promotions at the local level can involve local partners for both restaurants and hotels. *Merchandising* in food service involves selling at the point of purchase. Menu merchandising is especially powerful. Displays, banners, and other means of getting attention are also used. In-store merchandising reaches prospects who have already decided to buy and is intended to enhance the guests' experience and to lead guests to selections which will increase sales and profits. Four walls marketing treats the restaurant as a promotional medium. *Internal marketing* can be a form of indirect merchandising to the guest through employees. Personal selling, usually by the unit manager, can be used by restaurants to reach concentrations of customers. Lodging firms use personal selling to reach accounts which book multiple room-nights. Public relations and community involvement, while not free, are a cost-effective means of establishing a local identity for both restaurants and hotels.

◆ Key Words and Concepts

Community
Neighborhood marketing
Basis for local marketing
- Customer
- Competition
- Offering

Database marketing
Loyalty marketing
Field marketing manager
Adapting product to the locale
Merchandising
Descriptive menu copy
Boxing, shading, and icons
Merchandising zones
Four walls marketing
Internal marketing
On-site marketing
Turnkey merchandising programs
Advertising co-op
Frequent-diner club
Prime prospecting
Community relations
Yield management

◆ *Discussion Questions*

1. What forces are driving the increasing interest in local marketing in food service?
2. What problems does local marketing present for some chain organizations?
3. What resources are vital to the success of a local marketing program?
4. Describe the process of defining a customer in food service?
5. What are the purposes of "driving the area" when planning local marketing?
6. What means are available to "change" the product in hotel marketing without rebuilding the hotel?

7. What are the hotel property's key responsibilities with regard to pricing? What are the goals, special rates, and the decisions surrounding them?

8. What are the principal means of marketing communication at the property level?

9. What does the "inside out" focus in hotel sales mean?

10. What are the targets of personal selling in hotels?

Notes

Chapter 1

1. Christian Grönroos, *Service Management and Marketing* (Lexington, MA: Lexington Books, 1990).
2. George D. Rice, "Target Marketing: The Art of Segmentation," *Proceedings, Chain Operators Exchange, 1983* (Chicago: International Foodservice Manufacturers Association, 1983), pp. 5–6.
3. Peter Bennett, *Dictionary of Marketing Terms* (Chicago: American Marketing Association, 1988), p. 115.
4. For a brief critical discussion of the concept of the marketing mix, see Grönroos, *Service Management and Marketing,* pp. 134–136.
5. Peter Francese, "Income Winners," *American Demographics,* August 8, 1992, p. 2.
6. Diane Crispell, "The Real Middle Americans," *American Demographics,* October 1994, pp. 28–35.
7. Francese, "Income Winners."
8. Diane Crispell, "Dual Income Families," *American Demographics,* July 1995, pp. 32–37.
9. Greg J. Duncan, Timothy M. Smedding, and Willard Rodgers, "The Incredible Shrinking Middle Class," *American Demographics,* May 1992, pp. 34–38.
10. Peter Francese, "America at Mid Decade," *American Demographics,* February 1995, pp. 23–31.
11. James S. Mann, "Marketing to the Affluent," *Cornell Hotel and Restaurant Administration Quarterly,* October 1993, p. 55–58.
12. "The Future of Spending," *American Demographics,* January 1995, p. 14.
13. Ron Paul, "Top 100 Chains—An Update," *Technomic Foodservice Digest,* April 1995, p. 2.

14. For a fuller discussion of these issues, see Thomas F. Powers, "The Advent of the Megachain. A Case of the Emperor's New Clothes," *Hospitality Research Journal,* Volume 16, Number 1, 1992, pp. 1–12.

Chapter 2

1. *American Demographics,* September 1993, p. 9.
2. *American Demographics,* November 1992, p. 13.
3. *Fortune,* February 6, 1996, p. 130.
4. "The Future of Households," *American Demographics,* December 1993, pp. 27–40.
5. Margaret K. Ambry, "Childless Chances," *American Demongraphics,* April 1992, p. 55.
6. "The Future of Households," p. 34.
7. Abraham A. Maslow, *Motivation and Personality* (New York: Harper and Row, 1954). Maslow distinguished between two highest levels of need: esteem and status and, highest of all, self-actualization. We have treated these as a single category, personal need.
8. Carl R. Rogers, *Client Centered Therapy* (Boston: Houghton Mifflin, 1951).
9. Adapted from Leo Renaghan, "Consumer Behavior: The Forgotten Variable in Marketing," *Proceedings, Hospitality Leaders Conference* (Guelph, Ontario: School of Hotel and Food Administration, 1981).
10. Includes recreation and sports food service.
11. *Restaurants USA,* December 1995, p. 20.
12. Frederick E. Webster and Yram Wind, *Organizational Buying Behavior* (Englewood Cliffs, NJ: Prentice-Hall, 1972), pp. 12–20.
13. Ibid., pp. 78–79.
14. J. Dana Clark and Ken W. McCleary, "Influencing Associations' Site-Selection Process," *Cornell Hotel and Restaurant Administration Quarterly,* April 1985, p. 63.
15. Ibid., p. 63.
16. Ibid., p. 64.
17. Ibid.
18. Ibid., p. 68.

Chapter 3

1. I am indebted to Dianne Schmedley of the U.S. Census Bureau for her help in clarifying the distinction between census areas.
2. Geoffrey Meredith and Charles Shewe, "The Power of Cohorts," *American Demographics,* December 1994, pp. 22–31.
3. Harry Balzer, "Product Positioning," *Proceedings, Chain Operators Exchange, 1982* (Chicago: International Foodservice Manufacturers Association, 1982), p. 26.
4. Ken W. McCleary, Pamela Weaver, and Li Lan, "Gender-Based Differences in Business Travellers Lodging Preferences," *Cornell Hotel and Restaurant Administration Quarterly,* April 1994, pp. 51–58.
5. H. N. Fullerton, "The Baby Boom Moves On," *Monthly Labor Review,* November 1991, p. 37. The figures cited here pertain to the population aged 16 years and older.
6. Joseph T. Plummer, "The Concept and Application of Life Style Segmentation," *Journal of Marketing,* January 1974, p. 38.
7. "The VALS2 Typology," SRI International, Menlo Park, CA.

8. Robert J. Kimball, "American Values and Lifestyle Program," *Proceedings, Chain Operators Exchange, 1983* (Chicago: International Foodservice Manufacturers Association, 1983).
9. This discussion is based principally on George D. Rice, "Target Marketing: The Art of Segmentation," *Proceedings, Chain Operators Exchange, 1983* (Chicago: International Foodservice Manufacturers Association, 1983).
10. Rice, "Target Marketing."
11. Joan Viewager, "Beyond Demographics: Lifestyle Segmentation," *Proceedings, Chain Operators Exchange, 1987* (Chicago: International Foodservice Manufacturers Association, 1987), p. 2.
12. Peter Francese, "What Is Cluster Analysis For?" *Marketing Tools,* March–April 1994, p. 50.
13. Barbara Clark O'Hare, "The Art of Clustering," *Marketing Tools,* March–April 1994, p. 55.
14. Francese, "What Is Cluster Analysis For?" p. 55.
15. The description of the PRIZM segmentation system is based on *PRIZM: Lifestyle Segmentation* (New York: Claritas.)
16. Michael Mancini, "Putting the Pieces Together," *Marketing Tools,* March–April, 1984, p. 54.
17. For a fuller discussion of those segments, see R. C. Lewis, R. E. Chambers, and H. E. Chacko, *Marketing Leadership in Hospitality* (New York, Van Nostrand Reinhold, 1995), pp. 254-279.
18. Personal communication, Jeremy Paint, Vice President for Marketing, Commonwealth Hospitality.
19. For an extended discussion of these market segments, see Thomas F. Powers, *Introduction to Management in the Hospitality Industry,* 5th ed. (New York: Wiley 1995), pp. 176–200.
20. The discussion of contract segments is based on interviews with Joel Katz, Vice President, ARAMARK, and Ian Bell, Executive Vice President of Marketing, Versa Services, in July 1995.

Chapter 4

1. *Hotel Motel Management,* June 6, 1994, p. 6.
2. Susan M. Detwiler, "Secondhand Prose," *Marketing Tools,* January–February 1995, pp. 12–16.
3. Ibid., p. 12.
4. *Market Research for the Restaurateur* (Washington, DC: National Restaurant Association, 1982).
5. Thomas F. Powers', management case, "MIE Hospitality" (Guelph, Ontario: University of Guelph, Advanced Management Program for the Hospitality Industry, 1983), p. 8. The case describes the experience of an Arthur Treacher's franchisee during a period of rapid change in the franchisor company in which product changes figure prominently.
6. Gilbert A. Churchill, Jr., *Marketing Research: Methodological Foundations* (New York: CBS College Publishing, 1983), p. 85.
7. Ibid., p. 84.
8. Ibid., p. 85.

9. This section draws on Churchill, *Marketing Research,* pp. 59–65, 78–184.
10. William Dunn, "Building a Data Base," *Marketing Tools,* July–August, 1994, pp. 52–59.
11. Dan Peppers and Martha Rogers, "Welcome to the 1:1 Future," *Marketing Tools,* premier issue, p. 4.
12. *Restaurants and Institutions,* March 15, 1995, pp. 124–128.
13. Dan Peppers and Martha Rogers, "The End of Mass Marketing," *Marketing Tools,* March–April 1995, p. 45.
14. Paula A. Francese and Lee M. Renaghan, "Data-Base Marketing: Building Customer Profiles," *Cornell Hotel and Restaurant Administration Quarterly,* May 1990, p. 61.
15. Ibid.
16. Ibid.
17. Ibid., p. 62.
18. Restaurants and Institutions, March 15, 1995, p. 124.
19. Peppers and Rogers, "Welcome to the 1:1 Future," p. 4.

Chapter 5

1. Kenneth R. Andrews, *The Concept of Corporate Strategy* (Homewood, IL: Dow Jones–Irwin, 1971), p. 37.
2. Roland Christensen, Kenneth R. Andrews, and Joseph L. Bower, *Business Policy, Text and Cases,* 4th ed. (Homewood, IL: Richard D. Irwin, 1978), p. 125.
3. Adapted from Thomas V. Bonoma, *The Marketing Edge* (New York: Free Press, 1985), p. 7.
4. Kenichi Ohmae, *The Mind of the Strategist* (New York: McGraw-Hill, 1982), p. 36.
5. Mark J. Lawless and Christopher W. Hart, "Forces That Shape Restaurant Demand," *Cornell Hotel and Restaurant Administration Quarterly,* November 1983, p. 8.
6. Ron Paul, "The Value of Long-Range Planning," *Technomic Foodservice Digest,* January 1995.
7. Ibid.
8. David A. Aaker, *Strategic Marketing Management,* 4th ed. (New York: Wiley, 1995), p. 186.
9. Gary Hamel and C. K. Prahalad, *Competing for the Future* (Boston: Harvard Business School Press, 1994).
10. Ibid., p. 76.
11. Ibid., p. 73.
12. For a fuller discussion of the levels of organizational responsibility and its relationship to strategic planning in hospitality organizations, see Thomas F. Powers, "Hospitality Management Development for the 1980s," *Cornell Hotel and Restaurant Administration Quarterly,* February 1980, pp. 39–47.
13. *New Product News,* Marriott Hotels and Resorts, Summer 1987.
14. Michael E. Porter, *Competitive Strategy* (New York: Free Press, 1980), p. 34. His argument is summarized on pp. 5–33.
15. Ibid., p. 191.
16. Al Reis and Jack Trout, *Marketing Warfare* (New York: McGraw-Hill, 1986), pp. 4–5.
17. The early development of La Quinta Inns is chronicled by Christopher Lovelock in the case "La Quinta Motor Inns" (Boston: Harvard Business School, 1980).
18. Andrews, *The Concept of Corporate Strategy,* p. 38.

19. Philip Langdon, "Burgers, Shakes," *Atlantic Monthly,* December 1985, pp. 75–89.
20. For an example in case form of a hotel company employing this set of criteria to its operations, see Thomas F. Powers, "Atlific Inc." (Guelph, Ontario: University of Guelph, Advanced Management Program for the Hospitality Industry, 1983).
21. Porter, *Competitive Strategy,* p. 34.
22. Lawless and Hart, "Forces That Shape Restaurant Demand," p. 8.
23. Porter, *Competitive Strategy,* p. 37.
24. Ibid., p. 38.
25. The following discussion draws on Aaker, *Strategic Marketing Management,* especially pages 180–181 228–235.
26. Carlson Hospitality Group, "Global Power, Local Delivery."
27. Christopher H. Lovelock, *Services Management,* 2nd ed. (Englewood Cliffs, NJ:Prentice Hall, 1991) pp. 110–111.

Chapter 6

1. Christian Grönroos, "Designing a Long Range Marketing Strategy for Services," *Long Range Planning,* April 1980, pp. 36–42.
2. *Restaurants and Institutions,* February 5, 1986, p. 64.
3. This distinction is drawn from Grönroos, *Service Management and Marketing* (Lexington, MA: Lexington Books, 1990). Grönroos's point of view is discussed more fully in Chapter 7.
4. Christopher H. Lovelock, *Services Marketing* (Englewood Cliffs, NJ: Prentice-Hall, 1984), pp. 415, 417.
5. The kind of cross-training advocated here is a key benefit of senior executive programs. A number of hospitality schools are now committed to such programs. For a full description of the philosophy and content of one such program, see Thomas F. Powers, John W. Patterson, and Michiel J. Leenders, "Training at the Top," *Cornell Hotel and Restaurant Administration Quarterly,* February 1983, pp. 65–71. For a summary of executive reactions to this program, see Thomas F. Powers, Carl D. Riegel, and John W. Patterson, "Executive Education: Lessons from AMPHI," *Cornell Hotel and Restaurant Administration Quarterly,* August 1986, pp. 40–45.
6. Leonard R. Berry, "Services Marketing Is Different," in Lovelock, *Services Marketing,* p. 32.
7. Sid Feltenstein, "Menu Mix-Menu Magic," *Proceedings, Chain Operators Exchange, 1988* (Chicago: International Foodservice Manufacturers Association, 1988).
8. CREST is the acronym for Consumer Reports on Eating Out Share Trends, a series of market research studies based on consumer diaries.

Chapter 7

1. The definition is based on Christian Grönroos, *Service Management and Marketing* (Lexington, MA: Lexington Books, 1990), p. 27.
2. G. Lynn Shostock, "Breaking Free from Product Marketing," *Journal of Marketing,* April 1977.
3. Christopher H. Lovelock, *Services Marketing,* 2nd ed. (Englewood Cliffs, NJ: Prentice-Hall, 1991), pages 14–18. The operations and delivery systems in Figure 7.2

are essentially those Lovelock presents, but the communications system here is conceived of in a somewhat different way from Lovelock's "other contact points."

4. Grönroos, *Service Management and Marketing*, p. 36. He is quoting from R. Buzzell and B. Gale, *The PIMS Principle: Linking Strategy to Performance* (New York: Free Press, 1987).
5. Ibid., p. 40.
6. A. Parasuraman, Valerie A. Ziethaml, and Leonard L. Berry, "SERVQUAL: A Multiple-Item Scale for Measuring Consumer Perceptions of Service Quality," *Journal of Marketing*, Spring 1988, p. 23.
7. Valerie A. Ziethaml, Leonard L. Berry, and A. Parasuraman, "Communication and Control Processes in the Delivery of Service Quality," *Journal of Marketing*, April 1988, pp. 35–48.
8. Christopher W. L. Hart, James L. Heshelt, and W. Earl Sasser, Jr., "The Profitable Art of Service Recovery," *Harvard Business Review*, July–August 1990, p. 150.
9. Grönroos, *Service Management and Marketing*, p. 102.
10. Hart et al., "The Profitable Art of Service Recovery", p. 151.
11. Restaurants and Institutions, February 5, 1986, p. 64.
12. Philip Crosby, *Quality Is Free* (New York: McGraw-Hill, 1979), quoted in Grönroos, *Service Management and Marketing*.
13. Christopher W. L. Hart, "The Power of Unconditional Service Guarantees," *Harvard Business Review*, July–August 1988, p. 58.
14. Ibid., pp. 55–56.
15. Hart et al., "The Profitable Art of Service Recovery."
16. Grönroos, *Service Management and Marketing*, p. 203.
17. The term was used by Tom Feltenstein during the 1995 Marketing War College.
18. Grönroos, *Service Management and Marketing*, p. 233.
19. Ibid., p. 253.
20. S. M. Davis, *Managing Corporate Culture* (Cambridge, MA: Ballinger, 1985), quoted in Grönroos, *Service Management and Marketing*, p. 241.
21. William H. Davidow and Bro Uttal, *Total Customer Service: The Ultimate Weapon* (New York: Harper and Row, 1989), p. 85.
22. Ibid., p. 93.
23. Carol A. King, "Service-Oriented Quality Control," *Cornell Hotel and Restaurant Administration Quarterly*, November 1984, pp. 92–98.
24. G. Lynn Shostock, "Planning the Service Encounter," in John A. Czepiel, Michael R. Solomon, and Carol F. Surprenant, eds., *The Service Encounter* (Lexington, MA: Lexington Books, 1985), pp. 243–253.
25. Shostock, "Planning the Service Encounter," p. 247.
26. Ibid.
27. RSE is a ratio that was used by Dunphy Hotels and reported by Christopher Lovelock in the case "Parker House A" (Boston: Harvard Business School, 1980), p. 7. Lovelock prefers the term asset revenue generating efficiency (ARGE) which measures basically the same performance ("total revenues received divided by the theoretical maximum revenues"). See Lovelock, *Services Marketing*, pp. 122–123.
28. These estimates, high as they may seem, are probably *low*. The Rooms Department Operating Income is well above 70 percent and the costs deducted in that figure include a large component of *fixed costs* such as the wages for a minimum crew required if the establishment is to be kept open.

    In food service, food and payroll costs typically require on the order of 65 percent of sales, but here, too, much of the payroll costs are for fixed payroll and many operating costs do not vary directly with sales. As a single instance, the cost of cleaning supplies is unlikely to be increased measurably by the presence of one more diner.

29. David H. Maister, "Psychology of Waiting Lines," in John A. Czepiel et al., *The Service Encounter*, pp. 113–123. Maister is quoting from W. E. Sasser, J. Olsen, and D. D. Wyckoff, *Management of Service Operations: Text Cases and Readings* (New York: Allyn and Bacon, 1979), pp. 88–89.
30. The discussion here follows Sasser (W. Earl Sasser, "Match Supply and Demand in Service Industries," in Lovelock, *Services Marketing*, pp. 330–338). Sasser indicates that working conditions in chase demand are poor; "sweatshop" is the term he uses. This is not necessarily the case as amusement parks and enlightened fast-food operators demonstrate; thus, I have eliminated this characteristic.
31. Theodore Leavitt, "Management and the Post-Industrial State," *The Public Interest*, Summer 1976, p. 89.

Chapter 8

1. The author wishes to acknowledge his indebtedness to Professor Leo M. Renaghan of the Cornell Hotel School. This text draws heavily on his article, "A New Marketing Mix for the Hospitality Industry," *Cornell Hotel and Restaurant Administration Quarterly*, August 1981, pp. 32–33, though departing from it in some particulars.
2. The following section is derived principally from Christian Grönroos, *Service Management and Marketing* (Lexington, MA: Lexington Books, 1990), though I adopt a different definition than he advocates.
3. Ibid., p. 14.
4. G. Lynn Shostock, "Breaking Free from Product Marketing," *Journal of Marketing*, April 1997, p. 77.
5. Renaghan, "A New Marketing Mix," p. 34.
6. Christopher H. Lovelock, *Service Marketing*, 2nd ed. (Englewood Cliffs, NJ: Prentice-Hall, 1991), p. 14.
7. Philip Kotler, "Atmospherics as a Marketing Tool," *Journal of Retailing*, Winter 1973–1974, pp. 48–64.
8. Ibid.
9. Regina S. Baraban, "The Psychology of Design," Proceedings, *Chain Operators Exchange, 1984* (Chicago: International Foodservice Manufacturers Association, 1984).
10. Ibid.
11. William F. Babcock, "The Concept Comes to Life," *Proceedings, Chain Operators Exchange, 1985* (Chicago: International Foodservice Manufacturers Association, 1985).
12. William F. Babcock, "The Concept Comes to Life," *Proceedings, Chain Operators Exchange, 1984* (Chicago: International Foodservice Manufacturers Association, 1984).
13. Adapted from Ronald N. Paul, "Emerging Concepts . . . Picking the Winners," *Proceedings, Chain Operators Exchange, 1984* (Chicago: International Foodservice Manufacturers Association, 1984). Paul does not consider production strategy a separate variable. He identifies a sixth variable sometimes present that relates to special appeals such as video games or other entertainment features.
14. For a fuller discussion of lodging concepts and service levels, see Thomas F. Powers, *Introduction to Management in the Hospitality Industry*, 5th ed., (New York: Wiley, 1995), pp. 217–235.

15. This section draws on Ira Blumenthal, "Snapshots of Branding," *Proceedings, Chain Operators Exchange, 1994,* and "Brand on the Run," *Proceedings, Chain Operators Exchange, 1995.*
16. Blumenthal, "Brand on the Run," 1995.
17. Melvin Copeland, "The Relation of Consumers Buying Habits to Marketing Networks," *Harvard Business Review,* April 1923, pp. 282–289.
18. Ibid.
19. Blumenthal, "Brand on the Run," 1995.
20. Ibid.
21. Ibid.
22. *Restaurant Business,* January 1, 1994, p. 19.
23. *Nation's Restaurant News,* October 9, 1995, p. 9.
24. *Hotel and Motel Management,* November 2, 1992, p. 1.
25. *Hotel and Motel Management,* May 8, 1995, p. 25.
26. *Lodging,* October 1994, pp. 7–10.
27. Peter Krause and Morgan Grenfeld, Managing Director for Lodging and Leisure Products, quoted in *Lodging,* October 1994, p. 7.
28. A further possible reason for not highlighting the PepsiCo name on each of these chains is that PepsiCo is also a supplier to many restaurants which are in competition with PepsiCo's food service units. PepsiCo is probably not anxious to draw attention to the competition of its subsidiaries with its customers.
29. *Lodging,* December 1994, pp. 42–48.
30. *Amusement Business,* March 20, 1995, p. 26.
31. *Food Service Distributor,* August 15, 1993, p. 6.
32. *Food Service Distributor,* September 15, 1993, p. 20.
33. *Food Service Distributor,* January 1, 1995, p. 8.
34. Daryl Wyckoff, "Managing the Chain Restaurant Life Cycle," paper presented to the Chain Operators Exchange, March 3, 1980.
35. Nariman K. Dhalla and Sonia Yuspeh, "Forget the Life Cycle Concept," *Harvard Business Review,* January–February 1976, pp. 103–110. The words quoted are from p. 104.
36. *Time,* April 13, 1987, p. 58.
37. Ronald N. Paul, "New Product Development Overview," *Proceedings, Chain Operators Exchange, 1982* (Chicago: International Foodservice Manufacturers Association, 1982). This discussion follows Paul's line of reasoning closely. Paul adds a fourth category, acquisition, but that does not appear germane to the present discussion.
38. *Nation's Restaurant News,* July 14, 1986, p. 3.
39. Paul, "New Product Development Overview."
40. Ibid.
41. Tom Feltenstein, "New Product Development in Food Service: A Structural Approach," *Cornell Hotel and Restaurant Administration Quarterly,* November 1986, p. 61.

Chapter 9

1. *CKC Report,* April 1994, p. 14.
2. *CKC Report,* February 1995, p. 6.
3. Ibid., p. 4.

4. Ibid., p. 6.
5. *Hotel and Motel Management,* September 18, 1995, p. 35.
6. There is an important technical difference between a *franchise system* (in which a franchise company grants a licence) and a *membership system* (in which a property and its owner become members). Their mode of operation, however, is generally similar, although the membership group is characterized by considerable autonomy and tends to have lower charges than a franchise system. One result of these lower charges is a lower advertising budget. Best Western is the best known membership system.
7. Michael Levin, remarks during a panel discussion, "The Value of Branding," Hospitality Industry Investors Conference, June 7, 1994, New York.
8. *Lodging,* May 1994, pp. 21–24.
9. Levin, "The Value of Branding."
10. For a fuller discussion of these issues, see Thomas F. Powers, "The Advent of the Mega Chain: A Case of the Emperor's New Clothes," *Hospitality Research Journal,* Volume 16, Number 1, 1992, pp. 1–12.
11. *Hotel and Motel Management,* June 5, 1995, p. 46.
12. *Lodging,* March 1994, p. 52.
13. Patrick E. Culligan, "Toward a New Definition of Impact," *Cornell Hotel and Restaurant Administration Quarterly,* August 1995, pp. 38–47.
14. *Lodging,* April 1995, p. 41.
15. Rachel Rasinsky, "A Critical Analysis of Hotel Impact Issues," *Cornell Hotel and Restaurant Administration Quarterly,* August 1995, pp. 18–26.
16. Peggy Berg, "New Questions Address Impact Studies," *Hotel and Motel Management,* May 9, 1994, p. 26.
17. Peggy Berg, "Evaluating the Value of a Brand," *Lodging Hospitality,* May 1994, p. 13.
18. Data regarding franchising conversions are taken from *Lodging Outlook,* Smith Travel Research, March 1995. The exception to 1990–1994 statement was 1992 when the total number of conversions was 1,410.
19. *Lodging,* July 1994, p. 45. The source of the conclusion is Robert Mandelbaum, Research Director, PKF Consulting.
20. *Lodging,* May 1994, p. 65.
21. Lori Raleigh, Vice President, Liberty Real Estate Group, remarks during a panel discussion, "International Franchise Companies," Hospitality Industry Investment Conference, June 7, 1994, New York.
22. Christopher Schulz, "Hotels and Travel Agents: The New Partnership," *Cornell Hotel and Restaurant Administration Quarterly,* April 1994.
23. *Hotels,* July 1995, p. 62.
24. Schulz, "Hotels and Travel Agents," pp. 45–50.
25. *Hotel,* July 19, 1995, p. 78.
26. Schulz, "Hotels and Travel Agents," p. 48.
27. *Globe and Mail,* November. 24, 1995, p. B12.
28. Ira J. Blumenthal, "Brand on the Run," *Proceedings, Chain Operators Exchange* (Chicago: International Foodservice Manufacturers Association, 1994).
29. The source of this estimate is Robert Fox of McDonald's.
30. *Boston Chicken 1993 Annual Report,* p. 11.
31. *Nation's Restaurant News,* October 23, 1995, p. 2.
32. *Technomic Food Service Digest,* November 1995, p. 2.
33. *Boston Chicken 1993 Annual Report,* p. 11.
34. Ibid., p. 17.

35. More specifically, Boston Market "provides a loan to the area developer which is typically equal to 75 percent of the capital they need to reach a designated level of development in their market . . . . The loan is convertible into a majority ownership interest in the area developer, generally after two years." *Boston Chicken 1993 Annual Report,* p. 23.
36. *Nation's Restaurant News,* April 17, 1995, p. 3.
37. Andrew E. Serwer, "Trouble in Franchise Nation," *Fortune,* March 6, 1995, pp. 115–129.
38. *Nation's Restaurant News,* December 20, 1993, p. 107.
39. Serwer, "Trouble in Franchise Nation," p. 115.
40. This paragraph is based, in part, on Rupert M. Barkoff and W. Michael Garner, "Encroachment: The Thorn in Every Successful Franchisor's Side," paper presented to the American Bar Association Forum on Franchising, October 20–22, 1993, Dallas.
41. Serwer, "Trouble in Franchise Nation," p. 118.
42. *Nation's Restaurant News,* July 10, 1995, pp. 7 and 115, and September 11, 1995, p. 3.
43. Ira Blumenthal, "Snapshots of Branding," *Proceedings, Chain Operators Exchange 1995* (Chicago: International Foodservice Manufacturers Association, 1995).
44. Ibid.
45. Ibid.
46. The definition is extracted from Blumenthal, "Snapshots of Branding," but is my interpretation of his remarks since he does not offer a specific definition.

Chapter 10

1. *Boston Chicken 1993 Annual Report,* p. 11.
2. *Restaurants and Institutions,* November 15, 1994, p. 50.
3. Kenneth G. Hardy and Thomas F. Powers, "Wendy's of Canada," unpublished case.
4. Personal communication, Ronald J. Murphy, Marketing Manager, Scotts Restaurants.
5. The majority of the home meal replacement market indicate that if they had not eaten out, they would have cooked at home, which is not the case for Arby's QSR customers.
6. *Technomic Food Service Digest,* November 1995, pp. 6–7.
7. John S. Thompson, *Site Selection* (New York: Lebhar-Friedman, 1982).
8. Unless otherwise noted, the information in this discussion is from Thompson, *Site Selection.*
9. Ibid., p. 155.
10. David L. Huff, "Defining and Estimating a Trade Area," *Journal of Marketing,* July 1964, p. 36.
11. David L. Huff, "Retail Location Theory," in Staupfl and Hushman, eds., *Theory in Retailing* (Chicago: American Marketing Association, 1968), p. 109.
12. Ibid., p. 118.
13. Thompson, *Site Selection,* p. 66.
14. Rocco M. Angelo, *Understanding Feasibility Studies: A Practical Guide* (East Lansing, MI: American Hotel and Motel Association Educational Institute, 1985), p. 3.
15. Ibid.
16. Ibid.
17. Stephen Rushmore, *How to Perform an Economic Feasibility Study of a Proposed Hotel/Motel* (Chicago: American Society of Real Estate Counselors, 1986), p. 64.

18. Ibid., pp. 11–12, 19. The balance of this discussion draws on the work of Rushmore and Dean Angelo already cited.
19. Ibid., p. 64.
20. Ibid., p. 38.
20. Personal Communication, Simon Cooper, President, Delta Hotels.

Chapter 11

1. George D. Rice, "Target Marketing: The Art of Segmentation," *Proceedings, Chain Operators Exchange, 1983* (Chicago: International Foodservice Manufacturers Association, 1983).
2. The original formulation by Rice in "Target Marketing," is somewhat different in detail than that shown here and intended for food service alone. I have used different labels and added the notion of image. As proposed by Rice, value was defined as

$$\frac{\text{Products} + \text{Format} + \text{Decor}}{\text{Price}} = \text{Value}$$

3. Roger Hallowell and Leonard A. Schlessinger, "Taco Bell Corp" (Boston: Harvard Business School, 1991).
4. Martin R. Schlissel and Joseph Chasin, "Pricing of Service: An Interdisciplinary Review," *The Service Industries Journal,* pp. 271–285.
5. Hallowell and Schlessinger, "Taco Bell Corp," p. 22. The increase in profit was attributable to a number of factors other than increase in volume, including a restructuring to a more productive company at all levels.
6. See, for instance, *Nation's Restaurant News,* March 13, 1995, pp. 14–18.
7. *Nation's Restaurant News,* September 4, 1995, p. 1.
8. Eric B. Orkin, "An Integrated Menu Pricing System," *Cornell Hotel and Restaurant Administration Quarterly,* August 1978, p. 8.
9. Schlissel and Chasin, "Pricing of Service," p. 275.
10. As Schlissel and Chasin put it, "[i]nformation on such economic issues as elasticity of demand usually is not available to managers of small- and medium-sized businesses and therefore rarely enters into the decision process." Schlissel and Chasin, "Pricing of Service," p. 280.
11. Bill Main is co-owner of the Shore Bird Restaurant in Half Moon Bay, California. He has a broad based food service consulting practice that focuses, in large part, on menu-based marketing. In 1996, he was President of the California Restaurant Association. The material in this section draws on Mr. Main's remarks at the Marketing War College during a lecture on "Menu Marketing." The talk is available on tape from Wells Walker and Company, Inc., 7406 Allan Station Ct., B212, Springfield, VA.
12. Lee M. Kreul, "Magic Numbers: Psychological Aspects of Menu Pricing," *Cornell Hotel and Restaurant Administration Quarterly,* August 1982, pp. 70–75.
13. *Technomic Foodservice Digest,* November 1995, p. 5.
14. Roy Hubbart, *The Hubbart Formula for Evaluating Rate Structures of Hotel Rooms* (New York: American Hotel and Motel Association, 1952).
15. The categories are those used by Smith Travel Research, but I have changed the designation of one segment. Smith uses economy but I prefer the "limited service" designation as more descriptive in view of the fact that the main distinction between the midpriced and limited-service categories is *service,* principally the absence of food

service. The guest room and lobby facilities in the midpriced and limited-service segments are virtually identical.

16. J. M. Laitamaki and Leo Renaghan, "Value Based Pricing Strategies for Services: An Empirical Study of the Hotel Industry," in Carol Surprenant, ed., *Add Value to Your Service* (Chicago: American Marketing Association, 1988).
17. Schlissel and Chasin, "Pricing of Service," p. 272.
18. *Lodging Outlook,* Smith Travel Research, February 1995, p. 1.
19. Richard D. Hanks, Robert G. Cross, and R. Paul Norland, "Discounting in the Hotel Industry: A New Approach," *Cornell Hotel and Restaurant Administration Quarterly,* February 1992, p. 18.
20. Sheryl E. Kines, "The Basics of Yield Management," *Cornell Hotel and Restaurant Administration Quarterly.*
21. Sheryl E. Kines, "Perceived Fairness of Yield Management," *Cornell Hotel and Restaurant Administration Quarterly,* February 1994, p. 22–29.
22. *Travel Agent,* February 21, 1994, p. 76.
23. Schlissel and Chasin, "Pricing of Service," p. 282.

Chapter 12

1. Richard T. Good, "Making the Most of Your Advertising," *Proceedings, Chain Operators Exchange, 1986* (Chicago: International Foodservice Manufacturers Association, 1986).
2. Ibid.
3. Estimate provided to the author by Robert Fox, Staff Director, McDonald's, December 1995.
4. *Nation's Restaurant News,* October 19, 1987, p. F50.
5. Ibid.
6. *Nation's Restaurant News,* November 27, 1995, p. 14.
7. David W. Stewart, "Advertising in a Slow Growth Economy," *American Demographics,* September 1994, pp. 40–46.
8. Ibid., p. 46.
9. Ibid., p. 43.
10. Ibid., p. 43.
11. Michael S. Morgan, "Traveller's Choice: The Effects of Advertising and Prior Stay," *Cornell Hotel and Restaurant Administration Quarterly,* December 1991, pp. 41–49.
12. Thomas F. Powers, "The Standard World of 2005," *Hospitality Research Journal,* Volume 16, Number 1, 1992, p. 7.
13. *Nation's Restaurant News,* May 1, 1995, p. 12.
14. *Nation's Restaurant News,* Noember. 20, 1995, p. 18.
15. Glenn Withian, "Hotel Advertising in the 80's," *Cornell Hotel and Restaurant Administration Quarterly,* May 1986, p. 38.
16. *Nation's Restaurant News,* May 15, 1995, p. 14.
17. *Nation's Restaurant News,* July 24, 1994, p. 14.
18. *Nation's Restaurant News,* September 25, 1995, p. 15.
19. *Nation's Restaurant News,* April 6, 1987, p. 15.
20. *Nation's Restaurant News,* June 19, 1995, p. 14.
21. *Nation's Restaurant News,* March 27, 1996, p. 12.
22. Withian, "Hotel Advertising," p. 39.

23. Good, "Making the Most of Your Advertising."
24. *Restaurant Management,* March 1988, pp. 31–39.
25. The discussion occurred during the "Panel of the Pros" at the 1995 Marketing War College, March 25–28, 1995, Palm Beach. The panel was made up of chain restaurant marketing executives. The moderator was Tom Feltenstein, Chairman of the Neighborhood Marketing Institute.

Chapter 13

1. Robert H. Marriott, Jr., "Promotions—A Key Piece in Your Marketing Puzzle," *Proceedings, Chain Operators Exchange, 1987* (Chicago: International Foodservice Manufacturers Association, 1987). Mr. Marriott is President of Marriott and Associates, a marketing services firm.
2. Ibid.
3. William K. Irvine, "The Impact of Promotional Activity on the Restaurant Industry," *Proceedings, Chain Operators Exchange, 1982* (Chicago: International Foodservice Manufacturers Association, 1982).
4. George D. Rice, "An Analysis of Brand Loyalty for Chain Restaurants," *Proceedings, Chain Operators Exchange, 1986* (Chicago: International Foodservice Manufacturers Association, 1986). CREST is the acronym for Consumer Reports on Eating-Out Share Trends. It is the leading consumer behavior information service focused on the food service industry. CREST tracks consumer behavior at restaurants via a Diary Panel of 13,000 U.S. households.
5. Personal communication, Richard Benefield, Treacher's franchisee. I am indebted to Mr. Benefield for providing me with the smaller operator's perspective on couponing and for much of the discussion of bounce-back coupons.
6. Marriott, "Promotions."
7. Richard Benefield, personal communication.
8. Marriott, "Promotions."
9. Ibid.
10. Thomas F. Powers, "MIE Hospitality" (Guelph, Ontario: University of Guelph, Advanced Management Program for the Hospitality Industry, 1983).
11. The following section is based on Kathleen Hessert, "Preparing for Crisis and the Media Barrage," a presentation to the Chain Operators Exchange, February 28, 1994, and on Thomas F. Powers, "Red Lobster: the Mussel Crisis," a marketing case prepared in 1990 for executive training programs offered at the University of Guelph. This section also draws on the comments of senior executives involved in the discussion of the Red Lobster case at the university.
12. One of the leading texts on the subject is Frederick A. Russell, Frank H. Beach, and Richard H. Buskirk, *Selling Principles and Practices,* 11th ed. (New York: McGraw-Hill, 1982). An interesting short book designed for women interested in selling in industry—and that is the kind of selling hotel sales reps and contract catering sales staff engage in—is Richard H. Buskirk and Beverly Miles, *Beating Men at Their Own Game* (New York: Wiley, 1980). The latter contains an excellent short summary of the selling process. I have drawn on both of Buskirk's works for the structure of this chapter, though the applications, of course, are limited to the hospitality industry.
13. DeWitt Coffman, *Hospitality for Sale* (East Lansing, MI: American Hotel and Motel Association, 1980), p. 54.
14. Ibid, p. 6.

Chapter 14

1. This chapter is based on research which was sponsored by the Management Development Programs (MDP) of the School of Hotel and Food Administration, University of Guelph. The chapter draws on the following MDP cases and notes, which I wrote between 1993 and 1996. All are copyrighted by the University of Guelph.

   Pizza Hut A and B: The Promotional Vehicle (1993)
   Syracuse Swiss Chalet A and B (1993)
   Note on Restaurant Local Area Marketing (1995)
   Note on Property Level Marketing in Lodging (1996)

   I am happy to acknowledge my indebtedness to the MDP and to John Patterson, its director during those years, for his encouragement and support.
2. The Neighborhood Marketing Institute is devoted to research and professional education related to restaurant local area marketing. The institute sponsors an annual "Marketing War College" devoted principally to neighborhood marketing.
3. See Chapter 5 for a discussion of Kenichi Omhae's "strategic triangle" of customer, competition, and company (here interpreted as product offering).
4. For an extended discussion of the use of food service as a part of a marketing effort for rooms sales, see Christopher Lovelock, "Parker House A" (Boston: Harvard Business School, 1980).
5. William Dunn, "Building Database," *Marketing Tools,* July–August 1994, p. 55.
6. Paula A. Francese and Leo M. Renaghan, "Data Base Marketing: Building Customer Profiles," *Cornell Hotel and Restaurant Administration Quarterly,* May 1990, p.61.
7. This is the conclusion of Barbara Mowry in a presentation during the Marketing War College, March 25–28, 1995, Palm Beach. Ms. Mowry has been responsible for the launch and operation of six frequent-flyer programs, the development of many frequent-guest programs in the hotel industry, and the introduction of targeted marketing programs in other industries.
8. Tom Feltenstein, "Understanding Your Internal and External Customer" (Palm Beach: Neighborhood Marketing Institute, 1995), p. 6. Emphasis in the original.
9. Personal interview, Humphrey Kadaner, Director of Marketing, Pizza Hut Canada, October 1991.
10. *Restaurants USA,* April 1993, p. 14.
11. Information on advertising spending is taken from comments made during the "Panel of the Pros" at the 1995 Marketing War College. Among the panelists were Robert Charles, a McDonald's franchisee active in local marketing and recipient of the Neighborhood Marketing Institute's 1995 "Top Gun Award"; Roger Fishman, Vice President of Marketing and Sales, Hard Rock Cafes International; John R. Lauck, Vice President for Field Marketing and National Planning, Pizza Hut; and Alfred Thimm, Chief Operations Officer, Palm Management Corporation.
12. It is worth noting that the discount offered in this case was more than offset by the elimination of the cost of a disposable coffee cup.
13. Remarks by Thomas Salza, Director of Marketing, Red Robin International, during the Marketing War College, March 25–28, 1995, Palm Beach.
14. The information in this section draws extensively on a presentation by Bill Main titled "Menu Marketing" at the 1995 Marketing War College. Mr. Main is the author of *Menu Magic,* published by Mr. Main. See also note 11, Chapter 11.

15. The discussion of zone merchandising is drawn from Mr. Feltenstein's presentation, "The Newest Wave of Neighborhood Marketing," at the Marketing War College, March 25–28, 1995, Palm Beach. Tapes of this presentation are available from Wells Walker and Company, Inc., 7406 Allan Station Ct., B212, Springfield, VA.
16. For a discussion of buying centers and organizational buying behavior, see Chapter 2.
17. The discussion in this section is based, in large part, on interviews with Ian Bell, Executive Vice President of Marketing, Versus Services, March 1995. Versa Services, an affiliate of Aramark, is Canada's largest contract food service company.
18. *Restaurants USA,* March 1993, pp. 24–25.
19. Thomas F. Powers, "Red Lobster A and B" (Guelph, Ontario: University of Guelph, Advanced Management Program for the Hospitality Industry, 1990).
20. *Nation's Restaurant News,* April 26, 1993, p. 45.
21. See Chapter 13 for a discussion of sales call planning and execution.
22. See also note 4, above.
23. Personal interview, Michael Beckley, March 1995. Mr. Beckley is President of Commonwealth Hospitality which operates hotels under the Holiday Inn, Best Western, Radisson, and Ramada brands.
24. Personal interview, Simon Cooper, President, Delta Hotels, March 1995. Delta Hotels operates hotels in Canada, the United States, Latin America, and the Far East.
25. Ibid.
26. Christopher W. L. Hart and David A. Troy, *Strategic Hotel/Motel Marketing* (Lansing, MI: The American Hotel and Motel Association, 1986), p. 120.
27. Ibid., p. 120.

About the Author

Tom Powers is Professor Emeritus of the School of Hotel and Food Administration at the University of Guelph, where he taught Marketing for many years. Tom also served as director of the school and was founding director of the School's Advanced Management Program for the Hospitality Industry (AMPHI), an educational program for senior executives. He has served on the faculties of Morris Brown College, the Michigan State Hotel School, and headed the Hospitality Program at Penn State. He is a graduate of Harvard College and the Harvard Business School.

Tom began his hospitality career as an assistant manager with Stouffer Restaurants and then served on the consulting staff of the hotel accounting and consulting firm of Horwath and Horwath. He was a General Manager of franchised Holiday Inns in Illinois, Missouri, and Atlanta, Georgia. He was active in trade association affairs and served on the board of directors of the Illinois Hotel Association, the Georgia Hotel/Motel Association, and the Georgia Restaurant Association. He returned to school after 10 years in industry and received his Ph.D. from Georgia State University.

In addition to *Marketing Hospitality,* he is the author of the widely used *Introduction to Management in the Hospitality Industry,* now in its fifth edition. He also co-authored, with his wife Jo Marie, *Food Service Operations: Planning and Control.* Tom served as the founding editor of what is now the *Hospitality Research Journal.* He is author or co-author of over 35 papers and articles in professional journals, and his work has also appeared widely in the trade press. Since 1976, he has served as Consulting Editor of the *Wiley Service Management Series.*

Dr. Powers has served on CHRIE's Board of Directors, and, from 1978 to 1980, he was Executive Vice President of CHRIE. He is a member of the CHRIE Publications Council.

He was the first recipient, in 1982, of CHRIE's Research Scholar of the Year Award. He is a Foundation Diplomate of the Canadian Food Service and Hospitality Foundation. In 1992, Powers received the H.G. Meek Award for Lifetime Contribution to Hospitality Education, and, in 1993, he received the Van Nostrand Rheinhold Research Award.

Tom and Jo Marie Powers live near Guelph, Ontario. They have five sons.

Index